If it's APRIL 2007
and you are still using this Directory,
it's time to order the NEW Edition.

Please visit our website

www.cabells.com

or contact us at

Cabell Publishing Company
Box 5428, Beaumont, Texas 77726-5428
(409) 898-0575
Fax (409) 866-9554

Cabell's Directory
of Publishing Opportunities in

Educational
Psychology and Administration

VOLUME I   A thru J of B
SEVENTH EDITION 2005-2006

David W. E. Cabell, Editor
McNeese State University
Lake Charles, Louisiana

Deborah L. English, Editor
Twyla J. George, Assistant Editor
Lacey E. Earle, Assistant Editor

To order additional copies
visit our web site
www.cabells.com

or contact us at

Box 5428 Beaumont, Texas 77726-5428
(409) 898-0575 Fax (409) 866-9554

$99.95 U.S. for addresses in United States
Price includes shipping and handling for U.S.
Add $50 for surface mail to countries outside U.S.
Add $100 for airmail to countries outside U.S.

ISBN # 0-911753-28-1

TABLE OF CONTENTS

ii

iv

v

vi

Preface

The objective of *Cabell's Directory of Publishing Opportunities in Educational Psychology and Administration* is to help you publish your ideas.

The *Directory* contains the editor's name(s), address(es), phone and fax number(s), and e-mail and web address(es) for over 250 journals.

To help you in selecting those journals that are most likely to publish your manuscripts the **Index** classifies the journals into twenty-eight different topic areas. In addition, the Index provides information on the journal's type of review process, number of external reviewers and acceptance rate.

To further assist you in organizing and preparing your manuscripts, the *Directory* includes extensive information on the style and format of most journals. If a journal has its own set of manuscript guidelines, a copy of these guidelines is published in the *Directory*. Also, each entry indicates the use of a standard set of publication guidelines by a journal. For example, some journals use the *Chicago Manual of Style* or the *Publication Manual of the American Psychological Association.*

Furthermore, the *Directory* describes the type of review process used by the editor(s) of a journal, type of review, number of reviewers, acceptance rate, time required for review, availability of reviewers comments, fees charged to review or publish the manuscript, copies required and manuscript topics. Information on the journal's circulation, readership and subscription prices are also provided.

Although this *Directory* focuses on journals in the specialized area of **Educational Psychology and Administration**, other directories focus on **Psychology** and **Educational Curriculum and Methods**. The division of education journals into these two directories more appropriately meets the researcher's need for publishing in his area of specialization.

The decision to place journals in this directory is based on the manuscript topics selected by the editor as well as the journals' guidelines for authors.

Also, the *Directory* includes a section titled **"What is a Refereed Article?"** which tends to emphasize the value of a blind review process and use of external reviewers. However, this section cautions individuals using these criteria to also consider a journal's reputation for quality. Additionally, it indicates that differences in acceptance rates may be the result of different methods used to calculate these percentages and the number of people associated with a particular area of specialization.

How To Use the Directory

TABLE OF CONTENTS
Table of Contents provides over 250 journals to help your locate a publication.

INDEX
Index classifies the journals according to twenty-eight (28) different manuscript topics. It also includes information on the type of review, number of external reviewers, acceptance rate and page number of each journal.

ADDRESS FOR SUBMISSION
Address for Submission provides: the Editor's Name(s), Mailing Address(es), Telephone and Fax numbers(s), and E-mail and Web address(es).

PUBLICATION GUIDELINES
Manuscript Length refers to the length of the manuscript in terms of the number of double-spaced typescript pages.

Copies Required indicates the number of manuscript copies you should submit to the editor.

Computer Submission indicates whether the journal prefers hardcopy (paper) or electronic submissions such as disk, e-mail attachment, or a combination of methods.

Format refers to the type of word processing programs or computer programs the journal requires for reviewing the manuscript. Some examples of these programs are Microsoft Word, WordPerfect, PDF, or RTF.

Fees to Review refers to whether the journal charges a fee to review the manuscript. Knowing this item permits the author to send the required funds with the manuscript.

Manuscript Style refers to the overall style guide the journal uses for text, references within the text and the bibliography. This is usually either the *Chicago Manual of Style* or the *Publication Manual of the American Psychological Association (APA)*.

REVIEW INFORMATION
Type of Review specifies blind, editorial, or optional review methods. A blind review indicates the reviewer(s) does not know who wrote the manuscript. An editorial review indicates the reviewer knows who wrote the manuscript. The term "optional" indicates the author may choose either one of these types of review.

No. of External Reviewers and *No. of In House Reviewers*
These two items refer to the number of reviewers who review the manuscript prior to making a decision regarding the publication of the manuscript. Although the editor attempted to determine whether the reviewers were on the staff of the journal or were outside reviewers, many of the respondents had trouble distinguishing between internal and external reviewers. Thus it may be more accurate to add these two categories and determine the total number of reviewers.

Acceptance Rate refers to the number of manuscripts accepted for publication relative to the number of manuscripts submitted within the last year. The method of calculating acceptance rates varies among journals.

Time to Review indicates the amount of time that passes between the submission of a manuscript and notification to the author regarding the results of the review process.

Reviewer's Comments indicates whether the author can obtain a copy of the reviewer's comments. In some cases, the author needs to request that the editor send these remarks.

Invited Articles indicates the percentage of articles for which the editor requests an individual to write specifically for publication in the journal. The percentage is the number of invited articles relative to the total number of articles that appeared in a journal within the past year.

Fees to Publish refers to whether the journal charges a fee to publish the manuscript. Knowing this item assists the author in his decision to place the manuscript into the review process.

CIRCULATION DATA

Reader indicates the predominant type of reader the publication seeks to attract. These are divided into a group designated as practitioners and professionals, or another group referred to as administrators and counselors in the educational discipline.

Frequency of Issue indicates the number of times a journal will be published in a year.

Copies per Issue indicates the number of copies the journal distributes per issue.

Sponsor/Publisher indicates the journal's affiliation with a professional association, educational institution, governmental agency, and/or publishing company.

Subscribe Price indicates the cost to order a year's subscription unless otherwise indicated.

MANUSCRIPT TOPICS

Manuscript Topics indicates those subjects the journal emphasizes.

MANUSCRIPT GUIDELINES/COMMENTS

Manuscript Guidelines/Comments provides information on the journal's objectives, style and format for references and footnotes that the editor expects the author to follow in preparing his manuscript for submission.

How the Directory Helps You Publish

Although individuals must communicate their ideas in writing, the *Directory* helps the author determine which journal will most likely accept the manuscript. In making this decision, it is important to compare the characteristics of your manuscript and the needs of each journal. The following table provides a framework for making this comparison.

Information Provided by the Directory for Each Journal	Manuscript Characteristics
Topic(s) of Articles Manuscript Guidelines	Theme
Acceptance Rate Percentage of Invited Articles	Significance of Theme
Type of Reader	Methodology and Style
Circulation Review Process	Prestige
Number of Reviewers Availability of Reviewers Comments Time Required for Reviewer	Results of Review

This framework will help the author determine a small number of journals that will be interested in publishing the manuscript. The *Directory* can assist the author in determining these journals, yet a set of unwritten and written laws prevent simultaneous submission of a manuscript to more than one journal. However, a manuscript can be sent to another journal in the event of a rejection by any one publication.

Furthermore, copyright laws and editorial policy of a given publication often require the author to choose only one journal. Consequently, some journals will require the author to sign a statement indicating the manuscript is not presently under review by another publication.

Publication of the manuscript in the proceedings of a professional association does not prevent the author from sending it to a journal, however there usually are some restrictions attached. Most professional associations require that the author acknowledge the presentation of the manuscript at the associate meeting.

Since the author is limited to submission of a manuscript to only one journal and the review process for each journal requires a long period of time, a "query" letter may help the author determine the journal most likely to publish the manuscript.

The query letter contains the following information:
- Topic, major idea or conclusion of the manuscript
- The subject sample, research setting conceptual framework, methodology type of organization or location
- The reasons why the author thinks the journal's readers would be interested in your proposed article
- Asks the editor to make comments or suggestions on the usefulness of this type of article to the journal

While the query letter is helpful in selecting a journal that will be likely to publish the manuscript, the author could use the *Directory* and the framework presented to develop a set of journals which would be likely to publish the manuscript. With this number of possible journals, it makes the sending of a query letter more feasible and tends to achieve the objective of finding the journal most likely to publish the manuscript.

Relating the Theme of the Manuscript to the Topics of Articles Published by Each Journal

To begin the process of choosing the journals to receive the "query" letter and, at some future time, the manuscript, the author needs to examine the similarity between the theme of the manuscript and the editor's needs. The *Directory* describes these needs by listing the topics each publication considers important and the manuscript guidelines. To find those journals that publish manuscripts in any particular area, refer to the topic index.

In attempting to classify the theme, the author should limit his choice to a single discipline. With the increasing specialization in the academic world, it is unlikely that reviewers, editors, or readers will understand an article that requires knowledge of two different disciplines. If these groups do not understand a manuscript, the journal will reject it.

If a manuscript emphasizes an interdisciplinary approach, it is important to decide who will be reading the article. The approach should be to explain the theoretical concepts of one discipline to the specialist in another discipline. The author should not attempt to resolve theoretical issues present in his discipline and explain their implications for specialists in another discipline.

Although the discipline classifications indicate the number of journals interested in your manuscript topic, the manuscript guidelines help the author determine the journals that will most likely have the greatest interest in the manuscript. The manuscript guidelines provide a detailed statement of the criteria for judging manuscripts, the editorial objectives, the readership and the journal's content and approach. This information makes it possible to determine more precisely the congruence between the manuscript and the type of articles the journal publishes. **The *Directory* contains the manuscript guidelines for a large number of journals.**

The Relationship Between the Journal's Acceptance Rate and Significance of the Theme of the Manuscript

In addition to determining the similarity between the topic of the manuscript and the topic of articles published by the journal, an examination of the significance of the theme to the discipline is also an important criterion in selecting a journal. The journals with the lowest acceptance rate will tend to publish those manuscripts that make the most significant contributions to the advancement of the discipline. Since these journals receive a large number of manuscripts, the editors distinguish those manuscripts likely to make a significant contribution to the reader's knowledge.

Defining newness or the contribution of any one study to the understanding of a discipline is difficult. However, it is possible to gain some insights into this definition by asking the following questions:

1. Is the author stating the existence of a variable, trend or problem, not previously recognized by the literature?

2. Is the author testing the interactions of a different set of variables or events?

3. Is the author presenting a new technique to cope with a problem or test an idea not previously presented in the literature?

4. Is the author using a subject sample with different characteristics than previously presented in the literature?

If the manuscript does not satisfy one of the first two categories, it is unlikely that a journal with a low acceptance rate will accept it for publication. Thus, the author should send the manuscript to those journals where the acceptance rate is higher.

Although the *Directory* provides the acceptance rates of manuscripts for many different journals, it is important to examine the data on percentage of invited articles for each journal. A high acceptance rate may result because the editor has asked leaders in the discipline to write articles on a particular subject. These invited articles are usually accepted. Since the author of an unsolicited manuscript competes with the leaders in the discipline, the manuscript will have to make a significant contribution to receive the editor's approval.

The Relationship of the Manuscript's Style and Methodology to the Journal's Readership

Another factor in selecting the journal to receive the manuscript is the journal's readership. The readers of each journal include either, practitioners and professionals, academics, administrators and counselors in educational psychology and administration, or a combination of these groups.

Since the most important goal for an author is to publish the manuscript, the author should consider the prestige of the journal only after the manuscript has a relatively high probability of being published by more than one journal. This probability is determined by the responses the author received to his query letter and the similarity between the finished manuscript and the needs of the journal.

The method of determining the prestige of a journal varies depending on its readership and the goals of the author. If the readership is primarily administrators or practicing professionals and the goal of the author is to improve the author's image and that of the institution, the journal's circulation would probably be the best indicator of prestige.

In contrast, the author whose goal is to become known among the author's colleagues might consider the type of review process the journal uses as well as its circulation. With a few exceptions, the most prestigious journals with academic readership use a refereed review process.

The Possible Results of the Review Process and the Selection of a Journal to Receive the Manuscript

Despite the fact that a journal with lower prestige would most likely publish the article, the author might be willing to take a chance on a journal with a greater amount of prestige. Since this will decrease the chances of manuscript acceptance, the author should also consider the consequences of rejection. The consequences include the knowledge the author will gain from having his manuscript rejected.

To determine the amount of knowledge the author is likely to gain requires consideration of the number of reviewers the journal uses in the review process, the availability of the reviewer's comments and the time required for the review process. If the journal makes the reviewer's comments available to the author, this provides a great learning opportunity. Also, the more people that review the manuscript, the greater the author's knowledge will be concerning how to improve the present manuscript. Hopefully, the author will transfer the knowledge gained from writing this manuscript to future manuscripts.

Should the review process take a small amount of time relative to a long period of time, the author is provided with a greater opportunity to use this knowledge to revise the manuscript. To assist the author in determining those journals that provide a suitable learning opportunity, each journal in the *Directory* includes information on the number of reviewers, availability of reviewer's comments to the author and time required for review.

Sending the Manuscript

Before sending the manuscript to an editor, the author should write a cover letter, make sure the manuscript is correctly typed, the format conforms to the journal's guidelines and the necessary copies have been included. **The author should always keep a copy of the manuscript.**

The cover letter that is sent with the manuscript makes it easy for the editor to select reviewers and monitor the manuscript while it is in the review process. This letter should include the title of the manuscript, the author name(s), mailing address(es) phone and fax number(s) and e-mail addresses. In addition, this letter should provide a brief description of the manuscript theme, its applicability and significance to the journal's readership. Finally it should request a copy of the reviewer's comments regardless of whether the manuscript is accepted or rejected.

Receipt of the Reviewer's Comments

The reviewers may still reject the article although the author may have followed this procedure and taken every precaution to avoid rejection. When this occurs, the author's attitude should be focused on making those changes that would make the manuscript more understandable to the next editor, and/or reviewer. These changes may include providing additional information and/or presenting the topic in a more concise manner. Also, the author needs to determine whether some error occurred in selecting the journal to receive the manuscript. Regardless of the source of the errors, the author needs to make those changes that will improve the manuscript's chances of being accepted by the next journal to receive it.

Unless the journal specifically requests the author to revise the manuscript for publication, the author should not send the manuscript to the journal that first rejected it. In rejecting the manuscript, the reviewers implied that it could not be revised to meet their standards for publication. Thus, sending it back to them would not improve the likelihood that the manuscript will be accepted.

If your manuscript is accepted, go out and celebrate but write another one very quickly. When you find you're doing something right, keep doing it so you won't forget.

"What is a Refereed Article?"

With some exceptions a refereed article is one that is blind reviewed and has at least two external reviewers. The blind review requirement and the use of external reviewers are consistent with the research criteria of objectivity and of knowledge.

The use of a blind review process means that the author of the manuscript is not made known to the reviewer. With the large number of reviewers and journals, it is also likely that the name of the reviewers for a particular manuscript is not made known to the author. Thus, creating a double blind review process. Since the author and reviewers are frequently unknown, the manuscript is judged on its merits rather than on the reputation of the author and/or the author's influence on the reviewers.

The use of two (2) or more reviewers permits specialists familiar with research similar to that presented in the paper to judge whether the paper makes a contribution to the advancement of knowledge. When two reviewers are used it provides a broader perspective for evaluating the research. This perspective is further widened by the discussion between the editor and reviewers in seeking to reconcile these perspectives.

In contrast to these criteria, some journals that have attained a reputation for quality do not use either a blind review process or external reviewers. The most notable is *Academe: Bulletin of AAUP* that uses an editorial review process. Its reputation for quality results from its readership whose continual subscription attests to its quality.

In addition to these criteria, some researchers include the journal's acceptance rate in their definition of a refereed journal. However, the method of calculating acceptance rates varies among journals. Some journals use all manuscripts received as a base for computing this rate. Other journals allow the editor to choose which papers are sent to reviewers and calculate the acceptance rate on those that are reviewed that is less than the total manuscripts received. Also, many editors do not maintain accurate records on this data and provide only a rough estimate.

Furthermore, the number of people associated with a particular area of specialization influences the acceptance rate. If only a few people can write papers in an area, it tends to increase the journal's acceptance rate.

Although the type of review process and use of external reviewers is one possible definition of a refereed article, it is not the only criteria. Judging the usefulness of a journal to the advancement of knowledge requires the reader to be familiar with many journals in their specialization and make their own evaluation.

About Campus

ADDRESS FOR SUBMISSION:

Marcia Baxter Magdola, Editor
About Campus
Miami University
Department of Educational Leadership
350 McGuffey Hall
Oxford, OH 45056
USA
Phone: 513-529-6837
Fax: 513-529-1729
E-Mail: aboutcampus@muohio.edu
Web: www.myacpa.org/pub/pub_ac.cfm
Address May Change:

PUBLICATION GUIDELINES:

Manuscript Length: Varies
Copies Required: No Paper Copy Required
Computer Submission: Yes Email
Format: MSWord
Fees to Review: 0.00 US$

Manuscript Style:
    See Manuscript Guidelines

CIRCULATION DATA:

Reader: Academics
Frequency of Issue: 6 Times/Year
Copies per Issue: 5,001 - 10,000
Sponsor/Publisher: American College
    Personnel Association (ACPA)/Jossey-
    Bass (Wiley Publishers)
Subscribe Price: 60.00 US$ Individual

REVIEW INFORMATION:

Type of Review: Editorial Review
No. of External Reviewers: No Reply
No. of In House Reviewers: 2
Acceptance Rate: No Reply
Time to Review: 1 - 2 Months
Reviewers Comments: Yes
Invited Articles: 50% +
Fees to Publish: 0.00 US$

MANUSCRIPT TOPICS:
Counseling & Personnel Services; Curriculum Studies; Education
Management/Administration; Higher Education

MANUSCRIPT GUIDELINES/COMMENTS:

Submitting a Manuscript & Editorial Policy, and Submitted Manuscript Status
Contact Executive Editor, at the above address, or E-mail: **aboutcampus@muohio.edu**

Aims and Scope
About Campus is dedicated to the idea that student learning is the responsibility of all
educators on campus. Six times a year, *About Campus* offers an exciting and eclectic mix of
articles and features--all designed to illuminate the critical issues faced by both student affairs
and academic affairs staff as they work on the shared goal that brought them to the same
campus in the first place: to help students learn.

Academe: Bulletin of AAUP

ADDRESS FOR SUBMISSION:

Editor
Academe: Bulletin of AAUP
American Assn. of University Professors
Suite 500
1012 14th Street N.W.
Washington, DC 20005
USA
Phone: 202-737-5900 ext. 3014
Fax: 202-737-5526
E-Mail: academe@aaup.org
Web: www.aaup.org
Address May Change:

PUBLICATION GUIDELINES:

Manuscript Length: 11-15
Copies Required: Two
Computer Submission: Yes Disk, Email
Format: Any PC + 1 hardcopy
Fees to Review: 0.00 US$

Manuscript Style:
   Chicago Manual of Style

CIRCULATION DATA:

Reader: Academics
Frequency of Issue: Bi-Monthly
Copies per Issue: More than 25,000
Sponsor/Publisher: American Association
   of University Professors
Subscribe Price: 64.00 US$ Individual
   72.00 US$ Foreign (Including Canada)
   Free to AAUP Members

REVIEW INFORMATION:

Type of Review: Editorial Review
No. of External Reviewers: 0
No. of In House Reviewers: 2
Acceptance Rate: 0-5%
Time to Review: 2 - 3 Months
Reviewers Comments: Yes
Invited Articles: 50% +
Fees to Publish: 0.00 US$

MANUSCRIPT TOPICS:
Higher Education

MANUSCRIPT GUIDELINES/COMMENTS:

Manuscript Submissions
Academe explores topics in higher education from the perspective of faculty members. Most issues of the magazine focus on a particular theme but also include individual articles on separate subjects. Because *Academe*'s readership includes faculty members from many different disciplines, *Academe* seeks to publish thoughtful articles written in a lively, nontechnical style. The editors of *Academe* edit articles with such a style in mind. They also aim to break up long sentences, clarify confusing points, and remove any repetitions. Articles are first reviewed for content and substantive changes by *Academe*'s faculty editor, after which they are sent to the managing editor for copyediting.

Style. *Academe* uses the *Chicago Manual of Style* (14th ed.) and the *Merriam Webster Collegiate Dictionary* (10th ed.).

Preparation. Authors are asked to submit articles to *Academe*'s faculty editor, Ellen Schrecker (see address below). We can accept manuscripts in hard copy or by fax, but the editing process will require an electronic text, either as an e-mail submission or on disk. *Academe* can accommodate word-processing software compatible with Windows. Other formats must be converted before submission.

Length. Most features run between 2,000 and 3,000 words.

Biographical Statement. Include a brief biographical statement describing academic or other affiliation.

Notes. Avoid bibliographies, endnotes, and lengthy parenthetical references. Work any necessary citations into the text.

Illustrations. If your article is accepted for publication, we will need an author photo. *Academe* can accommodate color or black and white photos. Size does not matter. We welcome other graphic materials.

Contact Information. Please submit home and office addresses, telephone numbers, and e-mail addresses.

Note. We encourage you to contact *Academe*'s faculty editor before submitting a manuscript to determine if the manuscript's topic is compatible with *Academe*'s editorial program. An invitation to submit an article does not guarantee publication.

Letters To The Editor
Acdaeme welcomes letters to the editor of three hundred words or fewer. Submit letters by mail to the address above or by e-mail to **academe@aaup.org**. *Academe* reserves the right to edit letters. In order to be considered for publication, submissions must include the writer's name and telephone number.

For further information, contact Ellen Schrecker, Faculty Editor, *Academe*, 771 West End Ave., 7D, New York, NY 10025. E-mail: **schreckr@ymail.yu.edu**. You may also contact Wendi Maloney, Managing Editor, *Academe*, AAUP, 1012 Fourteenth St., NW, Suite 500, Washington DC 20005-3465. (202) 737-5900, ext. 3014. E-mail: **wmaloney@aaup.org**.

Adult Education Quarterly

ADDRESS FOR SUBMISSION:

B. Courtenay & R. Hill, Co-Editors
Adult Education Quarterly
University of Georgia
Department of Adult Education
River's Crossing, Room 422
850 College Station Road
Athens, GA 30602
USA
Phone: 706-542-2214
Fax: 706-542-4024
E-Mail: bcourt@coe.uga.edu
Web: http://www.uga.edu/aeq/
Address May Change:

PUBLICATION GUIDELINES:

Manuscript Length: 7,500 words maximum
Copies Required: One
Computer Submission: Yes Email, Disk
Format: MS Word
Fees to Review: 0.00 US$

Manuscript Style:
American Psychological Association

CIRCULATION DATA:

Reader: , Scholars & Practitioners
Frequency of Issue: Quarterly
Copies per Issue: 2,001 - 3,000
Sponsor/Publisher: American Association
of Adult & Continuing Education
(AAACE) / Sage Publications
Subscribe Price:
See Guidelines

REVIEW INFORMATION:

Type of Review: Blind Review
No. of External Reviewers: 3
No. of In House Reviewers: 0
Acceptance Rate: 11-30%
Time to Review: 2 - 3 Months
Reviewers Comments: Yes
Invited Articles: No Reply
Fees to Publish: 0.00 US$

MANUSCRIPT TOPICS:
Adult Career & Vocational

MANUSCRIPT GUIDELINES/COMMENTS:

AEQ Mission Statement
The *Adult Education Quarterly (AEQ)* is a scholarly refereed journal committed to advancing the understanding and practice of adult and continuing education. The journal strives to be inclusive in scope, addressing topics and issues of significance to scholars and practitioners concerned with diverse aspects of adult and continuing education. *AEQ* publishes research employing a variety of methods and approaches, including (but not limited to) survey research, experimental designs, case studies, ethnographic observations and interviews, grounded theory, phenomenology, historical investigations, and narrative inquiry as well as articles that address theoretical and philosophical issues pertinent to adult and continuing education. Innovative and provocative scholarship informed by diverse orientations is encouraged, including (but not limited to) positivism, post-positivism, constructivism, critical theory, feminism, race-based/Africentric, gay/lesbian, and poststructural/postmodern theories.

AEQ aims to stimulate a problem-oriented, critical approach to research and practice, with an increasing emphasis on inter-disciplinary and international perspectives. The audience includes researchers, students, and adult and continuing education practitioners of many orientations including teachers, trainers, facilitators, resource persons, organizational developers, community organizers, and policy designers.

Guidelines for Contributors

The *Adult Education Quarterly* is committed to the dissemination of knowledge produced by disciplined inquiry in the field of adult and continuing education. Three criteria are used in the review and selection process. First, articles must significantly advance knowledge and practice. Second, all material must be accurate and technically correct. Finally, articles must be well-crafted and well-written. To facilitate the preparation and submission of manuscripts, we offer the following information, guidelines, and procedures.

General Information

Journal Address:
University of Georgia
Department of Adult Education
River's Crossing, Room 422
850 College Station Road
Athens, GA 30602, USA
Phone: (706) 542-2214; Fax: (706) 542-4024
E-Mail: bcourt@coe.uga.edu; Web: http://www.coe.uga.edu/aeq/

EDITORIAL STAFF
Editors
Bradley Courtenay, University of Georgia
Robert Hill, University of Georgia

Book Review Editors
Mary Alfred, University of Wisconsin-Milwaukee
Barbara J. Daley, University of Wisconsin-Milwaukee

Editorial Associate
Elisabeth Bennett, University of Georgia

Organizational Sponsorship
American Association for Adult and Continuing Education (AAACE)
Commission of Professors of Adult Education (CPAE)
4380 Forbes Blvd.
Lanham, MD 20706 USA
Phone: 301-918-1913; Fax: 301-918-1846

Scope
AEQ is a blind-review scholarly journal committed to the dissemination of research and theory that advances the understanding and practice of adult and continuing education.

Types of Articles Published
- Research approaches including (but not limited to): survey research, experimental designs, case studies, ethnographic observations and interviews, grounded theory, phenomenology, historical investigations, and narrative inquiry
- Inquiry orientations including (but not limited to): positivism, post-positivism, constructivism, critical theory, feminism, race-based/Africentric, gay/lesbian, and poststructural/postmodern theories
- Theory building and philosophical analysis
- Critical integrative reviews of adult and continuing education literature
- Forum (position statements or reasoned critiques of articles previously printed in
- AEQ)
- Essay reviews (commissioned by the editors)
- Book reviews (contact the book review editor; see the book review section)
- "To the Editor" comments and contributions

Editorial Style
Publication Manual of the American Psychological Association (fourth edition).

Preparation for Submission
Prospective authors might consider the following strategies in preparing manuscripts for *AEQ:*
- Study the Editorial Policy and its sections on guidelines to ensure that your manuscript falls within the scope of the journal and will meet stylistic requirements.
- Consider the "Review Criteria" (see that section of the Editorial Policy) in developing and crafting your manuscript.
- Study back issues of *AEQ* and its predecessor, *Adult Education*, focusing especially on articles of purpose and form similar to your manuscript.
- Ask at least two colleagues who are insightful and constructive in their appraisals to critically review the manuscript before submitting it to *AEQ*.

Technical and Stylistic Requirements
For the editorial process to begin, all submissions must meet the following technical and stylistic requirements:

Typed Copy
Submit typed, **double-spaced** copy with numbered pages, using one inch margins on all sides.

Number of Copies
Submit one paper copy and one electronic (on either PC or Mac platform by either a disk or by email attachment). We would prefer that the manuscript be in MS Word. Be sure to label the disk or email message with the platform and word processing software you are using. Authors should retain a copy of their manuscripts. The editors are not responsible for returning copies to authors.

Article Length
Articles generally should not exceed 7500 words, including charts, tables, and bibliography.

Title Page
On the title page, indicate the following: title of paper; full name(s) of author(s), author titles and institutional affiliations, postal addresses, phone numbers, fax numbers, and email addresses; brief acknowledgement of the contribution of colleagues or students, if warranted; statement of place and date of previous oral presentation, if any; and date of submission.

Abstract
In 150 words or less, summarize the purpose, approach, and conclusions of the paper in an abstract immediately following the title page. Include only the title of the paper on   this   and subsequent pages.

Text
Repeat a shortened version of the title of the manuscript (a running head) on the top of each page of the text. The name of the author(s) must not appear on any page, other than through standard reference usage.

Stylistic Requirements
Manuscripts submitted to *AEQ* must be grammatically correct and stylistically consistent. *AEQ* uses the *Publication Manual of the American Psychological Association*, fourth edition. Consult this publication for rules governing references and citations as well as other elements of grammar and style.

Warrant Statement
Any submission must include a typed, dated, and signed warrant statement assigning first publication rights to AAACE effective if and when it is accepted for publication by the editors. Manuscripts cannot be processed for publication until the editors of *AEQ* have received this signed statement, worded as follows:

I hereby confirm the assignment of first publication rights only in and to the manuscript named above in all forms and media to AAACE effective if and when it is accepted for publication by the AEQ editorial board. I warrant that my manuscript is original work and has not bee accepted for publication by another periodical. I further warrant that my work (including tables, figures, photographs, and other illustrative material) does not infringe on the copyright or statutory rights of others, does not contain libelous statements, and that the editorial board members, staff, and officers of AAACE are indemnified against costs, expenses, and damages arising from any breach of the foregoing in regard to the manuscript. Finally, I acknowledge that AEQ is relying on this statement in any publishing of this manuscript's information.

Manuscripts submitted to *AEQ* should not be under consideration for publication by any other journals, nor should they have been published previously in any form. A paper may, however, have been presented at a meeting or conference. In such cases, the author should state where and when such a paper was presented. After acceptance, a paper may not be published elsewhere without written permission from AAACE and/or CPAE.

10

Letter of Transmittal
Attach a letter addressed to the editors indicating the title of the manuscript, date of submission, and all authors with their institutional affiliations.

Editorial Procedure
AEQ editorial staff initially reviews all manuscript submissions for compliance with *AEQ* editorial policy. If the manuscript fails to fall within the scope and stylistic guidelines of the journal, it is returned to the authors. If a manuscript is in accord with the scope of the journal and meets submission guidelines, all references to the author name and institution are removed from the manuscript, and it is submitted for blind reviews to three *AEQ* consulting editors. Each consulting editor is a professional scholar judged competent to appraise such manuscripts.

In compliance with advice of consulting editors, the editors make one of four decisions: *accept*; conditional accept, contingent upon major revisions; reject and encourage revision; or reject. In the case of conditional acceptance, the editors will specify necessary revisions in writing to the author. When revisions are completed and the editors accept a manuscript, the editors will then notify and inform the author(s) about the next steps in the publication process.

Review Criteria
In seeking to advance the understanding and practice of adult and continuing education, the journal strives to be inclusive in scope and aims to stimulate a problem-oriented, critical approach to research and practice, with an increasing emphasis on inter-disciplinary and international perspectives. The following are used to review scholarly papers submitted to *AEQ*:

Importance of the Problem
A problem or subject addressed by a manuscript should contribute to knowledge or theory pertinent to adult and continuing education. Importance is enhanced when a paper promotes understanding or improvement of practice.

Background
Through the abstract and a brief introduction, readers should be provided with sufficient background information to understand the problem being addressed.

Problem/Purpose
The purpose of the paper should be clearly and unambiguously stated. This typically requires a clearly described research problem.

Literature Review
Research and scholarship should be linked to relevant empirical and theoretical literature. The applicability of the research and the quality of the discussion are more important than the length of the literature review.

Methodology
The approach and procedures must be appropriate for addressing the stated research problem(s) and purpose(s).

Findings
Findings must be presented and documented to show clear relationships to the purpose(s) and research question(s). Evidence needed to support conclusions must be clearly identified and amply arrayed, including (but not limited to) the presentation of statistics, charts, and graphs; use of quotations; observational data; references; and citations.

Conclusions
Conclusions and logical inferences should be pertinent, clearly drawn, and convincingly supported by evidence.

Readability
All manuscripts must be well organized, well written, and readable.

Book Reviews
The book review editor solicits, edits, and manages the book review process. Suggestions for books to be reviewed or nominations to review books should be submitted to:

Book Review Editors
Mary Alfred and Barbara J. Daley
University of Wisconsin-Milwaukee
Adult & Continuing Education
Administrative Leadership, Enderis Hall
P.O. Box 413
Milwaukee, WI 53201-0413
Phone: 414-229-4311 or 414-229-5495; Fax: 414-229-5300

Subscription Prices:
Individual (Print Only) $67.00 US / £45.00 GBP
Institution: Combined (Print & E-access) $229.00 US / £153.00 GBP
Electronic only & Print only subscriptions are available at a discounted rate.

Adult Learning

ADDRESS FOR SUBMISSION:

Lillian Hill, Ralph Brockett, Editors
Adult Learning
410 N 12th Street, PO980533
Richmond, VA 23298-0533
USA
Phone: 804-828-3589
Fax: 804-827-0002
E-Mail: lhhill@vcu.edu
Web:
Address May Change: 10/31/2004

PUBLICATION GUIDELINES:

Manuscript Length: 11-15
Copies Required: Four
Computer Submission: Yes Disk, Email
Format: MSWord or RTF
Fees to Review: 0.00 US$

Manuscript Style:
    American Psychological Association

CIRCULATION DATA:

Reader: , Practitioners
Frequency of Issue: Quarterly
Copies per Issue: 3,001 - 4,000
Sponsor/Publisher: American Assn. for
    Adult and Continuing Education
Subscribe Price: 20.00 US$ Member
    45.00 US$ Non-Member US
    50.00 US$ Canada & $50 Foreign

REVIEW INFORMATION:

Type of Review: Blind Review
No. of External Reviewers: 3
No. of In House Reviewers: 1
Acceptance Rate: 21-30%
Time to Review: 2 - 3 Months
Reviewers Comments: No
Invited Articles: 21-30%
Fees to Publish: 0.00 US$

MANUSCRIPT TOPICS:
Adult Career & Vocational; Adult Education; Adult Learning

MANUSCRIPT GUIDELINES/COMMENTS:

Co-Editor Ralph Brockett
University of Tennessee
Department of Educational Psychology
439 Claxton Addition
Knoxville, TN 37996-3400
Phone: 865-974-2227; Email: **brockett@utk.edu**

Adult Learning is a magazine for adult educators designed to provide short, well-written, professionally oriented articles with a problem-solving emphasis. The audience *for Adult Learning* includes all individuals who design, manage, teach, conduct, and evaluate programs of adult and continuing education broadly defined.

Address of the Magazine
American Association for Adult and Continuing Education (AAACE) 4380 Forbes Blvd., Lanham, MD 20706

Suggested Length
Feature Articles: 1,500 words
Department Articles: 700-1,000 words

Format
Send three copies of the manuscript. The manuscript should be typed, double-spaced (keep a personal copy). Include a brief biography (current position and title) and a separate title page. Include the address and telephone number where you can be reached. Include the titled if the article on the actual manuscript page.

Where to Submit
All unsolicited manuscripts should be sent to the Editors at the **Address for Submission** address listed.

Photos
Photos to illustrate the article are accepted. Black and white glossy prints are preferred over color prints.

Editorial Procedure
Two members of the editorial board review articles. Authors receive a decision within three months of article submission. Reviewers make one of the following four recommendations: Publish, Revise, Rewrite, or Reject.

The magazine uses articles receiving recommendations to publish first. Articles receiving recommendations to Revise are published on a space available basis. It is the policy of *Adult Learning* to receive for review a second draft of articles that initially receive recommendations to Revise. These authors are given comments and suggestions on how substantive, content changes could be made successfully. Suggestions for organization and readability may also be offered. The same member of the editorial board who reviewed the first draft generally reviews second drafts. Second drafts that are acceptable in terms of content may be subject to further revision for organization and readability.

Copy Editing
Manuscripts accepted for publication will be edited.

Exclusivity
Manuscripts should not be under consideration for publication by other magazine or periodicals nor should they have been published previously (except as a part of a presentation at a meeting.) Articles should be submitted with a typed, dated, and signed warrant statement that reads as follows:

> I hereby confirm the assignment of first publication rights only in and to the manuscript named in all forms and media to AAACE effective if and When it is accepted for publication by another periodical. I warrant that my manuscript is original work and has not been accepted for publication by another periodical. /further warrant that my word does not infringe upon any copyright or statutory rights of others, does not contain

slightly different from that of regular paper publishing, the *APA* style will be followed as closely as possible. Indentions, spacing, and footnoting may vary in this journal.

2. Manuscripts should be typed, double-spaced, titled, and should be no more than a total of 30 pages in length. Do not put any identification of the author(s) within the text of the manuscript. Pertinent photographs, charts, or graphs need to accompany the manuscript.

3. Manuscripts submitted should be previously unpublished and not under consideration by another publication.

4. A cover page needs to be included containing such items as the title of the manuscript, all authors and their complete contact information such as address, telephone number, fax number, and e-mail addresses. Give a brief biography of each author stating affiliation, position, degree received, etc.

5. Submit manuscript either by e-mail or through the postal service.

E-mail to the Editors at: **edu_bid@shsu.edu** or **advancingwomen@shsu.edu**

Postal Mail. If mailed through the postal service, the author must submit three hard copies of the manuscript along with it saved on a disk. The document must be saved as a Word Document or as an RTF file.

Dr. Genevieve Brown/Dr. Beverly J. Irby, Editors
Advancing Women in Leadership On-line Journal
Sam Houston State University
P.O. Box 2119
Huntsville, Texas 77341-2119
Telephone: 936-294-1147; Fax: 936-294-3886

Manuscript Deadline: On a continuous basis

Copyright. Advancing Women in Leadership holds the copyright to each article; however, any article may be reproduced without permission, for educational purposes only, provided that the full and accurate bibliographic citation and the following credit line is cited: Copyright (year) by the *Advancing Women in Leadership*, Advancing Women Website, www.advancingwomen.com; reproduced with permission from the publisher. Any article cited as a reference in any other form should also report the same such citation, following APA or other style manual guidelines for citing electronic publications.

American Educational Research Journal: Social and Institutional Analysis

ADDRESS FOR SUBMISSION:

Maenette K. P. Benham, Editor
American Educational Research Journal:
Social and Institutional Analysis
ELECTRONIC SUBMISSION ONLY
Michigan State University
Sect. On Social & Institutional Analysis
419 A Erickson Hall
East Lansing, MI 48824
USA
Phone: 517-355-6613
Fax: 517-353-6393
E-Mail: aerjsia@msu.edu
Web: www.aera.net/pubs/aerj
Address May Change:

PUBLICATION GUIDELINES:

Manuscript Length: 50-75 not incl. Refs
Copies Required: Electronic only
Computer Submission: Yes
    www.aera.net/aerj
Format: Word or RTF
Fees to Review: 0.00 US$

Manuscript Style:
    See Manuscript Guidelines

CIRCULATION DATA:

Reader: Academics
Frequency of Issue: Quarterly
Copies per Issue: 10,001 - 25,000
Sponsor/Publisher: American Educational
    Research Association
Subscribe Price: 15.00 US$ AERA
    Member

REVIEW INFORMATION:

Type of Review: Blind Review
No. of External Reviewers: 3+
No. of In House Reviewers: 1
Acceptance Rate: 7-13%
Time to Review: 2 - 3 Months
Reviewers Comments: Yes
Invited Articles: 0-5%
Fees to Publish: 0.00 US$

MANUSCRIPT TOPICS:

Education Management/Administration; Higher Education; School Law; Social &
Institutional Analysis in Education; Tests, Measurement & Evaluation; Urban Education,
Cultural/Non-Traditional

MANUSCRIPT GUIDELINES/COMMENTS:

Statement of Purpose

The American Educational Research Journal has as its purpose to carry original empirical and
theoretical studies and analyses in education. The editors seek to publish articles from a wide
variety of academic disciplines and substantive fields; they are looking for clear and
significant contributions to the understanding and/or improvement of educational processes
and outcomes. Manuscripts not appropriate for submission to this journal include essays,
reviews, course evaluations, and brief reports of studies to address a narrow question.

The *Section on Social and Institutional Analysis (SIA)* publishes scholarly research that addresses significant political, cultural, social, economic, and organizational issues in education. It welcomes analyses of the broad contextual and organizational factors affecting teaching and learning, the links between those factors and the nature and processes of schooling, and the ways that such "external" domains are conceptualized in research, policy, and practice. The editors invite articles that advance the theoretical understandings of the social and institutional contexts of education and encompass the diverse communities of schooling and educational research. They welcome research across a wide range of methodological paradigms, including ethnographic, historical, narrative, legal, experimental/quantitative, critical, and interpretive approaches; they also invite studies that make the nature and uses of educational research itself a subject of social and cultural inquiry.

The *Section on Teaching, Learning, and Human Development (TLHD)* publishes research articles that explore the processes and outcomes of teaching, learning, and human development at all educational levels and in both formal and informal settings. This section also welcomes policy research related to teaching, learning, and learning to teach. It publishes articles that represent a wide range of academic disciplines and use a variety of research methods.

INFORMATION FOR CONTRIBUTORS

Submission of Manuscripts
Manuscripts are accepted for consideration with the understanding that they are original material and are not under consideration for publication elsewhere. All submissions must be properly formatted for blind reviewing (see *Publication Manual of the American Psychological Association*, 5th ed., 2001, for instructions).

The review process is conducted electronically. To submit manuscripts for the *SIA* section, go to **http://www.aera.net/aerj/**. All editorial correspondence and inquiries relating to this section should be sent to Maenette K. P. Benham, 419A Erickson Hall, Michigan State University, East Lansing, MI 48824 (e-mail **aerjsia@msu.edu**).

For the TLHD section, all editorial correspondence and manuscripts should be sent to Bruce Thompson, Department of Educational Psychology, Texas A&M University, 704 Harrington, College Station, TX 77843-4225. At present there are no arrangements for electronic submissions to the THLD section. To submit a manuscript to the TLHD section, please send five copies.

Specifications for Manuscripts
Style manuals. Submissions must follow the styles outlined in either the *Publication Manual of the American Psychological Association* (2001, 5th edition)—available from the American Psychological Association, Order Department, P.O. Box 2710, Hyattsville, MD 20784—or the *Chicago Manual of Style* (2003, 15th edition). IMPORTANT: Authors who follow *Chicago* must use the author-date citation system, described in chapter 16. Accepted manuscripts that do not use an author-date system of citation will need to be reformatted by the author for publication.

Abstract. All manuscripts should include an abstract of 100–120 words.

Author identification. The complete title of the article and the name(s) of the author(s) should be typed only on the first sheet to ensure anonymity in the review process. Subsequent pages should not have author names but may carry a short title at the top. Information in text or references that would identify the author should be deleted from the manuscript (e.g., text citations of "my previous work," especially when accompanied by a self-citation; a preponderance of the author's own work in the reference list.). These may be reinserted in the final draft. Complete contact information must be supplied for all authors and co-authors, including full street address and zip code, telephone and fax numbers, and e-mail address. The corresponding author should be identified.

Typescript. Manuscripts should be typed for 8½" x 11" paper, in upper and lower case, double-spaced, with 1½" margins on all sides. They should be in IBM-compatible MS Word format. Subheads should be used at reasonable intervals to break the monotony of text. Words and symbols to be italicized must be clearly indicated, by either italic type or underlining. Abbreviations and acronyms should be spelled out at first mention unless found as entries in their abbreviated form in Merriam-Webster's Tenth Collegiate Dictionary (e.g., "IQ" needs no explanation). Pages should be numbered consecutively.

Length. Manuscripts for the SIA section should typically run between 50 and 75 pages in typed form, not including the reference list. Manuscripts for the TLHD section should typically run between 35 and 60 pages in typed form, *including* the reference list.

Notes and references. Notes are for explanations or amplifications of textual material. They are distracting to readers and expensive to set and should be avoided whenever possible. They should be typed as normal text at the end of the text section of the manuscript rather than as part of the footnote or endnote feature of a computer program and should be numbered consecutively throughout the article.

A reference list contains only references that are cited in the text. Its accuracy and completeness are the responsibility of the author(s). Personal communications (letters, memos, telephone conversations) are cited in the text after the name with as exact a date as possible. Examples of references to a book, a chapter in a book, and a journal article follow, formatted in APA style:

Bobrow, D. G., & Collins, A. M. (Eds.). (1975). *Representation and understanding: Studies in cognitive science.* New York: Academic Press.

Crothers, E. (1972). Memory structure and the recall of discourse. In R. O. Freedle & J. B. Carroll (Eds.), *Language comprehension and the acquisition of knowledge* (pp. 201–238). Washington, DC: Winston.

Frase, L. T. (1968). Questions as aids to reading: Some research and a theory. *American Educational Research Journal, 5,* 319–322.

Tables, Figures, and Illustrations. Create tables, figures, and illustrations in their own electronic files, separate from the main text. (You may use one file for all of the tables, but place each figure or illustration in a separate file. Each table should begin on a new page.) Figures and tables should be keyed to the text. Do not describe the data in the text in such detail that tables become redundant. Figure captions should appear on a separate sheet, not on the original figures. One high-quality, camera-ready version of each figure must be submitted with the manuscript; photocopies may accompany the additional manuscript copies. Compositors will typeset the tables.

Review Process
The editor will acknowledge manuscripts upon receipt. After preliminary editorial review, articles will be sent to reviewers with expertise in the subject. The review process takes from 3 to 5 months, so authors should not expect to hear from editors before that time regarding the status of their manuscripts. AERA publications use the blind review system. The names of referees are published in the journals periodically.

Copyright
Authors who wish to use materials, such as figures or tables, for which they do not own the copyright *must* obtain written permission from the copyright holder (usually the publisher) and submit it to AERA with their manuscripts.

To protect the works of authors and the Association, AERA copyrights all of its publications. Rights and permissions for AERA-copyrighted materials are handled by the AERA Publications Department, 1230 17th Street, NW, Washington, DC 20036-3078.

Right of Reply
The right-of-reply policy encourages comments on articles recently published in AERA publications. The comments are subject to editorial review and decision. If a comment is accepted for publication, the editor informs the author of the original article. If the author submits a reply to the comment, the reply is also subject to editorial review and decision. The editor may allot a specific amount of journal space for the comment (ordinarily about 1,500 words) and for the reply (ordinarily about 750 words). The reply may appear in the same issue as the comment or in a later issue.

Grievances
Authors who believe that their manuscripts were not reviewed in a careful or timely manner in accordance with AERA's procedures should call the matter to the attention of the Association's president or executive officer.

Author Responsibilities
Please refer to the AERA link regarding Submission Guidelines
   http://35.8.171.42/aera/epubs/index.htm.

1. An author's obligation is to present a cogent and complete account of the research together with a discussion of its relevance to the field of education. The author's work must fit within the scope of AERJ:SIA.
2. The manuscript should include substantive detail and reference giving appropriate attribution.
3. The manuscript shall not include plagiarized material or falsified research data. In addition, it is inappropriate for the author to submit the same (or substantially similar) manuscript to more than one journal for publication consideration.

4. All manuscripts should be edited and copy edited to ensure appropriate style (*APA*, Fifth Edition), grammar, and coherent structure. It is inappropriate to submit manuscripts with an obvious commercial intent.

Editorial Obligations

Please also see http://35.8.171.42/aera/pub/aerj.

1. The primary responsibility of the *AERJ:SIA* editorial team is to ensure an efficient and fair peer review process of manuscripts that fall within the scope of the journal and to establish and maintain a high standard of technical and professional quality. Criteria of quality are originality of approach, profundity, rigorous research design and application, and relevance to the field of education.

2. The editorial team will judge the quality of the manuscript on its own merit respecting the intellectual independence of the author(s).

3. The editorial team shall disclose no information about a manuscript under consideration to anyone other than those from whom professional advice regarding the publication of the manuscript is sought. The names of the reviewers shall not be released.

4. The editorial team shall avoid conflicts of interest and/or the appearance thereof. A manuscript will not be sent to a reviewer who has a known bias in favor of or against the author or the subject matter of that manuscript.

5. If the editor is presented with convincing evidence that a manuscript contains plagiarized material, falsified research data, or appears in another journal, the editor, after notifying the author(s) and allowing them to respond in writing, shall facilitate immediate action per AERA policy.

American Educational Research Journal: Teaching, Learning and Human Development

ADDRESS FOR SUBMISSION:

Bruce Thompson, Co-Editor
American Educational Research Journal:
  Teaching, Learning and Human
  Development
Texas A&M University
Department of Educational Psychology
College Station, TX 77843-4225
USA
Phone: 979-862-6547
Fax:
E-Mail: aerj@coe.tamu.edu
Web: www.coe.tamu.edu/~bthompson/aerj
Address May Change:

PUBLICATION GUIDELINES:

Manuscript Length: No set length
Copies Required: Five
Computer Submission: Non-US only
Format:
Fees to Review: 0.00 US$

Manuscript Style:
  American Psychological Association,
  Chicago Manual of Style

CIRCULATION DATA:

Reader: Academics
Frequency of Issue: Quarterly
Copies per Issue: 20,000
Sponsor/Publisher: American Educational
  Research Association
Subscribe Price: 15.00 US$ Members

REVIEW INFORMATION:

Type of Review: Blind Review
No. of External Reviewers: 3+
No. of In House Reviewers: No Reply
Acceptance Rate: 7-13%
Time to Review: 3-4 Months
Reviewers Comments: Yes
Invited Articles: 0-5%
Fees to Publish: 0.00 US$

MANUSCRIPT TOPICS:

Educational Psychology; Elementary/Early Childhood; Gifted Children; Higher Education; Reading; Science Math & Environment; Secondary/Adolescent Studies; Social Studies/Social Science; Special Education

MANUSCRIPT GUIDELINES/COMMENTS:

Statement of Purpose

The *American Educational Research Journal: Teaching, Learning and Human Development (AERJ:TLHD)* has as its purpose to publish original empirical and theoretical studies and analyses in education. The editors seek to publish articles from a wide variety of academic disciplines and substantive fields. We are looking for contributions that are significant to the understanding and/or improvement of educational processes and outcomes. Quality and technical competence are important criteria in the review and selection processes. In addition, we consider the broader significance of the topic addressed. *AERJ* has a very diverse readership. Articles published in *AERJ* must be written in a style and format that will provide access to their content for researchers, practitioners, and policy makers in a broad range of education-related fields. Many articles are excellent examples of work, but are not necessarily important in advancing a field or to education in general. These articles are more appropriate for journals of a more specialized nature.

In recent years, *AERJ* has moved to increase the scope of the journal beyond the narrow band of disciplines traditionally represented. As a continuation of this trend, two distinct sections have been created within the journal, each with its own editor and editorial board.

Section on Teaching, Learning and Human Development
The Teaching, Learning, and Human Development section of *AERJ* publishes articles that explore the constructs, the processes and outcomes of teaching, learning, and human development at all educational levels and in formal and informal settings. This section also welcomes policy research related to teaching, learning, and learning to teach. The Teaching, Learning, and Human Development section seeks articles that represent a wide range of academic disciplines and use a variety of research methods.

Manuscript Submission Addresses
Please send manuscripts (five fully blinded copies) for the Teaching, Learning, and Human Development section to Bruce Thompson, AERJ:TLHD Co-Editor; TAMU Dept Educ Psyc; College Station, TX 77843-4225; Tel: (979) 862-6547, Email: **aerj@coe.tamu.edu**

Review Process
Manuscripts will be acknowledged by the editor upon receipt. *AERA* publications use the blind review system. The names of referees are published annually in the various journals.

American Indian Culture and Research

ADDRESS FOR SUBMISSION:

Editor
American Indian Culture and Research
UCLA American Indian Studies Center
3220 Campbell Hall, Box 951548
Los Angeles, CA 90095-1548
USA
Phone: 310-825-7315
Fax: 310-206-7060
E-Mail: editor@aisc.ucla.edu
Web: www.books.aisc.ucla.edu
Address May Change:

PUBLICATION GUIDELINES:

Manuscript Length: 26-30
Copies Required: Four
Computer Submission: No
Format: N/A
Fees to Review: 0.00 US$

Manuscript Style:
    Chicago Manual of Style

CIRCULATION DATA:

Reader: Academics
Frequency of Issue: Quarterly
Copies per Issue: 1,001 - 2,000
Sponsor/Publisher: UCLA American Indian
    Studies Center
Subscribe Price: 30.00 US$ Individual
    70.00 US$ Institution
    20.00 US$ Additional Foreign Postage

REVIEW INFORMATION:

Type of Review: Blind Review
No. of External Reviewers: 3+
No. of In House Reviewers: 1
Acceptance Rate: 21-30%
Time to Review: 2 - 3 Months
Reviewers Comments: Yes
Invited Articles: 6-10%
Fees to Publish: 0.00 US$

MANUSCRIPT TOPICS:
American Indian Studies; American Literature; Art/Music; Educational Psychology; History, Anthropology; Languages & Linguistics; Multicultural Education; Social Studies/Social Science; Urban Education, Cultural/Non-Traditional

MANUSCRIPT GUIDELINES/COMMENTS:

1. Submit four (4) copies of the manuscript to Editor, *American Indian Culture and Research Journal*, UCLA American Indian Studies Center, 3220 Campbell Hall, Box 951548, Los Angeles, CA 90095-1548.

Send copies; retain originals. Do not send original tables, pictures, figures, and the like, as we cannot guarantee they will be returned.

2. Since all manuscripts are evaluated by at least three anonymous referees, please keep identifying material out of the printed manuscript. Attach a cover page giving authorship, contact information (address, phone, and email), institutional affiliation, and acknowledgments.

3. All copies must be typed, double-spaced (including indented material, footnotes, and references) on 8-1/2-by-11 white paper. All margins must be at least one inch.

4. The review process ordinarily is completed within three months. If the process is delayed beyond that point, authors will be notified.

Multiple Submission Policy

The *American Indian Culture and Research Journal* regards as unacceptable the submission of a manuscript to one professional journal while that manuscript is under review by any other journal. It is further assumed by the *American Indian Culture and Research Journal* that work submitted for review has not been published previously and is not scheduled for publication elsewhere. If other published or submitted papers exist that are based on the same or closely related data sets, such papers should be noted and referenced in a cover letter to the editor, and their relation to the submitted paper should be briefly explained.

Final Submission of Article Manuscripts

1. After your article has been accepted, you will be asked to send a 3-1/2 inch computer disk containing your article. Please include a two-sentence bio and a hard copy of the manuscript. Manuscripts preferably should be on Macintosh-formatted disks with the text written and saved in Microsoft Word.

2. Manuscripts accepted for publication in the *American Indian Culture and Research Journal* are subject to editing for style and accuracy. Page proofs are sent to authors. All authors are required to assign copyright to the Regents of the University of California.

3. Manuscripts and disks will not be returned to authors. Submit original artwork upon acceptance for publication. We will make every effort to return original artwork, etc. to the author(s).

Guidelines for Manuscript Preparation, Documentation, and Illustration

Stylistic Matters

The *American Indian Culture and Research Journal's* primary guides are *The Chicago Manual of Style* (14th ed) for style and *Webster's Collegiate Dictionary* (10th ed.) for spelling and punctuation. This guide gives only general examples of documentation, including instances where AICRJ style diverges from *Chicago* style. For further guidance, please refer to chapter 15, sections 5457, 6567, and chapter 17 of the *Chicago Manual.*

Manuscript Preparation

- The following guidelines assume that you are using a computer and word-processing program to prepare your manuscript.
- Use numbered endnotes; see below for documentation style. Notes must be sequentially numbered in both the disk and hard copy.
- Indent block quotations half an inch from right and left margins.
- Indent new paragraphs half an inch.
- Type only one space after periods, questions marks, or other terminal punctuation marks.

- Center your title, typed in normal style. Underline or italicize any book or play titles contained within your own title. Do not include any note numbers in the title.
- If you use one level of subheads, CAPITALIZE and center each primary head. If you also use a secondary level of subheads, type each of such subheads flush-left.
- Use ragged right margins; don't use your word processor's justification or kerning features.
- Don't use automatic hyphenation and don't manually hyphenate words at the ends of lines. Put hyphens in the text only where you intend them to be kept (e.g., ten-mile hike).
- Use hard returns only at the ends of paragraphs, headings, list entries, etc.

Documentation

Use numbered endnotes, beginning on a separate page. Use the automated endnote function in your word-processing program to help ensure accurately numbered endnotes.

Please note that AICRJ always gives the author's name in a note, even when the name has appeared in the body of the paper.

First, Full Documentation for a Book

1. Sue-Ellen Case and Janelle Reinelt, ed., *The Performance of Power: Theatrical Discourse and Politics* (Iowa City: University of Iowa Press, 1991), 101-8.
- Note that the opening line is indented and begins with the note number in plain style (not superscripted). The note number is in the same font and size as the text.
- Note that *AICRJ* does not give the state in which the publisher is located, unless the city is likely to be unknown to a general audience (Thousand Oaks, CA: Sage Publications, 1989).
- AICRJ does not list multiple places of publication; use the city given first on the book's title page. Thus, a book published by Routledge in London & New York would be documented as London: Routledge.

First, Full Documentation for a Work in a Collection or Anthology

1. Bertolt Brecht, *Mother Courage and Her Children: A Chronicle of the Thirty Years' War, in Collected Plays: Volume 5*, ed. Ralf Manheim and John Willett (New York: Random House, Vintage Books, 1972), 196-97.
- Note that the title of the collection or anthology precedes the translator(s) or editor(s). Note, too, that "ed." precedes the editors' names when they are not in the author position.

First, Full Documentation for a Journal Article

1. James F. Powers, "Frontier Municipal Baths and Social Interaction in Thirteenth Century Spain," *American Historical Review* 84 (1993): 417.
- Note that a colon (not a comma) precedes the page number(s) for journal articles.

First, Full Documentation of Electronic Sources

3. Author's First and Last Name, "Title of Internet Site," [http://www.addaddresshere.org], Date viewed.
- Citations of documents on www should include the full reference to the exact page cited. The home page is not sufficient.

- Internet documents are often unattributed. If no individual author is indicated, add the organization sponsoring the document.

Subsequent References

- Ibid. (not italicized) refers to the immediately preceding note and indicates that all information is the same, with the possible exception of the page number: 4. Ibid.; or: 2. Ibid., 112.
- When a full citation has been given, but that citation does not immediately precede the subsequent reference, AICRJ uses the author-short title convention: 4. Brecht, *Mother Courage*, 20; or: 9. Dolan, "Geographies," 2001.

Illustrations, Photos, Figures, Tables, and Maps

Permissions
It is the author's responsibility to obtain proper permission for all artwork, photographs, etc. Permissions should be submitted with the completed manuscript and disk.

Special Fonts
Please provide on disk any special fonts used, e.g., a linguistic or non-European, foreign-language font.

Quality
Provide clean, black and white glossy prints of photographs, and clean copies of charts, graphs, figures, table, and artwork on bond paper, or have the image scanned as a TIFF file and provide on disk. In some cases, a high-quality laser-print can be used. Remember that such materials will not be improved in reproduction, so provide the best quality original you can.

Captioning and Documentation
Place a post-it or a taped sheet of paper to the back of the illustration, map, figure, etc. with the following typed or printed information.

The illustration's number (figure 1, 2, etc.).
A brief caption.
Any necessary documentation as to source, etc.
The photo credit or any other required copyright statement (e.g., "Reproduced by permission of the Barnes Foundation").

Placement
Please indicate placement of any outside media in the article's text:

[PLACE FIGURE 2 HERE].

American Journal of Distance Education

ADDRESS FOR SUBMISSION:

Michael G. Moore, Editor
American Journal of Distance Education
Pennsylvania State University
College of Education
409 Keller Bldg.
University Park, PA 16802-3202
USA
Phone:
Fax: 814-865-0128
E-Mail: mgmoore@psu.edu
Web: www.ajde.com
Address May Change:

PUBLICATION GUIDELINES:

Manuscript Length: 16-20
Copies Required: One Electronic
Computer Submission: Yes Email Preferred
Format: MSWord
Fees to Review: 0.00 US$

Manuscript Style:
      Chicago Manual of Style

CIRCULATION DATA:

Reader: Academics, Aministrators
Frequency of Issue: Quarterly
Copies per Issue: 1,001 - 2,000
Sponsor/Publisher: Lawrence Erlbaum
      Associates
Subscribe Price: 55.00 US$ Individual
      85.00 US$ Individual International
      120.00 US$ Inst., $150 International

REVIEW INFORMATION:

Type of Review: Blind Review
No. of External Reviewers: 2
No. of In House Reviewers: 3
Acceptance Rate: 11-20%
Time to Review: 4 - 6 Months
Reviewers Comments: Yes
Invited Articles: 0-5%
Fees to Publish: 0.00 US$

MANUSCRIPT TOPICS:
Curriculum Studies; Education Management/Administration; Educational Policy; Educational Technology Systems; Higher Education

MANUSCRIPT GUIDELINES/COMMENTS:

Statement of Purpose
The American Journal of Distance Education is published quarterly to disseminate information and act as a forum for criticism and debate about distant education research and practice in the Americas. In distance education, learners and teachers are separated by space and time, so instruction is by means of print, electronic, or other communications media. In recent years the predominant focus of articles has been on education via the Internet and Web.

AJDE's focus is on educational rather than technical issues. *AJDE* is concerned with subjects such as the effects of distance on learning; the history, theory, and social rationale for distance education; psychological and social characteristics of those who learn at a distance; analysis of learning styles; design of teaching programs; experimental and innovative teaching strategies using various communications media; student support and counseling; evaluation of effectiveness; management of distance education organizations; and national, state, and local policy issues.

AJDE's policy is to represent the interests of ALL sectors of education and training; therefore, the editor invites articles from practitioners and trainers in business and industry, the armed forces, public schools, and colleges and universities. While articles from international authors are welcome, the primary focus of *AJDE* is on developments in the United States and elsewhere in the Western Hemisphere. International articles should address the questions and concerns of this readership.

Submission of Manuscripts

The editor is always pleased to receive manuscripts for consideration. Submissions are accepted with the understanding that they will be subject to review and editorial revision, that they neither have been nor will be published elsewhere, and that copyright will be assigned to *The American Journal of Distance Education*

Authors are specifically advised to ensure that their work is appropriately grounded in a review of existing distance education literature.

Guidelines

1. *The Chicago Manual of Style*, Documentation Two should be used as the guide for manuscript style, especially for matters such as quotations, references, reference lists, punctuation, style, and grammar. If the *Manual* is not available, authors are advised to study previous issues of this journal.

2. All copy, including notes and references, should be typewritten, double-spaced, and in English.

3. The first paragraph of the manuscript should not be indented. Subsequent paragraphs should be indented five spaces from the left.

4. One-inch margins on all sides should be used.

5. The title should appear at the top of the first page, and all pages should be numbered.

6. The length should not exceed three to four thousand words, including captions, bylines, notes, and references.

7. Subtitles should be flush left, in upper- and lower-case type, and not underlined.

8. Photographs, figures, and illustrations should be used only if they are essential to explaining or supporting the manuscript. If used, such materials must be original black-and-white representations or quality halftone reproductions. Indicate clearly in the text where the table, figure, or illustration should be inserted, and follow the procedures in *The Chicago Manual of Style*.

9. A separate cover page should include the main author's name, address, phone number, and e-mail address; the name and address of all other authors; position and institutional affiliation for each author; and an abstract of 150 words or less.

10. The author(s) must NOT be identified in the manuscript (first page, headers, footers, etc.) so that our referees may be given "blind" copies of the manuscript.

11. Manuscripts should be submitted electronically by e-mail as an attachment and we prefer articles to be submitted in Microsoft Word with a minimum of formatting.

All manuscripts, materials, and letters of inquiry should be sent to: mgmoore@psu.edu

Citations
When referring to another work, give the author's last name and year of publication in parentheses and without punctuation, unless page numbers are included. References are placed before marks of punctuation when possible.

(Smith 1996), (Miller, McKenna, and Ramsey 1993), (Murphy et al. 1996), (Franklin 1990; Williams 1992), (Thomas 1997, 1989b), (Jones 1998, 69), Jones (1991) states . . .

Reference List
Citations are keyed to a reference list at the end of the manuscript which is alphabetically arranged by authors' last name. The year of publication follows the author's name. Title capitalization is used for journal titles, sentence capitalization for book and article titles. Documentation Two of *The Chicago Manual of Style* is used (chapter 16 of the 14th edition of the *Manual*). The basic reference list formats are:

Last name, Initials. Year. Article title: Article subtitle. *Journal Title* Volume (issue): pages.

Last name, Initials, Initials Last name2, and Initials Last name3. Year. *Book title.* City: Publisher.

Notes
Avoid the use of notes. If essential, notes are numbered consecutively in the text and listed at the **end** of the manuscript before the reference list. Do not use footnotes.

Long Quotations
Quotations over three lines should be indented from the left margin and clearly separated from the body of the text.

Review Procedures
Submissions are refereed by two individuals identified by the editor. A manuscript is judged on the basis of originality, scholarship, clarity of discourse, and significance, as well as the degree to which the subject matter contributes to the study and practice of distance education. Referees' notes and editorial comments are usually communicated to the author when revision is requested. Articles are submitted on the understanding that if rejected, the editor is NOT obliged to supply reviewers' comments, and WILL NOT enter into correspondence

concerning the merits of the article after a decision to reject it has been made. The editor retains the final authority to accept or reject manuscripts.

Copyright
Prior to publications, a copyright transfer form must be filled out, signed by the author, and returned to *AJDE.*

Compensation
Compensation for articles published in *AJDE* will be three copies of the issue in which the article appears for the main author and one copy each for all other authors.

Reference List Examples*
Journal Articles:
Cresswell, R., and P. Hobson. 1996. Fallacies and assumptions in use of student evaluation of distance learning teaching materials. *Distance Education* 17 (1): 132–214.

Sewart, D. 1993. Student support systems in distance education. *Open Learning* 8 (3): 3–12.

Sherry, L. 1994. Issues in distance education. *International Journal of Distance Education* 1:337–365.

Books, One Author (or Editor):
Cyrs, T. E. 1997. *Teaching and learning at a distance: What it takes to effectively design, deliver, and evaluate programs.* San Francisco: Jossey-Bass Publishers.

Holmberg, B. 1995. *Theory and practice of distance education,* 2nd ed. London and New York: Routledge.

Khan, B. H., ed. 1997. *Web-based instruction.* Englewood Cliffs, NJ: Educational Technology Publications.

Books, Two or More Authors:
Chute, A. G., M. M. Thompson, and B. W. Hancock. 1999. *The McGraw-Hill handbook of distance learning.* New York: McGraw-Hill.

Marshall, C., and G. B. Rossman. 1995. *Designing qualitative research.* Thousand Oaks, CA: Sage Publications.

Miller, J. W., M. C. McKenna, and P. Ramsey. 1993. An evaluation of student content learning and affective perceptions of a two-way interactive video learning experience. *Educational Technology* 33 (6): 51–55.

Chapters in Books:
Paul, R. 1995. Virtual realities or fantasies? Technology and the future of distance education. In *Why the information highway?* ed. J. M. Roberts and E. M. Keough, 201–225. Toronto: Trifolum Books.

32

Paulsen, M. F. 1995. Moderating educational computer conferences. In *Computer Mediated Communication and the Online Classroom.* Vol. 3, Distance education, ed. Z. L. Berge and M. P. Collins, 81–89. Cresskill, NJ: Hampton Press.

Papers:
Head, T., and B. Lockee. 1994. Forming the future from the past: Student-centered evaluation of distance learning at Virginia Tech. Paper presented at the Tenth Annual Conference of Distance Teaching and Learning, August, Madison, Wisconsin.

Kelly, K. 1997. The future of digital publishing. Paper presented at Digital Summit Conference, October, at the University of Minnesota, Minneapolis.

Dissertations:
Bunker, E. L. 1998. The ICCE/ICDE Conference Proceedings: A forum analysis of a distance education discourse community. Ed.D. diss., The Pennsylvania State University, University Park.

Learmont, D. 1990. Affective differences between host-site and remote-site distance learners participating in two-way interactive television classrooms for high school course credit. Ph.D. diss., University of South Dakota, Vermillion.

Miscellaneous:
El-Khawas, E. 1995. Campus trends 1995: New directions for academic programs. Higher Education Panel Report, No. 85. ERIC, ED 386089.

ELRA Group, Inc. 1986. Adoption of telecourses: The adoption and utilization of Annenberg/CPB Project telecourses. Annenberg/CPB Project. Photocopy.

McCartney, L. 1996. Virtual MBA: Going back to school doesn't mean sitting in a classroom again. *Information Week* [online], 4 November. Available online at http://www.informationweek.com

The American Journal of Distance Education follows *The Chicago Manual of Style,* Documentation Two.

American Journal of Evaluation

ADDRESS FOR SUBMISSION:

Robin Lin Miller, Editor
American Journal of Evaluation
Michigan State University
Department of Psychology
316 Psychology Building
East Lansing, MI 48824-1116
USA
Phone: 517-432-5640
Fax: 517-353-4873
E-Mail: aje@eval.org
Web: www.sagepub.com
Address May Change:

PUBLICATION GUIDELINES:

Manuscript Length: 26-40
Copies Required: Six (4 w/out ID, 2 w/ID)
Computer Submission: No
Format: N/A
Fees to Review: 0.00 US$

Manuscript Style:
American Psychological Association

CIRCULATION DATA:

Reader: Academics, Practitioners
Frequency of Issue: Quarterly
Copies per Issue: 3,001 - 4,000
Sponsor/Publisher: American Evaluation
Association (AEA) / Elsevier Science
Publishing Co.
Subscribe Price: 130.00 US$ Individual
393.00 US$ Institution

REVIEW INFORMATION:

Type of Review: Blind Review
No. of External Reviewers: 3+
No. of In House Reviewers: 1
Acceptance Rate: 21-30%
Time to Review: 3 Months
Reviewers Comments: Yes
Invited Articles: 20%
Fees to Publish: 0.00 US$

MANUSCRIPT TOPICS:
Program and Policy Evaluation; Tests, Measurement & Evaluation

MANUSCRIPT GUIDELINES/COMMENTS:

The *American Journal of Evaluation (AJE)* publishes original papers about the methods, theory, practice, and findings of evaluation. The general goal of *AJE* is to present the best work in and about evaluation, in order to improve the knowledge base and practice of its readers. Because the field of evaluation is diverse, with different intellectual traditions, approaches to practice, and domains of application, the papers published in *AJE* will reflect this diversity. Nevertheless, preference is given to papers that are likely to be of interest to a wide range of evaluators and that are written to be accessible to most readers.

Individuals interested in contributing to the Ethical Challenges, Exemplars, Teaching Evaluation, and Book Reviews sections should contact the relevant section editor (see Contribution Categories). All other manuscripts should be addressed to: Dr. Robin Lin Miller, Editor, *AJE*, Michigan State University, Department of Psychology, 316 Psychology Building, East Lansing, MI 48824-1116. Submission letters should specify that the manuscript is not currently under consideration elsewhere and has not been published elsewhere in the same or a substantially similar form.

A total of six double-spaced typewritten copies should be submitted. On two copies, each author's name, title, full mailing address, telephone number(s), and e-mail address should be listed. Author information should be omitted on four copies (for blind review).

Manuscripts should be prepared following the style of the *Publication Manual of the American Psychological Association*, 4th Edition. References, citations in text, tables, and figures should all conform to the *APA* style. Any figures should be camera-ready.

Authors whose works have been accepted for publication will be asked to submit the final manuscript on a disk prepared with an IBM-compatible word processor. Word is preferred, but others can be used. (Please contact Robin Miller for specific guidelines.)

If prospective contributors have questions or are uncertain about the appropriateness of possible submissions, they are welcome to contact Robin Miller via email at **aje@eval.org** or by phone at (517) 353-5010.

American Journal of Orthopsychiatry

ADDRESS FOR SUBMISSION:

Nancy Felipe Russo, Editor
American Journal of Orthopsychiatry
Arizona State University
Department of Psychology
Box 1104
Tempe, AZ 85287-1104
USA
Phone:
Fax:
E-Mail: nancy.russo@asu.edu
Web: www.amerortho.org
Address May Change:

PUBLICATION GUIDELINES:

Manuscript Length: 11-30
Copies Required: Four
Computer Submission: No
Format: N/A
Fees to Review: 0.00 US$

Manuscript Style:
American Psychological Association

CIRCULATION DATA:

Reader: No Reply
Frequency of Issue: Quarterly
Copies per Issue: 5,001 - 10,000
Sponsor/Publisher: American
Orthopsychiatric Association
Subscribe Price: 70.00 US$ Individual
90.00 US$ Institution

REVIEW INFORMATION:

Type of Review: Blind Review
No. of External Reviewers: 2
No. of In House Reviewers: 0
Acceptance Rate: 25%
Time to Review: 4 - 6 Months
Reviewers Comments: Yes
Invited Articles: 5%
Fees to Publish: 0.00 US$

MANUSCRIPT TOPICS:
Mental Health & Social Justice; Minority, Refugee & Family Mental Health; Public Policy & Professional Practice; Urban Education, Cultural/Non-Traditional

MANUSCRIPT GUIDELINES/COMMENTS:

Manuscript Topics. Mental Health Services and Policies; Human Rights and Mental Health; Minority and Mental Health; Refugees and Mental Health; Family and Social Systems.

The *Journal* is dedicated to informing public policy, professional practice, and knowledge production relating to mental health and social responsibility, from a multidisciplinary and interprofessional perspective. Clinical, theoretical, research, or expository papers that are essentially synergistic and directed at concept or theory development, reconceptualization of major issues, explanation, and interpretation are especially welcomed for Editorial Board consideration. Selection of articles for publication is based on their originality, adequacy of method, significance of findings, contribution to theory, relevance to service delivery and public policy, and clarity and brevity of presentation.

Submission should be in quadruplicate (four clean copies), typed on one side of firm paper, double spaced, with generous margins. Manuscripts should be in final form, with consistent headings and subheadings, in roman typeface (i.e., no boldface, italics, etc.), and should include a cover letter with mailing address, day-time telephone number, and fax number if available. Manuscripts should be prepared for blind review, and each should be accompanied by an abstract of approximately 50 words.

Original typescripts should be retained by authors. Only photocopies or computer-generated duplicates should be submitted, since rejected manuscripts are disposed of following review. In special circumstances that require return of a manuscript, return envelope and postage should accompany submission; however, the Journal assumes no responsibility for each return.

The entire manuscript must be double-spaced, including quotations, footnotes, references, and tables.

Footnotes should be worked back into the text or deleted where possible, where essential, they should appear at the bottom of the manuscript page on which they are cited and be indicated by the asterisk system.

References should be prepared in conformance with the style set forth in the *Publication Manual of the American Psychological Association*, Fourth Edition.

The American Orthopsychiatric Association *assumes no responsibility for any statements of fact or opinion in the papers printed, nor does acceptance of advertising in the Journal imply endorsement of the Association of any of the products or services advertised.*

The Editorial Board reserves the right to reject any manuscript, to suggest modifications prior to publication, and to edit accepted manuscripts in conformance with Journal style and standards.

American Journal of Pharmaceutical Education

ADDRESS FOR SUBMISSION:

Joseph T. DiPiro, Editor
American Journal of Pharmaceutical
   Education
Medical College of Georgia
CJ-1002
Augusta, GA 30912
USA
Phone: 706-721-4450
Fax: 706-721-3994
E-Mail: ajpe@mail.mcg.edu
Web: www.ajpe.org
Address May Change:

PUBLICATION GUIDELINES:

Manuscript Length: 10-20
Copies Required: Email
Computer Submission: Yes
Format: almost any PC or MAC
Fees to Review: 0.00 US$

Manuscript Style:
   See Manuscript Guidelines

CIRCULATION DATA:

Reader: Academics
Frequency of Issue: Bi-Monthly
Copies per Issue:
Sponsor/Publisher: American Association
   of Colleges of Pharmacy
Subscribe Price: 100.00 US$ Individual
   100.00 US$ Library
   100.00 US$ Foreign

REVIEW INFORMATION:

Type of Review: Blind Review
No. of External Reviewers: 2
No. of In House Reviewers: 1
Acceptance Rate: 60%
Time to Review: 1 - 2 Months
Reviewers Comments: Yes
Invited Articles: 0-5%
Fees to Publish: 0.00 US$

MANUSCRIPT TOPICS:
Book Reviews; Curriculum Studies; Educational Technology Systems; Instructional Design and Assessment; Research Articles; Statements and Reviews; Tests, Measurement & Evaluation

MANUSCRIPT GUIDELINES/COMMENTS:

Introduction
The *American Journal of Pharmaceutical Education* is devoted to providing relevant information for pharmaceutical educators and all others interested in the advancement of pharmaceutical education. The *Journal* provides a forum for communication among pharmaceutical educators. To be considered, manuscripts must provide useful information for the national or international audience of the *Journal*. If a submission has only local or regional relevance, its usefulness to the majority of our readers is limited. To assure that only accurate and substantive articles are included, all manuscripts undergo a peer review process and editorial approval prior to acceptance.

38
Manuscript Categories
Viewpoints. Viewpoints are short editorials and commentaries on educational policy, philosophical issues, or other pertinent subjects authored by the Editor, Editorial Board, AACP officers, or invited authors.

Statements. Statements are papers that present fully developed ideas, concepts, or recommendations on a topic of widespread interest to pharmacy education.

Reviews. Reviews are comprehensive, well-referenced descriptive papers on teaching or research topics directly related to pharmacy and graduate or post-graduate education and training. This section includes papers on the history of pharmacy education.

Instructional Design and Assessment. Instructional Design and Assessment papers describe novel methods for professional and graduate student instruction (lectures, laboratories, practice experiences, or courses), or informational manuscripts on programmatic and curriculum development.

Teachers' Topics. Teachers' Topics are invited manuscripts from the "Teachers of the Year" at AACP member institutions.

Innovations in Teaching. Innovations in Teaching are invited manuscripts from recipients of the AACP Innovations in Teaching Award.

AACP Reports. AACP Reports are summaries of activity of officers, delegates, and committee chairpersons within AACP.

Letters to the Editor. Letters to the Editor serve as a forum for the expression of ideas or for commenting on matters of interest. It is also an avenue for critiquing or expanding on the information presented in a previously published manuscript. Authors are required to identify themselves. The Editor reserves the right to reject, shorten, excerpt, or edit letters for publication.

Book and Software Reviews. Book and Software Reviews are brief documents that provide the reader with a clear understanding of content in a book or software program, as well as the product structure, scope, and limitations. The reviewer should state the value or utility of the product for instruction, research, or other academic activities.

Stylistic Considerations
The style specifications for the *Journal* must be followed. Below are general guidelines for manuscript format and style. If in doubt about style, authors should refer to the *American Medical Association* (AMA) Manual of Style, 9th ed, or consult a recent issue of the *Journal*.

Text. The text should be scholarly, readable, clear and concise. Standard nomenclature should be used. Unfamiliar terms and acronyms should be defined at first mention. Manuscripts that were prepared for oral presentation must be rewritten for print. Authors of research papers are discouraged from writing excessively long introduction or discussion sections.

Word style. Consult a current edition of Webster's dictionary for guidance on spelling, compounding, and word separation. Foreign words, not in general use, should be italicized. For proper use of chemical and biochemical terms, mathematical equations, mathematical expressions, special symbols, subscripts, superscripts, or Greek letters, please refer to the *AMA Manual of Style*.

Capitalization. The word "association" must be capitalized when referring to the American Association of Colleges of Pharmacy. When the word "journal" is capitalized and italicized as *Journal*, it can refer only to the American Journal of Pharmaceutical Education. In scientific writing, always capitalize the following: major words in titles and headings of manuscripts, designators (eg, Table 3), eponyms (but not the noun that follows them, eg, Gram stain, Babinski sign), names of tests (eg, Beck Depression Inventory), genus names of organisms (but not the name of species, varieties or subspecies), acts of legislation (eg, Medicare), awards (eg, Nobel Prize), proprietary names (eg, Xerox copier), the title of a person when followed by the person's name (eg, Chair John W. Jones), official names of organizations and institutions (eg, Centers for Disease Control and Prevention), geographic places (eg, United States of America), sociocultural designations (eg, Republicans, French people), historical events (eg, Vietnam War).

Abbreviations. In instances where repeated use of an organization or chemical name would become awkward, an official or accepted abbreviation may be substituted. The abbreviation should be placed in parentheses immediately following the first use of the name in the main body of the text. Abbreviations of common pharmaceutical organizations do not require periods or spaces between letters (eg, AMA). Abbreviations of "eg," "ie," and "viz" should not be seperated by periods. The names of US states and countries should be spelled out when they stand alone (eg, "...pharmacists throughout the United States..."). When the name of a state follows the name of a city or town, it should be abbreviated and periods should not be used (eg, Boston, Mass). Postal abbreviations for states are not used. Refer to the AMA Manual of Style for a list of proper abbreviations. The abbreviation "US" may be used as a modifier only when it directly precedes the word it modifies (eg, US health policies). Otherwise, it should be spelled out (eg, "...the population of the United States"). The names of all other cities, states, provinces, and countries should be spelled out when they occur within the text of the article.

Numbers. Numbers must be written as Arabic numerals unless they occur at the beginning of a sentence, in which case the number should be spelled out. The exception to this rule is when the number "one" is used in isolation within the text and substituting an Arabic number would seem awkward (eg, "there was only one logical solution to the problem"). A number containing a decimal must be styled as an Arabic number. All fractions must be written as decimal equivalents.

Measurements. The metric system will be used for all measurements; however, conventional units should be used instead of SI units. Do not use periods when abbreviating units of measure.

Reference numbers. These numbers should be superscript Arabic numerals placed at the end of the sentence, outside the final period or other punctuation. Subsequent citations to the same reference must be indicated by the same number originally assigned to that reference. Do not place parentheses around the reference numbers.

Personal Communications. If the source of material referred to in an article is from a personal communications, it should be referenced as such in parentheses immediately following reference to the material, followed by the date (eg, written communication, October 2, 2002).

Hypertext Links. Authors may identify uniform resource locators (URLs) for Internet web sites that provide the reader with additional information on the topic addressed in the manuscript. Although URLs are an important feature of electronic publishing, authors are encouraged to be selective in their choice of sites to include. Do not include URLs for web pages with newspaper or journal articles that will be removed or archived to another web page. Links to pharmaceutical manufacturers or other sources of product information are acceptable; however, providing a URL to the reader should not be substituted for adequate discussion within the manuscript itself. Do not include links to sites that are not accessible without a password.

Manuscript Organization
Within the document, each page of the manuscript should be arranged and numbered consecutively in the following order: title page, abstract, footnotes, text, references, tables, figure legends, and illustrations.

Title Page. The title page should have the following information: a concise title, name of each author, terminal degree, academic/professional title and affiliation, and city and state where located. If an author has relocated to another institution, please include his/her affiliation during the time the author worked on the manuscript. At the lower left of the page, indicate the name of the corresponding author and provide his/her mailing address, telephone number, facsimile number, and e-mail address. At the bottom of the title page, indicate 3 to 5 keywords.

Abstract. Each manuscript must include an abstract of 100 to 150 words. For Research Articles, the abstract should include a brief (1 to 3 sentences) statement for each of the following sections: Objectives, Methods, Results, and Conclusions. For Instructional Design and Assessment papers, the abstract should include a statement for the following sections: Objectives, Design, Assessment, and Conclusion. Each section within the abstract should be flushed left, followed by a period and the statements summarizing that section.

Main Body of Text. The use of subheadings to divide the text is encouraged. Primary headings should be in bold capital letters and should contain no more than 35 characters or spaces. Secondary headings should be in bold title case and appear above the paragraph. Tertiary headings should be in bold with only the initial letter capitalized. Tertiary headings should end with a period and should appear before the beginning of the first sentence in that section.

41

Acknowledgments
Any special funding received for research that is the subject of the manuscript should be included under a section entitled "Acknowledgments" at the end of the text. If the authors wish to thank colleagues or others who provided assistance with their research or manuscript preparation, those acknowledgments also should be included under this section. Any statements concerning liability for the content of the manuscript may be included here as well (eg, "the ideas expressed in this manuscript are those of the author and in no way are intended to represent the position of...").

Reference Section
References to a published source should be provided for all information in the manuscript that contains dates, facts, or opinions other than those of the author. Authors are responsible for the accuracy and completeness of all citations. References should be numbered consecutively in the order in which the information contained in the referenced publication appears or is referred to in the manuscript. Do not create a second abbreviated reference or use "ibid" to refer to information cited in a previous reference. Instead, if information from the same source is referred to a second time in the manuscript, cite the same reference number originally assigned to that source. For detailed information on reference style, refer to the section on Stylistic Concerns.

Each journal citation must include the surnames and complete initials of all authors. For manuscripts with 7 or more authors, the first 3 authors should be listed, followed by "et al." The names of all periodicals cited must be abbreviated in accordance with abbreviations adopted by the National Library of Medicine and used in Index Medicus. An example and special instructions for specific types of references are provided below. For additional guidance, please refer to the American Medical Association Manual of Style, 9th ed, or to a recent issue of the *Journal*.

Journal articles. For references to journal articles, first list the names of the authors beginning with the last name of the first author, followed by his/her initials. The authors' names are followed by the title of the article. The first letter of the title is capitalized, but the remainder of the title should be in lower case letters, except for the first letter of proper names. A period should be placed after the title. Next, give the properly abbreviated title of the journal being referenced. The title of the journal should be in italics followed by a period. One space should be left between the journal and the year of publication. A semicolon should be placed after the year of publication, followed by the volume number in which the article appeared. After the volume number, place a colon followed by the number of the first page of the article, then a dash, then the number of the last page of the article, followed by a period. If the article does not appear on consecutive pages, use a semicolon between each segment of pages (eg, 172-175;179-183;199.)

Example:
Stratton TP, Cochran GA. A rural geriatric experience. Am J Pharm Educ. 1990;62:151-5.

Reference to a book. List the last name of the first author of the book, followed by the first and middle initial if given, just as in a journal reference. The names of all authors of the book must be listed. Place a period after the last author's initials. Next, state the title of the book using standard rules for capitalization within titles. A period should be placed at the end of the title. If more than one edition of the book has been published, then the edition number must be given. An ordinal number should be used to indicate the edition number (eg, 9th), followed by a space and "ed." Next, provide the city and state where the publisher is located. Use the abbreviations for states provided in the AMA style manual rather than postal abbreviations. A colon should separate the city and state from the name of the publisher. The full name of the publisher should be given, followed by a semicolon. Next, provide the year of publication, followed by a colon and the page or page numbers referenced.

Example:
Martin AN. Physical Pharmacy. 4th ed. Philadelphia, Penn: Lea & Febiger; 1993:268.

Reference to a chapter in a book. To reference a single chapter in a book, first list the authors and state the title as you would if citing a journal article. The chapter title should be followed by the word "In" followed by a colon. Next, list the name(s) and initials of the editors of the book, followed by a comma and the abbreviation "ed" or "eds" if more than one editor, followed by a period. Next include the title of the book, location of the publisher, publisher's name, year of publication and page numbers in the same format as for a reference to an entire book (see previous example).

Example:
Lyon RA, Titeler M. Pharmacology and biochemistry of the 5-HT2 receptor. In: Sanders-Bush E, ed. The Serotonin Receptors. Clifton, NJ: Humana Press;1989: 59-88.

Thesis or Dissertation. For references to theses or dissertations, place the title of the thesis or dissertation in italics. Include the location of the institution, its name, and the year the thesis or dissertation was completed.

Example:
Thorn MD. A Comparative Review of the Statistical and Research Quality of the Medical and Pharmacy Literature [masters thesis]. Chapel Hill: University of North Carolina, 1982.

Reference to a Web Site. For references to journals, e-magazines, or other publications on the Internet, state the names of the authors, title of the article, publication title, and volume and publication date in the same format as you would for a journal reference. For references to other information, give the title of the web page, followed by the name of the organization or web site that published the information. For all references to online material, the author should include "Available at:" followed by the uniform resource locator (URL) for the page of the web site referenced (eg, www.hcfa.gov/stats.htm), followed by a period. Finally, write "Accessed" followed by the month, day, and year on which the information was obtained from the site, followed by a period.

Example:
Healthy People 2010, Office of Disease Prevention and Health Promotion, U.S. Department of Health and Human Services. Available at: http://health.gov/healthypeople. Accessed January 20, 2002.

Unpublished Works. References to unpublished material such as articles or abstracts presented at professional meetings but not published, provide the name of the meeting where the article was presented.

Articles in Press. For references to information in books or articles that are currently in press, provide all of the available information for the reference. In place of page numbers, designate that the publication is "in press."

Example:
Adamcik B, Hurley S, Erramouspe J. Assessment of pharmacy students' critical thinking and problem-solving abilities. Am J Pharm Educ. 1996;60:in press.

Tables and Figures
Tables. Table should be created in Microsoft Word© table format. Data must be placed in separate cells of the table to prevent text and numbers from shifting when the table is converted for publication on the Internet. You can insert empty cells to create spacing. Footnotes should be placed at the bottom of the table inside a single row or cell and should be indented. The following symbols are used to indicate footnotes: first footnote should be indicated by an asterisk (*); second, by a dagger (†); third, double dagger (‡); fourth, section mark (§); fifth, parallel mark (||), etc. Refer to a current issue of the *Journal* for more examples of table style.

Tables should not duplicate information provided in the text. Instead, tables should be used to provide additional information that illustrates or expands on a specific point the author wishes to make. Each table should be self-explanatory and begin on a separate page in the document. Tables should be numbered using Arabic numbers according to the order in which they are referred to in the text. The table number and a concise title should be placed above the body of the table.

Figures. Figures should be numbered using Arabic numbers, based on the order in which they are presented in the text. Figure legends should be concise and self-explanatory. All illustrative materials for the figures should be submitted as high-resolution gif or jpg files. The key to any symbols in a graph or chart should be included as part of the illustration itself, rather than in the legend. If figures contain illustrations that have been published elsewhere, a letter of permission to reprint from the original publisher must accompany the manuscript.

Figures should be included within the text file. If it is not possible to save the graphic for a figure or table within the main document because of its size or file format, send the document as a separate file.

Each figure should be sent in a separate file from the text of the manuscript. To insure the best quality possible, create the figure so that it is approximately 7 inches wide. Using the program in which it was created, save the figure in EPS or Postscript format. If that is not possible, TIFF, GIF and JPG formats also are acceptable. Ideally, figures should be saved at a resolution of at least 300 dpi. Although 72 dpi (computer screen resolution) is fine for publication online, when the PDF version of the article is printed, it will look blurry. Please keep an editable copy of each figure saved in the program in which it was created in case changes need to be made to the original.

Manuscript Submission

The manuscript should be created and saved in Microsoft Word for Windows. If you use WordPerfect or another word processing program, please use the "save as" option to save the file in Microsoft Word for Windows file format.

Copyright Form

Manuscript submitted to the *Journal* should be unpublished and not under consideration elsewhere. Under the terms of the Copyright Revision Act of 1976 (Public Law 94-533) it is necessary to have the rights of the authors transferred to the publisher in order to provide for the widest possible dissemination of professional and scientific literature. A transfer of copyright form must be received by the Editor before a manuscript can be accepted for publication.

Assurances

For all research manuscripts (including educational research), the author should indicate in the cover letter that the research has been reviewed and approved by the appropriate human research or ethics review committee, or that it has been determined to be exempt from such review. For research that has undergone such review and approval, a statement to that effect should be included in the methods section.

E-mail

Please submit your manuscript as an e-mail attachment. The body of the e-mail should contain a cover letter introducing your manuscript and should be addressed to Joseph DiPiro, PharmD, Editor, the American Journal of Pharmaceutical Education. The letter should include the name, postal address, telephone number, facsimile number, and email address of the author who will be responsible for correspondence regarding the manuscript. When your cover letter is complete and all documents attached to the file, the e-mail should be sent to **AJPE@mail.mcg.edu**.

Floppy Disk, CD-ROM or Zip Disk Submitted by Mail

All manuscripts should be submitted by e-mail as outlined above. If this is not possible, manuscripts may be submitted on a floppy disk, CD-ROM, or Zip disk. Please label the disk carefully with the last name of the corresponding author. If you send more than one disk, please label each disk carefully. Please include a printed cover letter in your packet. Do not send a printed copy of your manuscript. Send the packet to the following address: Joseph DiPiro, PharmD, Editor, American Journal of Pharmaceutical Education, CJ 1020, Medical College of Georgia, Augusta, GA 30912.

Proofing Process

With the *Journal*'s transition to an electronic format, tangible page proofs of the article will no longer be mailed to authors for approval. Instead the author will receive an e-mail with instructions on how to access the final copy of his or her article online, in a secure location, before it is published electronically.

American Psychologist

ADDRESS FOR SUBMISSION:

Norman B. Anderson, Editor-in-Chief
American Psychologist
750 First Street, N.E.
Washington, DC 2002-4242
USA
Phone: 203-336-5500
Fax:
E-Mail: Apeditor@apa.org
Web: www.apa.org
Address May Change:

PUBLICATION GUIDELINES:

Manuscript Length: 21-25 Max, double-
spaced
Copies Required:
Computer Submission: Yes See guidelines
Format:
Fees to Review: 0.00 US$

Manuscript Style:
American Psychological Association

CIRCULATION DATA:

Reader: Academics
Frequency of Issue: Monthly
Copies per Issue: 113,000+
Sponsor/Publisher: American Psychological
Association
Subscribe Price: 198.00 US$ Individual
449.00 US$ Institution

REVIEW INFORMATION:

Type of Review: Blind Review
No. of External Reviewers: 3
No. of In House Reviewers: 0
Acceptance Rate: 12%
Time to Review: 6 Months
Reviewers Comments: Yes
Invited Articles: 31-50%
Fees to Publish: 0.00 US$

MANUSCRIPT TOPICS:
Educational Psychology; Psychology

MANUSCRIPT GUIDELINES/COMMENTS:

Topics Include
Current issues, empirical, theoretical, and practical articles on broad aspects of psychology.

Manuscript Preparation. Authors should prepare manuscripts according to the *Publication Manual of the American Psychological Association* (5th ed.). Manuscripts should be no more than 25 double-spaced pages, including references. All manuscripts must include an abstract containing a maximum of 120 words. Formatting instructions, including instructions on preparing tables, figures, references, metrics, and abstracts, appear in the *Manual*. All manuscripts are copyedited for bias-free language. Comments should be submitted no later than two months from the date of the issue containing the article to which they respond. (Comments on comments are rarely considered.) Comments on matters of APA policy are also considered. Comments must be limited to 1,000 words (about five pages) and should contain no more than nine references. As in all manuscripts, authors should include page numbers and references for quotes. *APA* can now place supplementary materials online, which

46

will be available via the journal's Web page as noted above. To submit such materials, please see **www.apa.org/journals/supplementalmaterial.html** for details.

Publication Policy. APA policy prohibits an author from submitting the same manuscript for concurrent consideration by two or more publications. APA policy prohibits as well publication of any manuscript that has already been published in whole or substantial part elsewhere. Authors have an obligation to consult journal editors if there is any question concerning prior publication of part or all of their submitted manuscripts. Authors are required to obtain and provide to APA prior to production all necessary permissions to reproduce in print and electronic form any copyrighted work, including, for example, test materials (or portions thereof) and photographs of people. Also, authors of research reports submitted to APA journals are expected to have their data available throughout the editorial review process and for at least five years after the date of publication. Of course, APA expects authors submitting to this journal to adhere to the APA ethical standards regarding previous publication of data (Standard 8.13) and making research data available (Standard 8.14). Authors of research reports will be required to state in writing that they have complied with APA ethical standards in the treatment of their sample, human or animal, or to describe the details of treatment. A copy of the APA Ethical Principles may be obtained at www.apa.org/ethics/ or by writing the APA Ethics Office, 750 First Street, NE, Washington, DC 20002-4242. APA requires authors to reveal any possible conflict of interest in the conduct and reporting of research (e.g., financial interests in a test or procedure, funding by pharmaceutical companies for drug research).

Review Policy. The first step in the AP editorial review process is performed by the *AP* Editor-in-Chief/APA, CEO. Approximately 70% of author-submitted manuscripts are returned without review within 30 days for a host of reasons: Empirical manuscripts are more appropriate for one of the APA primary journals; topic of the manuscript or style of the writing is too specialized for the broad *AP* readership; the same topic was recently covered in the journal; inappropriate content or style; or other, more typical reasons such as the paper does not offer a major contribution to the field or is simply not written well enough. As a matter of policy, the identities of authors and reviewers are masked. Manuscripts that are peer reviewed are circulated without their title pages to mask the identity of the authors. Each copy of a manuscript should include a separate title page with authors' names and affiliations, and these should not appear anywhere else on the manuscript. Footnotes that identify the authors should be typed on a separate page. Authors should make every effort to see that the manuscript itself contains no clue to their identity.

Manuscript Submission. Submit manuscripts electronically via the Manuscript Submission Portal at **www.apa.org/journals/amp**. In addition to addresses and phone numbers, authors should supply electronic mail addresses and fax numbers, if available. Authors should keep a copy of the manuscript to guard against loss. General correspondence may be directed to Norman B. Anderson, Editor-in-Chief, *American Psychologist*, 750 First Street, NE, Washington, DC 20002-4242

E-Mail Address. To contact the editorial office of the *American Psychologist* via electronic mail (Internet), contact **APeditor@apa.org**.

American Scholar

ADDRESS FOR SUBMISSION:

Robert Wilson, Editor
American Scholar
The Phi Beta Kappa Society
1606 New Hampshire Avenue, NW
Washington, DC 20009
USA
Phone: 202-265-3808
Fax: 202-265-0083
E-Mail: scholar@pbk.org
Web: www.pbk.org/pubs/amscholar.htm
Address May Change:

PUBLICATION GUIDELINES:

Manuscript Length: N/A
Copies Required: One
Computer Submission: No
Format: N/A
Fees to Review: 0.00 US$

Manuscript Style:
Chicago Manual of Style

CIRCULATION DATA:

Reader: , Gerneral, college educated
Frequency of Issue: Quarterly
Copies per Issue: More than 25,000
Sponsor/Publisher: Phi Beta Kappa Society
Subscribe Price: 25.00 US$

REVIEW INFORMATION:

Type of Review: Editorial Review
No. of External Reviewers: No Reply
No. of In House Reviewers: 2
Acceptance Rate: 0-5%
Time to Review: 1 - 2 Months
Reviewers Comments: No
Invited Articles: 50% +
Fees to Publish: 0.00 US$

MANUSCRIPT TOPICS:
Art/Music; English Literature; General Issues in Education; Languages & Linguistics; Science Math & Environment; Secondary/Adolescent Studies; Social Studies/Social Science

MANUSCRIPT GUIDELINES/COMMENTS:

Articles. *The Scholar* is a quarterly journal published by Phi Beta Kappa for general circulation. Our intent is to have articles by scholars and experts but written in nontechnical language for an intelligent audience. The material that appears in the magazine covers a wide range of subject matter in the arts, sciences, current affairs, history, and literature. We prefer articles between 3,500 and 4,000 words, and we pay up to $500. To be accepted for publication, a manuscript must receive the affirmative votes of the editor and at least two members of the editorial board.

Poetry. Poems for submission to the Scholar should be typewritten, on one side of the paper, and each sheet of paper should bear the name and address of the author and the name of the poem. We have no special requirements of length, form, or content for original poetry. A look at several recent issues of the Scholar should give a good idea of the kind of poetry we publish and the way poems look on our pages. We suggest, too, that from the author's point of view, it is probably most effective if not more than three or four poems are submitted at any one time. We pay $50.00 for each accepted poem.

We do not have arrangements for sending sample copies of the *Scholar* to prospective contributors. It would be possible, of course, for you to purchase the latest issue for the regular price of $6.50. If you do not care to purchase a copy, your library would probably have copies you could see.

All manuscripts should be accompanied by a stamped, self-addressed envelope so that we may return them to you if we are unable to use them.

American School Board Journal

ADDRESS FOR SUBMISSION:

Sally Zakariya, Editor
American School Board Journal
National School Boards Association
1680 Duke Street
Alexandria, VA 22314
USA
Phone: 703-838-6231
Fax: 703-549-6719
E-Mail: szakariya@nsba.org
Web: www.asbj.com
Address May Change:

PUBLICATION GUIDELINES:

Manuscript Length: 10-20
Copies Required: Two
Computer Submission: Yes
Format: N/A
Fees to Review: 0.00 US$

Manuscript Style:
See Manuscript Guidelines

CIRCULATION DATA:

Reader: Administrators, School Board
  Members
Frequency of Issue: Monthly
Copies per Issue: More than 32,000
Sponsor/Publisher: National School Boards
  Association
Subscribe Price: 57.00 US$

REVIEW INFORMATION:

Type of Review: Editorial Review
No. of External Reviewers: 0
No. of In House Reviewers: 3
Acceptance Rate: 11-20%
Time to Review: 1 - 2 Months
Reviewers Comments: No
Invited Articles: 11-20%
Fees to Publish: 0.00 US$

MANUSCRIPT TOPICS:
Education Management/Administration; Education Trends

MANUSCRIPT GUIDELINES/COMMENTS:

As the nation's oldest education publication, founded in 1891, *American School Board Journal* has a reputation for independence, professionalism, and accuracy. Although *ASBJ* is published by the National School Boards Association, it is editorially independent and does not reflect the positions of the association.

These writer's guidelines are designed to lead you through the process we use to add outside writers to our mix of staff-written news and features.

We are not 'scholarly.' Although we are *American School Board Journal*, we are not a peer-reviewed journal. And, as a news and feature magazine, we generally do not publish footnotes and references.

What do we want? We strive to give the best, most comprehensive accounts of emerging education trends and solutions available. We are looking for good writing and good ideas, intelligently presented, aimed at our audience of school board members, superintendents, and other administrators. We don't publish theme issues; instead, we're always looking for a mix of practical, thought-provoking, and timely articles. We cover just about every educational topic, with special emphasis on district-level leadership.

What we don't want. Few teachers read our magazine, so articles aimed specifically at classroom educators aren't right for us. And we don't publish articles that push a particular product or service.

Getting Started

We feature two kinds of writers in *ASBJ*. One is the professional writer or journalist who researches and writes articles that are objective and present different viewpoints. The other kind of writer is the school board member, administrator, teacher, or professor who writes about what's going on in a local school, district, or community.

If you're a professional writer or journalist, query us with story ideas. Include clips that show you can handle education subjects and that you can write magazine-length articles. Your best chance of getting in the magazine is through our on-assignment stories, so if you have a controversy or interesting education story brewing in your backyard, let us know. Payment varies with the length and nature of the article. Also, we sometimes make assignments to journalists, so let us know you're out there.

If you're a school board member, administrator, teacher, professor, or anyone else who doesn't write for a living, send us your completed manuscripts. What we want from you is your experience and expertise. Did your board save your taxpayers $1 million this year? Write about it. Did your district raise achievement scores 10 points? Write about it. Did your university work with a local district to offer standards-based professional development? Write about it.

Before submitting a manuscript, look at Our Magazine. Check to see what subjects we've covered. Read the articles for subject matter, style, tone, and length. We can provide you with sample copies, or you can check out selected articles on this web site.

Our readers are school board members and administrators. Focus your article on how your subject might interest or affect them. For example, if you're a professor writing about a professional development program at your university, include information about how much the program will cost a district or school or how it can be tailored to fit local or state standards.

Forget the Jargon. Educators probably will know what you're talking about, but not all of our readers have education backgrounds. Avoid passive voice when you can. **Not good**: "A decision was made to effect paradigm shifts in educational teaming, in order to promote the impacting of educational outcomes." **Better**: "We formed teams to help students achieve."

Be specific. Provide facts, figures, and examples. **Not good:** "Few people in our community have children in school, and few citizens vote in bond elections." **Better**: "Only 20 percent of the people in our community have children in school, and well under half of our citizens voted in each of the last two bond elections."

Write from personal experience. Use the pronouns "I" or "we." Write as though you're having a conversation with a friend. When you make a point, give specifics. **Not good**: "The board made suggestions on how to change the program." **Better**: "The board suggested we lengthen the school day by seven minutes and give each ninth-grade teacher a laptop computer." If you don't know details, talk to people who do and include what they say in your article.

A lead is not a thesis statement. Instead of thinking back to your papers in English 101, pattern your manuscript after an interesting newspaper article or magazine story. Begin your article with an anecdote or a statement that focuses on your subject. Not good: "I'm writing this article to explain how education can be improved." Better: "Our principal issued a challenge to her teachers: Bring more parents into their classrooms."

A magazine article is not a graduate school paper. Leave out the "review of the literature" and the footnotes. If the topic warrants, include a short list of suggested readings. If you want to quote another author, include the citation in the text. Example: As John Smith pointed out in his 1998 book Raising Student Achievement,...

Don't worry. If your writing skills are rusty, but you have a great story to tell, we'll work with you.

Expect to be edited. If you believe every word in your manuscript is a jewel, don't send it to us. We edit everyone, in varying degrees, for length, style, clarity, even content.

After You Write
When preparing your manuscript, whether by typewriter or word processor:
- Double-space on white paper. Put your name on each page and number the pages.
- Include brief biographical information, including a daytime telephone number, a fax number, and your email address.

Your manuscript should be approximately five to 10 double-spaced pages, or 1,250 to 2,500 words.

If you want to submit your manuscript on a computer disk, please send it to us using Word 97. We cannot return disks. You also may send your manuscript as an e-mail attachment to **submissions@asbj.com**. Either way, please keep the formatting of the document simple.

Do not send your manuscript to multiple magazines at the same time. We do not accept simultaneous submissions. Also, we accept articles only when all copyrights -- including electronic ones -- are offered to our magazine.

Acceptance and Publication
We will acknowledge your manuscript when we receive it. We make decisions to accept or reject articles as quickly as possible. The review process usually takes between six to eight weeks, but sometimes longer when we receive large volumes of manuscripts.

As a monthly magazine, we plan months in advance for each issue, so expect several months between acceptance and publication. Once your article has been accepted, our editors will be in touch with you. We'll send you a copy of the edited manuscript before it goes to press, and we'll send you copies of the magazine in which it appears.

Send your manuscripts to:
Sally Banks Zakariya, Editor
American School Board Journal
1680 Duke St.
Alexandria, VA 22314
Phone: (703) 838-6739; Fax: (703) 549-6719
E-mail: editor@asbj.com

American Sociological Review

ADDRESS FOR SUBMISSION:

Jerry A. Jacobs, Editor
American Sociological Review
University of Pennsylvania
Department of Sociology
3718 Locust Walk
Philadelphia, PA 19104
USA
Phone: 215-898-6779
Fax: 215-898-3371
E-Mail: asrpenn@sas.upenn.edu
Web: www.asanet.org/journals/asr/
Address May Change:

PUBLICATION GUIDELINES:

Manuscript Length: 40-60 pages
Copies Required: Four
Computer Submission: Yes
Format: IBM
Fees to Review: 25.00 US$

Manuscript Style:
See Manuscript Guidelines

CIRCULATION DATA:

Reader: Academics
Frequency of Issue: Bi-Monthly
Copies per Issue: 10,001 - 25,000
Sponsor/Publisher: American Sociological
Association (ASA)
Subscribe Price: 90.00 US$ Individual
180.00 US$ Institution
35.00 US$ ASA Mem. / $20 Student
Mem.

REVIEW INFORMATION:

Type of Review: Blind Review
No. of External Reviewers: 2-4
No. of In House Reviewers: 1-2
Acceptance Rate: 6-10%
Time to Review: 2 - 3 Months
Reviewers Comments: Yes
Invited Articles: 0-5%
Fees to Publish: 0.00 US$

MANUSCRIPT TOPICS:
All Areas of Sociology/Not Social Studies; Social Studies/Social Science

MANUSCRIPT GUIDELINES/COMMENTS:

Scope and Mission
The *American Sociological Review* publishes original (not previously published) works of interest to the discipline in general, new theoretical developments, results of qualitative or quantitative research that advance our understanding of fundamental social processes, and important methodological innovations. All areas of sociology are welcome. Emphasis is on exceptional quality and general interest.

Ethics. Submission of a manuscript to another professional journal while it is under review by the *ASR* is regarded by the ASA as unethical. Significant findings or contributions that have already appeared (or will appear) elsewhere must be clearly identified. All persons who publish in ASA journals are required to abide by ASA guidelines and ethics codes regarding plagiarism and other ethical issues. This requirement includes adhering to ASA's stated policy on data-sharing: "Sociologists make their data available after completion of the project or its

54

major publications, except where proprietary agreements with employers, contractors, or clients preclude such accessibility or when it is impossible to share data and protect the confidentiality of the data or the anonymity of research participants (e.g., raw field notes or detailed information from ethnographic interviews)" (ASA *Code of Ethics*, 1997).

Manuscript format. Manuscripts should meet the format guidelines specified in the *Notice to Contributors* published in the February and August issues of each volume. The electronic files should be composed in MS Word, WordPerfect, and/or Excel. All text must be printed *double-spaced* on 8-1/2 by 11 inch white paper. Use Times New Roman, 12-point size font. Margins must be at least 1 inch on all four sides. On the title page, note the manuscript's total word count (include all text, references, and footnotes; do not include word counts for tables or figures). You may cite your own work, but do not use wording that identifies you as the author.

Submission requirements. Submit *four (4) print copies* of your manuscript and an *abstract* of 150 to 200 words. Include all *electronic files* on floppy disk or CD. Enclose a *$15.00 manuscript processing fee* in the form of a check or money order payable to the American Sociological Association. Provide *e-mail address* and *ASR* will acknowledge the receipt of your manuscript. In your *cover letter*, you may recommend specific reviewers (or identify individuals *ASR* should not use). Do not recommend colleagues, collaborators, or friends. *ASR* may choose to disregard your recommendation. Manuscripts are not returned after review.

Address for submission. *American Sociological Review*, University of Pennsylvania, Department of Sociology, 3718 Locust Walk, Philadelphia, PA 19104-6299 (**asrpenn@sas.upenn.edu**; 215-898-6779).

Editorial decisions. Median time between submission and decision is approximately twelve weeks. Please see the *ASR* journal web site for more information (http://www.asanet.org/journals/asr/).

Advertisements. Submit to Publications Department, American Sociological Association, 1307 New York Avenue NW, Suite 700, Washington, DC 20005-4701; (202) 383-9005 ext. 303; e-mail publications@asanet.org.

Subscription rates. ASA members, $35; ASA student member, $20; nonmembers, $90; institutions, $180. *Add $20 for postage outside the U.S./Canada*. To subscribe to *ASR* or to request single issues, contact the ASA Subscriptions Department (subscriptions@asanet.org).

Address change. Subscribers must notify the ASA Executive Office (customer@asanet.org) six weeks in advance of an address change. Include both old and new addresses. Claims for undelivered copies must be made within the month following the regular month of publication. When the reserve stock permits, ASA will replace copies of *ASR* that are lost because of an address change.

States Copyright Law. For all other purposes, permission must be obtained from the ASA Executive Office. (Articles in the American Sociological Review are indexed in *the Abstracts for Social Workers, Ayer's Guide, Current Index to Journals in Education, International Political Science Abstracts, Psychological Abstracts, Social Sciences Index, Sociological Abstracts, SRM Database of Social Research Methodology, United States Political Science Documents,* and *University Microfilms.*)

The American Sociological Association acknowledges with appreciation the facilities and assistance provided by the University of Pennsylvania.

MANUSCRIPT SUBMISSION

Package your manuscript securely and include the following:

- **Cover Letter.** Please provide complete contact information for the corresponding author (name, address, phone/fax, e-mail), the complete manuscript title, total word count (include all text, footnotes, and references; do not include word counts for tables or figures), and any other important and relevant information.
- **Biography Page.** On a separate page, provide short biography (less than 100 words) for each author. See previous issues for examples.
- **One (1) original manuscript.** Manuscript must be complete and typed double-spaced with 1 inch margins (see below).
- **Three (3) blinded copies.** Blinded copies start with the Abstract page headed by the full article title; but **do not include** the title page or the biography page (or any self identifying information—see below). Copies may be printed or photocopied.
- **Disk.** All manuscript materials must be included as electronic files on disk. Standard word processing files are preferred (MS Word, etc.) for text and tables.
- **$15.00 manuscript processing fee.** Please make check payable to the American Sociological Association. All manuscripts (new and revised) require a fee. No fee is required for *Comments* and *Replies* or for submissions by ASA student members.

Send your manuscript to the **ASR** editorial office at the following address:

American Sociological Review, University of Pennsylvania, Department of Sociology, 3718 Locust Walk, Room 394, Philadelphia, PA 19104-6299; phone 215-898-6779; fax 215-573-2081 (e-mail: **asrpenn@sas.upenn.edu**). The *ASR* editorial office will acknowledge the receipt of your manuscript via e-mail.

NOTE. Additional details on preparing and submitting manuscripts to *ASR* are published in the *ASA Style Guide* (2d ed., 1997) available from the American Sociological Association.

Preparation

All pages must be typed, double-spaced (including notes and references), on 8-1/2 by 11 inch white paper. Margins must be at least 1 inch (i.e., line length must not exceed 6-1/2 inches). Please use 12-point Times New Roman font.

ASR Articles may be any length, from short reports (e.g., 10 to 20 pages) to full-length articles (e.g., 30 to 40 pages) as well as qualitative and historical papers, which may need

56

more space (e.g., 50 to 60 pages). *ASR Comments/Replies* should not exceed 10 pages. Send *Comments* and *Replies* directly to the *ASR* office—*ASR* does not require that *Comments* first be sent to article authors.

Sections in a manuscript may include the following: (1) Title page, (2) Biography Page, (3) Abstract, (4) Text, (5) Notes, (6) References, (7) Tables, (8) Figures, and (9) Appendices.

1. **Title page.** Please include the following:
- Full article title
- Each author's complete name and institutional affiliation(s)
- Total word count
- Running head (short title, less than 55 characters w/spaces)
- Acknowledgments and credits
- Grant numbers and/or funding information
- Corresponding author (name, address, phone/fax, e-mail)

2.**Biography page.** On a separate page, provide short biography (less than 100 words) for each author. See previous issues for examples.

3. **Abstract page.** On a separate page headed by the full article title, print the abstract (150 to 200 words). *Omit author(s)'s name(s).*

4. **Text.** Begin article text on a new page headed by the full article title. Omit author(s)'s names. *ASR* uses anonymous peer review for manuscript evaluation. Delete or rewrite any text that identifies you as the author: when citing your own work, please write "Smith (1992) concluded . . . ," but do not write "I concluded (Smith 1992). . . ."
a. *Headings* and *subheadings.* Generally, three heading levels are sufficient to organize text. See recent issues for examples.

b. *Citations* in the text should provide the last name of the author(s) and year of publication. Include page numbers for direct quotes or specific passages. Cite only those works needed to provide evidence for your assertions and to refer to important sources on the topic. In the following examples of text citations, ellipses (. . .) indicate manuscript text:
- When author's name is in the text, follow it with the year in parentheses— . . . Duncan (1959).
- When author's name is not in the text, enclose the last name and year in parentheses— . . . (Gouldner 1963).
- Pages cited follow the year of publication after a colon— . . . (Ramirez and Weiss 1979:239–40).
- Provide last uthors, list all three last names in the first citation in the text— . . . (Carr, Smith, and names for joint authors— . . . (Martin and Bailey 1988).
- For three a Jones 1962). For all subsequent citations use "et al."— . . . (Carr et al. 1962). For works with four or more authors, use "et al." throughout.
- For institutional authorship, supply minimal identification from the complete citation— . . . (U.S. Bureau of the Census 1963:117).

- List a series of citations in alphabetical order or date order separated by semicolons— . . . (Burgess 1968; Marwell et al. 1971).
- Use "forthcoming" to cite sources scheduled for publication. For dissertations and unpublished papers, cite the date. If no date, use "n.d." in place of the date— . . . Smith (forthcoming) and Oropesa (n.d.).
- For machine-readable data files, cite authorship and date— . . . (Institute for Survey Research 1976).

c. *Notes* should be numbered in the text consecutively using superscript Arabic numerals. When referring to a note later in the text, use a parenthetical note— . . . (see note 3).

d. *Equations* in the text should be typed or printed. Use consecutive Arabic numerals in parentheses at the right margin to identify important equations. Align all expressions and clearly mark compound subscripts and superscripts. Clarify all unusual characters or symbols with notes circled in the margin.

5. **Notes** (footnotes or e t pages or in a separate "Endnotes" section. Begin each note with the superscript numeral to ndnotes) should be typed or printed, double-spaced, either as footnotes at the bottom of the tex which it is keyed in the text (e.g., "1 After 1981, there were . . ."). Notes can (a) explain or amplify text, (b) cite materials of limited availability, or (c) append information presented in a table or figure. *Avoid long notes*: consider (a) stating in the text that information is available from the author, (b) depositing the information in a national retrieval center and inserting a short footnote or a citation in the text, or (c) adding an appendix.

6. **References** are presented in a separate section headed "References." All references cited in the text must be listed in the reference section, and vice versa. Publication information for each must be complete and correct. List the references in alphabetical order by authors' last names; include first names and middle initials for all authors when available. List two or more entries by the same as been accepted for publication, use "Forthcoming" in place of the date and give the journal author(s) in order of the year of publication. When the cited material is not yet published but h name or publishing house. For dissertations and unpublished papers, cite the date and place the paper was presented and/or where it is available. If no date is available, use "N.d." in place of the date. If two or more cited works are by the same author(s) within the same year, list them in alphabetical order by title and distinguish them by adding the letters a, b, c, etc., to the year (or to "Forthcoming"). For works with more than one author, only the name of the first author is inverted (e.g., "Jones, Arthur B., Colin D. Smith, and James Petersen"). List all authors; using "et al." in the reference list is not acceptable. Refer to the *ASA Style Guide* (2d ed., 1997) for additional examples:

Books:
Bernard, Claude. [1865] 1957. *An Introduction to the Study of Experimental Medicine.* Translated by H. C. Greene. New York: Dover.

Mason, Karen O. 1974. *Women's Labor Force Participation and Fertility.* Research Triangle Park, NC: National Institutes of Health.

58

U.S. Bureau of the Census. 1960. *Characteristics of Population.* Vol. 1. Washington, DC: U.S. Government Printing Office.

Periodicals:
Goodman, Leo A. Are Unobservable. Part I—A Modified Latent Structure Approach." *American Journal* 1947a. "The Analysis of Systems of Qualitative Variables When Some of the Variables *of Sociology* 79:1179–1259.

———. 1947b. "Exploratory Latent Structure Analysis Using Both Identifiable and Unidentifiable Models." Biometrika 61:215–31.

Szelényi, Szonja and Jacqueline Olvera. Forthcoming. "The Declining Significance of Class: Does Gender Complicate the Story?" *Theory and Society.*

Collections:
Clausen, John A. 1972. "The Life Course of Individuals." Pp. 457–514 in *Aging and Society,* vol. 3, *A Sociology of Age Stratification,* edited by M.W. Riley, M. Johnson, and A. Foner. New York: Russell Sage.

Sampson, Robert J. 1992. "Family Management and Child Development: Insights from Social Disorganization Theory." Pp. 63–93 in *Advances in Criminology Theory,* vol. 3, *Facts, Frameworks, and Forecasts,* edited by J. McCord. New Brunswick, NJ: Transaction.

Dissertations:
Charles, Maria. 1990. "Occupational Sex Segregation: A Log-Linear Analysis of Patterns in 25 Industrial Countries." Ph.D. dissertation, Department of Sociology, Stanford University, Stanford, CA.

American Sociological
Web Sites: Race Relations" (ASA Action Alert, October 15). Washington, DC: American Sociological Association. Retrieved October 15, 1997 (http://www.asanet Association. 1997. "Call for Help: Social Science Knowledge on Race, Racism, and.org/racecall.htm). 2003. "Homeless Needs Outrun Success in Finding Shelter Site." *Washington Post* Boorstein, Michelle., October 19, 2003, p. C05. Retrieved October 20, 2003 (http://www.washingtonpost.com/wp-dyn/articles/A46989-2003Oct18.html).

Kao, Grace and Jennifer Thompson.2003. "Racial and Ethnic Stratification in Educational Achievement and Attainment." *Annual Review of Sociology* 29:417-42. Retrieved October 20,2003(http://arjournals.annualreviews.org/doi/abs/10.1146/annurev.soc.29.010202.1000 19).

7. **Tables** should be numbered consecutively in the order in which they appear in the text and must include table titles. Tables will appear in the published article in the order in which they are numbered initially. Each table must include a descriptive title and headings for all columns and rows. Gather general notes to tables as *"Note:"* or *"Notes:"*; use a, b, c, etc., for table footnotes. Use asterisks *, **, and/or *** to indicate significance at the $p < .05$, $p < .01$, and $p < .001$ levels, respectively, and *always* specify one-tailed or two-tailed tests.

8. **Figures** should be numbered consecutively in the order in which they appear in the text and must include figure captions. Figures will appear in the published article in the order in which they are numbered initially. All artwork must be submitted as computer files on disk. All figures must be black and white, no color. Contact the *ASR* office for further details regarding preferred file formats for computer-generated figures.

IMPORTANT: All figures (including all type) must be legible when resized to fit one or two column widths, 2-9/16 and 5-5/16 inches wide, respectively. **PERMISSION**: *The author(s) are responsible for securing permission to reproduce all copyrighted figures or any other materials before they are published by* ASR. *A copy of the written permission must be included with the manuscript submission.*

9. **Appendices** should be lettered to distinguish them from numbered tables and figures. Include a descriptive title for each appendix (e.g., "Appendix A. Variable Names and Definitions").

Applied Measurement in Education

ADDRESS FOR SUBMISSION:

Barbara Plake, James Impara, Co-Editors
Applied Measurement in Education
University of Nebraska, Lincoln
Buros Center for Testing
21 Teachers College Hall
Lincoln, NE 68588-0352
USA
Phone: 402-472-6203
Fax: 402-472-6207
E-Mail: bplake@unl.edu; jimpara@unl.edu
Web:
Address May Change:

PUBLICATION GUIDELINES:

Manuscript Length: 20-40
Copies Required: Four
Computer Submission: Yes International
 only
Format: DOS, MAC or Other
Fees to Review: 0.00 US$

Manuscript Style:
 American Psychological Association

CIRCULATION DATA:

Reader: Academics
Frequency of Issue: Quarterly
Copies per Issue: Less than 1,000
Sponsor/Publisher: Lawrence Erlbaum
 Associates
Subscribe Price: 50.00 US$ Individual
 405.00 US$ Institution
 75.00 US$ Add Outside US/Canada

REVIEW INFORMATION:

Type of Review: Blind Review
No. of External Reviewers: 3
No. of In House Reviewers: 1
Acceptance Rate: 21-30%
Time to Review: 2 - 3 Months
Reviewers Comments: Yes
Invited Articles: 11-20%
Fees to Publish: 0.00 US$

MANUSCRIPT TOPICS:
Tests, Measurement & Evaluation

MANUSCRIPT GUIDELINES/COMMENTS:

Applied Measurement in Education, sponsored by the Buros Center for Testing, is a scholarly journal dedicated to the application of educational and psychological measurement research to the educational process. Its intended audience consists of researchers and practitioners who are interested in research likely to have an impact on educational measurement practice. A major aim of the journal is to provide both a greater understanding of educational measurement issues and an improved use of measurement techniques in education.

Types of manuscripts that will be considered for publication in *Applied Measurement in Education* include (a) reports of original applied research focusing on measurement issues in educational contexts, (b) presentations of innovative strategies for solving existing educational measurement problems, and (c) integrative reviews of research pertaining to contemporary measurement issues. An additional section of the journal will be dedicated to providing comparative reviews of tests and methods currently used in addressing specific educational measurement needs. The editors also welcome proposals for special issues dealing with a focused treatment of a particular area of applied educational measurement. Manuscripts dealing exclusively with the validation of specific measures are not considered.

Manuscript Submission
Submit four manuscript copies to *Applied Measurement in Education*, 21 Teachers College Hall, University of Nebraska-Lincoln, Lincoln, NE 68588-0352. Only original manuscripts submitted to *Applied Measurement in Education* will be considered for publication. The cover letter should include a statement that the manuscript is not being simultaneously submitted elsewhere. Manuscripts will not be returned.

Format and Organization
Manuscripts should be prepared according to the guidelines in the *Publication Manual of the American Psychological Association* (5th Ed.). Double-space all text. On the first page, indicate the title of the manuscript, the names and affiliations of authors, and the name and address of the person to whom reprint requests are to be sent; suggest a shortened version of the title of the manuscript for use as a running head (40 characters or fewer, including spaces). On the second page, provide a 100 to 175-word abstract. On the third page (the first text page), type the title of the manuscript.

Permissions
Authors are responsible for all statements made in their work and for obtaining permission from copyright owners to use a lengthy quotation (100 words or more) or to reprint or adapt a table or figure published elsewhere. Authors should write to both author(s) and publisher of such material to request nonexclusive world rights in all languages for use in the article and in future editions of it.

Content
Do not use new technical words, psychological jargon or slang, or terminology not consistent with the style guidelines in the *Publication Manual of the APA*. Define any abbreviations or acronyms the first time they are used.

Figures and Tables
All figures and tables should be numbered separately using Arabic numerals and should be grouped at the end of the manuscript. Clearly visible notes within the text should indicate approximate placement of figures and tables. Figures must be professionally prepared and must be camera-ready. Type figure captions on a separate sheet. Write the article title and figure number lightly in pencil on the back of each piece of artwork. Refer to the *Publication Manual of the APA* for format of tables. Double-space.

References
Double-space. Compile references alphabetically (see the *Publication Manual of the APA* for multiple-author citations and references). Spell out names of journals. Provide page numbers of chapters in edited books. Text citations must correspond accurately to the references in the reference list.

Page Proofs

Authors are sent page proofs of their manuscripts and are asked to proofread them for printers errors and other defects. Correction of typographical errors will be made without charge; other alterations will be charged to the author.

Reprints

Authors may order article reprints of their articles when they receive page proofs. Printing considerations do not permit the ordering of reprints after authors have returned proofs.

Dear Journal Contributor

Now that your manuscript has been accepted for publication, we at Lawrence Erlbaum Associates, Inc. (LEA) would like to open the communication lines-offer our preproduction assistance, inform you of your responsibilities, and introduce you to our journal production process. We believe this early dialogue will get our collaboration off on the right foot.

This letter is divided into five sections: Keeping in Touch; Understanding the Publication Process; Preparing a Manuscript; Preparing the Word-Processed, Electronic File and Disk; and Taking Action.

Keeping In Touch

The Editor of the journal is your primary source of information and advice. However, if you have a question the Editor is unable to answer, feel free to contact the LEA Production Editor or Electronic Publishing Manager. (The Editor can put you in touch with these individuals.)

The journal is on a tight production schedule, so . . .
1. If you move or are away for an extended period during the time your manuscript is in production, please let the Editor and Production Editor know where you can be reached (address and phone number). You can imagine the delays that occur when the Production Editor (a) mails typeset page proofs to an old address or (b) phones a contributor with an important question, only to learn that the contributor is on overseas sabbatical and did not leave a forwarding number.

2. Call the Production Editor if you are unable to return page proofs within two days of receipt.

Understanding the Publication Process

1. You return a finalized, complete, correctly formatted manuscript – printout and disk – to the Editor.

2. The Editor compiles an issue of manuscripts and disks from several contributors and forwards the issue to the Production Editor.

3. The Production Editor reviews the manuscripts and disks. If your manuscript is not prepared correctly – see Preparing a Manuscript – the Production Editor returns it to the Editor so you can revise it. (Production on the issue is suspended until all manuscripts are ready.)

4. When all manuscripts are ready, the Production Editor copyedits and typesets the issue and sends each contributor (a) two sets of page proofs of the respective article, (b) a list of queries concerning the article, and (c) a reprint request form.

5. You proofread your typeset pages, indicate corrections on both sets, keep one set for your records, and return to the Production Editor (a) the other set, (b) answers to the queries and (c) the reprint request form (with payment if ordering reprints).

6. The Production Editor finalizes the issue and sends it to the printer.

Preparing the Manuscript

Take a few moments now to make certain that your manuscript is complete and that it complies with the editorial guidelines appearing in the *Publication Manual of the American Psychological Association* (5th ed.). (The manual is available from the APA Order Department, P.O. Box 92984, Washington, DC 20090-2984; tel: 800-374-2721; fax: 202-336-5502; e-mail: order@apa.org; online: www.apa.org/books/) You may find it helpful to consult "Appendix A: Checklist for Manuscript Submission" and "Appendix B: Checklist for Transmitting Accepted Manuscripts for Electronic Production" appearing on pages 379 through 386 of the *APA Manual*, the contributor information appearing in the journal, and/or the following summary of requirements for acceptable manuscripts. If you have any questions whatsoever, please ask for clarification.

Typing. Use 8 1/2- x 11-in. nonsmear paper. Set all margins at 1 in. Type all components double-spaced, including title page, abstract, text, acknowledgments, references, appendices, tables, figure captions, and footnotes. Indent all paragraphs and make sure the entire manuscript is neat and readable. Use superscript numbers to cite footnotes; type all footnotes on a separate page (not at the bottom of the pages on which they are cited). Indicate in the manuscript approximately where each figure or table is to be positioned; type all figure captions on a separate page.

Abstract. If an abstract is required, consult the Editor or the journal for the limit on length. Provide key words or phrases if required.

References. Provide complete, *APA*-formatted references and text citations and make sure the two correspond exactly. Pages 207 through 281 of the *APA Manual* provide (a) detailed guidelines on preparing references and citations and (b) many excellent sample references and citations. When typing a reference for a chapter in an edited book, be sure to add the inclusive page numbers of the chapter.

Tests, Scales, Subscales, Factors, Variables, Effects. See *APA Manual* regarding capitalization. *Statistics.* See *APA Manual* regarding presentation. *Acronyms.* Define on first mention.

Figures. Submit (a) high-quality laser prints, professionally prepared black-and-white originals or camera-ready glossy reproductions and (b) photocopies of all figures. (c) as many computer files for these figures as you have (see Preparing the Word-Processed, Electronic File and Disk). Please note that figures appearing in the journal will look only as good as what

64

you provide. Make sure lettering and details are crisp, clear, and large enough so that they will be legible upon reduction. (Figures are reduced in size in order to conserve space on the printed page.)

All hard copies for which we do not have computer files will be scanned electronically, so please avoid using gray shading or dot screens in graphs. Use solid black or white or diagonal lines to distinguish columns instead (for further examples and guidelines, see *APA Manual*, pp. 176-201).

Make sure each figure is identified. Assess whether textual information appearing on a piece of artwork might be best presented as part of the caption; alter artwork and caption accordingly.

Permissions. You are responsible for all statements made in your work and for obtaining permission from the copyright owner(s) to reprint or adapt a table or figure or to reprint quotes from one source totaling 500 words or more. Write to original author(s) and publisher to request nonexclusive world rights in all languages for use of the material in the article and in future print and nonprint editions. Please note that you must obtain permission for any lines of poetry or song lyrics you quote as well as for prose, and that you will be liable for any licensing fees required for such use. Provide copies of all permissions and credit lines obtained. Attached to this letter are (a) a sample permission request form you can copy/adapt and use in order to secure permissions and (b) sample credit lines from the *APA Manual*.

Concordance of Elements. Make sure your manuscript is complete and internally consistent. Each reference must be cited in text at least once; each citation must have a corresponding reference. Likewise, each figure, table, and footnote must be cited; if a figure, table, or footnote is cited in text, the corresponding element must be included with the manuscript.

Preparing the Word-Processed, Electronic File and Disk
Now is the time to submit the word-processed, electronic file (as well as an ASCII version) and a disk for copyediting and typesetting. Working with an electronic manuscript allows us to capture your keystrokes-thereby maintaining the accuracy of your article and reducing the time between research and publication.

Shortening the production schedule involves combining the stages of author review of copyedited articles and subsequent review of typeset page proofs into a single review of proofs made from copyedited disk files via desktop publishing. With timely publication the concern of all involved, we assume you will (a) accept minor editorial changes that do not alter intended meanings and (b) alter page proofs only to correct errors, update publication information, and respond to editors, queries. As substantial alterations will not be made after manuscripts have been typeset, please take the time now to make sure that your manuscript and its file are complete and identical and that they represent your 'final say."

Our first choice for format is WordPerfect or Word on an IBM-formatted disk. Other formats are acceptable.

IBM-Compatible Users. Submit a PC disk containing two files: (a) the file produced with your word processor and (b) the same file saved as ASCII DOS text or MS-DOS text. If we are unable to read the native file produced by your word processor, we can try the ASCII or MS-DOS file.

Macintosh Users. Submit a high-density Mac disk containing two files: (a) the file produced with your word processor and (b) the same file saved as ASCII DOS text or MS-DOS text. If we are unable to read the native file produced by your word processor, we can try the ASCII or MS-DOS file.

Other Computer Users. Please try to convert and transfer your file to an IBM-compatible or Mac disk; then follow directions for IBM-compatible or Mac users. If unable to do so, please contact the Electronic Publishing Manager.

However you submit your electronic manuscript, please (a) let us know computer type (IBM-compatible, Macintosh), word processor (including version number), and file name; and (b) make sure the content of the files exactly matches that of the printed, accepted, finalized manuscript.

In addition, if your figures were prepared using a computer and you can obtain files from which the hard copies were printed, please include these on your disk (or on additional disks if they are too large).

If you have any questions regarding disk preparation, please contact the LEA Electronic Journal Publishing Manager.

Taking Action
In a nutshell, now is the time for you to (a) make sure your manuscript is formatted correctly, (b) check on permissions, and (c) send the finalized manuscript--printout and disk--to the Editor.

We hope this letter has been informative, and we look forward to working with you. If you think of any way we can improve the production process, by all means let us know. We're here to help.

Sincerely,

Journal Production Office
Lawrence Erlbaum Associates, Inc.
10 Industrial Avenue
Mahwah, New Jersey 07430-3362
Voice: (201) 236-9500
FAX: (201) 236-0072
Production Fax: (201) 236-6396

Sample Permission Request Form

I am writing an article tentatively entitled:

_____

to be Published in the journal:

_____

by Lawrence Erlbaum Associates, Inc., and would like your permission to obtain nonexclusive world rights in all languages to reprint/adapt the following material in the article and the future editions of the article:

_____
_____
_____

Should I use the American Psychological Association format for credit lines? If not, type your credit line here:

_____
_____

A copy of this letter is enclosed. Please sign and return both copies to me at this address:

_____
_____

Thank you for granting this request.

Name:_____Signature:_____Date:_____

Copyright holder hereby grants permission to use the material in the manner described above.

Name:_____Signature:_____Date:_____

Sample Credit Lines From APA Manual

3.73 Tables From Another Source

Authors must obtain permission to reproduce or adapt all or part of a table (or figure) from a copyrighted source. It is not necessary to obtain permission from APA to reproduce one table (or figure) from an APA article provided you obtain the author's permission and give full credit to APA as copyright holder and to the author through a complete and accurate citation. When you wish to reproduce material from sources not copyrighted by APA, contact the copyright holders to determine their requirements for both print and electronic reuse. If you have any doubt about the policy of the copyright holder, you should request permission. Always enclose the letter of permission when transmitting the final version of the accepted manuscript for production.

Any reproduced table (or figure) must be accompanied by a note at the bottom of the reprinted table (or in the figure caption) giving credit to the original author and to the copyright holder. If the table (or figure) contains test items, see the cautionary note in section 3.93. Use the following form for tables or figures. (For copyright permission footnotes in text [see section 3.41 for permission to quote], use the following form, but substitute the indented superscript footnote number for the word Note.)

Material reprinted from a journal article
Note. From [or The data in column 1 are from] "Title of Article," by A. N. Author and C. O. Author, 2000, Title of Journal, 50, p. 22. Copyright 2000 by the Name of Copyright Holder. Reprinted [or Adapted] with permission.

Material reprinted from a book
Note. From [or The data in column 1 are from] Title of Book (p. 103), by A. N. Author and C. O. Author, 1999, Place of Publication: Publisher. Copyright 1999 by the Name of Copyright Holder. Reprinted [**or** Adapted] with permission.

Note. Guidelines are from *Publication Manual of the American Psychological Association* (5th ed., pp. 174-175), 2001, Washington, DC: American Psychological Association. Copyright 2001 by the American Psychological Association. Reprinted with permission.

Applied Psycholinguistics

ADDRESS FOR SUBMISSION:

Usha Goswami, Editor
Applied Psycholinguistics
University of Cambridge
Faculty of Education
Shaftesbury Road
Cambridge, CB2 2BX
United Kingdom
Phone: +44 (0) 1223 369631
Fax: +44 (0) 1223 324421
E-Mail: See Guidelines
Web:
Address May Change:

PUBLICATION GUIDELINES:

Manuscript Length: 20
Copies Required: Four
Computer Submission: Yes
Format: N/A
Fees to Review: 0.00 US$

Manuscript Style:
American Psychological Association

CIRCULATION DATA:

Reader: Academics
Frequency of Issue: Quarterly
Copies per Issue: No Reply
Sponsor/Publisher: University; Cambridge
University Press
Subscribe Price: 90.00 US$ Individual
195.00 US$ Inst Print Only
190.00 US$ Inst Electronic/ 218 +Print

REVIEW INFORMATION:

Type of Review: Editorial Review
No. of External Reviewers: 2
No. of In House Reviewers: 1
Acceptance Rate: 21-30%
Time to Review: 3 Months
Reviewers Comments: Yes
Invited Articles: 0-5%
Fees to Publish: 0.00 US$

MANUSCRIPT TOPICS:
Bilingual/E.S.L.; Higher Education; Language Development; Language Disorders; Languages
& Linguistics; Literacy Development; Psychological Processes in Language; Reading

MANUSCRIPT GUIDELINES/COMMENTS:

Applied Psycholinguistics publishes original articles on the psychological processes involved
in language. The articles address the development, use, and impairment of language in all its
modalities, including spoken, signed, and written, with a particular emphasis on cross-
linguistic studies. Studies appearing in *Applied Psycholinguistics* need to have a clear applied
relevance to professionals in a variety of fields, including linguistics, psychology, speech and
hearing, reading, language teaching, special education, and neurology. Contributors should
explicitly consider the relevance of their work to the larger community, as well as its
theoretical and psychological significance. Specific topics featured in the journal include:
language development (the development of speech perception and production, the acquisition
and use of sign language, studies of discourse development, second language learning);
language disorders in children and adults (including those associated with brain damage,
retardation and autism, specific learning disabilities, hearing impairment); literacy

development (early literacy skills, dyslexia and other reading disorders, writing development and disorders, spelling development and disorders); and psycholinguistic processing (lexical access, time course of language processing, semantics, and syntax).

In addition to research reports, theoretical reviews will be considered for publication, as will keynote articles and commentaries (the latter normally invited by the Editors) journal will occasionally publish issues devoted to special topics within its purview.

Manuscript Submission

Authors should send their manuscripts either electronically as an E-mail attachment or as four paper copies and an electronic file. (Authors who submit via E-mail should also send a paper copy.) Articles pertaining to language development (speech perception and production), literacy development, and psycholinguistic processing (lexical access and the time course of language processing) should be sent to Usha Goswami. Articles related to language development (sign language, bilingualism, and second language learning), language disorders, and psycholinguistic processing (semantics and syntax) should be sent to Martha Crago.

Usha Goswami, Faculty of Education, University of Cambridge, Shaftesbury Road, Cambridge, CB2 2BX, United Kingdom, Fax +44 (0) 1223 324421
    Email: **educ-applied-psycholinguistics@lists.cam.ac.uk**

Martha Crago, Beatty Hall, McGill University, 1266 Pine Avenue West, Montreal, Quebec H3G 1A8, Canada, Fax: +1 514 398 3878; E-mail: **applied.psycholinguistics@mcgill.ca**

Submissions may be full-length articles (original research or theoretical reviews), critical responses to articles previously published in *Applied Psycholinguistics*, or (usually) invited keynote articles with accompanying commentaries.

Spelling, Capitalization, and Punctuation should be consistent within each article and should follow the style recommended in the Fifth Edition of the *Publication Manual of the American Psychological Association*.

A Title should be given for each article. An **Auxiliary Short Title** should be given for any article whose title exceeds 50 characters. The author's name should be given in the form preferred for publication; the affiliation should include the author's full mailing address, telephone number, an email address or fax number.

An Abstract should be prepared for each article (limited to 120 words).

Author's personal note(s) should appear in the **Acknowledgement** section.

Notes should be numbered consecutively throughout the text and appear as a unit following the acknowledgment section.

Tables and Figures should be numbered consecutively throughout the article and appear as a unit following the reference section.

Bibliographic Citations in the text must include the author's last name and the date of publication and may include page references. Complete bibliographic information for each citation should be included in the list of references. Examples of correct styling for bibliographic citations are: Brown (1973), Ingram (1976, 54-55), Smith and Miller (1966), (Smith & Miller, 1966), (Peterson, Danner & Flavell, 1972) and subsequently (Peterson et al., 1972). If more than one, citations should be listed in alphabetical order.

References should be cited in the text and should be typed in alphabetical order using the following style:

Brown, R. (1973). Schizophrenia, language and reality. *American Psychologist*, 28, 395-403.
Ingram D. (1976). *Phonological disability in children*. New York: Elsevier,
Krashen, S.D. (1978). Individual variation in the use of the Monitor. In W.C. Ritchie (Ed.) *Second language acquisition research*. New York: Academic Press.
Smith, F. & Miller, G.A. (Eds.). (1966). *The genesis of language*. Cambridge, Mass: M.I.T. Press.

Titles of journals should not be abbreviated. Unpublished citations should be listed in the references.

Preparation of the Manuscript
The entire manuscript, including footnotes and references, must be typed double-spaced on 8-1/2 x 11 inch or A4 paper, with 1 inch margins Manuscript pages should be numbered consecutively. Each element of the article should begin on a new page and should be arranged as follows: title page (title, short title, author's full name, affiliation, and mailing address), abstract, text, appendices, acknowledgments, notes, references, tables and figures.

Each table and figure should be submitted on a separate page and should be titled. Figures should be ready for photographic reproduction; they cannot be redrawn by the publisher. Charts, graphs, or other artwork should be professionally rendered or computer generated. Photographs should be glossy black-and-white prints; 8 by 10 inch enlargements are preferred. All labels and details on figures should be clearly printed and large enough to remain legible after a 50% reduction.

Copyediting and Proofreading
The publisher reserves the right to copyedit and proofread all articles accepted for publication. The lead author will review the copyedited manuscript only if changes have been substantial. Page proof of an article will be sent to the lead author for correction of typographical errors only; authors must notify the editorial office of any changes within 48 hours or approval will be assumed.

The Fifth Edition of the *Publication Manual of the American Psychological Association* should be consulted for instructions on aspects of manuscript preparation and style not covered in these instructions. The Editors may find it necessary to return manuscripts for reworking and retyping that do not conform to requirements.

The lead author will receive 25 offprints of his or her article or note without charge; additional copies may be purchased if ordered at proof stage.

Submission of an article or note implies that it has not been published elsewhere. Authors are responsible for obtaining written permission to publish material (quotations, illustrations, etc.) for which they do not own the copyright. Contributors of accepted articles will be asked to assign their copyrights on certain conditions to Cambridge University Press.

Art Therapy: Journal of the American Art Therapy Association

ADDRESS FOR SUBMISSION:

Frances F. Kaplan, Editor
Art Therapy: Journal of the American Art
    Therapy Association
1202 Allanson Road
Mandelein, IL 60060-3808
USA
Phone: 503-407-2896
Fax: 847-566-4580
E-Mail: evefish37@earthlink.net
Web: www.arttherapy.org
Address May Change: 12/31/2005

PUBLICATION GUIDELINES:

Manuscript Length: 21-25
Copies Required: Five
Computer Submission:
Format:
Fees to Review: 0.00 US$

Manuscript Style:
    American Psychological Association

CIRCULATION DATA:

Reader: Counselors, Art Therapists
Frequency of Issue: Quarterly
Copies per Issue: 4,001 - 5,000
Sponsor/Publisher: The American Art
    Therapy Association
Subscribe Price: 125.00 US$ Individual
    200.00 US$ Indv Foreign
    200.00 US$ Inst/$225.00 Foreign

REVIEW INFORMATION:

Type of Review: Blind Review
No. of External Reviewers: 2
No. of In House Reviewers: 1
Acceptance Rate: 50%
Time to Review: 2 - 3 Months
Reviewers Comments: Yes
Invited Articles: 0-5%
Fees to Publish: 0.00 US$

MANUSCRIPT TOPICS:
Art Education; Art Therapy; Art/Music; Counseling & Personnel Services; Special Education

MANUSCRIPT GUIDELINES/COMMENTS:

The above mentioned topics as they relate to the therapeutic use of art.

All submissions will be acknowledged upon receipt by the AATA National Office. *Art Therapy: Journal of the American Art Therapy Association* uses a blind peer review procedure for articles, brief reports, and viewpoints. Final decisions regarding publication in these categories are made by the reviewers and the Editor. Decisions regarding submissions to other sections are made by the Editor, Associate Editor, and special section editors.

The following are guidelines for submissions. Submissions that do not conform to these guidelines will be returned to the author without review.

Submission Categories
1. **Articles**. Full-length articles may focus on the theory, practice, and research in art therapy or related areas. Articles must include an abstract of approximately 100-150 words

summarizing the major points of the article. Submissions should be no more than 5,500 words (about 22 typewritten, double-spaced pages).

2. **Brief Reports**. Short articles that focus on art therapy practice or the results of research are appropriate for this section. Research reports should include a short introduction, methodology, results, and conclusions. An abstract of approximately 100-150 words should also be included. Submissions should be no more than 3,500 words (about 14 typewritten, double-spaced pages).

3. **Viewpoints**. Short articles focusing on personal experiences, opinions, or reactions that express the viewpoint of the author and that have implications for the field. Poetry and original art relevant to art therapy may also be submitted to this section. No abstract is needed for viewpoint submissions. Submissions should be no more than 2,500 words (about 10 typewritten, double-spaced pages).

4. **Cover Art**. Artwork by AATA members in vertical format, either color or black and white. A slide, a 5" x 7" glossy print, five (5) photocopies, and a brief description of the artwork are required for consideration.

5. **Book Reviews**. Reviews of books of interest to art therapists may be submitted at any time. Books which authors wish to have considered for review may be sent directly to the AATA National Office. Submissions should be no more than 1,500 words (about 6 typewritten, double-spaced pages).

6. **Video Reviews**. Reviews of media (videos) may be submitted at any time. Media which producers wish to have considered for review may be sent directly to the AATA National Office. Submissions should be no more than 1,500 words (about 6 typewritten, double-spaced pages).

7. **Commentaries**. Brief comments on submissions published in Art Therapy, issues critical to the profession and practice of art therapy, or Letters to the Editor may be submitted to this section and should conform to the style of all other submissions. Submissions should be no more than 500 words (about 2 typewritten, double-spaced pages).

Other Requirements
1. Send five (5) clear copies of each submission to Editor, Art Therapy: Journal of the American Art Therapy Association, c/o American Art Therapy Association, Inc., 1202 Allanson Road, Mundelein, IL 60060-3808. Neither AATA nor the Editor can be responsible for submissions sent to any other address nor can Editor or AATA be responsible for submissions addressed to the proper address but not so delivered.

2. Only original submissions that are not under consideration by another periodical or publisher are acceptable.

3. Submissions must be typewritten on 8-1/2" x 11" white paper with margins of at least 1". The body of the paper, references, tables, and quotations must be double-spaced.

4. Submissions must be prepared in APA style. Please refer to the *Publication Manual of the American Psychological Association* (Fifth Edition) for more information.

5. An abstract of 100-150 words must be included with full-length articles and brief reports.

6. Please avoid footnotes, if possible.

7. A cover sheet should be prepared to include the full name(s) and degree(s) of the author(s); professional affiliations; the return mailing address of the author to whom correspondence can be sent; and any information authors would like to appear at the bottom of their submission in an Editor's Note (such as where they can be contacted for further information, if the material was presented at a conference, acknowledgements, etc.). Authors' names, positions, titles, and places of employment should not appear in the body of the paper to assure anonymity and to facilitate blind review.

8. Use tables sparingly and type them on separate pages. Refer to the *Publication Manual of the American Psychological Association* (Fifth Edition) for style of tabular presentations. All tables, charts, or diagrams must be legible and able to withstand reduction. Include originals and five (5) photocopies of each.

9. Photographs must be at least 5" x 7" black and white glossy prints, preferably with high contrast. Photocopies of illustrations or art expressions are not acceptable for publication. Figure numbers and captions should be noted on the back of photographs. Captions must be typed and submitted on a separate sheet of paper. Please refer to figures in the text as Figure 1, Figure 2, etc. Include five (5) sets of photocopies of original photographs.

10. No cases should the combined number of illustrations, graphs, and tables total more than eight (8) for any given manuscript in any of the publication categories.

11. Lengthy quotations (300 words or more from one source) or reproduction of works of art (this does not include client art expressions which are addressed below) require written permission from the copyright holder for reproduction. Adaptation of tables or figures from copyrighted sources also requires approval. It is the author's responsibility to secure such permissions. A copy of the copyright holder's written permission must be provided to the Editor immediately upon acceptance of the article for publication.

12. Client/patient confidentiality must be protected in the title, abstract, text, photos, illustrations, and other accompanying material. Proper releases for use of client art expressions and other client information must be obtained and kept on file by the author.

13. It is expected that any submission accepted for publication in Art Therapy will go through at least one revision before publication. Upon acceptance, authors are required to supply an electronic copy of the submission on either a 3.5" diskette generated from an IBM, IBM-compatible, or Macintosh computer or via e-mail to the AATA National Office. This will help speed processing, editing, and publication.

Note: Authors bear full responsibility for the accuracy of all references, quotations, and materials accompanying their submissions.

Assessing Writing

ADDRESS FOR SUBMISSION:

Liz Hamp-Lyons, Editor
Assessing Writing
University of Melbourne
School of Languages
Parkville, VIC 3010
Australia
Phone: +61 (-3) -8344 8991
Fax: +61 (-3) -8344 5163
E-Mail: lizhl@unimelb.edu.au
Web: www.elsevier.com
Address May Change:

PUBLICATION GUIDELINES:

Manuscript Length: 21-25
Copies Required: Three
Computer Submission: Yes by e-mail
Format: MSWord
Fees to Review: 0.00 US$

Manuscript Style:
    American Psychological Association

CIRCULATION DATA:

Reader: Academics
Frequency of Issue: 3 Times/Year
Copies per Issue: Confidential
Sponsor/Publisher: British Assn. of
    Lecturers in English for Academic
    Purposes/Elsevier Science Publishing Co.
Subscribe Price: 61.00 US$ Individual
    233.00 US$ Inst. / $227.00 Euro. Inst.
    60.00 US$ Indv. in European countries

REVIEW INFORMATION:

Type of Review: Blind Review
No. of External Reviewers: 2
No. of In House Reviewers: 0
Acceptance Rate: 21-30%
Time to Review: 2 - 3 Months
Reviewers Comments: Yes
Invited Articles:
Fees to Publish: 0.00 US$

MANUSCRIPT TOPICS:
Languages & Linguistics; Writing

MANUSCRIPT GUIDELINES/COMMENTS:

Description
The Editors welcome submissions that address writing assessment issues from diverse perspectives: classroom research, institutional, professional, and administrative. Journal articles explore various critical topics: assessment techniques from kindergarten through college classrooms; institutional, statewide, national and other large-scale assessment practices; evaluation in non educational settings; the research, theory and historical context of writing assessment; and the relationship between other literacies, technology, and writing assessment.

GUIDE FOR AUTHORS
Submission requirements
Submission of a paper requires the assurance that the manuscript is an original work which has not been published previously and is not currently being considered for publication elsewhere. Article submissions should not normally exceed 20 pages excluding tables. All

articles should have abstracts which summarize the scope and Purpose of the article and, if applicable, the results of the study. The abstracts should be between 100 and 200 words in length. Articles must be written in English. Manuscript pages should be consecutively numbered in the upper right hand corner. All artwork must be suitable for publication and need no further work. Submit your manuscript by email to either editor: Professor Liz Hamp-Lyons **lizhl@unimelb.edu.au** or William Condon **bcondon@wsu.edu**.

In a separate electronic file, please supply the senior author's telephone number, fax number and e-mail address along with a brief biographical sketch of about fifty words. The manuscript pages themselves must not indicate authorship. Receipt of manuscripts will be acknowledged, but they cannot be returned; therefore, authors should retain a copy of the paper exactly as it was submitted.

Authors unable to submit by e-mail should send three hard copies of their manuscript and a separate sheet of contact details to either editor at their address listed on the masterhead or below.

William Condon, Washington State University, 14204 SE Salmon Creek Avenue, Vancouver, Washington 98686-9600, USA

Style
Manuscripts must be typed double-spaced with wide margins on only one side of A4 or letter-size paper, and should follow the style of the *APA*. Grammatical, lexical, and orthographic features may conform to either British or American norms. Citations may be given of lexical material from languages other than English; however, citations from languages not employing a Roman alphabet must be given in a Romanized transliteration or in a transcription which uses standard symbols available in the International Phonetic Alphabet.

References and Footnotes
In the text, references are cited using author's last name, publication date (Wilkins, 1976). If quotations are cited, these should additionally have page numbers (Wilkins, 1976: 21-22). The reference list should be arranged in alphabetical order following the style sheet of the *American Psychological Association* and should appear on a separate page at the end of the article. The reference list should include only those items specifically cited in the body of the text. Generally speaking, comments and references should be incorporated into the text; but when necessary, footnotes should be typed at the bottom of the page on which the reference appears and should be set off from text with a horizontal line.

Keywords
Authors should provide up to six keywords, to appear just underneath the abstract. These keywords will be used to help provide efficient indexing, search and retrieval mechanisms as articles become available through electronic systems.

Tables
Prepare each table, figure, graph or illustration on its own page and number all such material clearly. Make sure that the text refers to the figures and tables in consecutive order. Tables should be numbered consecutively and titled, and should be referred to in the text and

78

submitted on separate sheets at the end of the manuscript. Please keep lines and frames to a minimum.

Electronic Submission

Authors should submit an electronic copy of their paper with the final version of the manuscript. The electronic copy should match the hardcopy exactly. Always keep a backup copy of the electronic file for reference and safety. Full details of electronic submission and formats can be obtained from **http://authors.elsevier.com** and from Author Support at Elsevier Science.

Proofs

Proofs will be sent to the author (first named author if no corresponding author is identified of multi-authored papers) and should be returned within 48 hours of receipt. Corrections should be restricted to typesetting errors; any others may be charged to the author. Any queries should be answered in full. Please note that authors are urged to check their proofs carefully before return, since the inclusion of late corrections cannot be guaranteed. Proofs are to be returned to the Log-in Department, Elsevier Science Ltd, Stover Court, Bampfylde Street, Exeter EX1 2AH, UK.

Offprints

Authors will receive 25 offprints of their own contributions. Writers of reviews will receive 10 offprints. If extra prints are desired, authors must request them with the offprint order form that the editorial office sends before publication of the journal. Additional offprints and copies of the issue can be ordered at a specially reduced rate using the order form sent to the corresponding author after the manuscript has been accepted. Orders for reprints (produced after publication of an article) will incur a 50% surcharge.

Copyright

All authors must sign the "Transfer of Copyright" agreement before the article can be published. This transfer agreement enables Elsevier Science Ltd to protect the copyrighted material for the authors, without the author relinquishing his/her proprietary rights. The copyright transfer covers the exclusive rights to reproduce and distribute the article, including reprints, photographic reproductions, microfilm or any other reproductions of a similar nature, and translations. It also includes the right to adapt the article for use in conjunction with computer systems and programs, including reproduction or publication in machine-readable form and incorporation in retrieval systems. Authors are responsible for obtaining from the copyright holder permission to reproduce any material for which copyright already exists.

Author Support

For queries relating to the general submission of manuscripts (including electronic text and artwork) and the status of accepted manuscripts, please contact Author Support at authorsupport@elsevier.ie Authors can also keep track of progress of their accepted article, and set up e-mail alerts informing them of changes to their manuscript's status, by using the "Track a Paper" feature of Elsevier's Author Gateway

Assessment for Effective Intervention

ADDRESS FOR SUBMISSION:

Linda & Nick Elksnin, Co-Editors
Assessment for Effective Intervention
The Citadel
Department of Education
171 Moultrie St.
Charleston, SC 29409
USA
Phone: 843-849-9306
Fax: 843-849-9306
E-Mail: assessmentei@citadel.edu
Web: www.cec.sped.org
Address May Change:

PUBLICATION GUIDELINES:

Manuscript Length: 15-30
Copies Required: Five
Computer Submission: No
Format: N/A
Fees to Review: 0.00 US$

Manuscript Style:
    American Psychological Association

CIRCULATION DATA:

Reader: Practicing Teachers, School
   Psychologists, Eductional Diagnosticians,
   Academics
Frequency of Issue: Quarterly
Copies per Issue: 1,001 - 2,000
Sponsor/Publisher: Council for Educational
   Diagnostic Services of the Council for
   Exceptional Children
Subscribe Price: 40.00 US$ Individual
   60.00 US$ Institution
   50.00 US$ Indv, $70 Inst. - Foreign

REVIEW INFORMATION:

Type of Review: Blind Review
No. of External Reviewers: 3
No. of In House Reviewers: 2
Acceptance Rate: 40%
Time to Review: 2 - 3 Months
Reviewers Comments: Yes
Invited Articles: 0-5%
Fees to Publish: 0.00 US$

MANUSCRIPT TOPICS:
Curriculum Studies; Gifted Children; Special Education; Tests, Measurement & Evaluation

MANUSCRIPT GUIDELINES/COMMENTS:

Manuscript Topics. Assessment of children and adolescents who are disabled and/or gifted and talented; Tests, measurement & evaluation; Curriculum-based assessment.

Tests Reviews should be submitted to
Matthew Burns, Ph.D., Associate Editor for Test Reviews
Central Michigan University
228 Rowe Hall, Mt. Pleasant, MI 48859
Email: **burns1mk@cmich.edu**

Book Reviews should be submitted to
Cathy Spinelli, Ph.D., Associate Editor for Book Reviews
Education Department, St. Joseph's University, Philadelphia, PA 19131
Email: **CathySpine@aol.com**

Assessment for Effective Intervention is the official journal of the Council for Educational Diagnostic Services, a division of the Council for Exceptional Children. The editorial board of *Assessment for Effective Intervention* will review manuscripts relevant for practicing educational diagnosticians, special educators, psychologists, academic trainers, and others interested in psycho-educational assessment.

The primary purpose of the journal is to publish empirically sound manuscripts that have implications for practitioners. The editors welcome manuscripts that center on practitioner-developed assessment procedures as well as papers that focus on published tests. Manuscripts that describe the relationship between assessment and instruction, innovative assessment strategies, diagnostic procedures, relationships between existing instruments, and review articles of assessment techniques, strategies and instrumentation are particularly desirable. Implications for the practitioner should be clearly communicated.

Five copies of each manuscript should be submitted to Dr. Linda Elsknin, Department of Education, The Citadel, 171 Moultrie Street, Charleston, SC 29404. One copy should be retained by the author(s). A submission letter should include contact information for the lead author and a statement that the manuscript has not been submitted for publication elsewhere.

The Associate Editors of *Assessment for Effective Intervention* will accept unsolicited book and test reviews. Guidelines for preparation of book/test reviews are available from the Associate Editors. When writing a test review, the author should address relevant test construction guidelines described in the most recent edition of Standards for Educational and Psychological Tests published by the American Educational Research Association, the American Psychological Association and the National Council for Measurement in Education. Book and test reviews should be written with the practitioner's needs in mind. Five copies of each book or test review should be submitted to the above addresses. One copy should be retained by the author(s). A submission letter should include contact information for the lead author and a statement that the manuscript has not been submitted for publication elsewhere.

Preparation of manuscripts should conform to guidelines established by the most recent (i.e., 5th) edition of the *Publication Manual of the American Psychological Association*. Each manuscript should be limited to approximately 4,500 words, or approximately 15 typewritten double-spaced pages, and should be accompanied by an abstract of 100 to 150 words. Because manuscripts are reviewed anonymously, only the cover sheet should include the author's identifying information such as name, affiliation, and address. Each test/book review should be limited to approximately 2,100 words.

It is understood that when an author submits a manuscript for review in Assessment for Effective Intervention, the author (a) assures that the manuscript is not being considered concurrently by another journal; (b) has not already published a substantial part of the article; (c) is responsible for the accuracy of all statements; (d) agrees that the editors have the right to edit the manuscript as necessary for publication; (e) will obtain permission, if appropriate, to quote and reproduce material owned by someone else; and (f) assign all rights for publication of the manuscript, if accepted for publication to *Assessment for Effective Intervention*.

Receipt of submissions will be acknowledged by mail. The editors will screen each manuscript for appropriateness of content and readability, as well as adherence to publication guidelines. A manuscript that meets criteria will be sent to three consulting or guest editors for review. The editors will consider reviewer's comments when making an editorial decision to accept with minor editing, conditionally accept pending minor revision, conditional accept pending major revision, or reject. The author is typically notified about status of the manuscript within ten weeks following submission.

There are no publication charges. However, should the Journal incur costs for preparing camera-ready figures, photographs, or other illustrations, they will be charged to the author. Reprints are available for purchase by authors.

Assessment in Education: Principles, Policy & Practice

ADDRESS FOR SUBMISSION:

Gordon Stobart, Editor
Assessment in Education: Principles, Policy
& Practice
University of Bristol - Grad Sch. of Edu
c/o Editorial Office
Helen Wodehouse Bldg
35 Berkeley Square
Bristol, BS8 1JA
UK
Phone: +44 (0) 2076 126157
Fax: +44 (0) 1179 251537
E-Mail: g.stobart@ioe.ac.uk
Web: www.tandf.co.uk/journals
Address May Change:

PUBLICATION GUIDELINES:

Manuscript Length: 26-30 (5,000-7,000
Words)
Copies Required: Four
Computer Submission: Yes Disk
Format: MS Word
Fees to Review: 0.00 US$

Manuscript Style:
See Manuscript Guidelines

CIRCULATION DATA:

Reader: Academics, Administrators
Frequency of Issue: 3 Times/Year
Copies per Issue:
Sponsor/Publisher: Taylor & Francis
Subscribe Price: 151.00 US$ Individual
568.00 US$ Institution

REVIEW INFORMATION:

Type of Review: Blind Review
No. of External Reviewers: 2
No. of In House Reviewers: 1
Acceptance Rate: 11-20%
Time to Review: 3-9 months
Reviewers Comments: Yes
Invited Articles: 30%
Fees to Publish: 0.00 US$

MANUSCRIPT TOPICS:
Curriculum Studies; Educational Psychology; Educational Technology Systems;
Elementary/Early Childhood; Higher Education; Secondary/Adolescent Studies; Teacher
Education; Tests, Measurement & Evaluation

MANUSCRIPT GUIDELINES/COMMENTS:

Journal's Website. www.tandf.co.uk/journals/titles/0969594x.asp

Note to Authors. please make sure your contact address information is clearly visible on the
outside of all packages you are sending to Editors.

Papers accepted become the copyright of the *Journal*, unless otherwise specifically agreed.

Manuscripts should be sent to The Editorial Office, Graduate School of Education, University
of Bristol, Helen Wodehouse Building, 35 Berkeley Square, Bristol BS8 1JA, UK.

brigid.walker@bristol.ac.uk. Articles can be considered only if **four complete copies of each manuscript** are submitted. (We prefer to receive disks in Microsoft Word PC format.) Articles should be typed on one side of the paper, double spaced, with ample margins, and bear the title of the contribution, name(s) of the author(s) and the address where the work was carried out. An abstract of 100-150 words should be included and a short note of bibliographical details for the 'Notes on Contributors' page. The full postal address of the author who will check proofs and receive correspondence and offprints should also be included. All pages should be numbered.

Footnotes to the text should be avoided wherever this is reasonably possible.

Profiles should be 3000-6000 words in length (including bibliography) and should be submitted to the journal as detailed above, indicating clearly that they are to be considered for publication within the section **Profiles of Educational Assessment Systems World-wide**.

Rejected manuscripts will not normally be returned to contributors unless sufficient international postal coupons have been sent.

Tables and captions to illustrations. Tables must be typed out on separate sheets and not included as part of the text. The captions to illustrations should be gathered together and also typed out on a separate sheet. Tables should be numbered by Arabic numerals. The approximate position of tables and figures should be indicated in the manuscript. Captions should include keys to symbols.

Figures. Please supply one set of artwork in a finished form, suitable for reproduction. Figures will not normally be redrawn by the publisher.

Citations of other work should be limited to those strictly necessary for the argument. Any quotations should be brief, and accompanied by precise references.

References should be indicated in the typescript by giving the author's name, with the year of publication in parentheses. If several papers by the same author and from the same year are cited, a, b, c, etc. should be put after the year of publication. The references should be listed in full, including pages, at the end of the paper in the following standard form:

For books
Kress, G. (2003) Literacy in the new media age (London, Routledge).

For articles
Cremin, L. A. (1983) The problematics of education in the 1980s: some reflections on the Oxford Workshop, Oxford Review of Education, 9, pp. 33-40.

For chapters within books
Willis, P. (1983) Cultural production and theories of reproduction, in: L. Barton & S. Walker (Eds) Race, Class and Education (London, Croom Helm), 25-50.

84

Titles of journals and names of publishers, etc. should **not** be abbreviated. Acronyms for the names of organisations, examinations, etc. should be preceded by the title in full.

If you have any further questions about the style for this journal, please submit your questions using the Style Queries form at www.tandf.co.uk/journals/authors/stylequeries.asp.

Proofs will be sent to authors if there is sufficient time to do so. They should be corrected and returned to the Publisher within three days. Major alterations to the text cannot be accepted.

Offprints. Fifty offprints of each paper are supplied free. Additional copies may be purchased and should be ordered when the proofs are returned. Offprints, together with a complete copy of the relevant journal issue, are sent by accelerated surface post about three weeks after publication.

Early Electronic Offprints. Corresponding authors can now receive their article by e-mail as a complete PDF. This allows the author to print up to 50 copies, free of charge, and disseminate them to colleagues. In many cases this facility will be available up to two weeks prior to publication. Or, alternatively, corresponding authors will receive the traditional 50 offprints. A copy of the journal will be sent by post to all corresponding authors after publication. Additional copies of the journal can be purchased at the author's preferential rate of £15.00/$25.00per copy.

Athletics Administration

ADDRESS FOR SUBMISSION:

Laurie Garrison, Editor
Athletics Administration
NACDA
PO Box 16428
Cleveland, OH 44116
USA
Phone: 440-892-4000
Fax: 440-892-4007
E-Mail: lgarrison@nacda.com
Web: www.nacda.com
Address May Change:

PUBLICATION GUIDELINES:

Manuscript Length: 6-10
Copies Required: One
Computer Submission: Yes
Format: MSWord for PC
Fees to Review: 0.00 US$

Manuscript Style:

CIRCULATION DATA:

Reader: Administrators
Frequency of Issue: Bi-Monthly
Copies per Issue: 5,001 - 10,000
Sponsor/Publisher: National Association of
    Collegiate Directors of Athletics; Host
    Communications, Inc.
Subscribe Price: 15.00 US$

REVIEW INFORMATION:

Type of Review: Editorial Review
No. of External Reviewers: 1
No. of In House Reviewers: 1
Acceptance Rate: 50%
Time to Review: 1 Month or Less
Reviewers Comments: No
Invited Articles: 50% +
Fees to Publish: 0.00 US$

MANUSCRIPT TOPICS:
Administration of Intercollegiate Athletics; Education Management/Administration

MANUSCRIPT GUIDELINES/COMMENTS:

Athletics Administration is the official publication of the National Association of Collegiate Directors of Athletics (NACDA). It is published six times annually and distributed to every athletics director at four-year and two-year colleges and universities in the United States and Canada. It is also distributed to all other individuals who are NACDA members, and to those who subscribe annually ($15).

Athletics Administration is primarily written by athletics directors for athletics directors. Manuscripts are carefully reviewed and printed under the following priority structure:

1.   NACDA members who are athletics directors
2.   NACDA members who are not athletics directors
3.   Athletics directors who are not NACDA members
4.   All others

Articles should contain in the neighborhood of 1,000 to 1,200 words, typed double-spaced, and preferably be broken with three to five sub-headings throughout the text. The contents should include bottom-line results of a study rather than explaining study design, variables, correlation coefficients, etc.

Our goal is to provide information to our members that they don't already know, and need to know. The best articles are the ones dealing with the most specific topics. Generic material dwelling on obvious management principles (planning, communicating, establishing goals and objectives, evaluating, etc. do not really tell anyone anything. On the other hand, a step-by-step outline for a ticket plan promoting women's basketball would be an ideal topic that can be very helpful to those who read the article.

Finally, articles should include a short,"catchy" title, and be submitted with a photo of the author and a 75-word (approx.) biography.

Behavior Research Methods, Instruments, and Computers

ADDRESS FOR SUBMISSION:

John H. Krantz, Editor
Behavior Research Methods, Instruments,
 and Computers
Hanover College
P.O. Box 890
Hanover, IN 47243
USA
Phone: 812-866-7316
Fax: 812-866-7114
E-Mail: krantzj@hanover.edu
Web: www.psychonomic.org/brm
Address May Change:

PUBLICATION GUIDELINES:

Manuscript Length: No Limit
Copies Required: Four
Computer Submission: Yes
Format:
Fees to Review: 0.00 US$

Manuscript Style:
 American Psychological Association

CIRCULATION DATA:

Reader: Academics
Frequency of Issue: Quarterly
Copies per Issue: 2,001 - 3,000
Sponsor/Publisher: Psychonomic Society
Subscribe Price: 79.00 US$ Individual
 194.00 US$ Institution

REVIEW INFORMATION:

Type of Review: Editorial Review
No. of External Reviewers: 2
No. of In House Reviewers: 1
Acceptance Rate: 46%
Time to Review: 2 - 3 Months
Reviewers Comments: Yes
Invited Articles: 21-30%
Fees to Publish: 0.00 US$

MANUSCRIPT TOPICS:
Educational Technology Systems; Instrument & Research Techniques; Operations
Research/Statistics; Program Abstracts

MANUSCRIPT GUIDELINES/COMMENTS:

Research Topics
Computers and Data Processing, Operations Research/Statistics, Research Methods,
Instrumentation Techniques, Computer Program Abstracts, Instructional Technology, Human-
computer Interaction.

Behavioral & Social Sciences Librarian

ADDRESS FOR SUBMISSION:

Mark Stover, Editor
Behavioral & Social Sciences Librarian
San Diego State University
5500 Campanile Drive
San Diego, CA 92182
USA
Phone: 619-594-2121
Fax: 619-594-3270
E-Mail: mstover@mail.sdsu.edu
Web: See Guidelines
Address May Change:

PUBLICATION GUIDELINES:

Manuscript Length: 5-50
Copies Required: Two
Computer Submission: Yes Disk, Email
Format: MS Word
Fees to Review: 0.00 US$

Manuscript Style:
    Chicago Manual of Style

CIRCULATION DATA:

Reader: , Academic Librarians
Frequency of Issue: 2 Times/Year
Copies per Issue: Less than 1,000
Sponsor/Publisher: Haworth Press, Inc.
Subscribe Price: 48.00 US$ Individual
    125.00 US$ Institution

REVIEW INFORMATION:

Type of Review: Blind Review
No. of External Reviewers: 1
No. of In House Reviewers: 1
Acceptance Rate: 80%
Time to Review: 1-3 Months
Reviewers Comments: Yes
Invited Articles: 21-30%
Fees to Publish: 0.00 US$

MANUSCRIPT TOPICS:
Educational Psychology; Library Science/Information Resources; Social Studies/Social Science

MANUSCRIPT GUIDELINES/COMMENTS:

About the Journal
Fore more that 20 years, scholars, educators, and professional information specialists have turned to a single journal for the information they need on behavioral and social sciences— *Behavioral & Social Sciences Librarian*. This landmark publication is the only journal that provides both professional information specialists and scholars with the latest research on the production, collection, organization, dissemination, and retrieval of the vital information they need in the social and behavioral sciences.

Since its first printing, *Behavioral & Social Sciences Librarian* has presented a unique range of material to a readership that includes librarians and information specialists, collection development administrators, and library educators, as well as scholars, teachers, policymakers, publishers, and database producers. The journal focuses on the core fields of anthropology, sociology, economics, psychology, education, political science, language and area studies, and population-specific studies such as Latin American studies, ethnic studies, and women's studies.

Behavioral & Social Sciences Librarian is built on a foundation of unusual and interesting biographies and checklists, as well as descriptions of collections or institutional resources. The *Journal* also seeks articles that study characteristics of social sciences literatures and studies of user behavior. The wide range of material includes:

* reference and bibliographic instruction
* publishing trends
* bibliographic and numeric databases
* descriptive and critical analyses of information resources
* indexing, abstracting, thesaurus building, and database construction

Behavioral & Social Sciences Librarian also features regular columns such as "The Internet Connection" and "Electronic Roundup" that present up-to-date information on the capacity and accessibility of electronic resources. Recent topics have included innovations in useful Web tools, electronic publishing, fair use, copyright law and digitized works, the impact of the Internet on research strategies, reviews of popular search engines, and ERIC (Educational Resources Information Center) resources online. The journal also offers tutorials on searching online databases and reviews of available Web content.

Behavioral & Social Sciences Librarian has been an essential resource for a generation of scholars and information specialists. Just as vital today as it was when first published in 1979, the journal is a fundamental source for information on human social life and behavior.

Instructions for Authors
1. **Original Articles Only**. Submission of a manuscript to this journal represents a certification on the part of the author(s) that it is an original work, and that neither this manuscript nor a version of it has been published elsewhere nor is being considered for publication elsewhere.

2. **Manuscript Length**. Your manuscript may be approximately 5-50 typed pages double-spaced (including references and abstract). Lengthier manuscripts may be considered, but only at the discretion of the Editor. Sometimes, lengthier manuscripts may be considered if they can be divided up into sections for publication in successive *Journal* issues.

3. **Manuscript Style**. References, citations, and general style of manuscripts for this *Journal* should follow the Chicago style (as outlined in the latest edition of the *Manual of Style* of the *University of Chicago Press*). References should be double-spaced and placed in alphabetical order.

If an author wishes to submit a paper that has been already prepared in another style, he or she may do so. However, if the paper is accepted (with or without reviewer's alterations), the author is fully responsible for retyping the manuscript in the correct style as indicated above. Neither the Editor nor the Publisher is responsible for re-preparing manuscript copy to adhere to the *Journal's* style.

4. Manuscript Preparation.
Margins. leave at least a one-inch margin on all four sides.
Paper. use clean white, 8 1/2 " x 11" bond paper.
Number of Copies. 4 (the original plus three photocopies).
Cover Page. Important--staple a cover page to the manuscript, indicating only the article title (this is used for anonymous refereeing).
Second "Title Page". enclose a regular title page but do not staple it to the manuscript. Include the title again, plus:
• full authorship
• a header or footer on each page with abbreviated title and pg number of total (e.g., pg2 of 7)
• an introductory footnote with authors' academic degrees, professional titles, affiliations, mailing addresses, and any desired acknowledgment of research support or other credit.

5. Return Envelopes. When you submit your four manuscript copies, also include:
• a 9" x 12" envelope, self-addressed and stamped (with sufficient postage to ensure return of your manuscript);
• a regular envelope, stamped and self-addressed. This is for the Editor to send you an "acknowledgement of receipt" letter.

6. Spelling, Grammar, and Punctuation. You are responsible for preparing manuscript copy which is clearly written in acceptable scholarly English, and which contains no errors of spelling, grammar, or punctuation. Neither the Editor nor the Publisher is responsible for correcting errors of spelling and grammar: The manuscript, after acceptance by the Editor, must be immediately ready for typesetting as it is finally submitted by the author(s). Check your paper for the following common errors:
• dangling modifiers
• misplaced modifiers
• unclear antecedents
• incorrect or inconsistent abbreviations

Also, check the accuracy of all arithmetic calculations, statistics, numerical data, text citations, and references.

7. Inconsistencies Must Be Avoided. Be sure you are consistent in your use of abbreviations, terminology, and in citing references, from one part of your paper to another.

8. Preparation of Tables, Figures, and Illustrations. Any material that is not textual is considered artwork. This includes tables, figures, diagrams, charts, graphs, illustrations, appendices, screen captures, and photos. Tables and figures (including legend, notes, and sources) should be no larger than 4 ½ x 6 ½ inches. Type styles should be Helvetica (or Helvetica narrow if necessary) and no smaller than 8 point. We request that computer-generated figures be in black and white and/or shades of gray (preferably no color, for it does not reproduce well). Camera-ready art must contain no grammatical, typographical, or format errors and must reproduce sharply and clearly in the dimensions of the final printed page (4 ½ x 6 ½ inches). Photos and screen captures must be on disk as a TIF file, or other graphic files format such as JPEG or BMP. For rapid publication we must receive black-and-white glossy or matte positives (white background with black images and/or wording) in addition to files on disk. Tables should be created in the text document file using the software's *Table* feature.

9. **Submitting Art**. Both a printed hard copy and a disk copy of the art must be provided. We request that each piece of art be sent in its own file, on a disk separate from the disk containing the manuscript text file(s), and be clearly labeled. We reserve the right to (if necessary) request new art, alter art, or if all else has failed in achieving art that is presentable, delete art. If submitted art cannot be used, the Publisher reserves the right to redo the art and to charge the author a fee of $35.00 per hour for this service. The Haworth Press, Inc. is not responsible for errors incurred in the preparation of new artwork. Camera-ready artwork must be prepared on separate sheets of paper. Always use black ink and professional drawing instruments. On the back of these items, write your article title and the journal title lightly in soft-lead pencil (please do not write on the face of art). In the text file, skip extra lines and indicate where these figures are placed. Photos are considered part of the acceptable manuscript and remain with the Publisher for use in additional printings.

10. **Electronic Media**. Haworth's in-house type-setting unit is able to utilize your final manuscript material as prepared on most personal computers and word processors. This will minimize typographical errors and decrease overall production time. Please send the first draft and final draft copies of your manuscript to the journal Editor in print format for his/her final review and approval. After approval of your final manuscript, please submit the final approved version both on printed format ("hard copy") and floppy diskette. On the outside of the diskette package write:
1). the brand name of your computer or word processor
2). the word-processing program that you used
3). the title of your article, and
4). file name

Note: Disk and hard copy must agree. In case of discrepancies, it is The Haworth Press' policy to follow hard copy. Authors are advised that **No Revisions** of the manuscript can be made after acceptance by the Editor for publication. The benefits of this procedure are many with speed and accuracy being the most obvious. We look forward to working with you on this, knowing we will be able to serve you more efficiently in the future.

11. **Alterations Required By Referees and Reviewers**. Many times a paper is accepted by the Editor contingent upon changes that are mandated by anonymous specialist referees and members of the Editorial Board. If the Editor returns your manuscript for revisions, you are responsible for retyping any sections of the paper to incorporate these revisions (if applicable, revisions should also be put on disk).

12. **Typesetting**. You will not be receiving galley proofs of your article. Editorial revisions, if any, must therefore be made while your article is still in manuscript. The final version of the manuscript will be the version you see published. Typesetter's errors will be corrected by the production staff of The Haworth Press. Authors are expected to submit manuscripts, disks, and art that are free from error.

13. **Reprints**. The senior author will receive two copies of the journal issue and 25 complimentary reprints of his or her article. The junior author will receive two copies of the journal issue. These are sent several weeks after the journal issue is published and in circulation. An order form for the purchase of additional reprints will also be sent to all authors at this time. (Approximately 4-6 weeks is necessary for the preparation of reprints.) Please do not query the Journal's Editor about reprints. All such questions should be sent directly to The Haworth Press, Inc. Production Department, 21 East Broad Street, West Hazleton, PA 18201 USA. To order additional reprints (minimum: 50 copies), please contact The Haworth Document Delivery Center, 10 Alice Street, Binghamton, NY 13904-1580 USA; 1-800-342-9678 or Fax (607) 722-6362.

14. **Copyright**. Copyright ownership of your manuscript must be transferred officially to The Haworth Press, Inc. before we can begin the peer-review process. The Editor's letter acknowledging receipt of the manuscript will be accompanied by a form fully explaining this. All authors must sign the form and return the original to the Editor as soon as possible. Failure to return the copyright form in a timely fashion will result in delay in review and subsequent publication.

Bilingual Family Newsletter (The)

ADDRESS FOR SUBMISSION:

Marjukka Grover, Editor
Bilingual Family Newsletter (The)
Multilingual Matters
Frankfurt Lodge
Clevedon Hall
Victoria Road
Clevedon, England
BS21 7HH
Phone: +44 (0) 1275 876519
Fax: +44 (0) 1275 871673
E-Mail: info@multilingualmatters.com
Web: multilingual-matters.com
Address May Change:

PUBLICATION GUIDELINES:

Manuscript Length: 1-5
Copies Required: Two
Computer Submission: Yes
Format: MSWord attachments
Fees to Review: 0.00 US$

Manuscript Style:
    American Psychological Association

CIRCULATION DATA:

Reader: Practicing Teachers, Parents
Frequency of Issue: Quarterly
Copies per Issue: 1,001 - 2,000
Sponsor/Publisher: Multilingual Matters
    Ltd.
Subscribe Price: 22.00 US$

REVIEW INFORMATION:

Type of Review: No Reply
No. of External Reviewers: 0
No. of In House Reviewers: 1
Acceptance Rate: 70%
Time to Review: 1 - 2 Months
Reviewers Comments: No Reply
Invited Articles: 11-20%
Fees to Publish: 0.00 US$

MANUSCRIPT TOPICS:
Bilingual/E.S.L.; Educational Psychology; Elementary/Early Childhood; Foreign Language; Gifted Children; Languages & Linguistics; Reading

MANUSCRIPT GUIDELINES/COMMENTS:

Aims of the Journal
The *Newsletter* publishes short, informative articles on current thoughts and research on language learning, bilingualism, biculturalism, mother tongue schools, cross-cultural marriage, intercultural living, etc. It publishes descriptions of how particular families have managed their situation, problems encountered and how these were overcome. The Newsletter also acts as a means of communication between similar families all over the world by providing answers to readers" queries, not only from experts, but also from other readers.

Guidelines
Articles should not normally exceed 7000 words. Note that it is our policy not to review papers that are currently under consideration by other journals. They should be typed,

double-spaced on A4 (or similar) paper, with ample left and right-hand margins, on one side of the paper only, and every page should be numbered consecutively. A cover page should contain only the title, thereby facilitating anonymous reviewing by two independent assessors. Authors may also wish to take precautions to avoid textual references which would identify themselves to the referees. In such cases the authors of accepted papers will have the opportunity to include any such omitted material before the paper is published.

Submissions for Work in Progress/ Readers' Response /Letters to the Editor sections should be approximately 500 words in length.

Main contact author should also appear in a separate paragraph on the title page.

An abstract should be included. This should not exceed 200 words (longer abstracts are rejected by many abstracting services).

A short version of the title (maximum 45 characters) should also be supplied for the journal's running headline.

To facilitate the production of the annual subject index, a list of keywords (not more than six) should be provided, under which the paper may be indexed.

Four copies of the article must be submitted.

Footnotes should be avoided. Essential notes should be numbered in the text and grouped together at the end of the article. Diagrams and Figures, if they are considered essential, should be clearly related to the section of the text to which they refer. The original diagrams and figures should be submitted with the top copy.

References should be set out in alphabetical order of the author's name in a list at the end of the article. They should be given in standard form, as in the Appendix below.

References in the text of an article should be by the author's name and year of publication, as in these examples: Jones (1997) in a paper on ...(commonest version); Jones and Evans (1997c:22) state that ...(where page number is required); Evidence is given by Smith et al. (1994)...(for three or more authors). Further exploration of this aspect may be found in many sources (e.g. Brown & Green, 1992; Jackson, 1993; White, 1991a) (note alphabetical order, use of & and semicolons).

Once the refereeing procedures are completed, authors should, if possible, supply a word-processor disc containing their manuscript file(s). If presented on disc, we require files to be saved:
- on an IBM-PC compatible 3.5 inch disc (or CD-ROM) or on an Apple Mac high-density 3,5 inch disc.
- Text should be saved in the author's normal word-processor format. The name of the word-processor program should also be supplied. Tables and Figures should be saved in separate files.

The author of an article accepted for publication will receive page proofs for correction, if there is sufficient time to do so. This stage must not be used as an opportunity to revise the paper, because alterations are extremely costly; extensive changes will be charged to the author and will probably result in the article being delayed to a later issue. Speedy return of corrected proofs is important.

Contributions and queries should be sent to the Editors, Multilingual Matters Ltd., Frankfurt Lodge, Clevedon Hall, Victoria Road, Clevedon, BS21 7HH, England. A very large majority of authors' proof corrections are caused by errors in references. Authors are therefore requested to check the following points particularly carefully when submitting manuscripts:

- Are all the references in the reference list cited in the text?
- Do all the citations in the text appear in the reference list?
- Do the dates in the text and the reference list correspond?
- Do the spellings of authors' names in text and reference list correspond, and do all authors have the correct initials?
- Are journal references complete with volume and pages numbers?
- Are references to books complete with place of publication and the name of the publisher?

It is extremely helpful if references are presented as far as possible in accordance with our house style. A few more typical examples are shown below. Note, especially, use of upper & lower case in paper titles, use of capital letters and italic (underlining can be used as an alternative if italic is not available) in book and journal titles, punctuation (or lack of it) after dates, journal titles, and book titles. The inclusion of issue numbers of journals, or page numbers in books is optional but if included should be as per the examples below.

Department of Education and Science (DES) (1985) *Education for All* (The Swann Report). London: HMSO

Evans, N.J. and Ilbery, B.W. (1989) A conceptual framework for investigating farm-based accommodation and tourism in Britain. *Journal of Rural Studies* 5 (3), 257-266.

Evans, N.J. and Ilbery, B.W. (1992) Advertising and farm-based accommodation: A British case-study. *Tourism Management* 13 (4), 415-422.

Laufer, B (2000) Vocabulary acquisition in a second language: The hypothesis of 'synforms'. PhD thesis, University of Edinburgh.

Mackey, W.F. (1998) The ecology of language shift. In P.H. Nelde (ed.) *Languages in Contact and in Conflict* (pp. 35-41). Wiesbaden: Steiner.

Marien, C. and Pizam, A. (1997) Implementing sustainable tourism development through citizen participation in the planning process. In S. Wahab and J. Pigram (eds) *Tourism, Development and Growth* (pp. 164-78). London: Routledge.

Morrison, D. (1999) Small group discussion project questionnaire. University of Hong Kong Language Centre (mimeo).

U.S. Census Bureau (1998) State profile: California. Online document: http/www.census.gov/statab/www/states/ca.txt.

Zahn, C.J. and Hopper, R (2000) The speech evaluation instrument: A user's manual (version 1.0a). Unpublished manuscript, Cleveland State University.

Zigler, E. and Balla, D. (eds) *Mental Retardation: The Developmental-Difference Controversy.* Hillsdale, N.J: Lawrence Erlbaum.

For more details, please e-mail us on **multi@multilingual-matters com**.

Brigham Young University Education and Law Journal

ADDRESS FOR SUBMISSION:

Solicitations Editor
Brigham Young University Education and
Law Journal
Brigham Young University
471 JRCB
Provo, UT 84602-8000
USA
Phone: 801-422-3671
Fax: 801-422-0401
E-Mail: lawed@lawgate.byu.edu
Web: www.law2.byu.edu/Jel/index.htm
Address May Change:

PUBLICATION GUIDELINES:

Manuscript Length: typically 20+
Copies Required: One
Computer Submission: Yes Preferred
Format: MSWord; Wordperfect
Fees to Review: 0.00 US$

Manuscript Style:
Chicago Manual of Style, ALWD
Citation Format

CIRCULATION DATA:

Reader:
Frequency of Issue: 2 Times/Year
Copies per Issue: Less than 1,000
Sponsor/Publisher: University
Subscribe Price: 16.00 US$

REVIEW INFORMATION:

Type of Review: Student
No. of External Reviewers: 0
No. of In House Reviewers: 3+
Acceptance Rate: Varies
Time to Review: 1 - 6 months
Reviewers Comments: Yes
Invited Articles: 33%
Fees to Publish: 0.00 US$

MANUSCRIPT TOPICS:
Education at All Levels and the Law; Gifted Children; School Law; Special Education

MANUSCRIPT GUIDELINES/COMMENTS:

As is often the case with law reviews, the editor and editorial board are for the most part, law students. The editor-in-chief serves for one year. The faculty advisor is a more constant conduit of information year to year. Permanent Faculty Advisor:
Scott Ferrin, J.D., Ed.D.
310-D MCKB
Brigham Young University
Provo, UT 84602-5002
801-422-4804, fax 801-422-7740
email: **ferrin@byu.edu**

The *Brigham Young University Education and Law Journal* is a unique publication in that both the J. Reuben Clark Law School and the BYU Department of Educational Leadership work jointly towards its publication. The *Journal* is published twice yearly in April and in

January of each academic year. This collaboration is vital to the *Journal's* mission, which is to discuss issues concerning education and the Law. These discussions range from issues affecting formative education, beginning with kindergarten, to those affecting higher education institutions. The *Journal* addresses controversial issues, examining the problems from both an educational and a Legal standpoint, and will help you remain in touch.

Submission Guidelines

We use the *ALWD Citation* format in the place of Blue Book. We consider the following things crucial for publication and would ask all contributors to review their submissions for the following:

- The paper must have a clear thesis statement on an educational issue.
- The topic sentence of every paragraph must relate back to the thesis statement.
- The conclusion must appropriately summarize the arguments of the paper and not add any new information.
- The paper must be written on a timely and current issue in the world of education and law.

All articles for the Fall edition of the *Journal* need to be submitted to the Solicitations Editor of the *Journal* no later than August 1, of each year (The submission deadline for the Spring Edition of the *Journal* is set for November 15, of each year) They will be reviewed by the Solicitations Editor initially for appropriateness of topic, duplication of articles, and consistency with theme and values of the *Journal*. Articles are then passed on the by the Solicitations Editor to the Editor-In-Chief who, with the help advise and counsel of the Management Committee, has the final decision as to publish-ability.

Each article is reviewed in a timely manner as they come in to the *Journal* staff. Authors of articles will be contacted by a member of the Committee upon receipt of the piece and a time frame for review will be set up with the author at that time, according to the necessities of the *Journal* as well as those of the author. All selections for the *Journal* will be made on a space-available basis. It is anticipated by the *Journal* staff that 5-6 professionals written works will be accepted in each edition, with an additional 4-5 student-written pieces accepted. Articles received and reviewed by the Committee early on in the solicitations period will have a better chance of publication, simply due to the rolling admission policy of the *Journal*.

All articles submitted for consideration must meet the following requirements:

- One hard copy of the article
- One computer diskette of the article, saved in WordPerfect 6.0 or MSWord 95 higher format OR
- Electronic copy of the article submitted to the Solicitations Editor via e-mail at lawed@lawgate.byu.edu
- Articles should be approximately 20-40 pages in length
- Double spaced
- Articles may be submitted by faculty, students, educators or other professionals with an interest in educational legal issues so Long as the writing is of publishable quality.

All articles published by the *Journal* will require a signed agreement by the author and the Solicitations Editor of the *Journal* waiving compensation and the right to publish the paper in any other form. All rights to the article will remain the property of the author. Also in the agreement the author will have to agree to allow Lexis-Nexis, WestLaw and other electronic services to publish the article as per the *Journal's* agreement with such services.

Please submit all articles to:
BYU Education and Law Journal
J. Reuben Clark Law School
4716 JRCB
Provo, Utah 84602-8000

British Educational Research Journal

ADDRESS FOR SUBMISSION:

Harry Torrance, Editor
British Educational Research Journal
Manchester Metropolitan University
Institute of Education
799 Wilmslow Road
Manchester, M20 2RR
UK
Phone: +44 1612 475191
Fax: +44 1612 476353
E-Mail: d.hustler@mmu.ac.uk
Web: www.tandf.co.uk/journals
Address May Change:

PUBLICATION GUIDELINES:

Manuscript Length: 21-30
Copies Required: Three
Computer Submission: No
Format: N/A
Fees to Review: 0.00 US$

Manuscript Style:
    See Manuscript Guidelines

CIRCULATION DATA:

Reader: Academics
Frequency of Issue: 6 Times/Year
Copies per Issue:
Sponsor/Publisher: Carfax (Taylor and
    Francis) SSCI Ranking 18/93
Subscribe Price: 209.00 US$ Individual
    1270.00 US$ Institution

REVIEW INFORMATION:

Type of Review: Blind Review
No. of External Reviewers: 2-3
No. of In House Reviewers: 1
Acceptance Rate: 11-20%
Time to Review: 1 - 2 Months
Reviewers Comments: Yes
Invited Articles: 0-5%
Fees to Publish: 0.00 US$

MANUSCRIPT TOPICS:

Curriculum Studies; Education Management/Administration; Educational Psychology; Educational Technology Systems; Elementary/Early Childhood; Gifted Children; Health & Physical Education; Higher Education; Interdisciplinary; Languages & Linguistics; Reading; Religious Education; Rural Education & Small Schools; Science Math & Environment; Secondary/Adolescent Studies; Special Education; Teacher Education; Tests, Measurement & Evaluation

MANUSCRIPT GUIDELINES/COMMENTS:

Journal's Website: www.tandf.co.uk/journals/titles/01411926.asp

Aims and Scope
The *British Educational Research Journal* is an international medium for the publication of articles of interest to researchers in education and has rapidly become a major focal point for the publication of educational research from throughout the world.

For further information on the association please connect directly to the British Educational Research Association web site: **www.bera.ac.uk**

The journal is interdisciplinary in approach, and includes reports of experiments and surveys, discussions of conceptual and methodological issues and of underlying assumptions in educational research, accounts of research in progress, and book reviews. The journal is the major publication of the British Educational Research Association, an organisation which aims to promote interest in education and to disseminate findings and discussions of educational research.

Notes for Contributors
Papers accepted become the copyright of the British Educational Research Association, unless otherwise specifically agreed.

Manuscripts should be sent to David Hustler, Institute of Education, Manchester Metropolitan University, 799 Wilmslow Road, Manchester M20 2RR UK. Articles can only be considered if three complete copies of each manuscript are submitted. They should be typed on one side of the paper, double spaced, with ample margins, and bear the title of the contribution, name(s) of the author(s) and the address where the work was carried out. Each article should be accompanied by an abstract/summary of 100-150 words on a separate sheet. The full postal address of the author who will check proofs and receive correspondence and offprints should also be included. All pages should be numbered. Footnotes to the text should be avoided.

Contributors will normally receive a decision on their article within six weeks of its receipt by the Editor. Rejected manuscripts will not normally be returned to contributors unless sufficient stamps/international postal coupons have been sent.

Tables and captions to illustrations. Tables must be typed out on separate sheets and not included as part of the text. The captions to illustrations should be gathered together and also typed out on a separate sheet. Tables should be numbered by Roman numerals, and figures by Arabic numerals. The approximate position of tables and figures should be indicated in the manuscript. Captions should include keys to symbols.

Figures. Please supply one set of artwork in a finished form, suitable for reproduction. Figures will not normally be redrawn by the publisher.

References should be indicated in the typescript by giving the author's name, with the year of publication in parentheses. If several papers by the same author and from the same year are cited, a, b, c, etc. should be put after the year of publication. The references should be listed in full at the end of the paper in the following standard form:

For books: SCOTT, P. (1984) **The Crisis of the University** (London, Croom Helm).

For articles: CREMIN, L.A. (1983) The problematics of education in the 1980s: some reflections on the Oxford workshop, **Oxford Review of Education**, 9, pp. 33-40.

102

For chapters within books: WILLIS, P. (1983) Cultural production and theories of reproduction, in: L. BARTON & S. WALKER (Eds) **Race, Class and Education** (London, Croom Helm).

Titles of journals should **not** be abbreviated.

Non-discriminatory writing. Please ensure that writing is free from bias, for instance by substituting 'he' or 'his' by 'he or she' or 's/he' or 'his/her' and by using non-racist language. Authors might wish to note the BERA Ethical Guidelines for Educational Research.

Proofs will be sent to authors if there is sufficient time to do so. They should be corrected and returned to the Editor within three days. Major alterations to the text cannot be accepted.

Offprints. Fifty offprints of each paper are supplied free together with a copy of the issue in which the paper appeared. Additional copies may be purchased and should be ordered when the proofs are returned. Offprints are sent about two weeks after publication.

Copyright. It is a condition of publication that authors vest copyright in their articles, including abstracts, in the British Educational Research Association. This enables us to ensure full copyright protection and to disseminate the article, and the journal, to the widest possible readership in print and electronic formats as appropriate. Authors may, of course, use the article elsewhere **after** publication without prior permission from Carfax Publishing, Taylor & Francis Limited is notified so that our records show that its use is properly authorized. Authors are themselves responsible for obtaining permission to reproduce copyright material from other sources.

Notes for Referees
Referees are asked to bear the following in mind when assessing papers for inclusion.

We want *BERJ* to represent the best of educational research and so it is important that referees are rigorous and demanding, taking into account the status of the journal as a premier international publication.

Articles are welcomed on all kinds and aspects of educational research, and addressing any form of education, formal or informal.

It is the policy of the journal that articles should offer original insight in terms of theory, methodology, or interpretation, arid not be restricted to the mere reporting of results. Submitted work should be substantially original, recent in reference, and unpublished.

It is important that referees pay particular attention to the appropriateness, accuracy, consistency and accessibility of tabular data, arid the specified referencing protocols.

We welcome original ways of presenting research findings, and support accessible, well written accounts.

It is important that referees are decisive in their judgments of submissions.

In writing up their comments on articles submitted to the journal, referees are asked, in a minimum of 250 words, or so, to address whatever is relevant in the following:

- offer a brief critical resume of theoretical, methodological, or substantive issues raised by the author;
- assess how adequately the research is located in terms of previous relevant research;
- make a reasoned appraisal of the overall quality of the submission in terms of its excellence, contribution to knowledge, or originality;
- provide feedback useful to the author (a) for resubmission (b) more generally in terms of the further development of the research. It is helpful in the resubmission process if specific numbered points are made by referees and addressed by authors;
- indicate where appropriate any limitations on their ability to comment.

We also expect referees to be able to report on submissions within a three week period. It is important that these deadlines are respected. Articles published in HERJ include information, on. 'date received' / 'date resubmitted' / 'date finally accepted' and we do not wish to exhibit unprofessional delays between receipt and acceptance/resubmission/ rejection.

Business Education Forum

ADDRESS FOR SUBMISSION:

Todd Crittendon, Editor
Business Education Forum
NBEA
1914 Association Drive
Reston, VA 20191-1596
USA
Phone: 703-860-8300
Fax: 703-620-4483
E-Mail:
Web: www.nbea.org
Address May Change:

PUBLICATION GUIDELINES:

Manuscript Length: 6-10
Copies Required: Two
Computer Submission: No
Format: N/A
Fees to Review: 0.00 US$

Manuscript Style:
American Psychological Association

CIRCULATION DATA:

Reader: Practicing Teachers, Academics,
   Administrators
Frequency of Issue: 4 Times/Year
Copies per Issue: 10,001 - 25,000
Sponsor/Publisher: National Business
   Education Forum
Subscribe Price:

REVIEW INFORMATION:

Type of Review: Editorial Review
No. of External Reviewers: 1
No. of In House Reviewers: 1
Acceptance Rate: 6-10%
Time to Review: 2 - 3 Months
Reviewers Comments: Yes
Invited Articles: 6-10%
Fees to Publish: 0.00 US$

MANUSCRIPT TOPICS:
Adult Career & Vocational; Business Education; Curriculum Studies

MANUSCRIPT GUIDELINES/COMMENTS:

How to Publish
Members of NBEA are encouraged to submit articles for publication in Business Education Forum. Here's what you need to know about writing for your association's journal.

What to Write
Write the kind of article you would like to read. Business Education Forum is geared toward teachers in the field of business education. The style of the publication is academic, and its aim is to improve learning for students or make teaching more effective and interesting. The information appearing in Business Education Forum should not be readily available in other magazines or journals. Ideas should be developed clearly and comprehensively with supporting graphs and tables, if necessary. Avoid excessive jargon in favor of concise, specific, and concrete prose. Use active, not passive, words and phrases. Be sure to proofread your article for errors in grammar, punctuation, and spelling. A list of references should be

included. Do not use footnotes. The closing paragraph in each article should be summarizing in nature and worthy of emphasis.

Length of Copy
Your manuscript should run from 1,500 to 2,000 words, or six to eight pages of double-spaced copy, using a 12-point font.

Manuscript Format
Use standard, 8-1/2 x 11 inches, white paper. Manuscripts should be legible and double-spaced, (except for long quotes of four or more lines). When printed, primary headings should be flush left and boldface on a single line. The *Publication Manual of the American Psychological Association* (Fifth Edition) should be consulted for further questions of style. For ease of editing, a disk version of your article, compatible with Microsoft Word for a PC, must be included.

Membership
In order to publish a manuscript in Business Education Forum, the author(s) must be a member of the NBEA. Articles must also be submitted exclusively to Business Education Forum; one article per year can be published by an author(s).

Acceptance
Please allow several months for your manuscript to be reviewed. Although Business Education Forum is not a refereed publication, the articles published are reviewed by a section editor who is a professional business educator and two NBEA staff editors. To speed up the review of your manuscript, please submit your article to the appropriate section editor.

Editing
Business Education Forum section editors often make suggestions for revisions to manuscripts accepted for publication. These suggestions can include cutting or adding material, as well as stylistic changes. Editors work in conjunction with the author(s) to make these changes, and, if time permits, changes are reviewed and approved by the author(s) before publication. A copyright release form is sent along as well. NBEA does not assume responsibility for the points of view or the opinions expressed by the author(s) unless such statements have been established by a resolution of the Association.

Photographs and Graphics
Tables, graphs, diagrams, and photographs should be used if they contribute to the article and enhance its clarity. Graphics, such as illustrations or photographs, may not be embedded in the word processing file; they must be submitted as a separate PC, EPS or TIFF, file.

Copyright Permission
Obtaining permission to use charts, photographs, or any book, magazine, or newspaper excerpts in an article is the author's responsibility.

Bylines
Authors should include their names, titles, and the schools where they teach. An e-mail address should also be provided, so that readers may contact the authors.

106

Examples

1. Byline for a single author
   - Margaret Smith is an assistant professor at the University of Florida, Gainesville, Florida. She can be contacted via e-mail at msmith@uf.edu.

2. Bylines for multiple authors
   - Elaine McPherson is an assistant professor at Boston College, in Boston, Massachusetts and can be contacted via e-mail at emcpherson@bc.edu. Brian Miller is a high school instructor at Delray High School in Delray Beach, Florida. His e-mail address is millerm@aol.com.

References

Authors should cite references in alphabetical order and in the following manner. References to periodicals should include:
- Author(s) with last name first, then first initial(s). (Year of publication). Article name. Journal title (in italics), Volume (Issue), Page number(s).

Examples

1. Journal article, one author
   - Baker, D. (1997). Business Software. Business Journal, 11, 31-34.
2. Journal article, multiple authors
   - Jensen, I., Polk, G., and Stevens, R. (1991). The Role of the Internet in Distance Learning. The Journal of Technology, 21, 201-209.
3. Magazine article
   - Skolnik, J. (1997, April 4). Statistics in Business. Science, 97, 151-156.
4. References to books should include:
   - Author(s) with last name first, then first initial(s) (Year of publication). Title of book (in italics). Place of publication: Publisher.

Examples

1. References to entire books
   - Allen, V., and Smith, J.P., (1982). Modern Survey of Business. New York: McGraw-Hill.
2. Edited book
   - Keller, S., and Tan A.S. (Eds.). (1994). International Business in the New Millennium. Boston: Allyn and Bacon, Inc.
3. Books with a group author, such as a government agency, as publisher
   - U.S. Bureau of Statistics. (1994). Population Shifts in the United States. Washington, D.C.: Author.

Online references should include: Author(s) with last name first, then first initial(s). (Date of access). Title of work. [Online]. Available: Specify path.

Examples
- Dodge, B. (1997, May 5). The WebQuest Page. [Online]. Available: http://edweb.sdsu.edu/courses/edtec597/aboutawebquests.html.

References to an NBEA yearbook should be formatted as follows:
- Smith, B. (1997). Evaluation: A Tool for Learning and Identifying Talent. In C. P. Brantley and B. J. Davis (Eds.), The Changing Dimensions of Business Education. Yearbook No. 35. (pp. 88-99). Reston, VA: National Business Education Association.

Sending Your Manuscript
Please submit two paper copies of your article and one disk, virus free and labeled with the software and operating system used. Remember to include your name, address, phone number, as well as fax number and e-mail address, if available. E-mail or fax cannot be used for submitting manuscripts. Your article should be sent to the appropriate section editor or to the Editor, NBEA, 1914 Association Drive, Reston, VA 20191-1596. For further information, call NBEA at 703-860-8300.

Career Development for Exceptional Individuals

ADDRESS FOR SUBMISSION:

David W. Test & Bob Algozzine, Co-Eds.
Career Development for Exceptional
   Individuals
University of North Carolina - Charlotte
Special Education Program
9201 University City Blvd.
Charlotte, NC 28223
USA
Phone: 704-687-3731
Fax: 704-687-2916
E-Mail: dwtest@email.uncc.edu
Web: www.dcdt.org/publications/index
Address May Change: 6/30/2006

PUBLICATION GUIDELINES:

Manuscript Length: 16-20
Copies Required: Four
Computer Submission: No
Format: NA
Fees to Review: 0.00 US$

Manuscript Style:
   American Psychological Association

CIRCULATION DATA:

Reader: Academics
Frequency of Issue: 2 Times/Year
Copies per Issue: 2,001 - 3,000
Sponsor/Publisher: Council for Exceptional
   Children's Division on Career
   Development and Transition
Subscribe Price:

REVIEW INFORMATION:

Type of Review: Blind Review
No. of External Reviewers: 3
No. of In House Reviewers: 1
Acceptance Rate: 21-30%
Time to Review: 2 - 3 Months
Reviewers Comments: Yes
Invited Articles: 0-5%
Fees to Publish: 0.00 US$

MANUSCRIPT TOPICS:
Adult Career & Vocational; Secondary/Adolescent Studies; Special Education; Transition to Adulthood

MANUSCRIPT GUIDELINES/COMMENTS:

Career Development for Exceptional Individuals (*CDEI*) is the official journal of the Division on Career Development and Transition (DCDT) of The Council for Exceptional Children (CEC). The journal is published twice yearly and specializes in the fields of secondary education, transition, and career development of persons with documented disabilities and/or special needs. Articles published in *CDEI* include original quantitative and qualitative research, scholarly reviews, and program descriptions and evaluations.

Manuscripts submitted for publication to *CDEI* should be prepared according to the *Publication Manual of the American Psychological Association*: Fifth Edition (2001). All manuscripts should be written as clearly and simply as possible, have a 75 to 120 word abstract, and have a narrative between 15 and 20 pages of typed, doubled spaced text in 12-

point font, excluding references, figures, and tables. Authors should use nonsexist language and person first terminology (e.g., adolescents with disabilities instead of disabled adolescents). CDEI prefers that manuscripts be written in the active voice, which usually can be achieved by writing in first person (e.g., We selected participants . . .). When submitting a manuscript describing a research or evaluation study, authors should ensure that (a) the research or evaluation method is connected closely to the question(s) being addressed; and (b) the setting, participants, and procedures are described in sufficient detail to allow for possible replication. All manuscripts should include recommendations for secondary education and transition practice that could be applied at the system, program, or individual level.

Manuscripts submitted to *CDEI* should be accompanied by a letter from the principal author indicating that the manuscript is not under consideration for publication elsewhere. The letter of transmittal should also include the names, degrees, titles, and affiliations of all authors, and contact information for the principal author (telephone, email, and mailing address).

Career Development Quarterly

ADDRESS FOR SUBMISSION:

Mark Pope, Editor
Career Development Quarterly
University of Missouri - Saint Louis
415 Marillac Hall
One University Boulevard
Saint Louis, MO 63121-4449
USA
Phone: 314-516-7121
Fax: 314-516-5784
E-Mail: cdq@ncda.org
Web: www.ncda.org
Address May Change:

PUBLICATION GUIDELINES:

Manuscript Length: 5-15 pages
Copies Required: One
Computer Submission: Yes preferred
Format: Microsoft Word
Fees to Review: 0.00 US$

Manuscript Style:
American Psychological Association

CIRCULATION DATA:

Reader: , Practicing Counselors
Frequency of Issue: Quarterly
Copies per Issue: 5,500
Sponsor/Publisher: National Career
   Development Association
Subscribe Price: 55.00 US$ Individual
   100.00 US$ Institution

REVIEW INFORMATION:

Type of Review: Blind Review
No. of External Reviewers: 3
No. of In House Reviewers: 0
Acceptance Rate: 19%
Time to Review: 1 Month or Less
Reviewers Comments: Yes
Invited Articles: 0-5%
Fees to Publish: 0.00 US$

MANUSCRIPT TOPICS:
Adult Career & Vocational; All topics as related to Career Development; Counseling & Personnel Services; Education Management/Administration; Elementary/Early Childhood; Secondary/Adolescent Studies; Tests, Measurement & Evaluation

MANUSCRIPT GUIDELINES/COMMENTS:

Topics Include:
All topics as related to Career Counseling; Individual and Organizational Career Development; Work and Leisure; Career Education; Career Coaching; Career Management

Information for Authors
The *Career Development Quarterly (CDQ)* invites articles regarding career counseling, individual and organizational career development, work and leisure, career education, career coaching, and career management. Methodologies can include but are not limited to literature reviews that make research accessible to practitioners, case studies, history and public policy analyses, qualitative research, and quantitative research that is of specific relevance to the practice of career development. Each article should include implications for practice because

111

CDQ is concerned with fostering career development through the design and use of career interventions.

Regular manuscripts must be double-spaced throughout (including references) and must not exceed 26,700 characters (including spaces), 3,750 words, or 15 pages. Occasionally, a longer manuscript may be considered. Provide, but do not count, a cover page with each author's name, position, and place of employment, and a clear abstract of essential information of up to 100 words. Authors should not place their names or other identifying information on the manuscript itself, as all manuscripts are peer-reviewed with a blind reviewing system. Manuscripts should be submitted electronically via email as an attachment to **cdq@ncda.org**. Manuscripts will be acknowledged by email when they are received.

Reports of demonstrably effective career counseling methods or programs are featured in the section "Effective Techniques." Articles in this section describe theoretically based techniques that advance career development for people of all ages. Qualitative or quantitative data providing evidence of the techniques' effectiveness will be included in these articles. Manuscripts submitted to the "Effective Techniques" section should be double-spaced throughout (including references) and should not exceed 21,360 characters (including spaces), 3,000 words, or 12 pages. Such articles should contain (a) a brief review of the literature related to the theoretically based intervention, (b) a clear description of the intervention, (c) a brief report of data supporting the techniques' effectiveness, and (d) a summary.

The "Personal Perspectives" section contains analyses of personal career development experiences and short editorials about critical issues in research or practice. Articles prepared for this section should be double-spaced throughout (including references) and should not exceed 12,460 characters (including spaces), 1,750 words, or 7 pages.

Responses to previously published articles appear in the "Reader Reactions" section. These responses should be double-spaced throughout (including references) and should not exceed 8,900 characters (including spaces), 1,250 words, or 5 pages.

"Brief Reports" manuscripts should be double-spaced throughout (including references) and should not exceed 8,900 characters (including spaces), 1,250 words, or 5 pages (excluding title page, an abstract of no more than 80 words, references, and no more than one table or figure) and should contain a clear and concise summary of the study (including rationale, objectives, design, instruments, sample, analyses, results, and implications for research and practice).

Manuscripts must be prepared carefully, such that ideas flow coherently and writing is clear and concise. Avoid jargon, acronyms, and sexist terminology. Headings and subheadings should be used to structure the content. Article titles and headings in the articles should be as short as possible. Use tables sparingly, include only essential data, and combine tables wherever possible. Authors should submit no more than three tables or two figures with each manuscript. The *Publication Manual of the American Psychological Association* (5th edition) serves as the style manual for *CDQ*. Authors are encouraged to reduce bias in language against persons on the basis of gender, sexual orientation, racial or ethnic group, disability, or age by referring to the guidelines in the fifth edition of the APA manual. Authors must address the clinical significance of their results using effect size indicators, narrative analyses, or both.

Authors who use lengthy quotations or adapt tables and figures from another source must secure written permission to do so from the copyrighted source. Manuscripts that include copyrighted material will not be accepted for publication in *CDQ* until the author provides the editor with written permission from the copyright holder.

Submit all manuscripts electronically through email to Dr. Mark Pope, Incoming Editor, *Career Development Quarterly* at **cdq@ncda.org**. If you do not have access to electronic mail services, please send an original and three photocopies of the manuscript to Dr. Mark Pope, Editor, *Career Development Quarterly*, Division of Counseling & Family Therapy, College of Education, University of Missouri - Saint Louis, 415 Marillac Hall, One University Boulevard, Saint Louis, Missouri 63121-4499, USA, 1.314.516.7121. Be sure to include your e-mail address on the title page of the manuscript. Never submit material that is under consideration by another journal or that has been previously published. About 10 weeks will elapse between acknowledgment of the manuscript's receipt and notification of its disposition. After the final acceptance of an article, authors should expect minor editing for style consistency. Authors of manuscripts accepted for publication will be asked to provide the final article electronically via email, specifying word processing software that was used to prepare the manuscript (MS Word or WordPerfect 5.0 or later version is preferred) along with a .txt file with no line breaks (e.g. popems.txt). After an article's publication, all authors of articles and senior contributors to sections will receive a complimentary copy of *CDQ* from ACA Publications.

CDQ Review Form – Research/Empirical Manuscripts

Please review the enclosed manuscript and include a narrative critique on the back of this form or on a separate page. Then use a checkmark to indicate your rating of the manuscript with regard to the following criteria:

1. Relevance of topic to CDQ	Excellent, extremely relevant to CDQ readers	Good, of interest to CDQ readers	Marginal, may be of interest to some CDQ readers	Poor, inappropriate for CDQ readership
2. Quality of the literature review	Excellent, little or no need to revise	Good, can be improved with revision	Marginal, requires major revisions	Poor, needs to be completely redone
3. Clarity/ organization of rationale	Excellent, little or no need to revise	Good, can be improved with revision	Marginal, requires major revisions	Poor, needs to be completely redone

4. Quality of design/ methodology	Excellent, well-designed study	Good, some minor problems	Marginal, problems which may be serious	Poor, unsalvageable
5. Adequacy of data analysis	Excellent, appropriate analyses	Good, some minor problems	Marginal, requires reanalysis	Poor, inappropriate methods chosen
6. Appropriateness of the interpretation of results and conclusions	Excellent, little or no need to revise	Good, can be improved with revision	Marginal, requires major revisions	Poor, needs to be completely redone
7. Contribution to theory or practice	Excellent, important timely contribution	Good, could be improved with revision	Marginal, questionable contribution as written	Poor, little or no contribution
8. Quality of writing style	Excellent, little or no need to revise	Good, can be improved with revision	Marginal, requires major revisions	Poor, needs to be completely redone

Recommendation: _____ Accept (minor revisions).
_____ Reject with encouragement to resubmit
(with substantive revisions).
_____ Reject with option to resubmit
(major revisions, will require new review).
_____ Definitely reject.
_____ Inappropriate for CDQ
(perhaps appropriate
for_____).

Confidential comments for editor:

_____ _____ _____
Signature   Date   Mail By

This form contains guidelines that reviewers use in evaluating manuscripts submitted to the *Career Development Quarterly*. When preparing a manuscript for submission to *CDQ*, please peruse the guidelines. Mark Pope, Editor.

114

CDQ Review Form – Conceptual Manuscripts

Please review the enclosed manuscript and include a narrative critique on the back of this form or on a separate page. Then use a check mark to indicate your rating of the manuscript with regard to the following criteria:

1. Relevance of topic to CDQ	Excellent, extremely relevant to CDQ readers	Good, of interest to CDQ readers	Marginal, may be of interest to some CDQ readers	Poor, inappropriate for CDQ readership
2. Importance of topic	Excellent, addresses a vital professional issue	Good, addresses a professional issue of merit	Marginal, addresses an issue of uncertain importance	Poor, addresses an unimportant issue
3. Relation to previous literature	Excellent, little or no need to revise	Good, can be improved with revision	Marginal, requires major revisions	Poor, needs to be completely redone
4. Quality of conceptualization	Excellent, little or no need to revise	Good, can be improved with revision	Marginal, requires major revisions	Poor, needs to be completely redone
5. Contribution to practice	Excellent, important and timely contribution	Good, could be improved with revision	Marginal, a questionable contribution as written	Poor, little or no contribution
6. Contribution to theory	Excellent, important and timely contribution	Good, could be improved with revision	Marginal, a questionable contribution as written	Poor, little or no contribution
7. Quality of writing style	Excellent, little or no need to revise	Good, can be improved with revision	Marginal, requires major revisions	Poor, needs to be completely redone revisions

Recommendation: _____ Accept (minor revisions).

_____ Reject with encouragement to resubmit (with substantive revisions).

_____ Reject with option to resubmit (major revisions, will require new review).

      _____   Definitely reject.

      _____   Inappropriate for CDQ

                                (perhaps appropriate

for_____).

Confidential comments for editor:

_____   _____   _____

Signature   Date   Mail By

This form contains guidelines that reviewers use in evaluating manuscripts submitted to the Career Development Quarterly. When preparing a manuscript for submission to CDQ, please peruse the guidelines. Mark Pope, Editor.

3. Articles should be typed, double spaced, and titled. Pertinent photographs, charts, or graphs should accompany the article. (No returns.)

4. Professional position of the author(s) should and details for contact should accompany the article.

5. Please use an author/date format for references (APA preferred).

6. A signed and dated statement of authorization to publish, verification of exclusive submission to the *Catalyst*, and no prior publication of the article should accompany the article.

7. Articles submitted in Microsoft Word 97 or 2000 is recommended; rich text can be used if there is a question of compatibility with Apple.

8. Articles should be mailed to the Editor.

Please call if you have any questions.

Change: The Magazine of Higher Learning

ADDRESS FOR SUBMISSION:

Nanette Wiese, Editor
Change: The Magazine of Higher Learning
1319 Eighteenth St. NW
Washington, DC 20036
USA
Phone: 202-296-6267
Fax: 202-296-5149
E-Mail: ch@heldref.org
Web: www.heldref.org
Address May Change:

PUBLICATION GUIDELINES:

Manuscript Length: 16-20
Copies Required: Three
Computer Submission: Yes
Format: MS Word
Fees to Review: 0.00 US$

Manuscript Style:
Associated Press Stylebook, and
Washington Post

CIRCULATION DATA:

Reader: Academics, Administrators,
Academic Libraries
Frequency of Issue: Bi-Monthly
Copies per Issue: 10,001 - 25,000
Sponsor/Publisher: American Assn. For
Higher Education; Heldref Publications,
Inc.
Subscribe Price: 58.00 US$ Individual
125.00 US$ Institution
141.00 US$ Outside US

REVIEW INFORMATION:

Type of Review: Editorial Review
No. of External Reviewers: 3+
No. of In House Reviewers: 2
Acceptance Rate: 6-10%
Time to Review: 2 - 3 Months
Reviewers Comments: Yes
Invited Articles: 50% +
Fees to Publish: 0.00 US$

MANUSCRIPT TOPICS:
College Costs; Curriculum Studies; Education Management/Administration; Educational
Technology Systems; Higher Education; Library Science/Information Resources; Policy;
Teaching & Learning; Technological Developments on Campuses; Urban Education,
Cultural/Non-Traditional

MANUSCRIPT GUIDELINES/COMMENTS:

Topics Include. Trend-setting institutions and individuals, innovative teaching methods,
technology, liberal learning, the curriculum, the financing and management of higher
education, for-profit and entrepreneurial higher education, faculty, the changing needs and
nature of students, the undergraduate experience, administrative practice and governance,
public policy, accountability, the social role of higher education, and other topics related to
changes in higher education. Those that have been exhausted (the culture wars) or that are too
broad (the history of universities in 2,000 words or less) or too specific for our broad audience
(preventing dormitory theft) will not be published.

Scope
Change is a magazine dealing with contemporary issues in higher learning. It is intended to stimulate and inform reflective practitioners in colleges, universities, corporations, government, and elsewhere. Using a magazine format rather than that of an academic journal, *Change* spotlights trends, provides new insights and ideas, and analyzes the implications of educational programs, policies, and practices.

The topics of the coming year's issues can be found on the Heldref Website, at **http://www.heldref.org/**. Since several articles in each issue on not on the issue's theme, we also invite articles on other topics. But even the best manuscripts compete for limited space: We publish just six times a year, and given that many of the articles are solicited, we can use but 20 or so of the hundreds of manuscripts submitted each year.

Audience
Change is intended for individuals responsible for higher learning in college, university, and other settings, including faculty, administrators, trustees, state and federal officials, and students, as well as corporation, union, and foundation officers.

Manuscripts
Owned by Heldref Publications, a division of the nonprofit Helen Dwight Reid Education Foundation in Washington, *Change* is one of the 43 journals and magazines published by Heldref. The magazine staff at Heldref includes a full-time managing editor, Nanette Wiese, and an associate editor, Brittany Engle. It is to Heldref that you direct all manuscripts, letters to the editor, and queries about guidelines for writers, as well as questions about advertising and subscriptions. (See below for relevant contact information.)

All manuscripts must be submitted in hard copy, on 8 ½"x 11" paper, 12-point font, double-spaced, with one-inch margins, and page numbers, in triplicate. If the article is accepted, we will request an electronic copy of the article.

Because *Change* is a magazine rather than a journal, footnotes should not be included. References can be worked into the text or given parenthetically when necessary. A short list of "Related Readings" or "Resources" can be provided with the article where appropriate, and URLs can be provided for Web sites containing more extensive documentation.

A separate title page should provide short biographical information (up to four or five lines) and contact information, including the complete address, telephone, and fax number, and e-mail of the author(s). The first-named author of a multi-authored article will receive the notification of acceptance, rejection, or need for revision. The cover page should also indicate the word count of the article.

Review Process
When we receive your manuscript, we will send you a postcard verifying that your article has entered the review process. By agreement with Heldref, AAHE is responsible for all editorial judgments about the magazine: its themes, articles, and editorial voice. AAHE exercises that judgment through its executive editor, Margaret Miller, or the guest editor of a particular issue. All manuscripts are read first by Margaret Miller to determine their suitability for

Change. If the fit is not good, you will hear within six weeks. Those that are promising she sends to two consulting editors for review. Those that are returned with positive reviews she or the guest editor considers for publication. This process takes from two to three months to complete. (Should the manuscript be held for longer than usual, you will be notified and offered the option of withdrawing the manuscript from consideration.)

If the article is accepted, you will be contacted to discuss editing procedures and the production schedule for the issue of the magazine in which your article will appear. Each author receives six complimentary copies of the issue in which the article is included. Authors may also order additional copies or reprints (minimum order of 100) at their expense.

Manuscripts should be submitted exclusively to this publication.

Contributing To *Change*
Change is a magazine, and the magazine article is a genre unto itself. A good article compels attention to an important matter. It shows a mind at work, one that reaches judgment and takes a stance. It is credible: it knows its subject and the context. And it is concrete: It names people, places, dates, and events. Articles written in the style of a journal—heavy on jargon and footnotes, light on analysis and point of view—will not be accepted. For a good idea of the kind of writing that works for *Change*, we encourage you to read a few past issues.

Change doesn't start with an ideological predisposition; we court good ideas from all sides. But tracts, broadsides, and grand plans seldom impress reviewers (or readers), who prefer real, usable ideas that someone has actually tried out and evaluated.

--Margaret Miller
Executive Editor

Send manuscripts to:
 Managing Editor
 Change magazine
 Heldref Publications
 1319 Eighteenth Street, NW
 Washington, DC 20036-1802
 Telephone: 202/296-6267, Extension 222;
 Fax: 202/296-5149, Email: **ch@heldref.org**

Chemical Engineering Education

ADDRESS FOR SUBMISSION:

Carole Yocum, Editor
Chemical Engineering Education
University of Florida
Department of Chemical Engineering
Gainesville, FL 32611
USA
Phone: 352-392-0861
Fax: 352-392-0861
E-Mail:
Web:
Address May Change:

PUBLICATION GUIDELINES:

Manuscript Length: 11-15
Copies Required: Three
Computer Submission: No
Format: N/A
Fees to Review: 0.00 US$

Manuscript Style:
    See Manuscript Guidelines

CIRCULATION DATA:

Reader: Academics
Frequency of Issue: Quarterly
Copies per Issue: 2,001 - 3,000
Sponsor/Publisher: Chemical Engineering
    Division of the American Society for
    Engineering Education (ASEE)
Subscribe Price: 40.00 US$

REVIEW INFORMATION:

Type of Review: Editorial Review
No. of External Reviewers: 3
No. of In House Reviewers: 1
Acceptance Rate: 48%
Time to Review: 2 - 3 Months
Reviewers Comments: Yes
Invited Articles: 0-5%
Fees to Publish: 0.00 US$

MANUSCRIPT TOPICS:
Chemical Engineering; Higher Education

MANUSCRIPT GUIDELINES/COMMENTS:

This guide is offered to aid authors in preparing manuscripts for *Chemical Engineering Education (CEE)* a quarterly journal published by the Chemical Engineering Division of the American Society for Engineering Education (ASEE).

CEE publishes papers in the broad field of chemical engineering education. Papers generally describe a course, a laboratory, a Che department, a Che educator, a Che curriculum, research program, machine computation, special instructional programs or give views and opinions on various topics of interest to the profession.

Specific Suggestions On Preparing Papers
Title. Use specific and informative titles. They should be as brief as possible, consistent with the need for defining the subject area covered by the paper.

Authorship: Be consistent in authorship designation. Use first name, second initial, and surname. Give complete mailing address of place where work was conducted. If current address is different, include it in the footnote on title page.

Text. Consult recent issues for general style. Assume your reader is not a novice in the field. Include only as much history as is needed to provide background for the particular material covered in your paper. Sectionalize the article and insert brief appropriate headings.

Tables. Avoid tables and graphs which involve duplication or superfluous date. If you can use a graph, do not include a table. If the reader needs the table, omit the graph. Substitute a few typical results for lengthy tables when practical. Avoid computer printouts.

Nomenclature. Follow nomenclature style of **Chemical Abstracts**; avoid trivial names. If trade names are used, define at point of first use. Trade names should carry an initial capital only, with no accompanying footnote. Use consistent units of measurement and give dimensions for all terms. Write all equations and formulas clearly, and number important equations consecutively.

Acknowledgment. Include in acknowledgment only such credits as are essential.

Literature Cited. References should be numbered and Listed on a separate sheet in order occurring in text.

Copy Requirements. Send three legible copies of manuscript, typed (double spaced) on 8 1/2 x 11 inch paper. Clear duplicated copies are acceptable. Submit original drawings (or sharp prints) or graphs and diagrams, and clear glossy prints of photographs. Prepare original drawings on tracing paper or high quality paper; use black India ink and a lettering set. Choose graph papers with blue cross-sectional lines; other colors interfere with good reproduction. Label ordinates and abscissas of graphs along the axes and outside the graph proper. Figure captions and Legends may be set in type and need not be lettered on the drawings. Number all illustrations consecutively. Supply all captions and Legends typed on a separate page. If drawings are mailed under separate cover, identify by name of author and title of manuscript. State in cover Letter if drawings or photographs are to be returned. Authors should include brief biographical sketches and recent photographs with the manuscript.

Child Development

ADDRESS FOR SUBMISSION:

Lynn S. Liben, Editor
Child Development
University of Michigan
3131 S. State St. Suite 302
Ann Arbor, MI 48108-1623
USA
Phone: 734-998-7310
Fax: 734-998-7282
E-Mail: cdev@umich.edu
Web: www.srcd.org/cd.html
Address May Change:

PUBLICATION GUIDELINES:

Manuscript Length: 25-40
Copies Required: Electronic
Computer Submission: Yes
Format: N/A
Fees to Review: 0.00 US$

Manuscript Style:
    American Psychological Association

CIRCULATION DATA:

Reader: Academics
Frequency of Issue: Bi-Monthly
Copies per Issue: 5,001 - 10,000
Sponsor/Publisher: Society for Research in
    Child Development / Black well
    Publishers, Inc.
Subscribe Price: 0.00 US$

REVIEW INFORMATION:

Type of Review: Blind Review
No. of External Reviewers: 2-4
No. of In House Reviewers: 0
Acceptance Rate: 21-30%
Time to Review: 2-4 Months
Reviewers Comments: Yes
Invited Articles: 0-5%
Fees to Publish: 0.00 US$

MANUSCRIPT TOPICS:
Educational Psychology; Elementary/Early Childhood; Interdisciplinary; International; School Law

MANUSCRIPT GUIDELINES/COMMENTS:

Notice to Contributors
Child Development publishes empirical, theoretical, review, applied, and policy articles reporting research on child development. Published by the interdisciplinary Society for Research in Child Development (SRCD), the journal welcomes relevant submissions from all disciplines. Further information is available at **http://www.srcd.org/cd.html**.

Types of Articles
Child Development considers manuscripts in formats described below. Inquiries concerning alternative formats should be addressed to the Editor prior to submission. All submissions are expected to be no more than 40 manuscript pages, including tables, references, and figures (but excluding appendices). Authors should provide a justification if the submission is substantially longer. Unless the editor finds that justification compelling, the submission will be returned to the author for shortening prior to editorial review.

Empirical articles comprise the major portion of the journal. To be accepted, empirical articles must be judged as being high in scientific quality, contributing to the empirical base of child development, and having important theoretical, practical, or interdisciplinary implications. Reports of multiple studies, methods, or settings are encouraged, but single-study reports are also considered. Empirical articles will thus vary considerably in length (approximately 8 to 40 manuscript pages); text and graphics should be as concise as material permits. All modes of empirical research are welcome.

Reviews focus on past empirical and/or on conceptual and theoretical work. They are expected to synthesize or evaluate a topic or issue relevant to child development, should appeal to a broad audience, and may be followed by a small number of solicited commentaries.

Essays describe original concepts, methods, trends, applications, and theories; these may also be accompanied by solicited commentaries.

Child Development and ... are articles that provide readers with tutorials about some new concept or academic specialty pertinent to research in child development. These papers should review the major definitions, methods, and findings of the concept or specialty and discuss past or potential links to child development.

From another perspective is a format in which papers on a focal topic, written by different authors, are published simultaneously. Papers represent diverse perspectives (e.g., authors whose work represents different populations; different disciplines; different theories, methods, or analytic tools). In some cases, calls for submissions on particular topics will be disseminated through SRCD (via e-mail or SRCD publications), and submissions will undergo normal editorial review. In some cases, a submitted manuscript (e.g., an empirical article) may be selected as a lead article for this format, with invited commentaries providing additional perspectives. The editors also welcome suggestions from readers for topics for this format.

Manuscript Submission
Please follow submission requirements carefully, as deviations may slow processing. *Child Development* will not consider for publication any manuscript under review elsewhere or substantially similar to a manuscript already published. At submission, please inform the Editor if the paper has been or is posted on a website. For more information on the SRCD policy on web publications, see website. Editors retain the right to reject manuscripts that do not meet established ethical standards.

Manuscripts should be submitted to cdev@umich.edu as an electronic attachment in a Word or WordPerfect file. The transmittal e-mail should contain the name(s) of the author(s) and affiliation(s), and the street address, telephone, fax, and electronic mail address of the corresponding author. A corresponding author's submission to *Child Development* implies that all co-authors have agreed to the content and form of the manuscript and that the ethical standards of SRCD have been followed (see the *Child Development* website or pp. 283-284 of the 2000 *SRCD Directory*). Any financial interest or conflict of interest must be explained to the Editor in the cover letter. The corresponding author is responsible for informing all co-authors, in a timely manner, of manuscript submission, editorial decisions, reviews, and revisions.

The manuscript file should be formatted with double spaced, 12-point type, and should include a single paragraph abstract of 100-120 words. Please follow all guidelines on format, style, and ethics provided in the Publication Manual (5th ed.) of the American Psychological Association. Figures included with initial submissions will not be returned. Therefore, please submit only electronic files or copies of figures. Authors should keep a copy of all correspondence, files, and figures to guard against loss.

Manuscript Review
If you have not received acknowledgment within two weeks of transmission, please inquire at *cdev@umich.edu* or call (734) 998-7310. Each manuscript is handled by the Editor or an Associate Editor who consults with one or more Consulting Editors and/or ad hoc reviewers who have relevant expertise. To ensure blind review, cover sheets are removed before review; authors should avoid including any other information about identity or affiliation in submissions. Copies of the submission and associated correspondence are retained in the SRCD archives. For accepted manuscripts, authors are required to prepare a 300-500 layperson's summary for public dissemination purposes. Details are provided to authors as part of final processing.

There is no charge for publication in *Child Development* unless tabular or graphic materials exceed 10% of the total number of pages. Charges are also levied for changes in proofs other than correction of printer's errors. Any inquiries relating to charges or business matters (including reprint orders) should be addressed to Blackwell Publishers, *Child Development*, Production Coordinator, 350 Main Street, Malden, MA 02148, (781) 388-8200.

Inquiries and suggestions regarding editorial policy may be addressed to: Dr. Lynn S. Liben, Editor, *Child Development*, Department of Psychology, The Pennsylvania State University, University Park, PA 16802, liben@psu.edu. *Please do not send electronic or paper manuscripts to the above address.* Doing so will delay the processing of your manuscript.

Children & Schools

ADDRESS FOR SUBMISSION:

Wilma Peebles-Wilkins, Editor-in Chief
Children & Schools
NASW Press
750 First Street NE, Suite 700
Washington, DC 20002-4241
USA
Phone: 202-408-8600
Fax: 202-336-8312
E-Mail: press@naswdc.org
Web:
Address May Change: 12/31/2006

PUBLICATION GUIDELINES:

Manuscript Length: 16-20
Copies Required: Five
Computer Submission: No
Format: N/A
Fees to Review: 0.00 US$

Manuscript Style:
   Chicago Manual of Style, American
   Psychological Association

CIRCULATION DATA:

Reader: Practicing Teachers, Counseors
Frequency of Issue: Quarterly
Copies per Issue: 1,001 - 2,000
Sponsor/Publisher: NASW Press, National
   Association of Social Workers
Subscribe Price: 89.00 US$ Individual
   125.00 US$ Institution
   54.00 US$ NASW Member

REVIEW INFORMATION:

Type of Review: Blind Review
No. of External Reviewers: 3
No. of In House Reviewers: 1
Acceptance Rate: 21-30%
Time to Review: 2 - 3 Months
Reviewers Comments: Yes
Invited Articles: 0-5%
Fees to Publish: 0.00 US$

MANUSCRIPT TOPICS:

Bilingual/E.S.L.; Counseling & Personnel Services; Educational Psychology; Health & Physical Education; Reading; Social Studies/Social Science; Special Education; Teacher Education; Tests, Measurement & Evaluation

MANUSCRIPT GUIDELINES/COMMENTS:

Children & Schools (formerly *Social Work In Education*, established in 1978) publishes professional materials relevant to social work services in education. The journal addresses school social workers, health and mental health agencies, educational institutions, the juvenile justice system, and others concerned about education.

Authors are invited to submit manuscripts related to early intervention programs; preschool, elementary, and secondary education; and transitions to adulthood. The editorial board particularly encourages practitioners to share their practice knowledge. The board welcomes articles on innovations in practice, interdisciplinary efforts, legislation, policy, planning, and administration. The journal seeks research articles including quantitative studies, such as single-subject designs, group designs, and program evaluation, and qualitative studies, such as case studies, ethnographic interviews, and focus groups.

As a practice-oriented journal *Children & Schools* seeks to represent the broad spectrum of activities related to schools, children, and families; controversial manuscripts that will encourage dialogue are welcomed. The editorial board particularly invites manuscripts that emphasize practice and cultural diversity. Because the journal represents the breadth of social work practice in education, the preference is to vary the content within a single issue. From time to time, however, the journal publishes special issues on themes of importance to the field.

Articles. Manuscripts for full-length articles should not exceed 20 pages, including all references and tables. The entire review process is anonymous. At Least three reviewers critique each manuscript; then the editor-in-chief makes a decision, taking those reviews into account.

Note: All submissions must be typed double-spaced, including references and tables, with one-inch margins on all sides.

COLUMNS
Trends & Issues provides program and policy updates on local, regional, or national developments. Authors are encouraged to address programmatic responses to social trends, changes in policy, innovative programs, reforms in the field, and other events that have generalizable implications for practice. Manuscripts should be short - no more than eight pages. The Trends & Issues editor may assist authors in developing potential articles for this column.

Practice Highlights describes exemplary social work services in educational settings. Authors are encouraged to submit descriptive case studies of their direct work with individuals and families. The editorial board encourages a strong emphasis on interdisciplinary collaboration. Intended as a practitioner-to-practitioner resource, the column is more relaxed in style than are the regular articles. Manuscripts should be short – up to six pages. The Practice Highlights editor may assist authors in developing potential articles for this column.

Resources for Practice provides reviews of books, films, videotapes, software, and other professional resources of interest to school social workers and their colleagues. The editor of this column selects materials for review, solicits reviews, and accepts or rejects the review. Although every effort is made to publish solicited reviews, reviews are not guaranteed publication. Unsolicited reviews are not accepted.

As Readers See It provides a forum for letters and comments from readers. The editorial board welcomes opinions of interest to the field as well as comments on articles published in the journal.

This section describes how to assemble and submit a manuscript. Adhering to NASW Press format and style will improve the chances of acceptance if the substance of a manuscript has merit.

MANUSCRIPT PREPARATION
Appropriate Content
To determine which journal is most appropriate for your manuscript, please refer to chapter 3 in this booklet. You also should be aware that the following submissions will be rejected automatically without peer review:

- Obituaries, biographical sketches, or testimonials
- Organizational reports
- Speeches that have not been recast in article format.

If the content is related to the mission of the journal and the manuscript is a scholarly article with utility for social work practice, the editorial boards generally will be interested in reviewing it. Editorial boards do not screen query letters.

Appropriate Length
Manuscripts submitted to any NASW Press journal should be no longer than 20 pages. You should be aware of the following information when you consider the length of your manuscript:

You should type the entire manuscript double-spaced with one-inch margins on all four sides.
- Every component of the manuscript (text, references, tables, figures) is included in the total page count.
- Editorial boards welcome short articles, and they do not equate length with quality.
- The NASW Press will return manuscripts in excess of 25 pages unreviewed.

Overwriting and excessive length for the subject at hand often result in rejection, even if the manuscript meets page limits. Consequently, you should review your manuscript carefully with an eye to tightening and condensing.

MANUSCRIPT COMPONENTS
Cover Sheet
The cover sheet should contain the following:
- The full title of the article
- Information on all authors: name; highest degree, credentials, and title; full address; telephone and fax numbers, and e-mail address if available
- The date of submission.

If there is more than one author, names should be listed in the order you would prefer for the byline of a published article. Designate one author as the corresponding author. The cover sheet is the only component of the manuscript that should identify the authors in any way.

Title Page
The title page will be circulated for review with the manuscript. An effective title expresses the essence of a manuscript in as few words as possible. Conciseness and precision, the hallmarks of good writing, are particularly important for titles. Try to use key words, without resorting to jargon, so that a title will attract readers and provide an accurate picture of the article. Do not attempt to communicate all of the article's content in the title.

130

Abstract

The abstract should provide a distillation of the key concepts in the manuscript. Whenever possible, the abstract should be informative, and it should include theoretical concepts, major hypotheses, and conclusions. Abstracts for research papers should include the purpose of the research, the study sample size and characteristics, the measurement instruments used, and the conclusions. You should present the value of the contribution without exaggerating the results.

A comprehensive yet concise abstract is important because readers and researchers often decide to read an article on the basis of the abstract. Write the abstract as a single paragraph of about 150 words. Do not include any tables or references.

If your manuscript is accepted, the abstract will be published at the beginning of the article. Following publication of the full article, the abstract will be entered into the *Social Work Abstracts* database and will appear in the print version, as well as in SWAB+, available on CD-ROM and on Internet.

Key Words

List up to five key words that describe the content of the manuscript on the abstract page.

Example: Key words: administration, health, Hispanic, people of color, women

The NASW Press uses authors' designations of key words to develop data on manuscript submissions. In addition, if the article is accepted, the key words will appear in the journal with the abstract and in the *Social Work Abstracts* database. Key words are not necessarily used for indexing.

Text

Reviewers are looking for new work that extends the knowledge base and builds on the contribution of others. There is, however, no one formula for a successful article. You may want to keep the following in mind.

State your purpose. You should state your purpose clearly within the first few paragraphs of the article. If the reader cannot recognize what you hoped to accomplish in writing the article easily, the manuscript is likely to be rejected.

Organize. Establish a clear framework for the article and organize the manuscript so that it flows coherently. Use subheadings judiciously to help the reader track the flow of the article. If the article is organized properly, it will proceed logically and directly from the opening statements to your conclusions.

Relate your work to existing knowledge. You must relate your work to existing knowledge on the subject. However, you should not be tempted to run voluminous electronic searches and incorporate every related reference you find. Instead, use those references that demonstrate best how the new information will fill gaps in the knowledge base.

Review and rewrite. Reviewing and rewriting are basic steps in developing a manuscript for publication. As you review your work, eliminate redundancies and superfluous language. The use of pretentious jargon interferes with communication and can conceal the importance of your work. Write precisely in the active voice, use jargon only when absolutely necessary to convey specialized knowledge, and eliminate any language that might convey the perception of bias or any kind of stereotyping of people and behavior (see chapter 7). Finally, review your manuscript for spelling, punctuation, and grammatical errors. Use electronic tools, such as spell-check and a thesaurus, to assure that you have used words correctly.

References

Authors are responsible for the completeness and accuracy of the references in their manuscripts. Generally, take reference data for published material from the title page of a book or pamphlet, first page of an article, or contents page of a periodical. Take dates from the copyright page.

In general, a citation in the reference list comprises the following components in the order listed: author surname(s); author initial(s); publication date; title of article or book; for periodicals, journal name, volume number, and inclusive page numbers for the article; for books, location of publisher (city and state) and publisher name. See the subsection Reference List for examples.

- General Style Points

Arrange entries in the reference list alphabetically (by surname of the first author), then chronologically (by earliest publication date first).

In a reference that appears in parenthetical text, use commas (not brackets) to set off the date.
Example: (see Table 2 of Philips & Ross, 1983, for complete data)

Within a paragraph, do not include the year in subsequent references to a study as long as the study cannot be confused with other studies cited in the article.
Example: In a recent study, Jones (1987) compared. . . . Jones also found. . . .

Use the past tense for in-text reference citations.
Example: Hartman (1981) discussed. . .

- In-Text Author-Date Citations

Reference citations in text primarily acknowledge original specific contributions or opinions of other writers. Indicate the source of quotations in text and, for any quotes more than three words long, provide page numbers. Arrange author-date citations alphabetically in text (by surname of the first author), then chronologically (by earliest publication date first). Use a semicolon to separate reference citations in text.
Examples: (Abramovitz, 1988a; Miller, 1989; Ozawa, 1982, 1986, 1990) (Duncan & Morgan, 1979; Lindquist, Telch, & Taylor, 1983; J. Smith, 1992; P. Smith, 1992)

- Citations of Same Surname

If two authors with the same surname and year of publication are cited in text and their first initials are different, include both authors' initials in all text citations to avoid confusion.
Example: (M. Henderson, 1990; P. Henderson, 1990)

- Personal Communications

Personal communications consist of letters, telephone conversations, interviews, and the like. Because they do not provide recoverable information, personal communications are not included in the reference list. Cite personal communications in text only. Use the following style: (personal communication with [first initials and last name], [title], [affiliation], [month, day, year of communication]).

Example: (personal communication with Jane Doe, professor of social work, University of California, Los Angeles, August 5, 1995)

If the reference citation is not parenthetical, then incorporate the name, title, and affiliation outside the parentheses and put the words "personal communication" and the date inside the parentheses.

Example: J. T. Jones, professor of sociology at the University of Maryland (personal communication, June 11, 1995), suggested. . . .

Reference List
- Citation Forms

Following are examples of citations found in reference lists.

Article in an edited book
Griss, B. (1988Ò1989). Strategies for adapting the private and public health insurance systems to the health-related needs of persons with disabilities or chronic illness. In B. Griss (Ed.), Access to health care (Vol. 1, pp. 1Ò38). Washington, DC: World Institute on Disability.
Jackson, A. (1995). Diversity and oppression. In C. Meyer & M. Mattaini (Eds.), The foundations of social work practice: A graduate text (pp. 42Ò58). Washington, DC: NASW Press.

Article in a journal
Chapin, R. K. (1995). Social policy development: The strengths perspective. Social Work, 40, 506Ò514.

Book
Feldman, D. A., & Johnson, T. M. (Eds.). (1986). The social dimensions of AIDS: Method and theory. New York: Praeger.
James, F. J. (in press). Factors which shape the risks of homelessness: Preliminary observation from Colorado. Denver: University of Colorado Graduate School of Public Affairs.
Martin, E. P., & Martin, J. M. (1995). Social work and the black experience. Washington, DC: NASW Press.
McReynolds, P., & Chelune, G. J. (Eds.). (1990). Advances in psychological assessment (Vol. 6). San Francisco: Jossey-Bass.

Legal references
Follow A Uniform System of Citation (14th ed., pp. 55Ò56 and inside front cover) for citation forms of legal references.

Cite the name and year of an act in the text. If possible, cite statutes to the current official code or supplement; otherwise, cite the official session laws (see A Uniform System of Citation, p. 55, for examples).

For citations of the Federal Register, attempt to cite the original source. If the Federal Register is the original or only source the author can provide, then use the following format:
Education for All Handicapped Children Act (P.L. 94-142). (1977). Federal Register, 42(163), 42474-42518. [Note: This act does have an original source and is used as an example only.]

Newspaper
Raymond, C. (1990, September 12). Global migration will have widespread impact on society, scholars say. New York Times, pp. A1, A6.

Nonprint media
When citing a review of nonprint media, include (if available) length (number of minutes) and format (such as videocassette, audiocassette).
Breaking silence. Produced and directed by Theresa Tollini. Berkeley, CA: Future Educational Film, 1986. 132 minutes. VHS videocassette.

Paper presented at a conference
DiCecco, J. (1990, November). Using interpreters: Issues and guidelines for the practitioner in a multilingual environment. Paper presented at NASW's Annual Conference, Boston.
Romero, J. (1990, May). Culturally appropriate interventions with Hispanics. Paper presented at the Cross Cultural Competence Conference, San Diego Mental Health Services, San Diego.

Report
Schafft, G., Erlanger, W., Rudolph, L., Yin, R. K., & Scott, A. C. (1987). *Joint study of services and funding for handicapped infants and toddlers, ages 0 through 2 years* (Final Report for Contract No. 300-85-0143). Washington, DC: U.S. Department of Education, Division of Innovation and Development, Office of Special Education Programs.

U.S. Bureau of the Census. (1984). Projections of the population of the United States, by age, sex, and race: 1983 to 2080. In R. J. Koski (Ed.), *Current population reports* (Series P-25, No. 952, Tables C and F, pp. 6, 8). Washington, DC: U.S. Government Printing Office.

Sections of journals (other than articles)
Use brackets around departments such as Letters, Editorial, and Book Reviews in the reference list:
Spickard, P. R., Fong, R., & Ewalt, P. L. (1995). Undermining the very basis of racism-Its categories [Editorial]. Social Work, 40, 581Ò584.

Unpublished manuscript
Farber, B. A. (1979). *The effects of psychotherapeutic practice upon psychotherapists: A phenomenological investigation.* Unpublished doctoral dissertation, Yale University, New Haven, CT.

- Use of Cities and States in Reference Citations

In reference citations and in text, NASW follows Associated Press style for the omission of states and countries, except for Washington, DC. Use DC with Washington in text and in references.

Notes

Footnotes often distract readers; consequently, you should use them sparingly and incorporate them into the text whenever possible. When footnotes are essential, number them consecutively to correspond with the numbers in the text and submit them on a separate sheet. If the article is published, footnotes will appear at the bottom of the columns in which they are cited.

Tables

If you cannot present data easily and clearly in text, use a table. Tables should be self-explanatory and should supplement, not duplicate, the text. The table title should describe the contents completely so that the table can remain independent of the text. Only the highlights of the table should be discussed in the text. When you are presenting a series of tables, be consistent in terminology and format, and number them in Arabic numerals in the order in which they should appear in the article. You may use standard abbreviations for nontechnical terms such as "no." for number and "%" for percent. Use notes to the table to explain any nonstandard abbreviations, such as "NS" for not significant and "NA" for not applicable.

Artwork

You must supply camera-ready artwork for figures and graphs that accompany articles. Artwork should not exceed 4 x 6 inches. You may be able to produce your artwork on your computer if you have access to a laser printer with a resolution of at least 300 dpi. Use a word-processing font, such as Times, instead of typewriter typefaces, such as Courier. If you cannot produce publication-quality art on your computer, lettering should be typeset or produced by a professional artist. All elements of each figure should be large enough to be legible even if the figures are reduced, as they generally are, for publication. Because reproduction reduces the legibility of any figure, you should start with a very clean, crisp figure. If you do not supply artwork, the NASW Press can prepare professional art and bill you for the cost. Staff can produce a cost estimate based on rough copy after an article is accepted.

GUIDELINES FOR PREPARING MANUSCRIPTS

In 1989 the *Health & Social Work* Editorial Board developed guidelines to assist both experienced and aspiring authors. The following is an adaptation of their work.

Content

- State your purpose early in the article.
- Develop an organizing theme and consistently relate the article to the theme.
- Start with an outline and refer to it regularly to help maintain a coherent flow.
- Prepare a short abstract to provide a general overview of the manuscript. Use an introduction to define the topic areas more specifically.
- Document all statistical statements and clearly identify opinions.

- Use case material to illustrate major theoretical concepts rather than to serve as the substance of the manuscript.
- Relate your review of the literature to your conclusion.
- Relate subject matter to the journals' editorial focus.
- Recognize that no one is as familiar with your topic as you are. Define terms and do not make too many assumptions about the reader's knowledge.
- Focus – do not try to write the definitive work on a subject in one manuscript.
- Define key concepts and relate your data to those concepts.

Writing Style
- Use the active voice whenever possible. Overuse of the passive voice takes the life out of an article. The use of the first person is appropriate for scholarly work so long as the focus is on the information in the article instead of on the author. Excessive use of "we feel," "I think," "I did," and so on emphasizes the author, whereas language such as "we studied" or "in the study we found" imparts information.
- Avoid jargon and multi-syllable words.
- Be concise. Omit unnecessary words.
- Aim for precision and accuracy. Eliminate qualifiers such as "very few" or "nearly all" that weaken the manuscript. Instead, provide comparisons that demonstrate what you mean.
- Eliminate language that might imply gender, ethnic, or other forms of discrimination, stereotyping, or bias.
- Use style manuals, a dictionary, and other resources to avoid poor grammar, misspellings, and incorrect punctuation. (Most word processors feature useful spell-check and thesaurus programs.)

Format
- Do not submit speeches unless they have been rewritten in article format.
- Use tables when they are the most efficient way to communicate information. Although tables appear impressive, sometimes the same information can be communicated more clearly and easily in a few sentences. Conversely, a well-designed table may enable you to eliminate many paragraphs.
- Make your manuscript flow logically from an interesting beginning to a justifiable conclusion.
- Use subheads to define carefully considered divisions of the topic.
- Review the journal you have selected to learn the range of topics, manuscript length, writing style, and style for footnotes and references.

Final Draft
- Ask a trusted colleague who has a publication record to review and comment before you submit.
- Incorporate comments from others as you rewrite and polish your manuscript.
- Be certain that your references and any footnotes are complete and accurate.
- Double space all sections of the manuscript, including tables, footnotes, and references.
- Proofread carefully.

- Take care with the appearance of the manuscript. It should be legible (no poor photocopies or unreadable typefaces) and clean, with no handwritten additions.
- Be certain the text contains no "About the Author" blurbs, bylines, or other references that identify you as author.
- Assemble the manuscript with cover sheet, title page, abstract, introduction, text, references, and tables and figures if used.
- Submit five copies of the manuscript.
- Notify the NASW Press immediately if you change your address or phone number.

Resubmissions
- Consider reviewers' comments objectively.
- Review the manuscript as objectively as possible.
- Use the revision to sharpen the focus of the manuscript.
- Incorporate as many of the reviewers' recommendations as possible.
- Attach a cover sheet that describes precisely how you have addressed reviewers' concerns. If you disagreed with a review and did not change some element of the manuscript, describe your rationale succinctly.

Ethics
- Obtain all necessary clearances and permissions for tables or illustrations borrowed from other sources before you submit your manuscript.
- Submit the same manuscript to only one journal at a time.
- If the manuscript is part of a series, reference all previous publications.
- Avoid overlapping submissions. Do not submit manuscripts that contain substantial portions of material contained in manuscripts already accepted or under review elsewhere.
- Submit only original material that has not been published or widely distributed elsewhere.

FORMAT FOR RESEARCH ARTICLES
1. Abstract--summarizes the entire article
- Provide five or six sentences.
- Limit to approximately 150 words.

2. Introduction--engages the reader
- State the specific purpose or goal of your study; include a statement of hypotheses.
- Review the literature of previous related research studies and indicate how your study is related to them. (This develops a rationale for your study.)

3. Method--explains how you conducted your study
- Describe subjects: who participated, how many, and how they were selected.
- Specify design by name or type: the arrangements for collecting data and how groups are collected for statistical analysis.
- Describe materials: measuring devices and special equipment, reliability and validity data.

- Detail procedures: how the study was conducted, what subjects did; also include a specific description of the intervention or independent variable sufficient for replication by others.

4. **Results--presents findings in the text and in tables and graphs**
- Use American Psychological Association (APA) format.
- Present results of all statistical tests (significant and nonsignificant) including means, standard deviations, degrees of freedom, calculated values (for example, F ratios), significance levels, and effect sizes.

5. **Discussion--gives a less technical interpretation of results, including why they turned out the way they did**
- Link results to literature reviewed earlier.
- Describe weaknesses in design and offer alternative explanations.
- Discuss the potential for generalizability and implications for research and practice.

6. **References--lists books and articles discussed in the text**

7. **Appendix--only if necessary for new or special materials such as a copy of a new scale or computer program**

Resources
Abbott, A. (1992). The quantitative research report. In L. Beebe (Ed.), *Professional writing for the human services* (pp. 63-85). Washington, DC: NASW Press.

American Psychological Association. (1994). *Publication manual of the American Psychological Association* (4th ed.). Washington, DC: Author.

Editor's note: Thanks are extended to Joel Fischer, University of Hawaii, Honolulu, for developing these guidelines. We offer them to readers for assistance in writing research articles and as a guide to our criteria for reviewing these articles.

MANUSCRIPT SUBMISSION
Authors should designate a journal when submitting a manuscript. Although we request computer disks when manuscripts are accepted, it is not necessary to submit a disk initially. Mail manuscripts for all NASW Press journals to
[Journal title]
NASW Press
750 First Street, NE, Suite 700
Washington, DC 20002-4241

Authors should submit five copies of their manuscript.

NASW Press journals practice strict anonymous reviews in which neither the reviewers nor the editor-in-chief learn the author's identity. Consequently, all manuscripts and correspondence regarding any article should be addressed to the NASW Press office. Editors are not able to engage in correspondence directly with authors, because doing so would abrogate the process. Manuscripts sent to an editor-in-chief at an address other than the NASW Press will be considerably delayed in review.

The NASW Press is not responsible for the loss of a manuscript in the mail. Authors should retain at least one copy of any manuscript. Manuscripts will not be returned. All manuscripts are acknowledged on receipt. The review process generally takes about three to four months.

GUIDELINES FOR PRACTICE HIGHLIGHTS AND OTHER PRACTICE DESCRIPTIONS

In 1994 the *Social Work in Education* Editorial Board developed the following guidelines for describing practice.

Purpose
- Am I doing something others should know about?
- What is the core of what I want to say?
- What should go away?

Getting Started
- Write a short paragraph and check it out with someone else. Do they understand it? Is it too broad? too narrow?
- Write an outline, laying out the various steps.
- Use outlines as a checklist.

Grab the Readers Attention
- State up front what you are attempting to do.
- Take the reader with you as you move along.
- Use existing practice as a springboard.
- Describe the problem or issue you will focus on in two paragraphs or so.

Tell What Happened
- Tell the reader what you did.
- Describe the case intervention or program in as much detail as readers need to replicate-- who was involved? what was the time span? what occurred?
- Include dialogue as appropriate.
- Use a flowchart if it makes the intervention clearer.

Help People Replicate the Practice
- What was the significance?
- Why is this practice intervention different? Is it unique?
- What impact does it have on others? On the practitioner?
- Answer the "So what?" question. What difference did it make?

Conclude the Article
- Don't just let it drop.
- Sum it up.
- Tell where you plan to go in the future--or suggest future efforts by others.

NASW PRESS GUIDELINES FOR DESCRIBING PEOPLE

To provide implementation strategies for its policy on unbiased communication (see page 19), the NASW Press has developed the following guidelines. The purposes of the guidelines are to help authors
- portray people as accurately and vividly as possible
- eliminate bias from their writing
- incorporate the richness of cultural diversity
- use language that is accessible and inviting to the reader.

All languages evolve over time, and it is likely that English will evolve to incorporate new terms for and better ways of describing people. In the meantime, the NASW Press expects authors and staff to follow the guidelines outlined in this document.

General Guidelines
Seek and use the preference of the people you write about.
Ask people you are working with how they prefer to be described and use the terms they give you. If, as often happens, people within a group disagree on preference, report the different terms and try to use the one most often used within the group. The NASW Press does not object to using alternate terms, such as black and African American, within one article or chapter as long as the content is clearly written so that readers are not confused. Be sensitive to real preferences and do not adopt descriptions that may have been imposed on people. For example, older people may say, "Oh, we're just senior citizens."

Be as specific as possible.
If you have studied work experiences among Cuban Americans, Mexican Americans, and Puerto Ricans, report on those three groups; do not lump them together as *Hispanics*. Whenever possible, use specific racial or ethnic identities instead of collecting different groups under a general heading. If you have researched drug use among a group of people whose ages range from 65 to 75, cite their ages rather than reporting on "drug use among older people."

Describe people in the positive.
Describe people in terms of what they are, instead of what they are not. For example, do not use the terms *nonwhite* or *nonparticipant*. Remember that you are writing about people.

Help the reader see that you are writing about people, not subjects or objects. Use the terms sample or subject for statistics and describe participants as *respondents, participants, workers,* and so forth. Keep in mind that a group of 100 people who share certain characteristics also have many traits unique to them, even though those individual traits are not included in your report. Pretend that you are a member of the group about whom you are writing and see how you would react to the terms you have used to describe them.

Avoid using terms that label people.
When adjectives that describe a person's condition or status are used as nouns, they become labels that often connote a derogatory intent. For example, people who do not earn enough money to provide for their needs are often referred to collectively as the poor; use poor people if you are referring to them in the aggregate. People who have lived a long time become *the elderly* or *the aged*; if you cannot use specific ages or age ranges, use terms such as elders or older people. Do not refer to people with disabilities as *the disabled* or *the handicapped*. Note that the use of "the" in front of a noun is a good warning sign that you may be using a label.

Guidelines for Specific Populations
Age
Use *boy* and *girl* only for children and adolescents, although even for high school students, *young man* and *young woman* may be preferable. Do not use terms such as *senior citizen* or *oldster* for people who are older than 65. Use specific age ranges whenever possible. Use *aging* and *elderly* as adjectives, not as nouns.

Class
Classism often creeps into our language. Instead of assigning class to people, you should describe their situations. This does not mean that you should pretend all people have the same socioeconomic advantages, but that you should describe the advantages or lack of advantages, rather than assigning attributes to the people.

Poor Usage	Better Usage
lower class	people who are poor
underclass	with low incomes
upper class	with high incomes
the disadvantaged	with socioeconomic disadvantages

Classism often is combined with bias toward people in terms of race or ethnicity; consequently, it is doubly important to take care with language that might perpetuate discrimination.

Disability
Remember that people *have* disabilities, they are not the disabilities; in addition, the disabilities may be barriers, such as stairs or curbs, that handicap people. The following are some commonly misused terms:

Poor Usage	Better Usage
the handicapped	people with disabilities
schizophrenics	people diagnosed with schizophrenia
challenged	person who has ___
wheelchair-bound	uses a wheelchair
the blind	people who are blind
hearing impaired	hard of hearing or deaf

HIV/AIDS
Say *people with AIDS*, not *AIDS victims* or *innocent victims of AIDS*. Avoid language that may imply a moral judgment on behavior or lifestyles. Instead of *high-risk groups*, which suggests that demographic traits may be responsible for AIDS exposure, use *high-risk behavior*.

Race and Ethnicity
• Issues and Dilemmas
Traditionally, authors in the social sciences have used *minority* as a shorthand term to describe people of various races and ethnicities collectively. In these cases the term has been used in the sense of a smaller number or a population that has been oppressed or subjected to differential treatment. Authors also have used *white* and *nonwhite*, particularly in research papers, to differentiate between population groups. *Nonwhite* appears to have been used to describe collectively a diverse group of people who differ in some ways from the greater number of a population.

Another complicating factor is that not all people within specific populations agree on nomenclature, and many people use different definitions for the same words. For example, some people prefer *African American*; others within the same population say, "I am not African American; I am *black*." Some scholars use the term race to describe broad classifications of people who are presumed to have common descent and share certain physical characteristics (generally American Indian, Asian, black, and white) and reserve *ethnicity* for people who share common culture, religion, or language (often people from specific nations or countries). Others use the terms interchangeably. Some eliminate the term race entirely because they believe it is racist in itself.

• Guidelines
Styles and preferences for nouns that refer to race and ethnicity change over time. The general guidelines for discussing all people are particularly helpful when you are describing race and ethnicity. Try to ascertain what the population group prefers and use that term; recognize and acknowledge that there may be disagreement about preference within the group. Whenever possible, be as specific as possible and describe individual population groups rather than collecting many different groups under an umbrella term. If the people in your study included Asian Americans, Hispanics, black Americans, and white Americans, do not compare the first three groups as a set with the last group. Describe them each as individual groups. If you researched experiences of a group of Asian Americans who included Chinese, Japanese, and Koreans, you should describe each national origin group individually.

You should avoid both *minority* and *nonwhite*. Many people who are described this way view the terms as pejorative and discriminatory. In addition, assuming that white people are the predominant population group is an inaccurate portrayal of most countries in the world and indeed of many areas in the United States. Some people prefer the use of people of color; however, you should be aware that this term also is imprecise and that not all people who might be included in the group under such a heading would describe themselves in this way.

Black and *white* are adjectives that should be used (in lowercase only unless they begin a sentence) to modify nouns, such as "black Americans" or "black men" or "white women." *African Americans, American Indians, Asian Americans,* and *Hispanics* are all proper nouns that should be capitalized; hyphens should never be inserted in multiword names even when the names are modifiers. Some individuals prefer to use Latino, instead of Hispanic, as the descriptive term for people of Latin American ancestry, and some use the two together. There has been considerable discussion about the use of *American Indian* versus *Native American*; many people prefer the former because it is a more precise term for the population in North America. Although the U.S. government combines *Asian* and *Pacific Islander*, most Pacific Islanders prefer that they be separated.

Poor Usage	Better Usage
minorities	specific population or "racial and ethnic groups"
tribes	people or nations
blacks	black people
nonwhites	specific populations

In addition to taking care with names of racial and ethnic groups, you should be careful with modifiers. For example, the passage "we compared the reactions of African American and Hispanic men with middle-class white men" suggests that the first two groups are in a different socioeconomic status, and given historical stereotyping, the perception is likely to be that they are in a lower status. Specify the status for all participants in your study. Describing someone as "the accomplished African American student" may suggest that this student is an exception. Describe people in terms of race or ethnicity only when the description is pertinent to the discussion.

Gender

Sexist language has no place in the professional literature. The most obvious manifestation of sexist language is the use of masculine pronouns, and there are numerous ways to avoid their use. One option is to use plural forms whenever possible. If you are writing a text or a how-to article, using the second person to address the reader directly will help you avoid having to select a masculine or feminine form and is likely to make the article more appealing to the reader. You can often substitute *we* for he and *our* or *their* for *his*. Another solution is to eliminate pronouns entirely. Inserting *him* or *her* or *he* or *she* throughout an article becomes cumbersome, although sparing use can sound natural. Do not use contrived forms such as *s/he* or *he/she*. In general, avoid alternating masculine and feminine pronouns within an article. Rather than demonstrating equality, the practice can suggest that they are interchangeable, and it is confusing to the reader.

Poor Usage	Better Usage
the social worker	social workers
will find that her	will find that they
he calls his children "kids"	we call our children "kids"
the teacher should encourage his students to write	encourage your students to write

Avoid words that suggest an overtone of judgment, that describe women in patronizing terms ("the little lady") or suggest second-class status ("authoress") or demean a woman's ability ("lady lawyer") or are rarely used to describe men ("coed"). Take care not to suggest that women are possessions of men or that they cannot carry out a role or perform a job that men do.

Poor Usage	Better Usage
policemen	police officers
man a project	staff a project
chairman	chair
housewife	homemaker
mankind	humans, human beings

It is not necessary or desirable to construct feminine versions of words that carry a masculine connotation. *Chair* or *representative* substitute much better for *chairman* or *spokesman* than *chairwoman* or *spokeswoman*. Do not specify sex unless it is a variable or it is essential to the discussion. Be sure to use parallel construction: *men* and *women*, not *men* and *females* or *girls* and *men*. *Men* and *women* are nouns, whereas *female* and *male* are best used as adjectives.

Sexual Orientation

Orientation is a state of being, and *preference* is a choice; consequently, you should not use the latter to refer to heterosexuality or homosexuality. The NASW Press uses the term *homosexual* only as an adjective. You should use *lesbians, gay men,* or *bisexual men* or *women* to refer to people whose orientation is not exclusively heterosexual.

It is important to distinguish between sexual orientation and sexual behavior. Consequently, you would not write "the client reported homosexual fantasies," but would substitute "the client reported same-gender sexual fantasies." The appropriate terms to use in describing sexual activity include *female-female, male-male,* and *same-gender,* in addition to *male-female.*

Accurate Historical Reporting

In their zeal to use appropriate language, authors sometimes try to change history. If you are quoting any document, you must quote it exactly as the words were written or said; and if you are describing a historical situation, you will likely want to use the words that were used in that context. You should, however, make the context clear. If you find the language too egregious, you may want to add a footnote saying this is not your language, but the language of the time in which it was written.

Clear, Accessible Writing

You are writing to communicate facts and ideas. Because you are writing for journals in the social sciences, you probably want to communicate those facts and ideas with the intent of improving human lives. To do so, you must write in such a way that you will engage readers so that they will absorb your content enough to use it.

There is no question that eliminating the old shorthand for describing people will add some length to a paper. Substituting *members of racial and ethnic groups* for *minorities* or *people with disabilities* for the *disabled* adds words, but it is more accurate and it eliminates bias. You can easily compensate for the additional length by practicing the principles of good writing. Use strong active verbs and eliminate all convoluted passive constructions. Strike out qualifiers and other redundancies:

Redundant	Simplified
successfully avoided	avoided
has the capability of	can
particularly unique	unique
most often is the case that	often is

Do not resort to euphemisms, which will weaken your message. Taking care to portray people with accuracy and sensitivity should enhance your critical analysis, not muddy it. The more clearly and simply you write, the easier you will make it for your readers to grasp complex ideas. Bring life to your writing by concentrating on the message. If you portray the people you are discussing vividly and truthfully, you will probably communicate the problems and solutions clearly.

Christian Higher Education: An Int'l Journal of Applied Research & Practice

ADDRESS FOR SUBMISSION:

D. Barry Lumsden, Editor
Christian Higher Education: An Int'l Journal
  of Applied Research & Practice
University of North Texas
College of Education
Box 311337
Denton, TX 76203
USA
Phone: 940-565-4074
Fax: 940-369-1337
E-Mail: lumsden@unt.edu
Web: www.tandf.co.uk/journals
Address May Change:

PUBLICATION GUIDELINES:

Manuscript Length: 16-20
Copies Required: Three
Computer Submission: Yes
Format: Accept All
Fees to Review: 0.00 US$

Manuscript Style:
  American Psychological Association

CIRCULATION DATA:

Reader: Practicing Teachers, Academics,
  Administrators, Counselors
Frequency of Issue: Quarterly
Copies per Issue:
Sponsor/Publisher: Higher Education
  Program at Univ. of North Texas / Taylor
  and Francis Publishers
Subscribe Price: 96.00 US$ Individual
  185.00 US$ Institution

REVIEW INFORMATION:

Type of Review: Blind Review
No. of External Reviewers: 3
No. of In House Reviewers: 0
Acceptance Rate: 21-30%
Time to Review: 1 - 2 Months
Reviewers Comments: Yes
Invited Articles: 0-5%
Fees to Publish: 0.00 US$

MANUSCRIPT TOPICS:

Adult Career & Vocational; Counseling & Personnel Services; Curriculum Studies; Education Management/Administration; Educational Psychology; Educational Technology Systems; English Literature; Higher Education; Library Science/Information Resources; Professional Development; Religious Education; School Law; Social Studies/Social Science; Teacher Education; Tests, Measurement & Evaluation; Urban Education, Cultural/Non-Traditional

MANUSCRIPT GUIDELINES/COMMENTS:

Aims and Scope

Christian Higher Education is a peer reviewed archival journal that features articles on developments being created and tested by those engaged in the study and practice of Christian higher education. This quarterly journal addresses issues in finance, enrollment management, innovative teaching methods, higher education administration, program assessment, faculty development, curriculum development, and student services. Each issue offers a balance of essays on current research as well as programs and methods at the cutting edge of progress.

Christian Higher Education is the only journal to be international, interdenominational, interdisciplinary, and to focus exclusively on Christian higher education.

Readership
Professors, scholars, administrators, practitioners, and scholarly societies throughout the world involved in the research, development, and practice of Christian higher education.

INSTRUCTIONS TO AUTHORS

Note to Authors. Please make sure your contact address information is clearly visible on the **outside** of all packages you are sending to Editors.

Manuscripts should be concise yet sufficiently detailed to permit critical review. All papers should contain an abstract, which should not exceed 250 words. Manuscripts should conclude with a section on Implications for Practice stating what the implications of the research findings are to practitioners in the field and including any recommendations for change indicated by the research results.

Manuscripts should be submitted to the Editor-in-Chief, D. Barry Lumsden, University of North Texas, P.O. Box 311337, Denton, Texas 76203.

Submission of Manuscripts
Original and two copies of each manuscript should be submitted to the editor. Authors are strongly encouraged to submit manuscripts on disk. The disk should be prepared using MS Word or WordPerfect and should be clearly labeled with the authors' names, file name, and software program. All parts of the manuscript should be typewritten, double-spaced, with margins of at least one inch on all sides. Number manuscript pages consecutively throughout the paper. Authors should also supply a shortened version of the title suitable for the running head, not exceeding 50 character spaces. Each article should be summarized in an abstract of 150-250 words, which should be typed, double-spaced, on a separate page. Avoid abbreviations, diagrams, and reference to the text within the abstract.

All papers, including figures, tables, and references, must conform to the specifications described in the *Publication Manual of the American Psychological Association* (5th ed., 2001). Any papers that do not adhere to this style will be returned for revision.

Each manuscript must be accompanied by a statement that it has not been published elsewhere and that it has not been submitted simultaneously for publication elsewhere. Authors are responsible for obtaining permission to reproduce copyrighted material from other sources and are required to sign an agreement for the transfer of copyright to the publisher. All accepted manuscripts, artwork, and photographs become the property of the publisher.

Tables and Figures
Tables and figures should not be embedded in the text, but should be included as separate sheets or files. A short descriptive title should appear above each table with a clear legend and any footnotes suitably identified below. All units must be included. Figures should be completely labeled, taking into account necessary size reduction. Captions should be typed, double-spaced, on a separate sheet. All original figures should be clearly marked in pencil on the reverse side with the number, author's name, and top edge indicated.

Illustrations
Illustrations submitted (line drawings, halftones, photos, photomicrographs, etc.) should be clean originals or digital files. Digital files are recommended for highest quality reproduction and should follow these guidelines:
- 300 dpi or higher
- sized to fit on journal page
- EPS, TIFF, or PSD format only
- submitted as separate files, not embedded in text files

Color illustrations will be considered for publication; however, the author will be required to bear the full cost involved in their printing and publication. The charge for the first page with color is $900.00. The next three pages with color are $450.00 each. A custom quote will be provided for color art totaling more than 4 journal pages. Good-quality color prints should be provided in their final size. The publisher has the right to refuse publication of color prints deemed unacceptable.

Reprints
The corresponding author of each article will receive one complete copy of the issue in which the article appears. Reprints of an individual article may be ordered from Taylor & Francis by using the reprint order form included with the page proofs.

Cognitive Psychology

ADDRESS FOR SUBMISSION:

Gordon Logan, Editor
Cognitive Psychology
Editorial Office
525 B Street, Suite 1900
San Diego, CA 92101-4495
USA
Phone: 619-669-6417
Fax: 619-699-6800
E-Mail: cogpsy@elsevier.com
Web:
Address May Change:

PUBLICATION GUIDELINES:

Manuscript Length: 30+
Copies Required: Five
Computer Submission: Yes Encouraged
Format:
Fees to Review: 0.00 US$

Manuscript Style:
    See Manuscript Guidelines

CIRCULATION DATA:

Reader: Academics
Frequency of Issue: 8 Times/Year
Copies per Issue: No Reply
Sponsor/Publisher: Academic Press
Subscribe Price: 475.00 US$ US & Canada
    520.00 US$ All Other Countries
    US$ Deep Discounts Available

REVIEW INFORMATION:

Type of Review: Editorial Review
No. of External Reviewers: 3
No. of In House Reviewers: 0
Acceptance Rate: 11-20%
Time to Review: 4 - 6 Months
Reviewers Comments: Yes
Invited Articles: 0-5%
Fees to Publish: 0.00 US$

MANUSCRIPT TOPICS:
Languages & Linguistics; Reading; Thinking, Reasoning, Memory, Attention, Perception

MANUSCRIPT GUIDELINES/COMMENTS:

Notice to Contributors
The publishers wish to call your attention to the following instructions for preparing manuscripts for *Cognitive Psychology*: Format and style of manuscript should conform to the conventions specified in the *Publication Manual of the American Psychological Association* (1200 Seventeenth Street, N.W., Washington, D.C. 20036; 1983 Revision), with the exceptions listed below. Please note that it is the responsibility of the author that manuscripts for *Cognitive Psychology* conform to the requirements of this journal.

Cognitive Psychology publishes original empirical, theoretical, and tutorial papers, methodological articles, and critical reviews dealing with memory, language processing, perception, problem solving, and thinking. This journal emphasizes work on human cognition. Papers dealing with relevant problems in such related areas as social psychology, developmental psychology, linguistics, artificial intelligence, and neurophysiology also are welcomed provided that they are of direct interest to cognitive psychologists and are written so as to be understandable by such readers. Minor or very specialized studies are seldom accepted.

All manuscripts should be submitted to:
Dr. Gordon Logan
Editorial Office
Cognitive Psychology
525 B Street, Suite 1900
San Diego, CA 92101-4495 USA

Original papers only will be considered. Manuscripts are accepted for review with the understanding that the same work has not been published, that it is not under consideration for publication elsewhere, and that its submission for publication has been approved by all of the authors and by the institution where the work was carried out; further, that any person cited as a source of personal communications has approved such citation. Written authorization may be required at the Editor's discretion. Articles and any other material published in *Cognitive Psychology* represent the opinions of the author(s) and should not be construed to reflect the opinions of the Editor(s) and the Publisher.

Authors submitting a manuscript do so on the understanding that if it is accepted for publication, copyright in the article, including the right to reproduce the article in all forms and media, shall be assigned exclusively to the Publisher. The Copyright Transfer Agreement, which may be copied from the pages following the Information for Authors or found on the journal home page listed here, should be signed by the appropriate person(s) and should accompany the original submission of a manuscript to this journal. The transfer of copyright does not take effect until the manuscript is accepted for publication.

A manuscript submitted for publication is judged by three main criteria: (a) appropriateness of the subject matter for this journal; (b) significance of its contribution to knowledge; and (c) clarity and conciseness of writing. No changes in a manuscript may be made once it has been accepted and is in press.

Form. Type at least double-spaced throughout, including tables, footnotes, references, and figure captions, with 1 inch margins on all sides. **Submit five complete copies**. Each copy *must* include all figures and tables.

Number the pages consecutively. *Page 1* should contain the article title, author(s) name(s), and affiliation; at the bottom of the page type a short title, not exceeding 35 characters and spaces, and the name and complete mailing address (including zip code) of the person to whom proofs should be sent. The address of correspondence should be given as a footnote to the appropriate author's name. *Page 2* should contain a short abstract, approximately 100 to 150 words in length. *Key Words* should be listed immediately after the abstract.

Headings. The organization of the paper must be clearly indicated by appropriate headings and subheadings.

Abbreviations. Do not use final periods with units of measure that are abbreviated (cm, s, kg, etc.) in text or in tables, except for "in." (inch).

Symbols. Underline letters that represent mathematical symbols; these will be set in *italic* type.

Equations. Number displayed equations consecutively, with the number placed in parentheses to the extreme right of the equation. Refer to numbered equations as Equation 1 or say "the first equation." Punctuate equations to conform to their place in the syntax of the sentence.

Footnotes. Use only when absolutely necessary, in which case type the footnotes consecutively, double-spaced, on a separate sheet of paper in the order of their appearance in the text. Use Arabic numbers 1, 2, etc. In the text, refer to footnotes by superscript 1, 2, etc.

Tables. Number tables consecutively with Arabic numerals in order of their appearance in the text. Type each table, double-spaced throughout, on a separate sheet; avoid vertical rules. Supply a short descriptive title below the table number. Type table footnotes, lettered *a, b,* etc., at the end of the table. For further information, see the *Publication Manual*, pages 83–94.

Illustrations. All illustrations are considered as figures, and must be supplied in finished form, ready for reproduction. Pages 94-105 of the "Publication Manual" describe concisely the proper preparation of line drawings and photographs. Plan figures to fit the proportion of the printed page (allowing for the legend under the figure), and take care that lettering on the original is large enough to be legible after a reduction of 50–60%.

Number the figures with Arabic numerals in order of mention in the text. Supply descriptive legends (captions) for all figures. Type these (double-spaced throughout) consecutively on a separate sheet of paper.

Illustrations in color can be accepted only if the authors defray the cost.

References. Cite references in the text by surname of the author, followed by year of publication.

> Smith (1982) found that . . .
> Contrary results (Brown, 1984) have been . . .

When a reference has two authors, cite both names, as (Harris & Cooper, 1980). When more than two are involved, cite the surnames of all authors, with the date, at first mention, but in subsequent citations of the same reference give the surname of the first author followed by et al. and the year, as

> (Colberg, Matthews, & Cooper, 1983) *first mention*
> (Colberg et al., 1983) *second mention*

In citing more than one publication by the same author or authors in the same year, add suffixes a, b, c, etc. after the year, as (Smith 1982a) and repeat the letter identification in the bibliography, at the end of the reference.

Under the heading REFERENCES, arrange the literature citations in the text in alphabetical order according to the surname of the first author. Do not abbreviate journal names; write them out in full. Full information on forms of literature citations may be found on pages 107-117 of the *Publication Manual*.

The following examples show style of capitalization and punctuation for journal articles, books, and edited books:

Biggs, J. B., & Collis, K. F. (1982). *Evaluating the quality of learning: The SOLO taxonomy.* New York: Academic Press.

Donchin, E., Ritter, W., & McCallum, C. (1978). Cognitive psychophysiology: The endogenous components of the ERP. In E. Calloway, P. Teuting, & S. Koslow (Eds.), *Brain event-related potentials in man* (pp. 349-441). New York: Academic Press.

Siegler, R. S., & Robinson, M. (1982). The development of numerical understandings. In H. W. Reese & L. P. Lipsitt (Eds.), *Advances in child development and behavior* (Vol. 16). New York: Academic Press.

Wilkinson, A. C. (1984). Children's partial knowledge of the cognitive skill of counting. *Cognitive Psychology, 16,* 28-64

[Use underline for journal names and book titles only.]

Author's alterations in excess of 10% of the cost of composition will be charged to the author.

Reprints. 50 reprints of each article will be supplied free of charge. Additional reprints can be ordered on the form accompanying the proofs.

Electronic Submission. Manuscripts may be submitted to *Cognitive Psychology* after all revisions have been incorporated and the manuscript has been accepted for publication. A hard-copy printout of the manuscript that exactly matches the electronic file must be supplied. The manuscript will be edited according to the style of the journal, and the proofs must be read carefully by the author. Complete instructions for electronic submission can be found on the Electronic Submission page.

Preparation of Electronic Files
Academic Press (AP) encourages all of its authors to prepare and transmit their manuscripts and associated materials electronically. **Please see the Information for Authors (IFA) section of the appropriate journal (either online or in print) for details regarding required formatting and whether electronic submission is acceptable when the manuscript is initially submitted for review or only upon acceptance.** Paper copies of each version of the manuscript are still required. Electronic versions must be transmitted in conjunction with and must exactly match the hard copy, including the abstract, key words, footnotes, references, tables, and figures. This guide describes how to prepare an electronic manuscript for transmission to AP.

Electronic manuscripts can be transmitted via FTP, e-mail, or computer disk. Electronic manuscripts should be accompanied by the appropriate number of hard copies, each time a version is transmitted.

New Submissions
AP encourages transmission of new submissions in PDF, DVI, or PostScript unless otherwise noted in the journal's Information for Authors (IFA) section. Although submission in these formats is preferred, transmission of new submissions as word-processing files or TeX is also acceptable. Files created in layout programs such as Adobe FrameMaker or PageMaker, QuarkXPress and Corel Ventura are unacceptable. Be advised that some journals also require the transmission of the manuscript at the time it has been accepted (see the journal's IFA section for details). Hard-copy printouts exactly matching the electronic file must be supplied. For the exact number of copies required see the IFA section of the appropriate journal. When submitting a revised version of a manuscript, please provide the file electronically along with a new hard copy of the revised manuscript. See the Electronic Artwork section below for instructions on preparing electronic artwork.

PDF Files
Adobe Portable Document Format (PDF) is a universal file format that preserves all of the fonts, formatting, colors, and graphics of any source document, regardless of the application and platform used to create it. PDF files are compact and can be shared, viewed, navigated, and printed exactly as intended by anyone with a free Adobe Acrobat Reader. You can convert any document to Adobe PDF using proprietary software including Adobe Acrobat.

DVI Files
Authors are requested to send Device Independent (DVI) files of their TeX or LaTeX files at initial submission as this will facilitate the review process. Please see the TeX Files section below for specific instructions for formatting the TeX file.

PS Files
Adobe PostScript files (PS) can be created from any application capable of printing files, provided a PostScript printer driver is used. Authors are encouraged to use PostScript Level 2, use ADSC structuring, include all fonts in the file and save it in ASCII rather than binary format.

AP requests PDF, DVI and PS submissions for review purposes only; they cannot be effectively edited and are unusable during the post acceptance production stage.

Accepted Manuscripts
AP strongly encourages authors to submit an electronic version of their accepted manuscript, as this will significantly speed the processing of the manuscript. Please bear in mind that this electronic version must exactly match the final hard copy that was accepted. Acceptable formats for this final transmission stage are described below. AP cannot use PDF, DVI, or PostScript files at this stage because they do not allow editing of the text. Files created in layout programs such as Adobe FrameMaker or PageMaker, QuarkXPress and Corel Ventura are unacceptable. Artwork should not be embedded within the manuscript. It must be supplied

in electronic files separate from the manuscript file. See the Electronic Artwork section below for instructions on preparing electronic artwork.

Word-Processing Files

Most word-processing packages are acceptable; however, AP prefers that authors use a recent version of Microsoft Word or Corel WordPerfect. Manuscripts saved with formatting intact are preferred. Rich-text format (.rtf extension) is acceptable, but plain text (.txt extension) files are discouraged. For some journals, it may be acceptable or preferable to prepare manuscripts in TeX; please see TeX Files (below) for instructions. Regardless of the software and file format used, one hard copy of the accepted version of the manuscript must be supplied.

Symbols and foreign characters can be set with word-processing software by altering typefaces to a corresponding font that displays the appropriate character. Use the Symbol font for Greek characters whenever possible. When special characters are unavailable, please note them on the hard-copy printout as not appearing properly in the electronic file. Do so by circling or making notes in the left margin.

Use the automatic word-processing wraparound feature and not hard returns (¶) for line breaks within a paragraph. Only use hard returns at the end of each paragraph and after heads. Use only one space between words and sentences. Use appropriate characters: do not use a lowercase "l" for a one or an "o" for a zero. Do not use double-byte characters for special symbols. Do not use automated bulleting, numbering, or internal linking.

The elements of the electronic file should be ordered so that all non-text elements, e.g., running title, figure legends, and footnotes, are out of the text stream. The running title should be placed above the article or chapter title, and the footnotes should be placed after the figure legends at the end of the manuscript. Do not use the footnote function of the software. Thus, the order should be running title, title, author(s), affiliation(s) including e-mail addresses, abstract, key words, text elements, references, figure legends, footnotes. Incorporate the above-listed components into one file.

AP may set tables from electronic files, typeset them conventionally, or scan them as art. Therefore, when providing tables electronically, please place them in a file separate from the manuscript.

Use the software's spell-checking and page-numbering capabilities before final transmission. Do not embed artwork into a word-processing file. See the Electronic Artwork section below for instructions on preparing electronic artwork.

TeX Files

TeX and LaTeX files are acceptable for electronic transmission provided they comply with the guidelines below. Deviation from these rules may cause inaccuracies in the article or a delay in publication, or may even result in the LaTeX file being discarded altogether so that the article is typeset conventionally.

154

AP prefers that authors prepare TeX manuscripts using LaTeX(2e). Use of specialized versions of TeX other than LaTeX, plain TeX, or AMSTeX or extensive use of packages or custom macros may render the electronic file unusable.

The most important thing to keep in mind while preparing a file for submission or publication is that it should be kept as simple as possible. Extensive formatting could render the file unusable to the typesetter. For this reason, restrict manual formatting to equations; page formatting will be done by the typesetter. Avoid manual coding of line breaks (except in displays), figure placement, and vertical and horizontal spacing. Such coding is difficult for typesetters to remove and increases the risk of errors in typesetting.

AP Preprint Class File and Templates
Where available, AP encourages authors who wish to use LaTeX(2e) to use our preprint style files. Check the journal home page to verify whether such files are available. The use of AP style files will speed the typesetting process and reduce the chance of typographical errors resulting from resetting text. However, AP does not require that submissions be prepared using our files. LaTeX manuscripts created without AP templates may be submitted if prepared according to the guidelines given below.

General TeX Guidelines
In order to enable the publisher to bring the article into the uniform layout and style of the journal in which it will appear, authors are kindly requested to follow the suggestions below.

So far as the journal style is concerned, if you can observe such matters as how references are cited (in parentheses or brackets, by numbers or by name and date), how equations are numbered and cited, how reference lists are styled, and how chemical terms (for example) are styled, this will be helpful. Such matters as single column vs. double column, or the typographic style of the section heads, are not important; the typesetter will impose the correct style for these in any case.

Extensive formatting could render the file unusable to the typesetter. Please use the usual LaTeX environments and sectioning commands, rather than explicit layout commands such as \hspace, \vspace, \large, \centering, etc. Also, do not redefine the page layout parameters. For this reason, restrict manual formatting to equations; page formatting will be done by the typesetter.

Do not be concerned with bad line breaks, page breaks, or under full or overfull boxes. These issues will be resolved during final production.

Custom macro definitions should be placed in the preamble of the article, and not at any other place in the document. Such custom definitions, i.e., definitions made using the commands \newcommand, \renewcommand, \newenvironrnment, or \renewenvironment, should be used with great care. Sensible, restricted usage of private definitions is encouraged. Large macro packages should be avoided. Definitions that are not used in the article should be omitted. Do not change existing environments, commands, or other standard parts of LaTeX.

It is preferable for you as the author to set the line breaks in equations, rather than having possibly undesirable breaks added during the production process. If you are not using Academic Press style files, check the printed width of your journal, and check that each equation will fit within that width. If you are using an AP style file, the text width will be set for the journal, and any equations that extend beyond the right margin will be obvious.

Lists should be produced with the usual itemize and enumerate environments. The itemize environment is used for unnumbered lists and the enumerate environment for numbered lists. The layout will be adjusted to match the journal style in the production process.

If you use BiBTeX, remember to send your .bbl file (not the .bib file). At this time, Academic Press does not provide bibstyles for our journals; please use one of the commonly available styles that closely resembles the format for your journal.

When you are done creating your LaTeX file, add the command \listfiles to the preamble, and run LaTeX again. In the log file, you will see a list of every file used in the typesetting process. If any of the listed files are not part of the basic LaTeX installation or not available on CTAN, please find those files on your local system and submit them along with your .tex file.

Submit the text of your manuscript as a single file whenever possible. If there are other files such as figures, tables, or style files, put all of the files into one archive file before submission.

TeX Figure and Table Guidelines
Use the LaTeX picture commands or other LaTeX drawing programs only for simple diagrams, as the quality is not acceptable for final typesetting.

Figures should be supplied as separate files, in .eps or .tif format, to ensure the best graphic output. Hard-copy printouts of the artwork, of reproduction quality, must be included with the printed manuscript. (For more information, see Electronic Artwork1 below.)

Floats such as figures and tables will be repositioned during our production process. Do not spend too much effort in adjusting float placement. Do ensure that each float is clearly cited in the text, and our typesetters will ensure that the figure is placed in the optimal position, as near to the first citation as possible.

Use of vertical lines within tables is strongly discouraged. Tables may be submitted within the main text of the manuscript or as separate tex files \input to the main file.

If you have further questions about TeX files, please see our TeX FAQ.

Electronic Artwork
In the interest of quality and accuracy, AP prefers to use author-supplied electronic artwork for all figures and complex tables. Each individual figure or graphic must be supplied as a separate, stand-alone file. Figure and table files must be named with their respective numbers and graphic types such as *SmithFig1.tif, SmithFig2a.tif, SmithTable1.eps*, etc. Long file names are acceptable.

Only EPS and TIFF file formats are considered acceptable; TIFF is preferred. Artwork submitted in TIFF should adhere to the following resolution settings: half tones (color/grayscale): 300 dpi; line art (black and white), and mixed images (halftones with text or line art): 600 to 1200 dpi. If it is necessary to import graphics from a vector-based drawing program (e.g., Adobe Illustrator) into a raster-based program (e.g., Adobe PhotoShop) in order to produce a TIFF file, a resolution of at least 600 dpi is required for quality reproduction.

Color artwork should be transmitted as CMYK color. RGB images must be converted to CMYK and all necessary color adjustments must be made prior to the transmission of the files. Authors must supply AP with a color-correct CMYK printout of all color electronic art.

When creating your figures, use font sizes and line weights that will reproduce clearly and accurately when figures are sized to the appropriate column width. The minimum line weight is 1/2 point (thinner lines will not reproduce well). Eliminate all excess white space from the borders of each figure. Do not include figure legends or other extraneous text in a graphic file; figure legends should be provided as text, placed after the reference section in the main manuscript file.

A hardcopy printout that **exactly** matches the electronic version of all artwork must be supplied.

All figures and complex tables not transmitted in electronic form must be sent as high-quality, camera-ready hard copies.

Transmission of Electronic Materials
Authors are requested to include in their electronic submission a cover letter and all ancillary materials.

Transmission of electronic files is quicker and more reliable if the files are first compressed or encoded. Files created using most popular compression/encoding schemes from the Windows, Macintosh and UNIX platforms are acceptable. Acceptable formats include:

ZIP, SIT, BIN, HQX, CAB, TAR, TGZ, TAZ, TZ, GZ, Z, UU, UUE, XXE, B64, BHX, MIM

All other formats, including LZH, ARJ, ARC, and self-extracting archives (EXE and SEA), are not acceptable.

Important. Please choose unique, descriptive file names. File names should include the corresponding author's last name, or the manuscript number (if available), or else the production number (if available). Examples: *SmithFig3.eps, DBIO2001-0439Fig1.tif,* or *DBIO4212Text.doc.* Upon successful completion of an FTP transmission, authors must send an e-mail message to the journal as notification that the files have been posted. The journal e-mail address uses the same journal abbreviation as the folder name prefixed to @acad.com (for example, jcat@acad.com for *Journal of Catalysis*). If you are unsure of the e-mail address, please see the IFA section of the appropriate journal. In the body of the e-mail, please include the name of the journal to which the manuscript has been transmitted, the title of the manuscript, the names of all the authors, the type of computer used to create the files, the type of software and version number used to create the files, and a list of all file names.

FTP

Because FTP (file transfer protocol) is fast, reliable, and convenient, AP considers it the preferred method for authors to transmit their electronic files. To access the proper location, authors log on anonymously to our FTP server at ftp://ftp.harcourtbrace.com/ and navigate to pub/academic press/saved. Within the "saved" directory are folders for most of our titles, named with the standard abbreviation for the journal. If you are unsure of the standard abbreviation, please see the Information for Authors section of the appropriate journal. Within each journal directory is a folder called "incoming." On some systems, it will appear as if access to the incoming folder is "denied"; this will not prevent correct transmission of the files. Anonymous users have write-only access to the incoming folder and will not be able to see anything inside, including their own materials. Alternatively, authors can place their files directly under the journal folder. Files placed here will not be protected and may be viewed by other anonymous users.

If you have not created a single archive file including all materials and you plan to transmit multiple files, you are strongly advised to create a new folder, appropriately named in accordance with the recommendations above, within the "incoming" folder on the FTP site.

E-mail

Manuscript files can be transmitted via e-mail if the total file size of all attached files does not exceed 2 megabytes. Address the e-mail to the journal and supply the information requested for FTP submission. If you are unsure of the e-mail address, please see the IFA section of the appropriate journal.

Storage Media

Although we prefer receiving files via the Internet, we also accept materials on 3.5-inch high-density (not double-density) disks, CD-ROMs, 100-MB Zip disks, 1-GB Jaz disks, and SyQuest disks (44, 88, or 200 MB). Disks should be formatted for DOS/Windows or Macintosh. Because we can access disks formatted for some, but not all, versions of UNIX, we strongly discourage transmission on UNIX disks. **Note on the disk label the operating system, software, file format, and version numbers used to create the disk: e.g., Windows 95 - Word 97; Windows 98 - WordPerfect 9; MacOS 8.6 - Word 98.** If you submit your electronic materials on one of these media, we recommend using the special packaging materials available and shipping them via a reputable express courier service.

We regret that storage media cannot be returned.

Cognitive Science

ADDRESS FOR SUBMISSION:

Robert Goldstone, Editor
Cognitive Science
Indiana University
Psychology Department
1101 East Street
Bloomington, IN 47405-7007
USA
Phone: 812-855-4853
Fax:
E-Mail: cogscij@indiana.edu
Web: www.cognitivesciencesociety.org
Address May Change: 12/31/2005

PUBLICATION GUIDELINES:

Manuscript Length: 30+
Copies Required: Electronic
Computer Submission: Yes Required
Format: See Guidelines
Fees to Review: 0.00 US$

Manuscript Style:
American Psychological Association

CIRCULATION DATA:

Reader: Academics
Frequency of Issue: Bi-Monthly
Copies per Issue: 2,001 - 3,000
Sponsor/Publisher: Cognitive Science
Society / Lawrence Erlbaum Associates,
Inc.
Subscribe Price: 90.00 US$ Non Members
65.00 US$ Cognitive Science Society

REVIEW INFORMATION:

Type of Review: Editorial Review
No. of External Reviewers: 3
No. of In House Reviewers: 0
Acceptance Rate: 11-20%
Time to Review: 2 - 3 Months
Reviewers Comments: Yes
Invited Articles: 6-10%
Fees to Publish: 0.00 US$

MANUSCRIPT TOPICS:
Artificial Intelligence; Computer Science; Education; Educational Psychology; Languages &
Linguistics; Reading; Science Math & Environment

MANUSCRIPT GUIDELINES/COMMENTS:

Topics Include: Anthropology, Biology, Neuroscience, Philosophy and Psychology

Submission Information for Authors
Cognitive Science is a bimonthly journal for the multidisciplinary study of minds and other
intelligent systems. It publishes articles on cognition from perspective in artificial intelligence,
education, linguistics, neuroscience, philosophy, psychology, and anthropology of
multidisciplinary concern. Editorial decisions are made on the basis of content, rather than
discipline or author, and papers in all areas of cognitive science are welcome. Research
reports which are specifically written for a multidisciplinary audience are given the highest
priority. Papers which are very general or speculative, which constitute parametric
refinements of well-known ideas, or which are accessible to only a narrow or discipline-

159

specific audience, will be given very low priority and may be returned to authors without formal review.

The following kinds of articles are appropriate for the journal: (a) theories or theoretical analyses of knowledge representation, cognitive processes, and brain theory; (b) experimental or ethnographic studies relevant to theoretical issues in cognitive science; (c) descriptions of intelligent programs that exhibit or model some human ability; (d) design proposals for cognitive models; (e) protocol or discourse analysis of human cognitive processing; (f) discussions of new problem areas or methodological issues in cognitive science; and (g) short theoretical notes or rebuttals. The journal will publish four categories of articles. *Regular articles* are approximately 30 published pages (12,000 words). *Extended articles* have a target length of approximately 45 pages (18,000 words), and are expected to present particularly noteworthy research that cannot be adequately described within the constraints of a regular article. *Brief reports* have a target length of about 10 pages (4,000 words). *Letters to the editor* will typically consist of approximately 2-3 page (1,000 words) commentaries to articles, responses to commentaries, and discussion items of general relevance to the cognitive science community.

Original articles only will be considered. Submission of an article is understood to imply that the article is original and unpublished, is not being considered for publication elsewhere, and will not be submitted elsewhere while it is under review by *Cognitive Science*. Distribution of a prepublication draft in paper or electronic form is not considered as prior publication, as long as the distributed article is clearly identified as a prepublication draft. Following publication, authors are entitled to distribute copies of their article for personal use, either on paper or electronically, through their own personal mailing or website, or through mailing or the website of an agency by which they are employed, but permission of the Cognitive Science Society is required to reproduce published papers in other sources, including electronic archives.

Cognitive Science uses a web-based submission and review process, Editorial Manager. Authors should log onto **http://www.editorialmanager.com/cogsci/** for instructions on how to register and submit manuscripts online. Paper copies of submissions are no longer acceptable. When submitting their manuscripts to Editorial Manager, authors will need to provide an electronic version of their manuscript and abstract, a set of keywords chosen from a set of classifications, and a category designation for their manuscript (letter to the editor, brief report, regular article, or extended article). Authors may send queries concerning the submission process, manuscript status, or journal procedures to the editorial office at **cogscij@indiana.edu**.

Illustrations. Color figures can now be reproduced on **www.leaonline.com** at no additional charge, regardless of whether or not these illustrations are reproduced in color in the printed version. In situations where figures make essential use of color, the journal also has the capacity to publish a limited number of color figures in the printed version. In these cases, costs incurred will be the author's responsibility. For further information on the preparation of electronic artwork, please see:

    https://www.erlbaum.com/shop/tek9.asp?pg=products&specific=0364-0213

160

Please note: Because of technical complications that can arise by converting color figures to 'gray scale' (for printed version should you not opt for color in print) please also submit usable black and white prints corresponding to all the color illustrations. For manuscripts submitted online, a file of a black and white version of each color should be uploaded, in addition to the color figure file.

Manuscripts should conform to APA 5th edition as specified in the *Publication Manual of the American Psychological Association* with the exceptions and considerations listed below. Authors may be asked to re-format manuscripts that do not conform to the following guidelines prior to editorial evaluation.

Preparation of Manuscript
Please double-space all material. Manuscripts should have 1-in. margins on all sides. Number pages consecutively with the title page as page 1 and include a brief abstract of 100 to 150 words as page 2. In departure from APA format, we accept and encourage submissions in which tables, figures, and figure captions are integrated into the text body rather than separated into sections. However, if authors choose to integrate these materials, they will still need to separate them for the version of the manuscript sent to the publisher. All tables and other end-of-paper matter except art should be numbered.

Figures
Figures must be supplied in electronic format and should be of sufficiently high resolution to appear sharp and artifact-free when printed. All figures must be in a form suitable for reproduction. Ideally, we would like authors to submit their figures in the actual final size. The maximum size allowed for this journal is 5½ by 7¼ inches (to allow room for the legend). Color illustrations are only available for the printed version of the journal. Figures captions should appear on a list separate from the text or on the figures themselves. The word "Figure" should always appear as Fig. in text and in legends.

Numbering of Figures and Tables
Each figure and table must be mentioned in the text and must be numbered consecutively using Arabic numerals in the order of its appearance in the text. On the reverse side of every figure write the name of the author and the figure number, unless figures are integrated with the text. A brief title should be typed directly above each table. Tables do not need any legends, and any explanations or clarifications of tabular material should be indicated as a footnote to the table by means of lower case letters.

References
Contributors should refer to the APA Publication Manual for the correct listing of references in the text and reference list. All references must be closely checked in text and lists to determine that dates and spellings are consistent. Please note that the names of all authors should be given in the list of references, and "et al." used only in the text. Examples for books, journals, and conference proceedings follow:

Reisen, A.H. (1966). Sensory deprivation. In E. Stellar & J.M. Sprague (Eds.), *Progress in physiological psychology* (Vol. 1). New York: Academic Press.

Atkinson, R.C., & Shiffrin, R.M. (1971). The control of short-term memory. *Scientific American*, 225, 82-90.

Keane, M.T.(1995). On order effects in analogical mapping: Predicting human error using IAM. In J.D. Moore & J.F. Lehman (Eds.), *Proceedings of the Seventeenth Annual Conference of the Cognitive Science Society* (pp. 449-454). Mahwah, NJ:Erlbaum.

Spelling, Terminology, and Abbreviations
American spelling, rather than British, is preferred. The Third Edition of Webster's Unabridged Dictionary is the standard reference work when in doubt. Please try to avoid jargon and, wherever possible, abbreviations that are not commonly accepted.

Permissions
Contributors are responsible for obtaining permission from copyright owners if they use an illustration, table, or lengthy quote from material that has been published elsewhere. Contributors should write to both the publisher and author of material they are seeking permission to reproduce.

Reprints
The only opportunity contributors have to order offprints is when page proofs are returned.

Please submit to http://cogsci.edmgr.com

Acceptable Formats. Word, WordPerfect, TXT, RTF, LaTeX2e, AMSTeX, TIFF, GIF, JPEG, EPS, Postscript, PICT, Excel and PowerPoint

College & Research Libraries

ADDRESS FOR SUBMISSION:

William Gray Potter, Editor
College & Research Libraries
University of Georgia
Main Library
Athens, GA 30602-1641
USA
Phone: 706-542-0621
Fax: 706-542-4144
E-Mail: wpotter@uga.edu
Web:
Address May Change:

PUBLICATION GUIDELINES:

Manuscript Length: 21-25
Copies Required: Three
Computer Submission: No
Format: N/A
Fees to Review: 0.00 US$

Manuscript Style:
     Chicago Manual of Style

CIRCULATION DATA:

Reader: Academics, Librarians
Frequency of Issue: Bi-Monthly
Copies per Issue: 10,001 - 25,000
Sponsor/Publisher: American Library
   Association; Association of College and
   Research Libraries
Subscribe Price: 65.00 US$ Individual
      25.00 US$ Member

REVIEW INFORMATION:

Type of Review: Blind Review
No. of External Reviewers: 2
No. of In House Reviewers: 1
Acceptance Rate: 40%
Time to Review: 2 - 3 Months
Reviewers Comments: Yes
Invited Articles: 0-5%
Fees to Publish: 0.00 US$

MANUSCRIPT TOPICS:
Library Science/Information Resources

MANUSCRIPT GUIDELINES/COMMENTS:

Manuscript Preparation
Manuscripts of articles should be sent to the editor, William Gray Potter, University of Georgia Libraries, Athens GA 30602-7412, Phone: 706-542-0621, Fax: 706-542 4144, Email: **wpotter@uga.edu**

Instructions for Authors
1. Submit original, unpublished manuscripts only. Authors are responsible for the accuracy of the statements and statistics included. Papers presented at a conference should be identified with the conference name and date in the cover letter.

2. Manuscripts should be machine-printed and double-spaced. Three copies should be provided. Disk copy will be requested from authors for accepted articles. Authors' titles, names, affiliations, and e-mail addresses should appear on a cover page only. Do not repeat this information in the text. Using key words from the title, put a header or footer on each

page and include the page number. A 75- to 100-word abstract should precede the body of the article. Although longer works may be considered, 1,000 to 5,000-word manuscripts are most suitable.

3. Clear, simple prose enhances the presentation of ideas and opinions. The editor especially encourages writing in the active voice.

4. Local peer review increases a manuscripts quality. Distribute the paper to colleagues, discuss it, and make revisions based on their comments.

5. Spelling will follow *Webster's Collegiate Dictionary*, 10th edition.

6. *College & Research Libraries* follows *The Chicago Manual of Style*, 14th ed. (Chicago: University of Chicago Pr., 1993) for capitalization, punctuation, quotations, tables, captions, and elements of bibliographic style.

7. The author is responsible for verifying all citations carefully. Bibliographic references should be consecutively numbered throughout the manuscript. Double-spaced endnotes should appear on separate pages at the end of the article. Use regular aligned numbers (1., 2., etc.) not superscripts. Authors are requested not to use the auto-footnoting feature on word processing programs.

8. *C&RL* follows the *Chicago* style of volume (date): pages. For example:

1. Larry R. Oberg, Mary Kay Schleiter, and Michael Van Houten, "Faculty Perceptions of Librarians at Albion College: Status, Role, Contribution, and Contacts," College & Research Libraries 50 (Mar. 1989): 215 30.

First mention of an article should use the author s full name; subsequent mentions will be by last name only.

9. Subsequent references should utilize surname, brief title, and page reference. If no other reference intervenes, "Ibid." will be used. Do not underline "Ibid." Op. cit. and loc. cit. are not used. For citations to book or journal page numbers, use 217-19 not p. 217-19. For example:

13. Oberg, Schleiter, and Van Houten, "Faculty Perceptions," 217-19.

Consult *C&RL* for further examples.

10. Tables and illustrations should appear on separate pages at the end of the paper. Indicate desired placement by adding an instruction, such as (Insert table 2), in parentheses. Each illustration or table should have a number and a brief title. Tables should be double-spaced, should follow examples in *The Chicago Manual of Style*, and should be submitted on disk.

11. Submit original, camera-ready art for illustrations, figures, and graphs.

164

Subject Content

College & Research Libraries includes articles in all fields of interest and concern to academic and research libraries. Well-written manuscripts on all aspects of academic and research librarianship will be considered. Manuscripts may include research studies, case studies, descriptive narratives of successful and unsuccessful ventures, thoughtful discussions of issues in librarianship, and other suitable subjects.

The editors and the Editorial Board invite submissions relevant to the goals stated in the ACRL Strategic Plan, 1996-2001 (*C&RL News*, September 1995; revised *C&RL News*, September 1996):
1. Provide development opportunities for academic and research librarians and other library personnel that enhance their ability to deliver superior services and resources.
2. Collaborate with other professional organizations and associations of higher education in order to promote mutual interests.
3. Maintain at the national level a prominent role in planning and decision-making for influencing information policy.
4. Ensure that ACRL s operating environment provides efficiency in its use of resources and effectiveness in the delivery of services to its members and constituent units.

Review of Manuscripts

College & Research Libraries is a refereed journal using double-blind reviewing. The editor peruses manuscripts and submits them to at least two reviewers. For this process, the cover sheet with authors names and other identifying materials is blocked out or deleted.

Reviewers address themselves to the content and style of the manuscript. Main areas of consideration are:
* Does the manuscript make a new contribution to the literature?
* Is the method used appropriate to the subject?
* Does the evidence presented support the hypothesis?
* Does the author communicate clearly with an educated, yet not necessarily specialized, audience?
* Does the literature review place the research or opinions in perspective?

This review process takes eight to ten weeks. After the decision has been made, the editor writes to the author accepting the manuscript, accepting it contingent on revisions, or rejecting it. Authors may not submit the manuscript to other publications while a *C&RL* review is in progress.

Publication

If accepted, manuscripts generally appear about ten months after completion of the review process. The editor may offer recommendations for changes when the article is accepted. Further editing may occur to tailor the article *to C&RL'* s style.

The American Library Association copyrights articles published in *College & Research Libraries*. Subsequent inquiries for reprinting articles should be referred to ALA s Office of Rights and Permissions. All copyrighted material in the journal may be photocopied for the noncommercial purpose of scientific or educational advancement.

Letters

Readers who wish to comment on articles in the journal should address the letters to the editor. Letters should be succinct, no longer than 200 words. Letters will be published on a space-available basis.

Reviews

College & Research Libraries includes reviews of new publications pertinent to academic and research librarians. Publishers are invited to send review copies and announcements to the Book Review Editor, Fred J. Hay, Appalachian State University, Belk Library, Boone, NC 28608; (704) 262-2887; e-mail: **hayfj@appstate.edu** Prospective reviewers may write to the book review editor indicating their qualifications and special areas of interest.

College & Undergraduate Libraries

ADDRESS FOR SUBMISSION:

Christopher Millson-Martula, Editor
College & Undergraduate Libraries
Lynchburg College
Director of the Library
1501 Lakeside Dr.
Lynchburg, VA 24501
USA
Phone: 434-544-8399
Fax: 434-544-8499
E-Mail: millsonmartula@lynchburg.edu
Web: www.haworthpressinc.com
Address May Change:

PUBLICATION GUIDELINES:

Manuscript Length: 5-50
Copies Required: Two
Computer Submission: Yes
Format: No Reply
Fees to Review: 0.00 US$

Manuscript Style:
    Chicago Manual of Style

CIRCULATION DATA:

Reader: Academics, Practicing Librarians
Frequency of Issue: 2 Times/Year
Copies per Issue: No Reply
Sponsor/Publisher: Haworth Press, Inc.
Subscribe Price: 28.00 US$ Individual
        60.00 US$ Institution

REVIEW INFORMATION:

Type of Review: Blind Review
No. of External Reviewers: 2
No. of In House Reviewers: 0
Acceptance Rate: 50%
Time to Review: 1-3 Months
Reviewers Comments: No
Invited Articles: 20%
Fees to Publish: 0.00 US$

MANUSCRIPT TOPICS:
Higher Education; Library Science/Information Resources

MANUSCRIPT GUIDELINES/COMMENTS:

Audience. Working college librarians who need solutions to immediate problems but lack a full complement of staff specialists.

Content. Practical and informative, not theoretical and exhaustive (a comprehensive literature review Isn't essential to make a useful point). References to research and university libraries can and should be made, but only to point out differences from college libraries. The emphasis is on undergraduate services, concerns and operations. Continuing education series that focus on specific issues and subjects are particularly welcome.

Style. A content analysis method for developing user-based objectives. The acculturation of librarians to faculty librarian positions is compared and contrasted to the socialization process of the professorate.

Abstract. In two or three clear sentences, summarize intent, findings and recommendations.

Bibliography. No footnotes. Use author-date system [e.g. (Smith 1978, 25) in the text. At end, In a section called "References," provide a single list of endnotes and/or citations in *The Humanities Style (Chicago Manual of Style,* latest edition).

Basics. Double space. Include a stamped, self-addressed postcard and envelope with each submission. As articles will be reviewed by outside readers, include your name and affiliation on the cover sheet only. Once manuscripts and/or proposal ideas are accepted, make revisions as requested. Hand-written additions and corrections are unacceptable. Submit three paper copies of fully revised, final manuscript; one disk copy in Word or ACSII (Indicate article title, your name, computer brand name and program/version); and signed, original copy of Publication Agreement form, **all by specified deadline**. Provide current job title, library/institution name/address and preferred reprint mailing address, and phone number.

Reprints. Senior authors receive one journal issue and 10 complimentary reprints. Junior authors receive one journal issue.

Proposals. The editors of College and Undergraduate Libraries prefer to see proposals rather than completed manuscripts. That helps to assure that article content matches editorial Intent and reduces the need for revisions.

Length. One page (single spacing permitted)

Content
1. Clearly state the general subject or topic. (a phrase)
2. Clearly state the main points of the article-what you are trying to prove or suggest. (one sentence)
3. Clearly state the arguments or evidence you will supply to support the main points and indicate the order in which each will be introduced. (four or five sentences. A simple list is acceptable.)

Submission. Send proposals to the editor.

Responses. Expect a response within 30 days.

Article References
A trademark of *C&UL* is a section preceding "References" called *Quick Bib*. This section highlights the three or four most important or useful sources cited in an article.

Quick Bib
Buschman, John, et al. "Smart Barcoding in a Small Academic Library." Information Technology and Libraries 7 (September 1988): 263-70.
Commings, Karen. "That B-Word"; or, Barcoding a Library." Library Journal 114 (October 1, 1989): 66-7.
Epstein, Susan Baerg, et al. "Custom Barcoding as a Better Way; How to Barcode Label your Collection Without Tears." Library Journal 114 (September 1, 1989):156-5.

168

Sluss, Sara B. "More Barcoding Counsel." Library Journal 115 (February 15, 1990): 108+.

About the Journal

College And Undergraduate Libraries is the only journal devoted to the needs of undergraduate libraries. A roadmap to excellence for these libraries, each issue includes highly readable articles on technical and public services, administration, and collections.

College & Undergraduate Libraries is the first journal to recognize that many college Libraries operate without the benefit of automation librarians, microcomputer librarians, subject specialists, preservation officers, security program officers, or microform Librarians available to large university research libraries. This unique journal will provide busy college Librarians, already saddled with an array of responsibilities, with practical, step by-step articles on subjects such as understanding statistics and purchasing and maintaining microcomputers, and columns on stretching library dollars. Topical areas to be covered by *College and Undergraduate Libraries* include:

- Assessment
- Monograph and serials collection development and management
- Faculty rank and status for college Librarians
- Preservation and conservation needs
- Innovations in library support for undergraduate courses
- Plagiarism
- Preparing the college library for accreditation
- College archives without an archivist
- Inexpensive staff development ideas
- Automating the college Library

About the Editor

Christopher Millson-Martula is Director of the Library at Lynchburg College, Lynchburg, VA since 1995. He is an active member of the College Library Section of the Association of College and Research Libraries and is the author of several publications on academic libraries. He received his M.L.S from Columbia University and has a bachelors and masters degree in history from Tufts and Trinity College (Hartford, CT) respectively.

INSTRUCTIONS FOR AUTHORS

1. **Original Articles Only**. Submission of a manuscript to this *Journal* represents a certification on the part of the author(s) that it is an original work, and that neither this manuscript nor a version of it has been published elsewhere nor is being considered for publication elsewhere.

2. **Content/Audience**. Practical, informative articles on undergraduate services, concerns, and operations written for busy Librarians. A comprehensive literature review isn't essential to make a useful point. Relevant research articles are welcome, but the emphasis must be on results and applications, not process. Short, reflective pieces, humor, and brief descriptions of innovative ideas that work are as welcome as full-length articles.

The editors encourage submissions from paraprofessionals, support staff, faculty, librarians, and students-anyone with a good idea for improving undergraduate library services.

3. **Style**. Simple, down-to-earth communication. Avoid language such as the following: a functional analysis methodology for developing user-based objectives.

4. **Manuscript Length**. Five-50 typed pages double-spaced (including references and abstract). Lengthier manuscripts may be considered, but only at the discretion of the Editor. Sometimes, lengthier manuscripts may be considered if they can be divided up into sections for publication in successive journal issues.

5. **Submissions/Return Postage**. Send three copies of manuscripts or proposals. Include a stamped, self-addressed postcard for acknowledging receipt and a 9" x 12" self-addressed, stamped envelope for return.

6. **Proposals**. The editors encourage proposals as well as completed manuscripts.
- Length: One page (single spacing permitted)
- Content:
  1. Clearly state the general subject or topic. (a phrase)
  2. Clearly state the main points of article-what you want to prove or suggest. (one sentence)
  3. Clearly state the arguments or evidence that you will supply to support the main points and indicate the order in which each will be introduced. (four or five sentences). A simple list is acceptable.

7. **Manuscript Preparation**.
Margins. leave at least a one-inch margin on all four sides.
Paper. use clean white, 8-1/2" x 11" paper.
Number of Copies. two
Cover Page. Important-staple a cover page to the manuscript, indicating only the article title (this is used for anonymous refereeing).
Second "Title Page" enclose a regular title page but do not staple it to the manuscript. Include the title again, plus:
- full authorship
- an ABSTRACT of about 100 words. (Below the abstract provide 3-10 key words for index purposes.)
- an introductory footnote with authors' academic degrees, professional titles, affiliations, mailing addresses, and any desired acknowledgment of research support or other credit.

References. No footnotes. Use the author-date system [e.g. Smith 1978, 257 in the text. At end, in a section called "References," provide a single list of endnotes and/or citations in The Humanities Style (The *Chicago Manual of Style*, latest edition). Before the references, list the three or four most important and relevant citations in a boxed section, labeled Quick Bib. This is a trademark of *C&UL*.

8. **Final Approved Manuscripts**. No galley proofs will be sent; therefore, editorial revisions must be made while an article is still in manuscript. Authors are expected to submit manuscripts, disks and art that are free from error. Final copy must:

• Be accurate
• Be free of punctuation, spelling, and grammatical errors
• Include all revisions recommended by referees and reviewers
• Be submitted in disk format (WordPerfect 5.1 or ASCII) as well as in paper (3 copies)-both versions must be exactly the same
• Provide camera-ready tables, figures, and illustrations, as outlined below

All tables, figures, and illustrations must be cleanly typed or artistically prepared so that they can be used either exactly as they are or else used after a photographic reduction in size. Figures, tables, and illustrations must be prepared on separate sheets of paper. Always use black ink and professional drawing instruments. On the back of these items, write your article title and the journal title lightly in pencil, so they do not get misplaced. In text, skip extra lines and indicate where these figures and tables are to be placed (please do not write on face of art). Photographs are considered part of the acceptable manuscript and remain with the publisher for use in additional printings.

9. **Reprints**. The senior author will receive one copy of the journal issue and 10 complimentary reprints of his or her article. The junior author will receive one copy of the issue. These are sent several weeks after the journal issue is published and in circulation. An order form for the purchase of additional reprints will also be sent to all authors at this time. (Approximately 4-6 weeks is necessary for the preparation of reprints.) Please do not query the journal's editor about reprints. All such questions should be sent directly to The Haworth Press, Inc., Production Department, 21 East Broad Street, West Hazleton, PA 18201. To order additional reprints (minimum: 50 copies), please contact The Haworth Document Delivery Center, 10 Alice Street, Binghamton, New York 13904-1580 (607) 722-5857.

10. **Copyright**. Copyright ownership of your manuscript must be transferred officially to The Haworth Press, Inc. before we can begin the peer-review process. The editor's letter acknowledging receipt of the manuscript will be accompanied by a form fully explaining this. All authors must sign the form and return the original to the editor as soon as possible. Failure to return the copyright form in a timely fashion will result in delay in review and subsequent publication.

Publication Agreement
1. **Copyright**: In consideration for review and possible subsequent publication of our Work in the journal noted on the reverse side of this page, the Author(s) agree to transfer copyright of the work to The Haworth Press, Inc., including full and exclusive rights to publication in all media now known or later developed, including but not limited to electronic databases and microfilm, and in anthologies of any kind. (*Note To U.S. Government Employees*: See Your Exemption, Paragraph 5 Below.)

2. **Author Re-Use Of Work**. As a professional courtesy, the authors retain the right to reprint their article submitted again, after publication in the journal in any work for which they are sole Author, or in any edited work for which the author is Senior Editor. No further

permission is necessary in writing from The Haworth Press, Inc., nor will the Press require fees of any kind for the reprinting. This statement is intended to provide full copyright release for the purposes listed above, and a photocopy of the release may be used when another Publisher requires a written release.

4. Author Warranties. The author(s) represent(s) and warrant(s):

a. That the manuscript submitted is his/her (their) own work;
b. That the work has been submitted only to this journal and that it has not been previously published;
c. That the article contains no libelous or unlawful statements and does not infringe upon the civil rights of others;
d. That the author(s) is (are) not infringing upon anyone else's copyright. The authors agree that if there is a breach of any of the above representations and warranties that (s)he (they) will indemnify the Publisher and Editor and hold them harmless.

4. Author Retention of Patents. The author(s) may have, within their article, descriptions of their own proprietary patents. It is not the intention of the Editor or Publisher to require copyright transfer of such materials. If any of these materials appear in the work, the authors may add their personal copyright notice to patents, with this understanding:

a. The author(s) retain copyright for said patents, with full and exclusive rights to their publication, not to include any other material from the article/publication;
b. The Publisher retains full and exclusive rights to publication to the article/publication in any format, including patents when published as part of the entire article or publication.
c. Photographs are considered part of the acceptable manuscript and remain with the Publisher for use in additional printings.

5. Note for U.S. Government Employees. If the article is single-authored by a U.S. government employee as part of his/ her official duties, it is understood that the article is not copyrightable. It is called a "Work of the U.S. Government." However, if the article was not part of the employee's official duties, it may be copyrighted. If the article was jointly written, the authors understand that they are delegating the right of copyright to the nongovernmental employee, who must sign this agreement.

6. "Work For Hire" Authors. If the article was written by an author who was hired by another person or company to do so, the article is called a "Work for Hire" manuscript. This agreement must then be signed by the "employer" who hired the author, as well as the author.

7. No Amendments. This form is not valid if the authors add any additional constraints and amendments. Please submit the article elsewhere for publication if the author(s) do not sign this form without alteration.

Name and exact Mailing Address of Contributor:

Special Note *This Will Be Used For Mailing Reprints*. You must include exact street address, name of your department if at a university, and Zip Code. The Haworth Press cannot be responsible for lost reprints if you do not provide us with your exact mailing address.

172

In reference to your journal article:

☐ If this box is checked . . .
Thank you for your article submission! Please allow 10-15 weeks for the review process. Before sending out your article for review, however, the Publisher requires us to obtain your signature(s) confirming that you have read the Publication Agreement on the reverse side of this page. All co-authors must sign and return the *Original* signed copy.

It Is Confirmed that I/we have read the **Publication Agreement** on the reverse side of the page, and agree and accept all conditions:

_____   _____
author's signature   date

_____   _____
author's signature   date

_____   _____
author's signature   date

_____   _____
authors signature   date

Other Comments:
Please reply to

_____
( ) Journal Editor:

_____
( ) Guest Editor / Special Issue Editor:

☐ If this box is checked . . .
Your article has been favorably reviewed. Our reviewers, however, require certain revisions which are indicated on the attached sheets. Please review and incorporate their suggestions, and return your manuscripts retyped within 14 days. A decision about publication will be made at that time. Thank you for your help and cooperation.

☐ If this box is checked . . .
We are pleased to inform you that your article has been accepted for publication in the journal noted above, or (if noted) by a special issue/ edition/monographic supplement to the journal.

Please note the following:
1. **Publication.** Your article is currently scheduled to appear in
   Volume: Number:
   Published during this season:

2. **Typesetting**. Your article will be sent to the Production Department of The Haworth Press, Inc., 21 East Broad Street, West Hazleton, PA 18201. They will typeset your article (preferably from your computer disk) exactly as submitted. Please note that you will not be receiving galley proofs. The production staff will proofread the galleys for typesetting errors against the final version of the manuscript as submitted. No revisions are allowed.

3. **Reprints.** Shortly after publication you will receive an order form for purchasing quantities of reprints. (About three weeks after publication, the senior author will receive two complimentary copies of the issue and ten copies of the article, and the junior author(s) will receive two complimentary copies of the issue.) Please note that preparation of reprints takes about eight weeks additional time after the actual issue is printed and in circulation.

☐ If this box is checked. . .

We are sorry, but the reviewers for this journal did not agree that your article was appropriate for publication in this periodical. If the reviewers consented in having their comments forwarded to you, their critiques are attached. Your submission is appreciated, and we hope that you will contribute again in the future.

The Haworth Press, INC.

College & University Media Review

ADDRESS FOR SUBMISSION:

Jeff Clark, Editor
College & University Media Review
James Madison University
Media Resources MSC 1701
Harrisonburg, VA 22807-0001
USA
Phone: 540-568-6770
Fax: 540-568-7037
E-Mail: clarkjc@jmu.edu
Web: http://www.ccumc.org
Address May Change:

PUBLICATION GUIDELINES:

Manuscript Length: 11-20 (typical)
Copies Required: One Paper on request
only
Computer Submission: Yes
Format: MSWord
Fees to Review: 0.00 US$

Manuscript Style:
See Manuscript Guidelines

CIRCULATION DATA:

Reader: Academics, Administrators
Frequency of Issue: 2 Times/Year
Copies per Issue: Less than 1,000
Sponsor/Publisher: Consortium of College
and University Media Centers (CCUMC)
Subscribe Price: 75.00 US$ Individual

REVIEW INFORMATION:

Type of Review: Peer Review
No. of External Reviewers: 1-3
No. of In House Reviewers: 2-4
Acceptance Rate: 80%
Time to Review: 1 - 2 Months
Reviewers Comments: Yes
Invited Articles: About 50%
Fees to Publish: 0.00 US$

MANUSCRIPT TOPICS:
Education Management/Administration; Educational Technology Systems; Higher Education;
Library Science/Information Resources; Teacher Education; Tests, Measurement &
Evaluation

MANUSCRIPT GUIDELINES/COMMENTS:

The College & University Media Review is the professional journal of the Consortium of
College and University Media Centers (CCUMC) and includes articles that focus on media
and technology, related research, instructional development, and management and
supervision, as related to the operation of instructional support service units in higher
education. If in doubt about the relevance of subject matter for a proposed contribution,
contact the editor. Interviews with leaders in the field or persons involved in interesting,
related practice may be submitted, as well as annotated bibliographies and case studies.

Persons interested in reviewing books, media, equipment, or software related to the foregoing
subjects should refer to "Reviews guidelines: Books, media, equipment, and software," which
can be found online at http://www.ccumc.org/pubs/reviews.html.

Manuscripts submitted and requests for information should be sent to the Editor (address above).

Submission Process

Manuscript Format. Manuscripts may be submitted in paper or electronic text form (MS Word for Windows preferred). Manuscripts are not restricted as to length but should conform to the style of the *Publication Manual of the American Psychological Association* (5th ed., 2001). Citations of electronic documents not covered by the APA manual should conform to the style specified by *APA Style.org* (http://www.apastyle.org/elecref.html), or in *Electronic Style: A Guide to Citing Electronic Information* by Nancy B. Crane and Xia Li (2nd ed., Information Today, 1996). Name(s), title(s), address(es), phone and FAX numbers, Internet address(es), and affiliation(s) of all authors should appear on a separate cover page.

Manuscripts submitted will not be returned unless special arrangements are made in advance with the editor.

Abstract. A descriptive abstract of 100-150 words, double-spaced, should be included on a separate page.

Review and Editing Process

Peer Review. All solicited and unsolicited contributions submitted for publication will be peer reviewed by members of the editorial staff, as well as external academic reviewers when necessary. All submissions to the *College & University Media Review* will be acknowledged promptly. It is anticipated that author(s) will be advised of the editorial staff's decision within two months after receipt of the contribution. The editorial staff will recommend one of the following: (1) Accept with no (or minor) revisions, (2) Accept conditionally with specified revisions, or (3) Reject.

Editing. The editor reserves the right to edit all contributions and will only contact authors for clarification, as needed.

Final Acceptance. The final decision as to whether a contribution will be published lies with the editor and editor-in-chief.

Publication Process

If the manuscript is accepted for publication, the author(s) will be expected to provide the following.

Submission. Each contribution, edited in its final form, should be submitted to the editor either as an attachment to an e-mail message (send to clarkjc@jmu.edu) or on disk (PC or Macintosh). Most common word processing software can be accepted; MS Word for Windows is preferred. One hard copy version of the manuscript sent to the editor by FAX or mail may be required so that the author(s)' intended formatting can be determined. Authors should keep document formatting to an absolute minimum. Do not use headers or footers, page numbers, indents other than tabs, or line spacing other than single or double spacing. The preferred format for graphics files is TIFF. GIF, JPEG, and PICT files are not acceptable.

Disks submitted should be clearly labeled with author name(s), file name(s), software used, and date.

Release Form. A signed release form must be received by the editor before a contribution can be published. The form certifies that the contribution has not been published or submitted for publication elsewhere, and authorizes CCUMC for first publication in the *College & University Media Review,* as well as in subsequent CCUMC publications under a non-exclusive license. Authors otherwise retain copyright in their individual articles and reviews. This release form will be mailed to the author(s) at the time the contribution is accepted for publication in the *Review.*

Photo. Although not required, a recent b&w photograph of each author (in electronic file format) is desired and strongly encouraged.

Other Information
Complimentary Copies. Each author will receive three complimentary copies of the issue in which his or her contribution appears.

Permissions. The *College & University Media Review* is copyrighted by the Consortium of College and University Media Centers. Copyright in individual articles and reviews are retained by their respective authors. Contributions may be reproduced without permission only for the uses allowed under copyright law (Title 17, *U. S. Code*); permission for other uses should be requested by letter or e-mail from the editor. All reproduction of contents, whether by permission or otherwise under copyright law, should display a copyright notice and full credit acknowledgments for this publication and the author(s) involved.

Back Issues. Back issues may be ordered from the CCUMC Executive office (see address below). Copies are $30 (U.S. funds) in the U.S. and Canada. Persons in other countries should contact the Executive Office for pricing information. Orders must be prepaid with checks made payable to CCUMC. Purchase orders cannot be accepted.

Other Correspondence. Subscriptions and business correspondence should be sent to the following address: Consortium of College and University Media Centers (CCUMC), Executive Office, Instructional Technology Center, 1200 Communications Building, Iowa State University, Ames, IA 50011-3243. E-mail: ccumc@ccumc.org

College and University

ADDRESS FOR SUBMISSION:

Louise Lonabocker, Editor
College and University
Boston College
102 Lyons Hall
Chestnut Hill, MA 02467
USA
Phone: 617-552-3318
Fax: 617-552-4889
E-Mail: louise@bc.edu
Web: See Guidelines
Address May Change:

PUBLICATION GUIDELINES:

Manuscript Length: 11-15
Copies Required: One
Computer Submission: Yes Email
Format: Word, Excel
Fees to Review: 0.00 US$

Manuscript Style:
    Chicago Manual of Style

CIRCULATION DATA:

Reader: , Higher Education Administrators
Frequency of Issue: Quarterly
Copies per Issue: 10,000
Sponsor/Publisher: American Assn. of
    Collegiate Registrars and Admissions
    Officers
Subscribe Price: 50.00 US$ one year

REVIEW INFORMATION:

Type of Review: Blind Review
No. of External Reviewers: 3+
No. of In House Reviewers: 1
Acceptance Rate: 21-30%
Time to Review: 1 Month
Reviewers Comments: Yes
Invited Articles: 0-5%
Fees to Publish: 0.00 US$

MANUSCRIPT TOPICS:
Enrolment Management; Financial Aid; Higher Education; Registration and Records; Student
Record Systems; Student Recruitment & Retention

MANUSCRIPT GUIDELINES/COMMENTS:

Website: www.aacrao.org/publications/candu/write.htm

Write for *College and University*
What's the best way to share your ideas, innovations, and opinions with registrars, admissions
officers, and enrollment managers nationwide? Contribute to AACRAO's prestigious College
and University (C&U) quarterly journal.

Give your research and experience a voice by writing for the "Feature" section, or address
best practices, how-tos, new technologies, the latest books, and other pertinent topics in "The
Forum" section. With a substantial circulation base, C&U is an excellent vehicle for shaping
the profession and gaining recognition.

AACRAO members are especially encouraged to submit articles, but non-members, faculty, graduate students, and members of the corporate sector are also welcome to share their work. Authors will receive copies of the issue in which their article appears, and will be issued an author honorarium.

MANUSCRIPT PREPARATION FOR C&U

Feature Articles (refereed articles)

The editor will acknowledge receipt of manuscripts and will forward them to the Editorial Board for review. The Committee will consider the appropriateness of the article for AACRAO's membership, the usefulness of the information, the nature and logic of the research methodology, clarity, and the style of presentation. This review may take as long as three months, after which the C&U editor will inform the author of the manuscript's acceptance or rejection.

- Manuscripts for **feature articles** should be no longer than 4,500 words.
- All submissions must be sent as an attachment via e-mail.
- Because the Editorial Board has a blind review policy, the author's name should not appear on any text page. *A separate cover sheet should be sent via e-mail and include the title of the manuscript and the author's name, address, phone, fax, and e-mail, if applicable.*
- References should be formatted in author-date style and follow guidelines provided on page 526 of *The Chicago Manual of Style*, 14th edition, published by the University of Chicago Press. A list of references should appear at the end of the article. Text citations also follow the author-date format; examples may be found on page 641 of the *Manual*. For more information or for samples, please contact the editor.
- In addition to being placed in the manuscript, the data for essential tables and charts should also be included in a separate Microsoft Excel (spreadsheet) file.
- Articles are accepted for publication with the understanding that the editors and Editorial Board reserve the right to edit for clarity and style.
- Authors whose manuscripts are selected for submission will be asked to submit a short biographical statement and an abstract of their article, both no more than 35 words.
- Do not submit articles that are under consideration for publication in another periodical.
- Submit manuscripts, letters, and direct inquiries to:

> Louise Lonabocker, *C&U* Editor-in-Chief
> Director, Student Services
> Boston College
> Lyons 102
> Chestnut Hill, MA 02467
> Tel: (617) 552-3318; E-mail: louise@bc.edu

Forum Articles (commentary, analysis, book reviews, international resources)

College & University also welcomes comments on articles, timely issues in higher education, new technologies, and other topics of interest to the journal's readers in the form of commentary, policy analysis, international observations, and book reviews. This is an excellent venue for individuals to share their knowledge and experience, and for companies to share corporate know-how and the latest techniques and technologies.

- Manuscripts for "The Forum" should not exceed 2,000 words.
- Companies submitting articles should not have a sales-oriented focus to the article, but rather, provide a general overview.
- All other guidelines follow as above.
- Submit commentary, book reviews, and other non-refereed pieces to:

> Saira Burki, *C&U* Managing Editor
> AACRAO
> One Dupont Circle, NW, Suite 520
> Washington, DC 20036
> Tel: (202) 293-9161; E-mail: burkis@aacrao.org

College Language Association Journal

ADDRESS FOR SUBMISSION:

Cason L. Hill, Editor
College Language Association Journal
Morehouse College
Atlanta, GA 30314
USA
Phone: 404-681-2800, ext. 2160
Fax: 404-688-3700
E-Mail: chill@morehouse.edu
Web: www.clascholars.org
Address May Change:

PUBLICATION GUIDELINES:

Manuscript Length: 11-15
Copies Required: Two
Computer Submission: No
Format: N/A
Fees to Review: 0.00 US$

Manuscript Style:
, MLA Handbook, Latest Edition

CIRCULATION DATA:

Reader: Academics
Frequency of Issue: Quarterly
Copies per Issue: 1,001 - 2,000
Sponsor/Publisher: Professional Association
& University
Subscribe Price: 50.00 US$ Individual
51.50 US$ Canada
55.50 US$ Other Countries

REVIEW INFORMATION:

Type of Review: Editorial Review
No. of External Reviewers: 1
No. of In House Reviewers: 3
Acceptance Rate: 75%
Time to Review: 4 - 6 Months
Reviewers Comments: Yes
Invited Articles: 0-5%
Fees to Publish: 0.00 US$

MANUSCRIPT TOPICS:
Adult Career & Vocational; African-American Literature; American Literature; Curriculum Studies; English Literature; Foreign Language; Foreign Literature; Languages & Linguistics

MANUSCRIPT GUIDELINES/COMMENTS:

Manuscripts sought on the following:
•   Language and Literature* (criticism)
•   Book Reviews
*English, American, Foreign (In English Translation)

Manuscripts submitted for consideration and possible publication should conform to the *MLA Handbook*, latest edition, in all matters of form.

The *CLA Journal* primarily publishes:
1.   Articles on language and literature (all periods and all countries)
2.   Literary criticism and book reviews (all periods and all countries)

College Student Affairs Journal

ADDRESS FOR SUBMISSION:

Tony W. Cawthon
College Student Affairs Journal
Clemson University
305 Tillman Hall Box 340710
Clemson, SC 29634-0710
USA
Phone: 864-656-0328
Fax: 864-656-1322
E-Mail: cawthot@clemson.edu
Web: www.sacsa.org
Address May Change: 11/1/2007

PUBLICATION GUIDELINES:

Manuscript Length: 21-25
Copies Required: Five
Computer Submission: Yes
Format: Microsoft Word
Fees to Review: 0.00 US$

Manuscript Style:
American Psychological Association

CIRCULATION DATA:

Reader: Academics, Administrators
Frequency of Issue: 2 Times/Year
Copies per Issue: 1,001 - 2,000
Sponsor/Publisher: Southern Association
For College Student Affairs
Subscribe Price: 25.00 US$

REVIEW INFORMATION:

Type of Review: Blind Review
No. of External Reviewers: 0
No. of In House Reviewers: 3+
Acceptance Rate: 21-30%
Time to Review: 2 - 3 Months
Reviewers Comments: Yes
Invited Articles: 0-5%
Fees to Publish: 0.00 US$

MANUSCRIPT TOPICS:
Education Management/Administration; Higher Education; Student Affairs

MANUSCRIPT GUIDELINES/COMMENTS:

Purpose. The College Student Affairs Journal publishes articles related to research, concepts, and practices that have implications for both practitioners and scholars in college student affairs work.

Types of Manuscripts Accepted. General articles may be research reports, updates on professional issues, examinations of legislative issues, dialogues and debates, historical articles, literature reviews, opinion pieces, or projections of future trends. Developmentally Speaking articles are descriptions of successful campus programs, including evidence to support claims of their success. Authors may also submit reviews of works in any medium, such as books or films.

Publication Schedule. Twice yearly, fall and spring.

Circulation. 1,200.

Index. Current Index to Journals in Education and Higher Education Abstracts.

Concurrent Submissions to Other Publications. Not accepted.

Style Guide. The Journal adheres to the guidelines of the *Publication Manual of the American Psychological Association* (5th ed.). Authors should particularly note this manual's recommendations to use active voice and first person narration.

Special Format Guidelines. The first page of the manuscript should include the article title; the name, position, and institutional affiliation of each author; and appropriate contact information for editorial response. The article's first text page should include the manuscript title, but no information that would identify any author.

Recommended Length. Manuscripts submitted for the Articles section generally range between 3,000 and 6,500 words including abstract, tables, figures, and references. Developmentally Speaking manuscripts may be between 1,000 and 3,000 words. Reviews should not exceed 1,000 words.

Figures and Graphs. Supply camera-ready art.

Manuscript Submission. Electronic submission is strongly preferred, using Microsoft Word. Send email attachments to **cawthot@clemson.edu**, or mail diskettes to Dr. Tony W. Cawthon, Associate Professor, Clemson University, 305 Tillman Hall Box 340710, Clemson, SC, 29634-0710. For those who must supply hard copies (original plus four copies) instead of electronic files, the USPS address is the same as for diskettes above.

Review Process. All submissions are refereed using a blind review system. Evaluative criteria include significance of topic, clarity of presentation, style of writing, usefulness to practitioners and/or importance for scholarship, contribution to the student affairs profession, and quality of methodology or program. Notification of acceptance or rejection of all manuscripts will be made by the editor. All manuscripts received and approved for publication become the property of the association. All others will be returned on request. The editor reserves the right to edit or rewrite accepted articles to meet the Journal's standards.

Questions or Comments. Email info@sacsa.org

College Student Journal

ADDRESS FOR SUBMISSION:

George E. Uhlig, Editor
College Student Journal
c/o Project Innovation of Mobile
PO Box 8508
Spring Hill Station
Mobile, AL 36689-8508
USA
Phone: 251-343-1878
Fax: 251-343-1878
E-Mail: pfeldman@gulftel.com
Web: See Guidelines
Address May Change:

PUBLICATION GUIDELINES:

Manuscript Length: 11-15
Copies Required: Two
Computer Submission: Yes
Format: 1 data diskette + 1 hard copy
Fees to Review: 0.00 US$

Manuscript Style:
    American Psychological Association

CIRCULATION DATA:

Reader: Academics, Administrators
Frequency of Issue: Quarterly
Copies per Issue: 1,001 - 2,000
Sponsor/Publisher: Project Innovation, Inc.
Subscribe Price: 40.00 US$ Institution
    20.00 US$ Additional for Foreign

REVIEW INFORMATION:

Type of Review: Editorial Review
No. of External Reviewers: 2
No. of In House Reviewers: 1
Acceptance Rate: 60%
Time to Review: 1 - 2 Months
Reviewers Comments: Yes
Invited Articles: 0-5%
Fees to Publish: 30.00 US$ per double-
    spaced page

MANUSCRIPT TOPICS:
Curriculum Studies; Education Management/Administration; Higher Education; Urban Education, Cultural/Non-Traditional

MANUSCRIPT GUIDELINES/COMMENTS:

Journal's Website://journals825.home.mindspring.com

College Student Journal publishes original investigations and theoretical papers dealing with college student values, attitudes, opinions, and learning. This includes the areas of undergraduate, graduate, and professional schools, and may include selected contributions dealing with college preparation.

Manuscript Submission
Manuscripts must be submitted in duplicate and should be prepared to conform to the style and procedures described in the *Publication Manual of the American Psychological Association*. Manuscripts must be accompanied by an abstract of 100 to 200 words typed on a

184

separate sheet of paper. The abstract should contain statements of the (a) problem, (b).method, (c) results, (d) conclusions when appropriate.

The abstract should provide the reader with an idea of the theme and scope of the article.

At least one copy of the manuscript and the abstract must be original with clear, clean typing or printing. We prefer disk-based manuscripts in either Macintosh or MS-Dos format. However, at least one printed copy of the manuscript must be included with the disk.

Review Process
Manuscripts are reviewed by at least two reviewers knowledgeable in the field of study. An attempt is made to review manuscripts within two weeks of receipt when possible.

Fees to Publish
This *Journal* is not supported by either membership or association dues, or advertising. Authors or their institutions share the cost of publication. Except for invited articles, authors will be invoiced for their share of publication costs at the time the manuscript is accepted for publication. The article will be scheduled for publication after payment or an institutional purchase order is received.

Reprints
Information concerning reprints and reprint policy is disseminated with page proofs/galleys.

College Teaching

ADDRESS FOR SUBMISSION:

Wendy Rubin, Editor
College Teaching
Heldref Publications
1319 Eighteenth St. NW
Washington, DC 20036
USA
Phone: 202-296-6267
Fax: 202-296-5149
E-Mail: wrubin@heldref.org
Web: www.heldref.org
Address May Change:

PUBLICATION GUIDELINES:

Manuscript Length: 4000 words max
Copies Required: Two
Computer Submission: Yes Email
Format: No Reply
Fees to Review: 0.00 US$

Manuscript Style:
    Chicago Manual of Style

CIRCULATION DATA:

Reader: Academics
Frequency of Issue: Quarterly
Copies per Issue: 2,001 - 3,000
Sponsor/Publisher: Heldref Publications,
    Inc.
Subscribe Price: 47.00 US$ Individual
    93.00 US$ Institution

REVIEW INFORMATION:

Type of Review: Editorial Review
No. of External Reviewers: 2
No. of In House Reviewers: 0
Acceptance Rate: 40%
Time to Review: 4 - 6 Months
Reviewers Comments: Yes
Invited Articles: 6-10%
Fees to Publish: 0.00 US$

MANUSCRIPT TOPICS:
Higher Education; Professional Development; Teacher Education; Teaching Technique

MANUSCRIPT GUIDELINES/COMMENTS:

College Teaching provides an interdisciplinary forum on issues related to teaching at the undergraduate and graduate levels. This journal is interested in articles that explore: (1) Aims and outcomes of teaching philosophy and practices that have significance beyond a specific discipline. These may include teaching techniques, new classroom procedures, evaluations of innovative programs, and examination of contemporary developments. (2) Teachers' roles, education, professional development, preparation to teach, and evaluation. (3) Incentives that encourage good teaching and ways good teaching is evaluated and rewarded. The editors welcome thoughtful reactions to articles appearing in the journal.

The journal welcomes articles on research in one field as long as it has applications to others as well. However, the journal cannot use: (1) Articles that are purely descriptive without any critical evaluation or analysis. (2) Those that are limited to one specific discipline. (3) Those that show no awareness of current work and literature in the field.

Articles range from 750 to 5,000 words, depending on the nature of the topic. Discussion of promising practices should be short, while articles on research material may be longer. **Commentaries**, of no more than 850 words, will be considered. The journal is refereed. Each article is read by two reviewers, with a total review time of two to three months. Accepted manuscripts usually are published within one year.

Manuscripts must be submitted exclusively to *College Teaching*. We cannot review or publish multiple submissions.

Contributors should submit two hard copies of each manuscript to be considered for publication. In addition, the author should keep an exact copy so the editors can refer to specific pages and lines if a question arises. The manuscript should be double spaced with wide margins of about 1 1/2 inches each.

If the manuscript is accepted, we will send the author directions for sending us a diskette.

The Chicago Manual of Style, 15th ed., University of Chicago Press, 2003, should be used as a style reference in preparation of manuscripts. REFERENCES at the end of the manuscript should be unnumbered and listed alphabetically according to the author's last name, followed by the year of publication, as in Smith, J. 1989. Citation in the text should list author and date, as in (Smith 1989).

Reproductions of figures (graphs and charts) may be submitted for review purposes, but the originals must be supplied if the manuscript is accepted for publication. Tables should be prepared exactly or adapted as they are to appear in the journal. For tables reproduced or adapted from another publication, permission must be obtained by the author and noted on the ms.

Avoid explanatory notes whenever possible by incorporating their content in the text. For essential notes, identify them with consecutive superscripts and list them in a section entitled NOTES at the end of the text.

We reserve the right to make editorial changes in style and format.

Authors receive two complimentary copies of the issue in which their article appears and permission to reproduce additional copies of that article. Reprints are available through the journal.

Send manuscripts to:
COLLEGE TEACHING
Heldref Publications
1319 Eighteenth St., NW
Washington, D.C. 20036-1802

Phone 202-296-6267, ext. 1272
Fax:202-296-5149

Community & Junior College Libraries

ADDRESS FOR SUBMISSION:

Susan Anderson, Editor
Community & Junior College Libraries
St. Petersburg College
PO Box 13489
St. Petersburg, FL 33733
USA
Phone: 727-341-3719
Fax: 727-341-5638
E-Mail: andersons@spcollege.edu
Web:
Address May Change:

PUBLICATION GUIDELINES:

Manuscript Length: 11-15
Copies Required: Two
Computer Submission: Yes Disk, Email
Format: MS Word
Fees to Review: 0.00 US$

Manuscript Style:
   Chicago Manual of Style

CIRCULATION DATA:

Reader: Academics, Administrators,
   Librarians
Frequency of Issue: Quarterly
Copies per Issue: Less than 1,000
Sponsor/Publisher: Haworth Press, Inc.
Subscribe Price: 25.00 US$

REVIEW INFORMATION:

Type of Review: Editorial Review
No. of External Reviewers: 1
No. of In House Reviewers: 0
Acceptance Rate: 80%
Time to Review: 1 - 2 Months
Reviewers Comments: Yes
Invited Articles: 50% +
Fees to Publish: 0.00 US$

MANUSCRIPT TOPICS:
Educational Technology Systems; Information Literacy; Library Management; Library Science/Information Resources

MANUSCRIPT GUIDELINES/COMMENTS:

Community & Junior College Libraries is a refereed journal especially for professionals working in two-year academic and technical libraries, learning or media centers, library training programs, and library organizations. The distinctive, dynamic nature of learning resources centers in two-year colleges is focused on, and the various professional contributions being made by these colleges are highlighted. Contributors to this fundamental resource present profiles of LRCs around the country and address news of special relevance-legislation; systems development, and various concerns faced by professionals in the libraries and information centers of two-year colleges.

Community & Junior College Libraries also features several noteworthy columns that serve to inform readers about the people and the programs making headlines in the profession. The journal contains informative and scholarly sections that will help improve the skills of LRC librarians, such as:

188

- *Nothing But Net* column that describes websites of interest to community college librarians and recommends list servers or internet search engines that may prove useful.
- *Librarian Abroad* column focusing on brief descriptions of two-year libraries and Learning Resource Centers.

Through research and interviews with professionals in the field, *Community & Junior College Libraries* provides a coherent voice for community college librarians. It addresses the need to define and enhance the leading edge of LRC planning and practice in the United States and abroad. Readers receive information on pertinent topics such as the Internet in the LRC, LRC standards, proven policies, conference reports, and networks and consortia. This savvy journal offers comprehensive and authoritative information that will benefit any community or junior college librarian.

Instructions for Authors
1. **Original Articles Only**. Submission of a manuscript to this journal represents a certification on the part of the author(s) that it is an original work, and that neither this manuscript nor a version of it has been published elsewhere nor is being considered for publication elsewhere.

2. **Manuscript Length**. Your manuscript may be approximately 5-50 typed pages double-spaced (including references and abstract). Lengthier manuscripts may be considered, but only at the discretion of the Editor. Sometimes, lengthier manuscripts may be considered if they can be divided up into sections for publication in successive Journal issues.

3. **Manuscript Style**. References, citations, and general style of manuscripts for this Journal should follow the Chicago style (as outlined in the latest edition of the *Manual of Style* of the University of Chicago Press). References should be double-spaced and placed in alphabetical order.

If an author wishes to submit a paper that has been already prepared in another style, he or she may do so. However, if the paper is accepted (with or without reviewer's alterations), the author is fully responsible for retyping the manuscript in the correct style as indicated above. Neither the Editor nor the Publisher is responsible for re-preparing manuscript copy to adhere to the Journal's style.

4. **Manuscript Preparation**.
Margins. leave at least a one-inch margin on all four sides.
Paper. use clean white, 8 1/2 " x 11" bond paper.
Number of Copies. 2 (the original plus one photocopy).
Cover Page. Important--staple a cover page to the manuscript, indicating only the article title (this is used for anonymous refereeing).
Second "Title Page." enclose a regular title page but do not staple it to the manuscript. Include the title again, plus:
- full authorship
- an ABSTRACT of about 100 words. (Below the abstract provide 3-10 key words for index purposes)

- an introductory footnote with authors' academic degrees, professional titles, affiliations, mailing addresses, and any desired acknowledgment of research support or other credit. Manuscripts may be submitted to the editor via e-mail.

5. **Return Envelopes**. When you submit your manuscript copies by mail, also include:

- a 9" x 12" envelope, self-addressed and stamped (with sufficient postage to ensure return of your manuscript);
- a regular envelope, stamped and self-addressed. This is for the Editor to send you an "acknowledgement of receipt" letter.

6. **Spelling, Grammar, and Punctuation**. You are responsible for preparing manuscript copy which is clearly written in acceptable scholarly English, and which contains no errors of spelling, grammar, or punctuation. Neither the Editor nor the Publisher is responsible for correcting errors of spelling and grammar: the manuscript, after acceptance by the Editor, must be immediately ready for typesetting as it is finally submitted by the author(s). Also, check the accuracy of all arithmetic calculations, statistics, numerical data, text citations, and references.

7. **Inconsistencies Must Be Avoided**. Be sure you are consistent in your use of abbreviations, terminology, and in citing references, from one part of your paper to another.

8. **Preparation of Tables, Figures, and Illustrations**. All tables and figures, illustrations, etc. must be "camera-ready". That is, they must be cleanly typed or artistically prepared so that they can be used either exactly as they are or else used after a photographic reduction in size. Figures, tables, and illustrations must be prepared on separate sheets of paper. Always use black ink and professional drawing instruments. On the back of these items, write your article title and the journal title lightly in pencil, so they do not get misplaced. In text, skip extra lines and indicate where these figures and tables are to be placed (please do not write on the face of art). Photographs are considered part of the acceptable manuscript and remain with the publisher for use in additional printings. If submitted art cannot be used, the Publisher reserves the right to redo the art and to charge the author a fee of $35.00 per hour for this service.

9. **Alterations Required By Referees and Reviewers**. Many times a paper is accepted by the Editor contingent upon changes that are mandated by anonymous specialist referees and members of the Editorial Board. If the Editor returns your manuscript for revisions, you are responsible for retyping any sections of the paper to incorporate these revisions (if applicable, revisions should also be put on disk).

10. **Typesetting**. You will not be receiving galley proofs of your article. Editorial revisions, if any, must therefore be made while your article is still in manuscript. The final version of the manuscript will be the version you see published. Typesetter's errors will be corrected by the production staff of The Haworth Press. Authors are expected to submit manuscripts, disks, and art that are free from error.

11. **Electronic Media**. Haworth's in-house typesetting unit is able to utilize your final manuscript material as prepared on most personal computers and word processors. This will

190

minimize typographical errors and decrease overall production timelag. Please send the first draft and final draft copies of you manuscript to the journal Editor in print format for his/her final review and approval.

It is The Haworth Press' policy to follow hard copy. Authors are advised that **No Revisions** of the manuscript can be made after acceptance by the Editor for publication. The benefits of this procedure are many with speed and accuracy being the most obvious. We look forward to working with you on this, knowing we will be able to serve you more efficiently in the future.

12. **Reprints**. The senior author will receive two copies of the journal issue and 25 complimentary reprints of his or her article. The junior author will receive two copies of the journal issue. These are sent several weeks after the journal issue is published and in circulation. An order form for the purchase of additional reprints will also be sent to all authors at this time. (Approximately 4-6 weeks is necessary for the preparation of reprints.) Please do not query the Journal's Editor about reprints. All such questions should be sent directly to The Haworth Press, Inc. Production Department, 21 East Broad Street, West Hazleton, PA 18201 USA. To order additional reprints (minimum: 50 copies), please contact The Haworth Document Delivery Center, 10 Alice Street, Binghamton, NY 13904-1580 USA; 1-800-342-9678 or Fax (607) 722-6362.

13. **Copyright**. Copyright ownership of your manuscript must be transferred officially to The Haworth Press, Inc. before we can begin the peer-review process. The Editor's letter acknowledging receipt of the manuscript will be accompanied by a form fully explaining this. All authors must sign the form and return the original to the Editor as soon as possible. Failure to return the copyright form in a timely fashion will result in delay in review and subsequent publication.

Community College Journal

ADDRESS FOR SUBMISSION:

Cheryl Gamble, Editor
Community College Journal
Amer Association of Community Colleges
One Dupont Circle, Suite 410
Washington, DC 20036
USA
Phone: 202-728-0200 ext 215
Fax: 202-223-9390
E-Mail: cgamble@aacc.nche.edu
Web: www.aacc.nche.edu
Address May Change:

PUBLICATION GUIDELINES:

Manuscript Length: 6-10
Copies Required: One
Computer Submission: Yes Disk, Email
Format: MS Word, Wordperfect, Rich Text
Fees to Review: 0.00 US$

Manuscript Style:
      Chicago Manual of Style

CIRCULATION DATA:

Reader: Administrators
Frequency of Issue: Bi-Monthly
Copies per Issue: 10,001 - 25,000
Sponsor/Publisher: American Association
    of Community Colleges
Subscribe Price: 29.00 US$

REVIEW INFORMATION:

Type of Review: Editorial Review
No. of External Reviewers: 0
No. of In House Reviewers: 2
Acceptance Rate: 21-30%
Time to Review: 2 - 3 Months
Reviewers Comments: No
Invited Articles: 50% +
Fees to Publish: 0.00 US$

MANUSCRIPT TOPICS:
Adult Career & Vocational; Curriculum Studies; Higher Education; Urban Education, Cultural/Non-Traditional

MANUSCRIPT GUIDELINES/COMMENTS:

The *Community College Journal* is published six times yearly, on the first day of every other month: August/September, October/November, December/January, February/March, April/May, and June/July. AACC welcomes *Journal* submissions. All manuscripts, solicited or unsolicited, are subject to review by the editorial board and **may be published or not according to the editors' discretion**. AACC assumes no responsibility for the receipt, return, or publication of unsolicited manuscripts. AACC reserves the right to edit all articles for length, style, and accuracy. All articles published in the *Journal* become the property of AACC.

A. **Topics**
1. Each issue of the *Journal* focuses on a theme. See Section E for 2004-2006 themes and deadlines.

2. Journal articles examine in-depth trends, problems and solutions, innovations, new technologies, and new ideas in higher education. The *Journal* avoids articles on empirical research and favors essays offering an objective look at problems and solutions of contemporary community colleges.

3. Articles should involve community and junior colleges, technical institutes, and independent schools. Issues should be of current interest to presidents, board members, administrators, faculty, and staff at two-year institutions. The *Journal* does not accept articles on K–12 or four-year education and rarely accepts articles about general higher education unless they are germane to the two-year college audience.

4. Book reviews should describe the book's scope, content, arguments, and structure.

5. For a guest editorial, write an opinion piece on a topic of concern to community colleges. The topic should be controversial, not a statement with which everyone obviously agrees. Query the *Journal* editor for topics of interest.

B. Length

1. Features: **1,100 – 1,200 words** on national perspectives, long-term trends, analysis.

2. News in Brief: approximately **200-300 words** on exemplary programs at individual campuses or current news items of pertinence to community colleges. News should be national in scope. Candid, publication-quality photographs required.

3. New in Print: approximately **500-1,000 words**; book reviews should describe the scope, content, basic arguments, and structure of the book.

4. Feedback: (Guest Editorial) **500-1,000 words**; opinion pieces on a topic of concern to community colleges; be controversial.

C. Style

1. *Chicago Manual of Style*. For references, refer to chapter 16 (reference style 2, author-date style).

2. *American Heritage Dictionary*

D. Tips for Writers

1. Add to the current literature or research. Original, even controversial articles are more desirable than well-written pieces on outworn issues. Discuss cutting-edge trends, not programs that have already been implemented on community college campuses.

2. Provide a nuts-and-bolts look at how to implement programs in the real world.

3. Present a national perspective, long-term trends, or analysis.

4. Submit well-written, coherent, and logical articles.

5. Avoid self-promotional articles. The *Journal* does not run public relations pieces for colleges, outside organizations, or companies that provide products or services to colleges. The only exceptions to this rule are paid advertising and house ads.

6. Include appropriate, complete bibliographical references. Articles that contain incomplete citations will be rejected. Do not cite your own previous publications, however. Readers will assume that the ideas are the author's unless otherwise noted. Rewrite the material rather than quote your own previous publications. Articles that are otherwise excellent but do not follow *Chicago Manual of Style* for references may be accepted, but the author will be asked to rewrite the reference section.

7. Include candid, publication-quality photographs illustrating the article. For News in Brief, photographs are required for the article to be considered. Avoid posed photographs, "grip and grin," etc. **All photos must have an accompanying caption identifying its subject**. With feature articles, accompanying charts, graphs and tables are a definite plus. Submitted graphic elements **should not be embedded** in the article copy. Please send graphics as separate electronic files. Consult *Journal* editor first if you wish to send photographs or other art electronically.

E. **Deadlines**
To be considered for publication, manuscripts must be received at least two and a half months before the issue date, **no later than** the following:

Writer's Due Date	Issue Date	Theme
September 6, 2004	December/January 2004-05	Policy
November 8, 2004	February/March 2005	Security
January 17, 2005	April/May 2005	Access in the Balance
March 14, 2005	June/July 2005	Economic & Workforce Dev./Entrepreneurship
May 16, 2005	August/September 2005	Why Community Colleges Work/ Student Success
July 11, 2005	October/November 2005	Technology
September 12, 2005	December/January 2005-06	Access to the Baccalaureate

194

F. Submission
1. Electronic files sent as an e-mail attachment are the preferred method of delivery. Submissions sent by snail mail must include hard copy and electronic file. Microsoft Word for PC platform preferred. Send art by fast, traceable service. Consult the *Journal* editor if you wish to send photographs or other art electronically. Photographs must be high resolution tagged image file format (TIFF) or encapsulated postscript (EPS) file of at least **300 dpi**.

2. Insert a running header in the text that includes filename, article name, your name, date, and page numbers. Double-space text.

3. LABEL ALL DISKS with filename, name of program, and your name.

4. Address for Submissions:
   Cheryl Gamble, Editor
   Community College Journal
   One Dupont Circle, NW, Suite 410
   Washington, DC 20036-1176
   Phone: (202) 728-0200, ext 215
   Fax: (202) 223-9390
   E-mail: **cgamble@aacc.nche.edu**

Community College Journal of Research and Practice

ADDRESS FOR SUBMISSION:

D. Barry Lumsden, Editor
Community College Journal of Research
  and Practice
University of North Texas
College of Education
Box 311337
Denton, TX 76203
USA
Phone: 940-565-4074
Fax: 940-369-711337
E-Mail: lumsden@unt.edu
Web: http://www.tandf.co.uk/journals
Address May Change:

PUBLICATION GUIDELINES:

Manuscript Length: 15-20
Copies Required: Three
Computer Submission: Yes Disk, Email
Format: any and all
Fees to Review: 0.00 US$

Manuscript Style:
  American Psychological Association

CIRCULATION DATA:

Reader: Academics, Administrators,
  Practicing Teachers
Frequency of Issue: 10 Times/Year
Copies per Issue:
Sponsor/Publisher: Higher Education
  Program, University of North Texas /
  Taylor & Francis
Subscribe Price: 150.00 US$ Individual
  557.00 US$ Institution

REVIEW INFORMATION:

Type of Review: Blind Review
No. of External Reviewers: 3
No. of In House Reviewers: 0
Acceptance Rate: 21-30%
Time to Review: 1 - 2 Months
Reviewers Comments: Yes
Invited Articles: 0-5%
Fees to Publish: 0.00 US$

MANUSCRIPT TOPICS:
Adult Career & Vocational; Counseling & Personnel Services; Curriculum Studies; Education Management/Administration; Educational Psychology; Educational Technology Systems; Health & Physical Education; Higher Education; Professional Development; School Law

MANUSCRIPT GUIDELINES/COMMENTS:

Aims and Scope
The only two-year college journal that is international in scope and purpose, *Community College Journal of Research and Practice* is published ten times per volume year. The journal is a multidisciplinary forum for researchers and practitioners in higher education and the behavioral and social sciences. It promotes an increased awareness of community college issues by providing an exchange of ideas, research, and empirically tested educational innovations. The journal is sponsored by the Bill J. Priest Center for Community College Education in association with the Higher Education Program at the University of North Texas.

Readership
Community college educators, curriculum specialists, teachers, counselors, behavioral and social scientists, and researchers studying the broad field of higher education.

INSTRUCTIONS FOR AUTHORS

Note to Authors. Please make sure your contact address information is clearly visible on the **outside** of all packages you are sending to Editors.

Timely reviews of subjects and books of interest to community and junior college administrators, teachers, counselors, researchers, and scholars in the social and behavioral sciences will be considered for publication. Letters to the editor will be published on approval by the editorial board. Announcements of general interest to the journal's readership will also be accepted for publication.

Manuscripts should be concise yet sufficiently detailed to permit critical review. All papers should contain an abstract, which should not exceed 250 words. Manuscripts should conclude with a section on Implications for Practice stating what the implications of the research findings are to practitioners in the field and including any recommendations for change indicated by the research results.

Submission of Manuscripts
Original and two copies of each manuscript should be submitted to the editor. Authors are strongly encouraged to submit manuscripts on disk. The disk should be prepared using MS Word or WordPerfect and should be clearly labeled with the authors' names, file name, and software program.

All parts of the manuscript should be typewritten, double-spaced, with margins of at least one inch on all sides. Number manuscript pages consecutively throughout the paper. The length must not exceed 20 pages. All titles should be as brief as possible, 6 to 12 words. Authors should also supply a short-ended version of the title suitable for the running head, not exceeding 50 character spaces. Each article should be summarized in an abstract of not more that 100 words. Avoid abbreviations, diagrams, and reference to the text.

All papers, including figures, tables, and references, must conform to the specifications described in the *Publication Manual of the American Psychological Association* (4th ed., 1994). Any papers that do not adhere to this style will be returned for revision. Copies of the *Manual* can be obtained from the Publication Department of the American Psychological Association, 750 First Street, N.E., Washington, D.C. 20002-4242. Phone: (202) 336-5500.

Each manuscript must be accompanied by a statement that it has not been published elsewhere and that it has not been submitted simultaneously for publication elsewhere. Authors are responsible for obtaining permission to reproduce copyrighted material from other sources and are required to sign an agreement for the transfer of copyright to the publisher. All accepted manuscripts, artwork, and photographs become the property of the publisher.

A Microsoft Word author template file, which also includes more detailed instructions in its "**Read Me**" file, can be downloaded from the website.

Tables and Figures

Tables and figures should not be embedded in the text, but should be included as separate sheets or files. A short descriptive title should appear above each table with a clear legend, and any footnotes suitably identified below. All units must be included. Figures should be completely labeled, taking into account necessary size reduction. Captions should be typed, double spaced, on a separate sheet. All original figures should be clearly marked in pencil on the reverse side with the number, author's name, and top edge indicated.

Illustrations

Illustrations submitted (line drawings, halftones, photos, photomicrographs, etc.) should be clean originals or digital files. Digital files are recommended for highest quality reproduction and should follow these guidelines:

- 300 dpi or higher
- sized to fit on journal page
- EPS, TIFF, or PSD format only
- submitted as separate files, not embedded in text files

Four-color illustrations will be considered for publication; however, the author will be required to bear the full cost involved in their printing and publication. The charge for the first figure is $1,200. Subsequent figures, totaling no more than 4 text pages, are $500.00 each. Good quality color prints should be provided, in their final size. Figures needing reduction or enlargement will be charged an additional 25 percent. The publisher has the right to refuse publication of color prints deemed unacceptable.

Reprints

The corresponding author of each article will receive one complete copy of the issue in which the article appears. Reprints of an individual article may be ordered from Taylor & Francis. Use the reprint order form included with the page proofs.

Community College Review

ADDRESS FOR SUBMISSION:

George Vaughan, Editor
Community College Review
North Carolina State University
Dept. of Adult & Community College Edu.
Box 7801
Raleigh, NC 27695-7801
USA
Phone: 919-515-6248
Fax: 919-515-4039
E-Mail: nicolle_leney@ncsu.edu
Web: See Guidelines
Address May Change:

PUBLICATION GUIDELINES:

Manuscript Length: 12-20
Copies Required: Three
Computer Submission: No
Format:
Fees to Review: 0.00 US$

Manuscript Style:
    American Psychological Association

CIRCULATION DATA:

Reader: Academics
Frequency of Issue: Quarterly
Copies per Issue: 1,001 - 2,000
Sponsor/Publisher: University
Subscribe Price: 90.00 US$ US
    45.00 US$ Student
    92.00 US$ Canada / $94.00 US$
    Foreign

REVIEW INFORMATION:

Type of Review: Blind Review
No. of External Reviewers: 2
No. of In House Reviewers: 3
Acceptance Rate: 21-30%
Time to Review: 1 - 2 Months
Reviewers Comments: Yes
Invited Articles: 0-5%
Fees to Publish: 0.00 US$

MANUSCRIPT TOPICS:
Adult Career & Vocational; Bilingual/E.S.L.; Educational Technology Systems; Scheduling; Serving Unique Popluations w/the Community College; Tests, Measurement & Evaluation; Transfer & Articulation

MANUSCRIPT GUIDELINES/COMMENTS:

Nicolle Leney, Managing Editor (address, phone, fax, email same as above.) The *Community College Review* (circulation 1,000), a quarterly academic journal dedicated to community college education, publishes manuscripts from scholars and practitioners who would like to present their research and experiences in community college education to readers. One way to become familiar with the kinds of articles published in the *Review* is to study recent issues.

As a fully refereed journal, the *Review* relies on a nine-member editorial board composed of community college educators and scholars to evaluate manuscripts. Submissions to the *Review's* editorial office are reviewed initially by the editorial staff. The staff assigns those manuscripts that meet style and topic guidelines to at least two reviewers for evaluation.

Reviewers include members of the editorial board and researchers who are interested in the topic being presented.

Decisions to publish a manuscript are based on the reviewers recommendations. Exceptions to this policy occasionally are made for manuscripts based on personal experiences or opinion rather than on research or literature reviews.

The editor selects such essays for publication, and they are designated as editor's selections when they are published.

Content
The *Review's* readers include a broad national audience of community college presidents, administrators, and faculty, as well as university faculty and graduate students involved in community college education. Thus, the most important criteria for evaluating a manuscript are the timeliness and relevance of its topic for community colleges in general.

Most manuscripts accepted for publication describe original qualitative or quantitative research that involves community colleges. Essays that combine authors' personal experiences with their knowledge of the existing literature on specific topics or issues constitute a small percentage of accepted submissions.

Authors of acceptable research reports document design and methodology before presenting results and conclusions. They interpret findings in the context of existing theory and research, and they discuss implications for community colleges in general as part of the manuscript's conclusion.

Style
The *Review's* editorial staff generally uses the most recent edition of the *Publication Manual of the American Psychological Association* as a style guide. The following brief instructions summarize some basic guidelines.

Provide three copies of the manuscript for evaluation. Limit manuscripts to 20 typed (double-spaced) pages with one-inch margins, indented paragraphs, and pages clearly numbered.

Include a cover page that lists the manuscript's title along with each author's name, position, affiliation, complete mailing address, email address and phone number below it. A second page should bear the title of the manuscript only with an abstract of approximately 50 words.

Do not use footnotes. Cite material from other sources in the text, and list the sources in a reference list at the end of the manuscript. Citations within the text should be in parentheses with the last name(s) of the author(s) cited and the publication year. Citations for quotations and statistics must include page numbers (for example, Jones, 1987, pp. 2-4).

Alphabetize the reference list of cited sources by authors' last names according to American Psychological Association style. Entries for journals and edited volumes should include article or chapter page numbers, and entries for edited anthologies should include editors' names.

Declined manuscripts will be returned if stamped, self-addressed envelopes are enclosed with submissions. Requests for detailed guidelines for submitting manuscripts and questions about what is required should be directed to the managing editor at the following location:

Community College Review
ced.ncsu.edu/ace/ccr/ccreview.htm
Telephone (919) 515-6248
Box 7801
N. C. State University
Raleigh, NC 27695-7801
Facsimile (919) 515-4039
Telephone (919) 515-6248
Email **Nicolle_Leney@ncsu.edu**

Computers and Composition

ADDRESS FOR SUBMISSION:

G. Hawisher and C. Selfe, Co-Editors
Computers and Composition
Michigan Technological University
Humanities Department
1400 Townsend Drive
Houghton, MI 49931-1295
USA
Phone: 217-333-3251
Fax:
E-Mail: candc@mtu.edu
Web: http://www.elsevier.com
Address May Change:

PUBLICATION GUIDELINES:

Manuscript Length: 11-30
Copies Required: Five
Computer Submission: No
Format:
Fees to Review: 0.00 US$

Manuscript Style:
American Psychological Association

CIRCULATION DATA:

Reader: Practicing Teachers, Academics
Frequency of Issue: Quarterly
Copies per Issue: No Reply
Sponsor/Publisher: Elsevier Science
Publishing Company
Subscribe Price: 72.00 US$ Individual
296.00 US$ Institution

REVIEW INFORMATION:

Type of Review: Blind Review
No. of External Reviewers: 3
No. of In House Reviewers: 3
Acceptance Rate: 30%
Time to Review: 3 Months
Reviewers Comments: Yes
Invited Articles: Occasional
Fees to Publish: 0.00 US$

MANUSCRIPT TOPICS:
Higher Education; Languages & Linguistics; Tests, Measurement & Evaluation; Writing

MANUSCRIPT GUIDELINES/COMMENTS:

Topics Include
Information Technologies and New Media as they relate to the impact they are making on writing, teaching, academics, and everyday lives

Guidelines for Submission
Manuscript Preparation. Submissions should be between 15 and 30 pages in length, typed, double-spaced, on 8-1/2 x 11 inch paper with 1 inch margins on all sides and include a 200-word abstract, 5-10 relevant key words, and a short (50-100 words) biography statement.

Manuscript Submission. Five copies of the manuscript, accompanied by a cover letter that includes the author's (or authors') name, affiliation, postal address, e-mail address, and home and office phone numbers, should be submitted to Cynthia L. Selfe, Humanities Department, Michigan Technological University, 1400 Townsend Drive, Houghton, MI 49931-1295.

Style. The style guidelines of the most recent edition of the Publication Manual of the American Psychological Association (4th ed., 1994) should be followed, especially for reference lists and text citation of sources, with the following exception. Authors must provide first names and middle names or initials for authors in references (see **References** below).

Review. Since manuscripts are submitted for blind review, all identifying information must be removed from the body of the paper.

Tables and Figures. Tables and figures should be completely understandable, independent of the text. Each table and figure must be mentioned in the text, given a title, and consecutively numbered with Arabic numerals. Authors must provide good-quality originals of all figures to be directly reproduced for publication. Originals must be legible after reduction to a maximum size of 5 inches wide by 8 inches high. Graphs and charts must be professionally prepared and may be submitted as original black ink drawings or as sharp black and white photographic reproductions. Color originals, which will be published in black and white, are discouraged.

Notes. Notes should be used sparingly and indicated by consecutive numbers in the text. Acknowledgments, grant numbers, or other credits should be given as a separate footnote.

References. All sources cited in the text must be included alphabetically in the reference list, and all reference items must appear in text. *Computers and Composition* varies from the APA style by including first names in all references. Below are examples of entries.

Flinn, Jane Zeni & Madigan, Chris (1989). The gateway writing project: Staff development and computers in St. Louis. In Cynthia L. Selfe, Dawn Rodrigues & William R. Oates (Eds.) *Computers in English and the language arts: The challenge of teacher education* (pp. 55-68). Urbana, IL: National Council of Teachers of English.

McDaid, John. (1990, March). *The shape of texts to come: Response and the ecology of hypertext.* Paper presented at the convention of the Conference on College Composition and Communication, Chicago, IL.

Strenski, Ellen. (1995). Electronic tutor training with a local e-mail LISTSERV discussion group. *Computers and Composition, 12,* 246-256.

Guyer, Carolyn & Petry, Martha (1991) IZME PASS [Computer program] Boston: Eastgate Systems.

Permissions. Copies of any letters granting permission to reproduce illustrations, tables, or lengthy quoted passages should be included with the manuscript.

Copyright. Your acceptance copyright must be assigned to Elsevier Science Inc. The author will supply a Macintosh or IBM compatible disk, spell checked and stripped of all embedded graphics. Graphics should be saved as separate files in postscript (.ps), encapsulated postscript (.eps), or tagged image file (.tif) format.

Author Enquiries. Authors can also keep a track on the progress of their accepted article, and set up e-mail alerts informing them of changes to their manuscript's status, by using the "Track a Paper" feature of Elsevier's Author Gateway

Offprints: Each lead author will receive 25 free offprints.

Contemporary Educational Psychology

ADDRESS FOR SUBMISSION:

Patricia Alexander, Editor
Contemporary Educational Psychology
University of Maryland
Dept. of Human Development
Benjamin Bldg
College Park, MD 20742
USA
Phone: 301-405-6493 or 301-405-2821
Fax: 301-405-2891
E-Mail: palexand@umd.edu
Web: www.elsevier.com/locate/yceps
Address May Change:

PUBLICATION GUIDELINES:

Manuscript Length: 30+
Copies Required: Four + 1 Disk Copy
Computer Submission: No
Format: MSWord or WordPerfect
Fees to Review: 0.00 US$

Manuscript Style:
American Psychological Association

CIRCULATION DATA:

Reader: Academics
Frequency of Issue: Quarterly
Copies per Issue: 2,001 - 3,000
Sponsor/Publisher: Elsevier
Subscribe Price: 243.00 US$ Individual
525.00 US$ Institution
114.00 US$ Student

REVIEW INFORMATION:

Type of Review: Blind Review
No. of External Reviewers: 3
No. of In House Reviewers: 0
Acceptance Rate: 11-15%
Time to Review: 2 - 3 Months
Reviewers Comments: Yes
Invited Articles: 0-5%
Fees to Publish: 0.00 US$

MANUSCRIPT TOPICS:
Bilingual/E.S.L.; Educational Psychology; Gifted Children; Languages & Linguistics;
Reading; Science Math & Environment; Social Studies/Social Science; Special Education;
Tests, Measurement & Evaluation

MANUSCRIPT GUIDELINES/COMMENTS:

Contemporary Educational Psychology publishes articles that involve the application of
psychological theory and science to the educational process. Of particular relevance are
descriptions of, research reviews of, and the presentation of theory designed to either explicate
or enhance the educational process. The journal publishes quantitative, qualitative, and single-
subject design studies that involve the application of psychological science to an important
educational process, issue, or problem.

The journal does not limit its scope to any age range. Articles dealing with the education of
preschoolers, K-12 children, adults, and the elderly are all relevant if they apply psychological
theory and science to the process of education. Likewise, articles that make a substantial
contribution to the understanding of individual differences in the process of learning are also

appropriate. The journal does not focus on a particular educational setting. Articles applying psychological theory and research methods in school settings, industry, or other formal or informal settings involving adults or children are relevant, assuming they are judged in the review process to advance the science of education.

Submission of Manuscripts

Manuscripts must be written in English and should be submitted in quadruplicate along with an electronic copy of the manuscript prepared as a Word or Rich Text File (RTF) on a computer disk to:

Contemporary Educational Psychology
Patricia Alexander, Editor
University of Maryland
Department of Human Development
Benjamin Building
College Park, MD 20742-1131, USA

The Editor can also be reached at:
Patricia Alexander
Telephone (301)405-2821
Fax: (301)405-2891
E-mail: **pa34@umail.umd.edu**

Manuscripts are accepted for review with the understanding that the same work has not been and is not currently submitted elsewhere, and that it will not be submitted elsewhere prior to the journal's making an editorial decision. At the time of submission, authors must notify the Editor if any part of the data on which their article depends has been published elsewhere. Moreover, it must be the case that submission of the article for publication has been approved by all of the authors and by the institution where the work was carried out; further, that any person cited as a source of personal communications has approved such citation. Written authorization may be required at the Editor's discretion. Articles and an other material published in Contemporary Educational Psychology represent the opinions of the author(s) and should not be construed to reflect the opinions of the Editor or the Publisher.

Upon acceptance of an article, authors will be asked to transfer copyright (for more information on copyright, see http://authors.elsevier.com). This transfer will ensure the widest possible dissemination of information. A letter will be sent to the corresponding author confirming receipt of the manuscript. A form facilitating transfer of copyright will be provided after acceptance.

If excerpts from other copyrighted works are included, the author(s) must obtain written permission from the copyright owners and credit the source(s) in the article. Elsevier has preprinted forms for use by authors in these cases: contact Elsevier Global Rights Department, P.O. Box 800, Oxford OX5 1DX, UK; phone: (+44) 1865 843830, fax: (+44) 1865 853333, e-mail: permissions@elsevier.com.

Electronic Transmission of Accepted Manuscripts. Authors are requested to transmit the text and art of the manuscript in electronic form via either computer disk or e-mail, after all revisions have been incorporated and the manuscript has been accepted for publication. Submission as an e-mail attachment is acceptable provided that all files are included in a single archive the size of which does not exceed 2 megabytes (**pa34@umail.umd.edu**). Hardcopy printouts of the manuscript and art must also be supplied. The manuscript will be edited according to the style of the journal, and authors must read the proofs carefully.

Type of Articles That *CEP* Publishes
The journal publishes three types of articles: Research Studies, Brief Research Reports, and Reviews.

Research Studies report a quantitative, qualitative, or single-subject design study. Articles that contain multiple studies are seen as particularly desirable contributions. For quantitative studies, authors should report effect sizes. Methods for calculating and interpreting effect sizes are presented in *Contemporary Educational Psychology* in Volume 25 (Number 3) on pages 241-286.*Brief Research Reports* are relatively short articles that provide a needed replication of a previous research effort or that extend the boundaries of earlier research. Brief Research Reports are initially submitted as full Research Studies and identified as Brief Research Reports during the review process.

Review Articles are primarily based on other published work and include reviews of existing literature, methodological reviews of research in a particular area, or theoretical presentations that advance or clarify psychological theory or science as it applies to education.

Preparation of the Manuscript
Manuscripts should be prepared on 8.5 x 11-inch or A4 white paper, using double spacing throughout. Authors are requested to follow the instructions given in the most recent edition of the *Publication Manual of the American Psychological Association*. Four copies of the manuscript should be submitted; each copy must include all figures and tables. Each page of the manuscript should be numbered consecutively.

The title page (p. 1) should contain the article title, authors' names and complete affiliations, footnotes to the title, and the address for manuscript correspondence (including e-mail address and telephone and fax numbers).

The second page (p. 2) should contain only the article title and footnotes to the title. These items should be placed in the same position as they were on the title page.

The abstract (p. 3) must be a single paragraph that summarizes the main findings of the paper in less than 150 words. After the abstract a list of up to 10 keywords that will be useful for indexing or searching should be included.

References in the text should be cited by author's surname and the year of publication, e.g., Hum (1994); Hum et al. (1993); Hum and St. Clair (1993, p. 128) (for references to a specific page); Hum & St. Clair (1993) (ampersand for references in parentheses). If more than one paper was published by the same author in a given year, the correct style is Smith (1985a) and

Smith (1985b). References cited in the text should be listed alphabetically and typed double-spaced at the end of the article. Journal titles should be written out in full according to the form followed in the most recent edition of the *Publication Manual of the American Psychological Association*. Personal communications should be cited as such in the text and should not be included in the reference list. Please note the following examples:

Gagne, R. M., & Driscoll, M. P. (1988). *Essentials of learning for instruction*. Englewood Cliffs, NJ: Prentice-Hall.

Griffin, M. M., & Griffin, B. W. (1995, April). *An investigation of the effects of reciprocal peer tutoring on achievement, self-efficacy, and test anxiety*. Paper presented at the Annual Meeting of the National Consortium for Instruction and Cognition, San Francisco, CA.

Kulhavy, R. W., Schwartz, N. H., & Peterson, S. (1986). Working memory: The encoding process. In G. D. Phye & T. Andre (Eds.), *Cognitive classroom learning: Understanding, thinking, and problem solving* (pp. 115-140). Orlando, FL: Academic Press.

Zeidner, M., & Schleyer, E. J. (1999). The big-fish-little-pond effect for academic self-concept, test anxiety, and school grades in gifted children. *Contemporary Educational Psychology*, 24, 305-329.

Figures should be in a finished form suitable for publication. Number figures consecutively with Arabic numerals, and indicate the top and the authors on the back of each figure. Lettering on drawings should be professional quality or generated by high-resolution computer graphics and must be large enough to withstand appropriate reduction for publication. Please visit our Web site at http://authors.elsevier.com/artwork for detailed instructions on preparing electronic artwork.

If, together with your accepted article, you submit usable color figures, then Elsevier will ensure, at no additional charge, that these figures will appear in color on the Web (e.g., ScienceDirect and other sites) regardless of whether these illustrations are reproduced in color in the printed version. For color reproduction in print, you will receive information regarding the costs from Elsevier after receipt of your accepted article. For further information on the preparation of electronic artwork, please see http://authors.elsevier.com/artwork.

Please note: Because of technical complications that can arise in converting color figures to "gray scale" (for the printed version should you not opt for color in print), please submit in addition usable black-and-white prints corresponding to all the color illustrations.

Tables should be numbered consecutively with Arabic numerals in order of appearance in the text. Type each table double-spaced on a separate page with a short descriptive title typed directly above and with essential footnotes below. Authors should submit complex tables as camera-ready copy.

Preparation of Supplementary Material
Elsevier now accepts electronic supplementary material to support and enhance your scientific research. Supplementary files offer additional possibilities for publishing supporting applications, movies, animation sequences, high-resolution images, background datasets, sound clips, and more. Supplementary files supplied will be published online alongside the electronic version of your article in Elsevier Web products, including ScienceDirect (http://www.sciencedirect.com). To ensure that your submitted material is directly usable, please provide the data in one of our recommended file formats. Authors should submit the material in electronic format together with the article and supply a concise and descriptive caption for each file. Please note, however, that supplementary material will not appear in the printed journal. Files can be stored on 3?-inch diskette, ZIP disk, or CD (either MS-DOS or Macintosh). For more detailed instructions, please visit our Author Gateway at http://authors.elsevier.com, click on "Artwork instructions," and then click on "Multimedia files."

Proofs
PDF proofs will be sent by e-mail to the corresponding author. To avoid delay in publication, only necessary changes should be made, and corrections should be returned promptly. Authors will be charged for alterations that exceed 10% of the total cost of composition.

Reprints
Twenty-five reprints will be provided to the corresponding author free of charge. Additional reprints may be ordered. A reprint order form will accompany your proofs.

Author Inquiries
For inquiries relating to the submission of articles (including electronic submission where available) please visit the Elsevier Author Gateway at http://authors.elsevier.com. The Author Gateway also provides the facility to track accepted articles and set up e-mail alerts to inform you of when an article's status has changed, as well as detailed artwork guidelines, copyright information, frequently asked questions, and more. Contact details for questions arising after acceptance of an article, especially those relating to proofs, are provided after registration of an article for publication.

Continuing Higher Education Review

ADDRESS FOR SUBMISSION:

Wayne Ishikawa, Associate Editor
Continuing Higher Education Review
Harvard University
Division of Continuing Education
51 Brattle Street
Cambridge, MA 02138-3722
USA
Phone: 617-495-2478
Fax: 617-496-2680
E-Mail: ishikawa@hudce.harvard.edu
Web:
Address May Change:

PUBLICATION GUIDELINES:

Manuscript Length: 6-10 1500 Words
Copies Required: One
Computer Submission: Yes
Format: MSWord 6.0+
Fees to Review: 0.00 US$

Manuscript Style:
    See Manuscript Guidelines

CIRCULATION DATA:

Reader: Academics, Administrators
Frequency of Issue: 1 Time/Year
Copies per Issue: 2,001 - 3,000
Sponsor/Publisher: Professional Association
    & University
Subscribe Price: 27.00 US$
    35.00 US$ Foreign

REVIEW INFORMATION:

Type of Review: Internal
No. of External Reviewers: No Reply
No. of In House Reviewers: 2
Acceptance Rate: 50%
Time to Review: 1 - 2 Months
Reviewers Comments: Yes
Invited Articles: 90%
Fees to Publish: 0.00 US$

MANUSCRIPT TOPICS:
Higher Education

MANUSCRIPT GUIDELINES/COMMENTS:

Continuing Higher Education Review (ISSN 0893-0384) Published once a year by Harvard University, in affiliation with the University Continuing Education Association (UCEA). Michael Shinagel, Editor.

Guidelines for contributors: The *Continuing Higher Education Review,* a journal that supports the mission of the University Continuing Education Association (UCEA), is intended for leaders in higher education nationally and internationally as well as continuing education professionals. The *Review* solicits articles for publication and also considers non-solicited articles and notes to ensure a broad range of essays on topics of relevance to the profession. Editorial criteria include the article's relevance to issues of national and international importance in continuing education, its potential for stimulating the readership to engage not only in further scholarly discourse but also in meaningful institutional action, and its substantive content and clarity of exposition. Solicited articles will contain 4,000–6,000

210
words. Other articles will range from 1,500–4,000 words. Notes will generally not exceed 1,500 words. In all cases, manuscripts must conform to the style guidelines contained in the latest edition of the *Chicago Manual of Style*. A hard copy of the manuscript should be sent to Michael Shinagel, Editor, Continuing Higher Education Review, 51 Brattle Street, Cambridge, MA 02138-3722; an electronic version can be sent to **ishikawa@hudce.harvard.edu**. All submitted articles will be acknowledged upon receipt of the manuscript, and every effort will be made to ensure timely review. Once a decision has been reached, a notification will be sent out immediately.

Continuous Improvement Monitor

ADDRESS FOR SUBMISSION:

J.R. Llanes, Editor
Continuous Improvement Monitor
University of Texas Pan American
SEND ALL SUBMISSIONS VIA EMAIL
SEE EMAIL BELOW
1201 West University Drive-EDC125
Edinburg, TX 78539-2999
USA
Phone: 956-381-3415
Fax: 956-381-2927
E-Mail: llanes@panam.edu
Web: llanes.panam.edu/journal/cim1
Address May Change: 9/1/2006

PUBLICATION GUIDELINES:

Manuscript Length: 26-30
Copies Required: No Paper Copy Required
Computer Submission: Yes Email
Format: MSWord Attachment Only
Fees to Review: 0.00 US$

Manuscript Style:
    American Psychological Association,
    Chicago Manual of Style, Salamca Style

CIRCULATION DATA:

Reader: Academics, Administrators,
    Business Managers
Frequency of Issue: Continuosly
Copies per Issue: Exclusively Online
Sponsor/Publisher: University of Texas-Pan
    American
Subscribe Price: 0.00 US$ Online

REVIEW INFORMATION:

Type of Review: Blind Review
No. of External Reviewers: 3
No. of In House Reviewers: 1
Acceptance Rate: 11-20%
Time to Review: 1 Month or Less
Reviewers Comments: Yes
Invited Articles: 11-20%
Fees to Publish: 0.00 US$

MANUSCRIPT TOPICS:
Education Management/Administration; Higher Education

MANUSCRIPT GUIDELINES/COMMENTS:

General Information
Contributions are solicited world-wide from scholars and practitioners of educational quality improvement for the current Edition of the International Journal: *Continuous Improvement Monitor*, which is published continuously, as articles are reviewed and approved for publication

The *Continuous Improvement Monitor* is a peer-reviewed, electronic journal published by the Department of Educational Leadership at the University of Texas Pan American

The Journal is interested in research, theory and analysis of practice. It is mainly interested in restructuring of public education, reorganization of schools and school curricula, school-reform networks and their effectiveness, and the transformation of educational institutions to quality systems at the K-12 and Post-secondary levels.

Quality improvement systems are better known in industry and global trade, but hundreds of applications have been noted in K-16 education. It is the vision of the Journal to help educators and those involved in human services understand the dynamics of quality systems within their own practice, and it will be the mission of the Journal to act as a communications link between research and experiences with quality systems in global organizations and educational institutions, educational researchers and educators worldwide.

Journal Objectives
1. To serve as a Forum for exchange of opinion, information, theses, research findings, and qualitative or quantitative analysis of quality in education, such as:
- Quality Standards in education
- Restructuring and reform of public education
- Leadership of school-based teams
- Management of Change

2. To relate the new findings and the fresh understandings of quality in education to what has been previously attempted and to draw parallels between quality efforts in business and industry to those being attempted in public-sector agencies.

3. To serve as a source of impartial research-based data on school reform programs, projects and practices.

Article Submission Process
Before submitting an article for publication, the author is encouraged to contact the Journal's Managing Editor via e-mail or regular mail, or fax and to submit a one-page outline of the article's main idea.

We accept articles continuously and send them to editors for review without regard as to which may be published first. The speed of the individual editors and our own internal editorial process would determine in which issue your article will appear. In order to speed up the process articles must be submitted in Microsoft Word format, or as part of an e-mail format, or as a text file in ASCII format or as an html file and addressed to: **llanes@panam.edu**.

Peer-Review Process
Articles will be received by the Managing Editor and if they meet the Journal's criteria will be forwarded anonymously to at least three reviewers (Associate Editors) whose educational background, experiences, research and/or training has enabled them to evaluate the significance, adequacy and completeness of scholarly contributions to the field. A current list of the Associate Editors may be found at http://llanes.panam.edu/journal/aeinfo . Please do not contact Associate Editors directly regarding your article. All reviews must remain anonymous or be judged invalid.

Features and Limitations

There's no page limit for the articles, but in every case, the author will be asked to complete a one-page summary.

Because the articles will be available through the World Wide Web, the publishers have added a feature, which will enable the Journal reader to access the full text (or the relevant portion) of the references used by the authors in the article. A hyperlink is made between each citation and either the full text of the article quoted, or the relevant portion of that article or book, will be stored in our server and made available to the reader. In order to enable us to include this feature, and after the article has been approved for publication, authors should submit scanned or camera-ready copies of the references cited. We will obtain necessary permission to post the article in the Web from the copyright holder.

We will also furnish to the readers, the back-up data authors utilize in the articles. If the author's article is based upon a database which was collected by the author(s), the publishers would like to make the database available to readers who may want to replicate the study. We will accept these data in any widely used spreadsheet or statistical program, such as SPSS, Excel, 1-2-3, or any other similar program. The Web server will make available these data via a hyperlink to the writer's text.

The above features will enable the Journal to be more useful to scholars in small institutions lacking reference materials, to researchers in foreign universities who may not subscribe to U.S. journals, and to of those wanting a more thorough reading of your contribution.

Editorial Policy

The current Editorial Policy is very inclusive, and the following guidelines are only suggestive. The journal will publish mainly two types of articles:

Scholarly articles in either *APA*, *Chicago* or *MLA* format which may be based upon research studies, meta-analysis of research and/or evaluation data, qualitative review of programs in place, theoretical pieces on quality systems, and program descriptions of quality systems. These may also be historical articles on the evolution of school management theories, humanistic assessments of quality systems, reviews of literature on quality or quality systems, or theoretical analyses of quality programs or philosophies. We have accepted several opinion pieces by recognized experts in their fields and also welcome future submission in this area.

The Journal will also publish Program Reviews which involve an in-depth analysis of a school reform or quality improvement program which promises to improve the quality of instruction in K-16. These program reviews should be in a specific format which is available upon request from the Managing Editor. There are 60 School Reform Networks nationwide which qualify for Program Review. A list of those Networks is contained here. If you are interested in preparing a review of one of these, please contact the Managing Editor, via e-mail, via fax or phone.

News and Comments. From time to time we will also publish a Reader's Forum, which will consist of items contributed by readers and likely to be of interest to other readers,

214

commentaries on previous articles, and whatever happens to be in the minds of our readers. Your contributions are solicited.

Deadlines
We accept articles on a continuous basis and publish (electronically) as soon as the editorial team concludes its review, usually 60 days after original submission if there are no major corrections to be made.

Electronic Journal editions are available on the World Wide Web as soon as they are edited and placed on-line. As a result, we can publish your article 9-12 months before it can appear in any paper-bound edition.
- Volume 1 Number 1 January –December 1996
- Volume 1 Number 2 January - December 1997
- Volume 1 Number 3 January - December 1998
- Volume 1 Number 4 January - December 1999
- Volume 2 Number 1 January - December 2000

Article Review Process
Articles may be reviewed in three categories
1. accepted for publication as is
2. accepted with changes
3. rejected.

If accepted as is, the article will be published in the current edition immediately. If the article is accepted with changes, the author will be informed and formal changes requested. The author then has 30 days to resubmit the article. Resubmissions are sent back to the reviewers for comments and approval.

Advantages of Publishing in Our Journal
Fast. We expect that most articles will be reviewed and if approved be ready for publishing within 60 days.

Peer-Review. To support the author, our team of associate editors, a multi-national group (8 countries), collaborate to improve the quality of each article submitted.

Widely Distributed. The Journal's web pages have been accessed by over 200,000 visitors in the past four years. The current number of accesses is contained in the Journal's Home Page. You may link your author's name with your own web page or an e-mail feature which allows feedback. If there's something in the article for which you require feedback, we would flag that section inviting comments from readers and often our authors get them.

International Scope. The 200,000 visitors come from over 65 countries and our contributions come from 19 countries. Our ability to serve reference material makes us 1) a truly accessible source of information in other nations where US reference materials are not as common as in the United States and 2) cross-disciplinary, insofar as no technical expertise in one or another of the disciplines of quality is required to read and understand our articles. We are listed and abstracted in web servers in Spanish, Japanese, Dutch and German.

Flexible Copyrights. The Journal accepts for electronic publication articles which have been previously published in hardbound journals (particularly those of limited --less than 1,000-- distribution), providing the subject of the article meets the guidelines for significance and the author holds intellectual property rights. The Journal also grants the author the right to republish in other journals or magazines. For additional information you may contact:

J. R. Llanes Ph. D.Professor, University of Texas Pan American 1201 West University Drive - EDC 125 Edinburg, Texas 78539-2999 Phone: (956) 381-3415 Fax: (956) 381-2927 e-mail: **llanes@panam.edu** World Wide Web: **http://llanes.panam.edu**

Counseling and Values

ADDRESS FOR SUBMISSION:

Christopher Sink, Editor
Counseling and Values
Seattle Pacific University
School of Education
Dept. of School Counseling & Psychology
3307 3rd Avenue West
Seattle, WA 98119
USA
Phone: 206-281-2453
Fax: 206-281-2756
E-Mail: csink@spu.edu
Web:
Address May Change:

PUBLICATION GUIDELINES:

Manuscript Length: 10-20
Copies Required: Three
Computer Submission: No
Format: N/A
Fees to Review: 0.00 US$

Manuscript Style:
American Psychological Association

CIRCULATION DATA:

Reader: Academics, Counselors
Frequency of Issue: 3 Times/Year
Copies per Issue: 2,300
Sponsor/Publisher: Professional Association
Subscribe Price: 41.00 US$ Individual
50.00 US$ Institution

REVIEW INFORMATION:

Type of Review: Blind Review
No. of External Reviewers: 2
No. of In House Reviewers: 0
Acceptance Rate: 15-20%
Time to Review: 2 - 3 Months
Reviewers Comments: Yes
Invited Articles: 0-5%
Fees to Publish: 0.00 US$

MANUSCRIPT TOPICS:
Adult Career & Vocational; Counseling & Personnel Services; Religious Education; Social Studies/Social Science

MANUSCRIPT GUIDELINES/COMMENTS:

Topics Include. Spiritual, Ethical, Religious and Values Issues as these relate to Counseling, Counseling Theory and Counselor Preparation

The Association for Spiritual, Ethical and Religious Values in Counseling (ASERVIC) is one of 17 divisions of the American Counseling Association. Originally the National Catholic Guidance Conference, ASERVIC was chartered in 1974. ASERVIC is devoted to professionals who believe that spiritual, ethical, religious, and other human values are essential to the full development of the person and to the discipline of counseling.

To Contact ASERVIC: ASERVIC, A Division of the American Counseling Association, 5999 Stevenson Avenue, Alexandria, VA 22304-3300, 1-800-347-6647.

ASERVIC's Journal is *Counseling and Values.*

Counseling and Values is a professional journal of theory, research and informed opinion concerned with relationships among counseling, ethics, philosophy, psychology, religion, personal and social values and spirituality. *Counseling and Values'* mission is to promote free intellectual inquiry across these domains. Its vision is to attract a diverse readership reflective of a growing diversity in the membership of ASERVIC and to effect change leading to the continuing growth and development of a more genuinely civil society. *Counseling and Values* welcomes theoretical, philosophical, empirical or methodological manuscripts dealing with significant moral, ethical, religious, spiritual and values issues as these relate to counseling and related mental health work. Manuscripts must be submitted in triplicate along with a disk in Word or via email with the editor's prior consent.

Journal Editor
Christopher Sink, Ph.D., LMHC, Professor and Chair; Department of School Counseling, School of Education, Seattle Pacific University; 3307 3rd Ave West, Seattle, WA 98119; Phone: 206 281-2453 (W), Fax: 206 281-2756; Email: **csink@spu.edu**

Guidelines for Authors
Articles
Manuscripts should be well organized and concise so that the development of ideas is clear. Avoid dull, clichéd writing and use of jargon.

- Authors are required to submit a disk of the current revised copy in MS Word.
- Provide an abstract of the article of approximately 100 words. Do not use footnotes. Most footnote material can be incorporated into the body of the manuscript.
- Manuscripts are typically between 10 and 20 pages, typewritten, and double spaced. This does not include title page, abstract, and references.
- Double space all material, including direct quotations and references.
- Authors' names, positions, and places of employment should appear only on the title page. Authors' names should not appear on the manuscript.
- Manuscript style is that of the fifth edition of the *Publication Manual of the American Psychological Association* (available from APA, 750 First St. N.E., Washington, DC 20002-4242). All items cited in articles should be listed as references. Reference notes are not used. Provide page numbers for direct quotations.
- Authors should not submit more than three tables or two figures with each manuscript. Include only essential data and combine tables where possible. Tables should be typed on separate pages. Figures (graphs, illustrations, line drawings) should be supplied as camera-ready art (prepared by a commercial artist). Figure captions should be attached to the art and will be set in the appropriate type.
- Authors should reduce bias in language against persons on the basis of gender, sexual orientation, racial or ethnic group, disability, or age by referring to the guidelines in the fifth edition of the *APA Publication Manual.*
- Manuscripts must be submitted in the original and two clear copies. If you wish to have your manuscript returned, you must include a stamped, self-addressed envelope.

- Never submit material for concurrent consideration by another periodical. Manuscripts that meet the guidelines and are appropriate for the focus of the journal are ordinarily submitted to a blind review by the Editorial Board members. Two or 3 months may elapse between acknowledgment of receipt of a manuscript and notification of its disposition. After publication of an article, each author receives a copy of the journal.

Forum

- *Forum* articles will be published in concert with preannounced special topic(s) subject headings. Please consult ACA's newspaper *Counseling Today* for special topic(s) to be addressed in future issues.
- Reactions to editorials, articles, and other *Forum* subjects will be considered for publication in this section as space is available. The editor reserves the right to edit and abridge responses published as reactions to original articles.
- All other guidelines for articles apply to *Forum*.

Issues and Insights

- Philosophical and practical applications of first person narratives that are written in accordance with *APA Publication Manual* standards for publication will be featured.
- Manuscripts must be clearly referenced and represent an author's attempt to offer fresh information.
- "New" counseling interventions and accompanying "techniques that work" will be considered for publication in this section.
- All other guidelines for articles apply *to Issues and Insights*.

Send all manuscripts and correspondence to: Christopher Sink, Ph.D., LMHC, Professor and Chair, Department of School Counseling, School of Education, Seattle Pacific University, 3307 3rd Ave West, Seattle, WA 98119, Phone: 206 281-2453 (W), FAX: 206 281-2756, Email: **csink@spu.edu**

Counselor Education and Supervision

ADDRESS FOR SUBMISSION:

William B. Kline, Editor
Counselor Education and Supervision
Ohio University, College of Education
Dept. of Counseling & Higher Education
ELECTRONIC SUBMISSION
McCracken Hall, Room 201
Athens, OH 45701-2979
USA
Phone: 740-593-0115
Fax: 740-593-0477
E-Mail: ces@ohio.edu
Web: www.ohiou.edu/che/ces
Address May Change:

PUBLICATION GUIDELINES:

Manuscript Length: 24 Max
Copies Required: One
Computer Submission: Yes
Format: MSWord, rtf format
Fees to Review: 0.00 US$

Manuscript Style:
American Psychological Association

CIRCULATION DATA:

Reader: Academics
Frequency of Issue: Quarterly
Copies per Issue: 3,000
Sponsor/Publisher: ACA Publications
Subscribe Price: 50.00 US$ Members
    70.00 US$ Nonmembers

REVIEW INFORMATION:

Type of Review: Blind Review
No. of External Reviewers: 33
No. of In House Reviewers: 1
Acceptance Rate: 8.5%
Time to Review: 3-5 Months
Reviewers Comments: Yes
Invited Articles: 0-5%
Fees to Publish: 0.00 US$

MANUSCRIPT TOPICS:
Counseling & Personnel Services; Education Management/Administration

MANUSCRIPT GUIDELINES/COMMENTS:

Topics Include
Research, theory development, or program applications related to counselor education and supervision. Preparation and supervision of counselors in agency or school settings, in colleges and universities, or at local, state, or federal level.

Counselor Education and Supervision is dedicated to publishing manuscripts concerned with research, theory development, or program applications related to counselor education and supervision. The journal is concerned with the preparation and supervision of counselors in agency or school settings, in colleges and universities, or at local, state, or federal levels.

Manuscripts are acknowledged on receipt by the Editor, who then sends them out for review. The journal uses an anonymous review procedure. Final decisions regarding publication are made by the Editor. Generally, authors can expect a decision regarding a manuscript within 3 to 5 months of the acknowledgment of receipt.

Following are guidelines for developing and submitting a manuscript. Manuscripts that do not conform to these guidelines will be returned to the author without review.

Manuscript Categories

1. *Counselor Preparation*. Research and theory articles on counseling curriculum and counselor training.

2. *Supervision*. Research and theory articles on counseling supervision.

3. *Professional Development*. Research articles and position papers related to ongoing professional development for counselors by counselor educators and supervisors.

4. *Current Issues*. Research articles and position papers relevant to counselor education and supervision. Relevant areas include diversity, accreditation, licensure, counselor function, supervision issues, and other timely topics.

5. *Innovative Methods*. Clearly delineated and substantiated descriptions of new methods, ideas, and innovations in counselor education and supervision. Manuscripts must include a review of the literature establishing a basis for the methods, a description of the methods including the context in which the methods are used, and a qualitative or quantitative evaluation of the method.

6. *Comments*. A section of carefully composed brief comments on articles recently appearing in the journal.

Manuscript Requirements

1. Manuscripts are not to exceed 24 pages total, including all references, tables, etc. Manuscripts should include a 50-100 word abstract. All manuscripts are to be double-spaced including references and extensive quotes. Allow 1" margins on all sides.

2. Manuscript files should be submitted in Microsoft Word or WordPerfect for Windows. We do not accept Macintosh formats. For re-submissions only, please combine the cover letter and manuscript into one complete file, which is prepared for blind review. Files must be submitted in a 12-point Times Roman Font.

3. Use the *Publication Manual for the American Psychological Association* (5th edition) as a manual for style and manuscript format, including style for all figures, tables, and references. Figures that are not camera-ready will be returned to the author and may cause a delay in publication. Authors bear responsibility for the accuracy of references tables and figures.

4. Authors are encouraged to use guidelines to reduce bias in language against persons based on gender, sexual orientation, racial or ethnic group, disability, or age by referring to the fifth edition of the *Publication Manual for the American Psychological Association*.

5. Do not submit previously published or in press material or a manuscript that is under consideration for publication in another periodical.

6. Lengthy quotations (300-500 words) require written permission from the copyright holder for reproduction. Adaptation of tables and figures also requires reproduction approval. It is the author's responsibility to secure such permission. A copy of the publisher's permission must be provided to the journal Editor immediately on acceptance of the article for publication.

7. Submission Procedures: Submit your manuscript and cover by email attachment. Please be sure the manuscript is prepared for blind review. Send your manuscript to **ces@ohio.edu**. All tables and figures must be included and properly formatted within the electronic file (i.e., they will not be accepted separately). For additional information regarding submission requirements, please refer to our website: **http://www.ohio.edu/che/ces**

Creativity Research Journal

ADDRESS FOR SUBMISSION:

Mark A. Runco, Editor
Creativity Research Journal
California State University
EC 105
Calif State Univ
PO Box 6868
Fullerton, CA 92834
USA
Phone: 714-278-3376
Fax: 714-278-3314
E-Mail: runco@exchange.fullerton.edu
Web: www.erlbaum.com
Address May Change:

PUBLICATION GUIDELINES:

Manuscript Length: 15-40
Copies Required: Five
Computer Submission: Yes
Format: See Guidelines
Fees to Review: 0.00 US$

Manuscript Style:
American Psychological Association

CIRCULATION DATA:

Reader: Academics, Organizational, social,
and experimental psychologists
Frequency of Issue: Quarterly
Copies per Issue: 1,001 - 2,000
Sponsor/Publisher: Lawrence Erlbaum
Associates
Subscribe Price: 55.00 US$ Individual
260.00 US$ Institution
49.50 US$ / 234.00 US$ for Electronic

REVIEW INFORMATION:

Type of Review: Blind Review
No. of External Reviewers: 2
No. of In House Reviewers: 2
Acceptance Rate: 11-20%
Time to Review: 2 - 3 Months
Reviewers Comments: Yes
Invited Articles: 6-10%
Fees to Publish: 0.00 US$

MANUSCRIPT TOPICS:
Art/Music; Creativitiy, High Achievement; Educational Psychology; Educational Technology Systems; Gifted Children; Special Education; Tests, Measurement & Evaluation

MANUSCRIPT GUIDELINES/COMMENTS:

Topics Include. Behavioral, clinical, cognitive, developmental, educational historical, personality, or psychometric research on Creativity and related topics (e.g., Innovation, Originality, the Arts, Aesthetics, Entrepreneurship, Problem solving, Brainstorming, Giftedness).

Editorial Scope
This well-established journal publishes high quality, scholarly research capturing the full range of approaches to the study of creativity – behavioral, clinical, cognitive, cross-cultural, developmental, educational, genetic, organizational, psychoanalytic, psychometric, and social. Interdisciplinary research is also published, as is research within specific domains such as art and science, as well as on critical issues such as aesthetics, genius, imagery, imagination,

incubation, insight, intuition, metaphor, play, and problem finding and solving. Integrative literature reviews and theoretical pieces that appreciate empirical work are welcome, but purely speculative articles will not be published.

Audience. Behavioral, clinical, cognitive, developmental, and educational psychologists, and others interested in the study of creativity.

Instructions to Contributors
Manuscript Preparation. Prepare manuscripts according to the Publication Manual of the *American Psychological Association* (5th ed., 1994; American Psychological Association, P.O. Box 2710, Hyattsville, MD 20784), especially with regard to reference lists and text citations. Follow "Guidelines to Reduce Bias in Language" (APA Manual, pp. 46-60). Report exact probabilities (e.g., $p = .03$) and effect sizes. Using 8½ x 11-in. non-smear paper and 1-in. margins, type all components double-spaced and in the following order: title page (p. 1), abstract (p. 2), text (including quotations), references, appendices, footnotes, tables, and figure captions. On page 1, type article title, author name(s) and affiliation(s), running head (abbreviated title, no more than 45 characters and spaces), author notes and acknowledgments, submission date (month, day, and year on original manuscript and on any revisions), and name and address of the person to whom requests for reprints should be addressed; on page 2, type an abstract of 150 to 200 words. Indent all paragraphs. Use footnotes sparingly. Attach photocopies of all figures. Number all manuscript pages (including photocopies of figures). Cover Letter, Permissions, Credit Lines.

In a cover letter, include the contact author's complete mailing address, e-mail address, and telephone and fax numbers. State that the manuscript includes only original material that has not been published and that is not under review for publication elsewhere. Authors are responsible for all statements made in their work and for obtaining permission to reprint or adapt a copyrighted table or figure or to quote at length from a copyrighted work. Authors should write to original author(s) and original publisher to see if permission is required and to request nonexclusive world rights in all languages to use the material in the current article and in future editions. Include copies of all permissions and credit lines with the manuscript. (See p. 140 of the APA Manual for samples of credit lines.)

Manuscript Submission. Prepare manuscript on a word processor and submit five (5) high quality printouts to the Editor, Mark A. Runco, EC 105, Calif State Univ, PO Box 6868, Fullerton, CA 92834, USA. E-mail: **runco@exchange.fullerton.edu**. Manuscripts are not returned. Accepted Manuscripts and Computer Disk Submission: After manuscripts are accepted, authors are asked to sign and return copyright-transfer agreements and submit uniquely labeled, highly legible, camera-ready figures (use Times Roman font for text appearing in figures). It is the responsibility of the contact author to ascertain that all co-authors approve the accepted manuscript and concur with its publication in the journal. Submit a disk containing two files: word-processor and ASCII versions of the manuscript. File content must match the printed manuscript exactly, or there will be a delay in publication. Disks are not returned. Production Notes: Files are copyedited and typeset into page proofs. Authors read proofs to correct errors and answer editors' queries. Authors may order reprints at that time.

CUPA-HR Journal

ADDRESS FOR SUBMISSION:

Missy King, Editor
CUPA-HR Journal
CUPA-HR
Tyson Place
2607 Kingston Pike, Suite 250
Knoxville, TN 37919
USA
Phone: 865-637-7673
Fax: 865-637-7674
E-Mail: communications@cupahr.org
Web: www.cupahr.org
Address May Change:

PUBLICATION GUIDELINES:

Manuscript Length: 1,500 - 3,500 Words
Copies Required: One
Computer Submission: Yes Prefer E-mail
Format: MS Word
Fees to Review: 0.00 US$

Manuscript Style:
See Manuscript Guidelines

CIRCULATION DATA:

Reader: , Higher Education HR
Professionals
Frequency of Issue: 2 Times/Year
Copies per Issue: 2,500
Sponsor/Publisher: College and University
Professional Association for Human
Resources
Subscribe Price: 75.00 US$ Nonmember
40.00 US$ Member
20.00 US$ Single Issue

REVIEW INFORMATION:

Type of Review: Peer Review
No. of External Reviewers: 3+
No. of In House Reviewers: 2
Acceptance Rate: 70%
Time to Review: 4 - 6 Months
Reviewers Comments: Yes
Invited Articles: 20%
Fees to Publish: 0.00 US$

MANUSCRIPT TOPICS:
Higher Education; Higher Education Human Resources

MANUSCRIPT GUIDELINES/COMMENTS:

Two types of articles are of interest to our readers. The first type of article is on an HR topic from a practical approach. This kind of how-to article describes an innovative program that has been put in place at a member institution and that could be implemented on other campuses as well. Senior practitioners in HR management are encouraged to submit articles of this nature. The second type of article presents information or observations of universal importance to higher education HR professionals. Rather than focusing on a practice at a particular university, this type of article addresses a recently emerging trend in human resource management; a technical area in need of clarification, such as immigration law; or an issue that just won't go away, such as sexual harassment or merit pay. This type of article is written by experts in a particular area of HR management or by attorneys, compensation specialists, and the like.

All articles should be double-spaced and all pages should be numbered consecutively. Paragraphs should be indented 1/2 inch and should not be separated from other paragraphs by an extra line space. Major subheads should be initial capped, boldfaced, and flush left (that is, unindented). Subheads between major subheads should be initial capped, boldfaced and italicized, and flush left. Tables and figures should be typed on separate pages and presented at the end of the manuscript. They should be numbered consecutively as they appear in the text. Their positions in the manuscript should be indicated-for example, Table 1, Table 2, Figure 1, Figure 2. Footnotes should not be used. The *Journal* now uses the author-date reference system, which is described in Chapter 16 of *The Chicago Manual of Style*, 14th edition. This system has two parts: the text citation (which appears parenthetically just before the period at the end of a sentence and which consists of the author's last name followed by the year of publication) and the reference list (which appears at the end of the article and which contains the full bibliographic citation for each source referred to in the main text of the article).

Please send articles as a Word attachment via e-mail to **communications@cupahr.org**. Include all author names, professional titles, addresses (including e-mail addresses), and telephone numbers on the cover page. Also include a brief, one-paragraph biography of all authors on a separate page. Include current title, place of employment, academic degrees, and the names of institutions conferring them.

Decision Sciences Journal of Innovative Education

ADDRESS FOR SUBMISSION:

Barbara B. Flynn, Editor
Decision Sciences Journal of Innovative
    Education
Wake Forest University
Babcock Graduate School of Management
PO Box 7659, Reynolda Station
Winston-Salem, NC 27109-7659
USA
Phone: 336-758-3672
Fax: 336-758-4514
E-Mail: barb.flynn@mba.wfu.edu
Web: http://www.mba.wfu.edu/dsjie/
Address May Change: 12/31/2006

PUBLICATION GUIDELINES:

Manuscript Length: 26-30
Copies Required: Five
Computer Submission: Yes Disk, Email
Format:
Fees to Review: 0.00 US$

Manuscript Style:
    See Manuscript Guidelines

CIRCULATION DATA:

Reader: Academics, Professors,
    Researchers
Frequency of Issue: 2 Times/Year
Copies per Issue: 3,001 - 4,000
Sponsor/Publisher: Decision Sciences
    Institute
Subscribe Price: 85.00 US$ Members
    281.00 US$ US Libraries
    374.00 US$ International Libraries

REVIEW INFORMATION:

Type of Review: Blind Review
No. of External Reviewers: 2
No. of In House Reviewers: 0
Acceptance Rate: 21-30%
Time to Review: 2 - 3 Months
Reviewers Comments: Yes
Invited Articles: 0-5%
Fees to Publish: 0.00 US$

MANUSCRIPT TOPICS:
Education Management/Administration; Educational Psychology; Educational Technology
Systems; Higher Education; Tests, Measurement & Evaluation

MANUSCRIPT GUIDELINES/COMMENTS:

The Decision Sciences Journal of Innovative Education is a peer-reviewed journal published
by the Decision Sciences Institute. Its mission is to publish significant research relevant to
teaching and learning issues in the decision sciences. The decision sciences is the union of the
quantitative and behavioral approaches to managerial decision making, encompassing all of
the functional areas of business, including (but not limited to) accounting, business strategy
and entrepreneurship, economics, finance, international business and globalization, marketing,
MIS/DSS and computer systems, organizational behavior/organizational design, operations
and logistics management, quantitative methods and statistics.

Types of articles suitable for publication in the *Decision Sciences Journal of Innovative
Education* include the following:

Empirical Research Articles
An empirical research article describes high quality empirical research related to innovative education in the decision sciences. It should begin with an in-depth review of the literature and development of hypotheses, drawing upon theory in the functional area to support details of the innovative approach, as well as upon the educational and psychological theory, to support the intended learning effects of the innovation. The hypotheses will typically refer to the effect of the innovation, in terms of measures of student learning, measures of course effectiveness, etc. Empirical research articles should include a description of the innovative approach and its rationale, a description of the methodology used for gathering data to test the effectiveness of the approach, description of the statistical analysis of the data, and a discussion of the findings, including suggestions for readers who would like to implement the approach in their classroom.

Case Study Research Articles
A case study research article describes high quality research related to innovative education in the decision sciences that employs a class as a case. This approach allows in-depth study of a single class or several classes and is based on careful and detailed documentation of the use and impact of an educational innovation in the decision sciences. The multiple case study, which contains detailed information on several classes or several sections of a class, is preferred. In analyzing the data, similarities and differences between the classes should be noted and documented, to the extent possible. The following article provides a good guide to case study research:

Eisenhardt, K.M. "Building Theories from Case Study Research." Academy of Management Review, vol. 14., no 4, 1989, 532-550.

A case study research article should begin with an in-depth review of the literature, drawing upon theory in the functional area to support details of the innovative approach, as well as upon the educational and psychological theory to support the intended learning effects of the innovation. It should include a structured approach for analyzing the data and should lead to a set of propositions providing a foundation for future research. Either quantitative or qualitative analysis of the data may be appropriate. A case study research article should include a description of the innovative approach and a description of the cases (classes), highlighting their similarities and differences. Tables should be used to present summaries of the quantitative or qualitative comparisons. It should also include a thorough discussion of the findings, including suggestions for readers who would like to implement the innovative approach in their classrooms.

A good example of a case study research article is provided by McLahlin, Ron, "Management Initiatives and Just-in-Time Manufacturing." *Journal of Operations Management*, vol. 15, no 4 (1997), 271-292., although it doesn't deal with teaching or learning issues.

The *Decision Sciences Journal of Innovative Education* does not publish case studies designed for classroom use.

Conceptual/Theoretical Articles
A conceptual article describes an approach to innovative education or a learning issue relevant to the decision sciences. A conceptual article should be strongly grounded in the relevant theoretical literature in functional areas such as education, organization behavior or psychology, as well as in the literature specific to the innovative approach or learning issue being described. It may focus on a single approach or issue, or it may be based on a comparison and contrast of alternative approaches or issues. Because it should lay the groundwork for future research in the area, a conceptual/theoretical article should develop a set of propositions about the effectiveness of the innovative approach or learning issue. It is important that conceptual/theoretical research articles focus on cutting-edge topics and present significant new insight.

Teaching Briefs
Teaching briefs *briefly* describe an innovative approach for teaching in the decision sciences. Limited to five double-spaced pages (12-pt. font) of text, it should describe the innovative approach in sufficient detail so that it could be replicated in the reader's classroom. It should also provide a brief summary of evidence of the effectiveness of the innovative approach. Teaching briefs should focus on the innovative approach itself, and do not need to include a literature review or statistical analysis of the data. They should have more of a "how to" flavor than the empirical or case study research articles. Teaching briefs may refer readers to the authors' website for additional detail about how to use the innovative approach.

Submission
Five copies of the manuscript should be submitted to:

Professor Barbara B. Flynn, Editor
Decision Sciences Journal of Innovative Education
Wake Forest University
Babcock Graduate School of Management
P.O. Box 7659, Reynolda Station
3102 Worrell Professional Center
Winston-Salem, North Carolina 27109-7659
336 758-3672, fax 336 758-4514
Email: **barb.flynn@mba.wfu.edu**

Your submission certifies that none of the contents are copyrighted, published or accepted for publication by another journal, under review by another journal or submitted to another journal while under review by *Decision Sciences Journal of Innovative Education*. All manuscripts should be printed in Times Roman (12 pt), double-spaced on 8 ½ x 11 paper and accompanied by an abstract of not more than 180 words (except for teaching briefs, which do not require an abstract) and an author's vita of no more than 150 words. The author's name and affiliation should appear on a separate page.

Figures, charts and tables should be consecutively numbered in Arabic. *Decision Sciences Journal of Innovative Education* does not allow the use of footnotes or endnotes. References should be listed alphabetically by author at the end of the paper and referred to in the body of the text by Name (date).

Should the manuscript be accepted for publication, the author will be asked to submit a copy on a disk containing the final post-review version of the paper. The word processing file (or ASCII text file) will be used in the typesetting process.

Authors will be required to assign copyright in their paper to the Decision Sciences Institute. Copyright assignment is a condition of publication, and papers will not be passed to the publisher for production unless copyright has been assigned. (Papers subject to government or Crown copyright are exempt from this requirement). To assist authors, an appropriate copyright form will be supplied by the editorial office.

Website-http://www.mba.wfu.edu/dsjie/
The *Decision Sciences Journal of Innovative Education* website contains abstracts of all empirical research, case study research and conceptual/theoretical articles, as well as teaching briefs in their entirety. It also contains information for contributors and a site where authors can check on the status of articles in process. The website also contains announcements about upcoming events related to innovative education in the decision sciences and a section for personal news about DSI members, such as news about winners of teaching awards. Please send your news to the Editor, at the address listed above.

Review Process
Each manuscript submitted to the *Decision Sciences Journal of Innovative Education* is subjected to the following reviewing process:

1. An initial screening by the Editor to determine the suitability of the article for the journal. Suitable articles are assigned to two or three referees, according to their functional and methodological content. If the manuscript is deemed inappropriate for the journal because it is not a match for the *Decision Sciences Journal of Innovative Education's* audience or mission, it will be promptly returned to the author.
2. A careful review by the referees, each of whom makes a recommendation to the Editor and provides comments for authors.
3. An appraisal of the reviews by the Editor. If the Editor feels the paper has potential for publication, the author is invited to make revisions, following the suggestions of the reviewers.
4. Upon receipt of the revisions, the Editor will make a final decision. The Editor will appraise the entire review process, making sure that all revisions suggested by the referees have been addressed.

The Editor reserves the right to deviate from the above procedures when the situation warrants and as it is deemed appropriate.

Delta Pi Epsilon Journal

ADDRESS FOR SUBMISSION:

Nancy Groneman, Editor
Delta Pi Epsilon Journal
EmporiaState University
1200 Commercial
Emporia, KS 66801
USA
Phone: 620-341-5415
Fax: 620-341-6345
E-Mail: groneman@emporia.edu
Web:
Address May Change: 1/31/2006

PUBLICATION GUIDELINES:

Manuscript Length: 21-25
Copies Required: Five
Computer Submission: Yes Disk, Email
Format: MS Word
Fees to Review: 0.00 US$

Manuscript Style:
   American Psychological Association

CIRCULATION DATA:

Reader: Academics, Practicing Teachers
Frequency of Issue: Quarterly
Copies per Issue: 4,001 - 5,000
Sponsor/Publisher: Delta Pi Epsilon
Subscribe Price:

REVIEW INFORMATION:

Type of Review: Blind Review
No. of External Reviewers: 3
No. of In House Reviewers: 1
Acceptance Rate: 21-30%
Time to Review: 2 - 3 Months
Reviewers Comments: Yes
Invited Articles: 11-20%
Fees to Publish: 0.00 US$

MANUSCRIPT TOPICS:
Business Teacher Education; Higher Education; Teacher Education

MANUSCRIPT GUIDELINES/COMMENTS:

The Delta Pi Epsilon Journal publishes articles that build the knowledge base for both business and education and that relay ways the two reinforce each other. Articles reporting sound quantitative or qualitative research are selected for publication.

Manuscript reviews for this refereed publication occur on a continual basis, so you are welcome to submit them at any time.

All manuscripts must:
1. Be research based and contain actual research data to support findings and conclusions.
2. Be reliable, generalizable, and adequate.
3. Be sufficiently well written to require minimal editing and revision.
4. Be 2,000 to 5,000 words in length.

Specific Procedures for Preparing a Manuscript for *The Delta Pi Epsilon Journal*

a. Use the *Publication Manual for the American Psychological Association*, 5th Edition, to prepare the manuscript. Obtain this manual at most bookstores, or order it from the American Psychological Association, 1200 Seventeenth Street, N.W., Washington, DC 20036.

b. Include a title page *and* abstract (maximum 150 words) with the manuscript.

c. Include a brief biographical statement for each author. Include titles (e.g., Dr., Mr., Mrs., Ms., or Miss); full names; position titles; phone numbers; places of employment; and cities, states, and zip codes. If appropriate, include an acknowledgment statement for agencies that assisted with authorship or research funding.

d. Conclude research manuscripts with a section that elaborates on the findings and how they contribute to the body of knowledge in the area being investigated. Also, provide recommendations for further research that would build upon and complement this study.

e. Send *FIVE* copies of the manuscript, including the title page and abstract to the editor:
Dr. Nancy J. Groneman, Editor
The Delta Pi Epsilon Journal
310 Cremer Hall
Emporia State University
Emporia, KS 66801
Phone: (620) 341-5415 E-mail: **groneman@emporia.edu**

Developmental Review

ADDRESS FOR SUBMISSION:

C.J. Brainerd, Editor
Developmental Review
University ofTexas
Department of Psychology
Life Sciences Building
Arlington, TX 76019
USA
Phone:
Fax:
E-Mail: brainerd@uta.edu
Web: www.apnet.com
Address May Change:

PUBLICATION GUIDELINES:

Manuscript Length: 30+
Copies Required: Four
Computer Submission: No
Format: N/A
Fees to Review: 0.00 US$

Manuscript Style:
American Psychological Association

CIRCULATION DATA:

Reader: Academics
Frequency of Issue: Quarterly
Copies per Issue: 5,001 - 10,000
Sponsor/Publisher: Academic Press, Inc.
Subscribe Price:
80.00 US$ IDEAL/Deep Discount
320.00 US$ All Countries/Institutional

REVIEW INFORMATION:

Type of Review: Editorial Review
No. of External Reviewers: 3
No. of In House Reviewers: 1
Acceptance Rate: 11-20%
Time to Review: 2 - 3 Months
Reviewers Comments: Yes
Invited Articles: 11-20%
Fees to Publish: 0.00 US$

MANUSCRIPT TOPICS:
Developmental Psychology; Educational Psychology

MANUSCRIPT GUIDELINES/COMMENTS:

Description
Presenting research that bears on important conceptual issues in developmental psychology, Developmental Review: Perspectives in Behavior and Cognition provides child and developmental, child clinical, and educational psychologists with authoritative articles that reflect current thinking and cover significant scientific developments. The journal emphasizes human developmental processes and gives particular attention to issues relevant to child developmental psychology. The research concerns issues with important implications for the fields of pediatrics, psychiatry, and education, and increases the understanding of socialization processes.

Features
- Analyses of method and design
- Analyses of social policy as it affects human development

- Essays on major books
- Historical analyses
- Integrated collections of papers on a single theme
- Provocative empirical findings of particular importance for developmental theory
- Reviews of the literature
- Summaries of programmatic research
- Theoretical statements

Guide for Authors

Developmental Review (DR), an international and interdisciplinary journal, publishes original articles that bear on conceptual issues in psychological development. Appropriate papers include (1) theoretical statements, (2) reviews of literature, (3) summaries of programmatic research, (4) empirical findings that are provocative and of particular relevance for developmental theory, (5) integrated collections of papers on a single theme, (6) analyses of social policy as it affects human development, (7) historical analyses, (8) essays on major books, and (9) analyses of method and design. Discussions and commentaries are welcomed. Subject matter may be from the disciplines of psychology, sociology, education, or pediatrics, may be basic or applied, and may be drawn from any species or age range as long as it speaks to issues of psychological development.

Submission of Manuscripts

Manuscripts must be written in English. We strongly encourage authors to transmit an electronic version of their manuscript each time a new version of the manuscript is submitted. Initial submissions should be formatted as Microsoft Word or PDF files. Submitting an electronic manuscript will expedite the review process and facilitate communication among authors, reviewers, and editors. Submission as an e-mail attachment is acceptable provided that all files are included in a single archive the size of which does not exceed 2 megabytes. Authors should include in their electronic submission a cover letter and all ancillary materials. Electronic submissions should be sent to **brainerd@u.arizona.edu**. If an electronic version is not available, three complete copies of the manuscript, including three sets of good-quality figures, should be submitted to:

Developmental Review
C.J. Brainerd, Editor
Department Psychology
Life Sciences Building
University of Texas
Arlington, TX 76019, USA
E-mail: **brainerd@uta.edu**

There are no submission fees or page charges. Each manuscript should be accompanied by a letter outlining the basic findings of the paper and their significance.

Original papers only will be considered. Manuscripts are accepted for review with the understanding that the same work has not been and is not currently submitted elsewhere, and that it will not be submitted elsewhere prior to the journal making an editorial decision.

234

Moreover, submission of the article for publication has been approved by all of the authors and by the institution where the work was carried out, and any person cited as a source of personal communications has approved such citation. Written authorization may be required at the Editor's discretion. Articles and any other material published in Developmental Review represent the opinions of the author(s) and should not be construed to reflect the opinions of the Editor(s) and the Publisher.

Manuscripts fitting the objectives of *Developmental Review* will ordinarily be submitted to at least two reviewers for comments. Authors are invited to suggest potential reviewers with the understanding that present or former students or collaborators should not be suggested and that these recommendations are subject to the Editor's discretion. Authors wishing blind review should specifically request it and should remove identifying material from the abstract and the body of the manuscript. Persons interested in organizing a thematic collection of papers, submitting a book review, or preparing a commentary on previously published material are invited to make a preliminary inquiry to the Editor.

Upon acceptance of an article, authors will be asked to transfer copyright (for more information on copyright, see http://authors.elsevier.com). This transfer will ensure the widest possible dissemination of information. A letter will be sent to the corresponding author confirming receipt of the manuscript. A form facilitating transfer of copyright will be provided.

If excerpts or material from other copyrighted works are included, the author(s) must obtain written permission from the copyright owners and credit the source(s) in the article. Elsevier has preprinted forms for use by authors in these cases: contact Elsevier Global Rights Department, P.O. Box 800, Oxford OX5 1DX, UK; phone: (+44) 1865 843830, fax: (+44) 1865 853333, e-mail: permissions@elsevier.com.

Preparation of Manuscript
Manuscripts should be double-spaced throughout. Authors are requested to follow the instructions given in the most recent edition of the *Publication Manual of the American Psychological Association*. Pages should be numbered consecutively and organized as follows:

The *title page* (p. 1) should contain the article title, authors' names and complete affiliations, footnotes to the title, and the address for manuscript correspondence (including e-mail address and telephone and fax numbers).
The *abstract* (p. 2) must be a single paragraph that summarizes the main findings of the paper in less than 150 words. After the abstract a list of up to 10 keywords that will be useful for indexing or searching should be included.

The *Introduction* should be as concise as possible, without subheadings.

Materials and methods should be sufficiently detailed to enable the experiments to be reproduced.

Results and *Discussion* may be combined and may be organized into subheadings.

Acknowledgments should be brief.

References. Literature references in the text should be cited by author's surname and the year of publication, e.g., Smith (1980); Smith et al. (1981); Smith and Jones (1982, p. 250) (for references to a specific page); (Smith & Jones, 1983) (ampersand for references in parentheses). If a reference has more than two authors, the citation includes the surnames of all authors at the first mention, but later citations of the same reference include only the surname of the first author and the abbreviation "et al." Suffixes a, b, etc., should be used following the date to distinguish two or more works by the same author(s) in the same year, e.g., Smith (1984a, 1984b). References cited in the text should be listed alphabetically and type double-spaced at the end of the article. Journal titles should be written out in full. Personal communication should be cited as such in the text and should not be included in the reference list. Please note the following examples:

Cohen, J. (1977). Statistical power analysis for the behavioral sciences. New York: Academic Press.

Treiman, R., & Baron, J. (1981). Segmental analysis ability: Development and relation to reading ability. In G. Waller & T. MacKinnon (Eds.), Reading research: Advances in theory and practice (Vol. 3, pp. 159-198). New York: Academic Press.

Waterman, A.S. (1999). Issues of identity formation revisited: United States and The Netherlands. Developmental Review, 19, 462-479.

Figures. Number figures consecutively with Arabic numeral. Please visit our Web site at http://authors.elsevier.com/artwork for detailed instruction on preparing electronic artwork.

Free color on the Web. If, together with your accepted article, you submit usable color figures, then Elsevier will ensure, at no additional charge, that these figures will appear in color on the Web (e.g., ScienceDirect and other sites) regardless of whether these illustrations are reproduced in color in the printed version. For color reproduction in print, you will receive information regarding the costs from Elsevier after receipt of your accepted article.

Please note: Because of technical complications that can arise in converting color figures to "gray scale" (for the printed version should you not opt for color in print), please submit in addition usable black-and-white files corresponding to all the color illustrations.
Tables should be numbered consecutively with Arabic numerals in order of appearance in the text. Type each table double-spaced on a separate page with a short descriptive title typed directly above and with essential footnotes below.

Preparation of Supplementary Material
Elsevier now accepts electronic supplementary material to support and enhance your scientific research. Supplementary files offer additional possibilities for publishing supporting applications, movies, animation sequences, high-resolution images, background datasets, sound clips, and more. Supplementary files supplied will be published online alongside the electronic version of your article in Elsevier Web products, including ScienceDirect

236

(http://www.sciencedirect.com). To ensure that your submitted material is directly usable, please provide the data in one of our recommended file formats. Authors should submit the material in electronic format together with the article and supply a concise and descriptive caption for each file. Please note, however, that supplementary material will not appear in the printed journal. Files can be stored on 3.5-inch diskette, ZIP disk, or CD (either MS-DOS or Macintosh). For more detailed instructions, please visit our Author Gateway at http://authors.elsevier.com, click on "Artwork instructions," and then click on "Multimedia files."

Proofs
PDF proofs will be sent by e-mail to the corresponding author. To avoid delay in publication, only necessary changes should be made, and corrections should be returned promptly. Authors will be charged for alterations that exceed 10% of the total cost of composition.

Reprints
Twenty-five reprints will be provided to the corresponding author free of charge. Additional reprints may be ordered. A reprint order form will accompany your proofs.

Economics of Education Review

ADDRESS FOR SUBMISSION:

Elchanan Cohn, Editor
Economics of Education Review
University of South Carolina
The Moore School of Business
Department of Economics
Columbia, SC 29208
USA
Phone: 803-777-2714
Fax: 803-777-6876
E-Mail: feu00004@moore.sc.edu
Web: www.elsevier.nl/inca/publications
Address May Change:

PUBLICATION GUIDELINES:

Manuscript Length: Reasonable
Copies Required: One
Computer Submission: Yes
Format: Word on CD
Fees to Review: 0.00 US$

Manuscript Style:
See Manuscript Guidelines

CIRCULATION DATA:

Reader: Academics
Frequency of Issue: Bi-Monthly
Copies per Issue: Less than 1,000
Sponsor/Publisher: Elsevier Science, Ltd.
Subscribe Price: 173.00 US$ Individual
620.00 US$ Institution

REVIEW INFORMATION:

Type of Review: Blind Review
No. of External Reviewers: 2
No. of In House Reviewers: 0
Acceptance Rate: 21-30%
Time to Review: 4 - 6 Months
Reviewers Comments: Yes
Invited Articles: 0-5%
Fees to Publish: 0.00 US$

MANUSCRIPT TOPICS:
Economics and Finance of Education; Education Management/Administration

MANUSCRIPT GUIDELINES/COMMENTS:

Notes for Contributors
Authors are requested to submit one copy of their manuscript along with two electronic files (one for the full text, one anonymous, with all identifying information removed, submitted in Word on a CD) to the Editor, Elchanan Cohn, Department of Economics, The Moore School of Business, University of South Carolina, Columbia, SC 29208, USA.

Proposals for book reviews should be sent to William H. Phillips, Book Review Editor, Department of Economics, University of South Carolina, SC 29208, USA.

Submission of a paper implies that it has not been published previously, that it is not under consideration for publication elsewhere, and that if accepted it will not be published elsewhere in the same form, in English or in any other language, without the written consent of the publisher.

238

Manuscript Preparation

General. Manuscripts must be typewritten, double-spaced with wide margins on one side of white paper. Good quality printouts with a font size of 12 or 10 pt are required. The corresponding author should be identified (include a Fax number and E-mail address). Full postal addresses must be given for all co-authors. Authors should consult a recent issue of the journal for style if possible. An electronic copy of the paper should accompany the **final** version. The Editors reserve the right to adjust style to certain standards of uniformity. Authors should retain a copy of their manuscript since we cannot accept responsibility for damage or loss of papers. Original manuscripts are discarded one month after publication unless the Publisher is asked to return original material after use.

Abstracts. Manuscripts must contain an abstract briefly summarizing the essential contents, followed by the relevant JEL classification. This should not exceed 150 words.

Keywords. Authors should select 2-6 keywords to describe their paper from the following list: costs, demand for schooling, economic development, economic impact, economics of scale, educational economics, educational finance, educational vouchers, efficiency, expenditures, grants, human capital, input output analysis, privatization, productivity, rate of return, resource allocation, salary wage differentials, school choice, state and federal aid, student financial aid, teacher salaries.

Text. Follow this order when typing manuscripts: Title, Authors, Affiliations, Abstract, Keywords, Main text, Acknowledgements, Appendix, References, Figure Captions and then Tables. Do not import the Figures or Tables into your text. The corresponding author should be identified with an asterisk and footnote.

Footnotes. All other footnotes (except for table footnotes) should be identified with superscript Arabic numbers. Short footnotes may be included at the foot of a manuscript page. Longer notes should be numbered and grouped together in a "Notes" section at the end of the text.

References. All publications cited in the text should be present in a list of references following the text of the manuscript. In the text refer to the author's name (without initials) and year of publication, e.g. "Since Peterson (1993) has shown that..." or "This is in agreement with results obtained later (Kramer, 1994)". For 2-6 authors, all authors are to be listed at first citation, with "&" separating the last two authors. For more than six authors, use the first six authors followed by et al. In subsequent citations for three or more authors, use author et al. in the text. The list of references should be arranged alphabetically by authors' names. The manuscript should be carefully checked to ensure that the spelling of authors names and dates are exactly the same in the text as in the reference list.

References should be given in the following form:

Becker, G.S. (1964). *Human capital*. New York, National Bureau of Economic Research.

Hansen, W.L., & King, M.A. (1971). A new approach to higher education finance. In: M.O. Orwig, *Financing higher education: Alternatives for the Federal Government* (pp. 206-236). Iowa City: American College Testing Program.

Stanovnik, T. (1997). The returns to education in Slovenia. *Economics of Education Review 16* (4) , 443-449.

Illustrations. All illustrations should be provided in camera-ready form, suitable for reproduction (which may include reduction) without retouching. Photographs, charts and diagrams are all to be referred to as "Figure(s)" and should be numbered consecutively in the order to which they are referred. They should accompany the manuscript, but should not be included within the text. All illustrations should be clearly marked on the back with the figure number and the author's name. All figures are to have a caption. Captions should be supplied on a separate sheet.

Line drawings. Good quality printouts on white paper produced in black ink are required. All lettering, graph lines and points on graphs should be sufficiently large and bold to permit reproduction when the diagram has been reduced to a size suitable for inclusion in the journal. Dye-line prints or photocopies are not suitable for reproduction. Do not use any type of shading on computer-generated illustrations.

Photographs. Original photographs must be supplied as they are to be reproduced (e.g. black and white or colour). If necessary, a scale should be marked on the photograph. Please note that photocopies of photographs are not acceptable.

Colour. Authors will be charged for colour at current printing costs.

Tables. Tables should be numbered consecutively and given a suitable caption and each table typed on a separate sheet. Footnotes to tables should be typed below the table and should be referred to by superscript lowercase letters. No vertical rules should be used. Tables should not duplicate results presented elsewhere in the manuscript, (e.g. in graphs).

Electronic Submission
Authors should submit an electronic copy of their paper when requested after the final version of the manuscript. The electronic copy should match the hardcopy exactly.

Always keep a backup copy of the electronic file for reference and safety. Full details of electronic submission and formats can be obtained from http://www.elsevier.nl/locate/disksub or from Author Services at Elsevier Science.

Proofs
Proofs will be sent to the author (first named author if no corresponding author is identified of multi-authored papers) and should be returned within 48 hours of receipt. Corrections should be restricted to typesetting errors; any others may be charged to the author. Any queries should be answered in full. Please note that authors are urged to check their proofs carefully before return, since the inclusion of late corrections cannot be guaranteed. Proofs are to be

returned to the Log-in Department, Elsevier Science, Stover Court, Bampfylde Street, Exeter, Devon EX1 2AH, UK.

Offprints
Twenty-five offprints will be supplied free of charge. Additional offprints and copies of the issue can be ordered at a specially reduced rate using the order form sent to the corresponding author after the manuscript has been accepted. Orders for reprints (produced after publication of an article) will incur a 50% surcharge.

Copyright
All authors must sign the "Transfer of Copyright" agreement before the article can be published. This transfer agreement enables Elsevier Science Ltd to protect the copyrighted material for the authors, without the author relinquishing his/her proprietary rights. The copyright transfer covers the exclusive rights to reproduce and distribute the article, including reprints, photographic reproductions, microfilm or any other reproductions of a similar nature, and translations. It also includes the right to adapt the article for use in conjunction with computer systems and programs, including reproduction or publication in machine-readable form and incorporation in retrieval systems. Authors are responsible for obtaining from the copyright holder permission to reproduce any material for which copyright already exists.

Author Services
For queries relating to the general submission of manuscripts (including electronic text and artwork) and the status of accepted manuscripts, please contact Author Services, Log-in Department, Elsevier Science, The Boulevard, Langford Lane, Kidlington, Oxford OX5 1GB, UK. E-mail: authors@elsevier.co.uk, Fax: +44 (0) 1865 843905, Phone: +44 (0) 1865 843900. Authors can also keep a track of the progress of their accepted article through our OASIS system on the Internet. For information on an article go to this Internet page and key in the corresponding author's name and the Elsevier reference number.

Education and the Law

ADDRESS FOR SUBMISSION:

Geoffrey J. Bennett, Editor
Education and the Law
Notre Dame University
London Law Centre
One Suffolk Street
London, UK SW1Y 4HG
UK
Phone: +44 (0) 20 7484 7822
Fax: +44 (0) 20 7484 7854
E-Mail: bennett.24@nd.edu
Web: www.tandf.co.uk/journals
Address May Change:

PUBLICATION GUIDELINES:

Manuscript Length: 4-20
Copies Required: One
Computer Submission: Yes
Format: WordPerfect or Word
Fees to Review: 0.00 US$

Manuscript Style:
　　See Manuscript Guidelines

CIRCULATION DATA:

Reader: Academics, Administrators,
　　Lawyers
Frequency of Issue: Quarterly
Copies per Issue:
Sponsor/Publisher: Carfax Publishing
　　(Taylor & Francis Group)
Subscribe Price: 177.00 US$ Individual
　　325.00 US$ Institution

REVIEW INFORMATION:

Type of Review:
No. of External Reviewers: 1
No. of In House Reviewers: 2
Acceptance Rate: No Reply
Time to Review: 1 Month or Less
Reviewers Comments: No
Invited Articles: 31-50%
Fees to Publish: 0.00 US$

MANUSCRIPT TOPICS:
Education Management/Administration; Higher Education; School Law; Special Education

MANUSCRIPT GUIDELINES/COMMENTS:

Editor's Comments
We are flexible about length. A rough average might be 5,000 words but many of our articles are shorter and some being considerably longer, have been spread over several issues.

Education and the Law is an academic journal addressing all aspects of the law relating to primary, secondary, tertiary and higher education. Papers accepted become the copyright of the journal unless otherwise agreed.

Author's Guidelines
Manuscripts should be sent to: Professor Geoffrey Bennett, Editor. All submissions will normally be sent anonymously for the observations of referees. Submissions should be typed, double-spaced, on one side of the paper only. Each paper should be accompanied by an abstract of 100-150 words on one page together with the title of the article and the names of

242

the authors. The full postal address of the author who will check proofs and receive correspondence and offprints should also be included. All pages should be numbered. Papers will, be considered provided that they are nor submitted simultaneously elsewhere for publication, and have not previously been published elsewhere.

Tables and Captions should be typed out on separate sheets and not included as part of the text. Tables should be numbered by roman numerals and figures by Arabic numerals. The approximate position of tables and figures should be indicated in the manuscript. Captions should include keys to any symbols.

Figures and any line drawings should be of a quality suitable for printing and will not normally be redrawn by the publishers.

References should follow the Harvard system, i.e. they should be indicated in the typescript by giving the author's name, with the year of publication in parentheses, e.g. smith (1994); or if there are more than two authors--Smith et al. (1994). If several papers from the same author(s) and from the same year are cited, (s), (b), (c), etc. should be put after the year of publication. The references should then be listed in full alphabetically at the end of the paper on a separate sheet in the following standard form:

HARRIS, N. S. (1993) Local complaints procedures under the Education Reform Act 1988, Journal of Social Welfare and Family Law, pp. 19-39.

JACKSON, B. S. (1993) Piaget, Kohlberg and Habermas: psychological and comunicational approaches to legal theory, in: V. FERRARI & C. FARALLI (eds), laws and Rights; pp. 571-592 (Milan; Giuffre).

LYON, C. M. (1993) The Law Relating to Children (London, Buterworths).

Titles of Journals should not be abbreviated.

Cases should be cited in the usual English law form with the name of the case and its date in the text and a list of cases in alphabetical order at the end of the article.

Proofs will be sent to authors, if there is sufficient time to do so. they should be corrected and returned within three days. Proofs are supplied for checking and making essential corrections, not for general revision or alteration.

Offprints. Fifty offprints of each paper are supplied free of charge. Additional copies may be purchased an should be ordered when the proofs are returned. Offprints, together with a complete copy of the relevant journal issue, are sent about three weeks after publication.

Printed and bound in Great Britain by Wace Journals, Abingdon, Oxfordshire, England.

Education and Urban Society

ADDRESS FOR SUBMISSION:

Charles J. Russo, Editor
Education and Urban Society
University of Dayton
School of Education & Allied Professions
Department of Educational Administration
324 Chaminade Hall
Dayton, OH 45469-0534
USA
Phone: 937-229-3722
Fax: 937-229-3392
E-Mail: charles_j_russo@hotmail.com
Web: www.sagepub.com
Address May Change:

PUBLICATION GUIDELINES:

Manuscript Length: 21-25
Copies Required: Three
Computer Submission: Yes Disk/ Prefer
  Email
Format: WordPerfect, MSWord
Fees to Review: 0.00 US$

Manuscript Style:
  American Psychological Association

CIRCULATION DATA:

Reader: Academics
Frequency of Issue: Quarterly
Copies per Issue: 1,001 - 2,000
Sponsor/Publisher: Corwin Press, 2455
  Teller Road, Thousand Oaks, CA 91320
Subscribe Price: 88.00 US$ Individual
  325.00 US$ Institution

REVIEW INFORMATION:

Type of Review: Blind Review
No. of External Reviewers: 3
No. of In House Reviewers: 1
Acceptance Rate: 30%-/+
Time to Review: 2 - 3 Months
Reviewers Comments: Yes
Invited Articles: Less then 10%
Fees to Publish: 0.00 US$

MANUSCRIPT TOPICS:
Education Management/Administration; In Urban Context; Teacher Education

MANUSCRIPT GUIDELINES/COMMENTS:

Editor's Note: Please note that we just changed format from invited to peer review.

Policy
During recent years, an increasing number of social scientists have been conducting research on education as a social institution. Research studies have not been limited to the workings of the institution but have begun to explore educational institutions and processes as agents of social change. Much of this work, of course, centers on the problems and needs resulting from the national concern with improving the urban environment but also involves the role of education in a society that is urban. *Education and Urban Society* exists to foster such research and to provide a multidisciplinary forum for communication.

244

Submission Guidelines

Manuscripts. *Education and Urban Society* has now shifted from a themed issue format to a traditional, peer-reviewed journal. Unsolicited manuscripts are now accepted. Four (4) copies should be submitted along with an IBM-compatible disk. Manuscripts must be prepared in accordance with the *American Psychological Association* (APA) guidelines (4th ed.).

Tables, charts, notes, and references must all be on separate pages, also completely double-spaced. A double-spaced abstract of approximately 150 words as well as a double-spaced brief biographical paragraph describing each author's affiliation, research interest, and recent publications should accompany the manuscript. Because the manuscripts are sent out anonymously for editorial evaluation, the author's name, affiliation, and biographical paragraph should appear on a separate cover page. In addition, to help ensure anonymity in the review process, three (3) of the four (4) copies should have all references to the author(s) left blank. This includes any references in the manuscript, the notes, the title, and reference sections.

Please send manuscripts to

Charles Russo, Editor
Department of Educational Administration
School of Education and Allied Professions
324 Chaminade Hall
Dayton, OH 45469-0534
937/229-3722 (office)
937/229-3392 (fax)
russo@keiko.udayton.edu

Submission of a manuscript implies commitment to publish in the journal. Authors submitting manuscripts to the journal should not simultaneously submit them to another journal, nor should manuscripts have been published elsewhere in substantially similar form or with substantially similar content.

Education Economics

ADDRESS FOR SUBMISSION:

Steve Bradley, Editor
Education Economics
Lancaster University
The Management School
Department of Economics
Lancaster, LA1 4YX
UK
Phone: +44 1524 593880
Fax: +44 1524 594244
E-Mail: s.bradley@lancaster.ac.uk
Web: http://www.tandf.co.uk/journals
Address May Change:

PUBLICATION GUIDELINES:

Manuscript Length: 26-30
Copies Required: Three
Computer Submission: No
Format: N/A
Fees to Review: 0.00 US$

Manuscript Style:
See Manuscript Guidelines

CIRCULATION DATA:

Reader: Academics
Frequency of Issue: 4Times/Year
Copies per Issue:
Sponsor/Publisher: Routledge Journals
(Taylor and Francis)
Subscribe Price: 1009.00 US$ Individual
1038.00 US$ Institution
611.00 Pounds Indv. & 629 Pounds Inst.

REVIEW INFORMATION:

Type of Review: Editorial Review
No. of External Reviewers: 1
No. of In House Reviewers: 1
Acceptance Rate: 21-30%
Time to Review: 2 - 3 Months
Reviewers Comments: Yes
Invited Articles: 21-30%
Fees to Publish: 0.00 US$

MANUSCRIPT TOPICS:
Economics and Finance of Education; Education Management/Administration

MANUSCRIPT GUIDELINES/COMMENTS:

Aims and Scope
Education Economics serves as a forum for debate in all areas of the economics and management of education. Particular emphasis is given to the 'quantitative' aspects of educational management which involve numerate disciplines such as economics and operational research. The content is of international appeal and is not limited to material of a technical nature. Applied work with clear policy implications is especially encouraged.

Readership of the journal includes academics in the field of education, economics and management; civil servants and local government officials responsible for education and manpower planning; educational managers at the level of the individual school or college.

Manuscripts to be considered for publication should be sent to the Editor. Three complete copies of each manuscript should be submitted. They should be typed on one side of the paper, double-spaced, with ample margins, and bear the title of the contribution and name(s) of the author(s). The full postal address of the author who will check proofs and receive correspondence and offprints should also be included. All papers should be numbered. Contributions should not normally be more than 5000 words in length and should be written in the English Language. They should also include an abstract of 100 words. Footnotes to the text should be avoided wherever this is reasonably possible.

Rejected manuscripts will not normally be returned unless a self-addressed envelope and international postal coupons have been sent.

Tables and Captions to Illustrations. Tables must be typed out on separate sheets and not included as part of the text. The captions to illustrations should be gathered together and also typed out on a separate sheet. Tables and figures should be numbered by Arabic numerals. The approximate position of tables and figures shouts be indicated in the manuscript. Captions should include keys to symbols.

Figures. Artwork must be submitted in suitable condition for publication.

References. These should be indicated in the typescript by giving the author's name and the year of publication, as follows: Weaver (1978) or (Weaver, 1978). If several papers by the same author and from the same year are cited, a, b, c, etc. should be put after the year of publication. The references should be listed in full at the end of the paper in the following standard form:

Blaug, M. (Ed.) (1992) **The Economic Value of Education: Studies in the Economics of Education** (Aldershot, Edward Elgar).

Grubel, H. G. (1987) The economics of the brain drain, in Psacharopoulos, G. (Ed.) **Economics of Education: Research and Studies** (Oxford, Pergamon).

Halsey, A. H. (1991) **The Decline of Donnish Dominion** (Oxford, Oxford University Press).

Murnane, R. J. & Olsen, R. J. (1989) Will there be enough teachers? **American Economic Review**, 79, pp. 242-246.

Titles of journals should not be abbreviated.

Proofs. These will be sent to authors if there is sufficient time to do so. They should be corrected and returned to the publishers within three days. Major alterations to the text cannot be accepted.

Offprints. Fifty offprints of each paper are supplied free. Additional copies may be purchased and should be ordered when the proofs are returned. Offprints, together with a complete copy of the relevant journal issue are sent about three weeks after publication.

247

Education Policy Analysis Archives

ADDRESS FOR SUBMISSION:

Gene V. Glass, Editor
Education Policy Analysis Archives
Arizona State University
College of Education
  SUBMIT ONLY BY EMAIL BELOW
Box 870211
Tempe, AZ 85287-0211
USA
Phone: 480-965-2692
Fax:
E-Mail: glass@asu.edu
Web: http://epaa.asu.edu
Address May Change:

PUBLICATION GUIDELINES:

Manuscript Length: 30+
Copies Required: No Paper Copies Req.
Computer Submission: Yes Email
Format: Word/WordPerfect; Eng/Span/Port
Fees to Review: 0.00 US$

Manuscript Style:
  American Psychological Association

CIRCULATION DATA:

Reader: Academics
Frequency of Issue: 50 Times/Year
Copies per Issue: N/A
Sponsor/Publisher: College of Education,
  Arizona State University
Subscribe Price: Electronic

REVIEW INFORMATION:

Type of Review: Blind Review
No. of External Reviewers: 3+
No. of In House Reviewers: 1
Acceptance Rate: 21-30%
Time to Review: 2 - 3 Months
Reviewers Comments: Yes
Invited Articles: 0-5%
Fees to Publish: 0.00 US$

MANUSCRIPT TOPICS:
Curriculum Studies; Education Management/Administration; Education Policy; Higher Education

MANUSCRIPT GUIDELINES/COMMENTS:

How to Submit an Article to EPAA
EPAA welcomes submitted articles for consideration for publication. Articles should deal with education policy in any of its many aspects, and may focus at any level of the education system in any nation. Articles may be written in either English or Spanish or Portuguese.

Please prepare manuscripts in accord with the format recommended in the *Publication Manual of the American Psychological Association*. Articles may be of any length, though contributions of fewer than 1,500 words are discouraged.

Either include articles as text in email letters to the Editor, or attach word processor files to email letters addressed to the Editor (**glass@asu.edu**). Rich Text Format is the preferred word processor format, but Microsoft WORD or Word Perfect is acceptable. Files sent through regular postal mail on floppy diskettes are also acceptable.

Email submitted articles to the Editor, Gene Glass at **glass@asu.edu**.

Or mail articles on floppy diskettes via regular mail to

Gene V Glass, Editor
Education Policy Analysis Archives
College of Education
Arizona State University
Box 870211
Tempe, AZ 85287-0211

Articles written in Spanish or Portugese may be submitted to the Associate Editors for Spanish & Portuguese Language, Gustavo Fischman (**fischman@asu.edu**) or Pablo Gentili (**Pablo@lpp-uerj.net**).

Authors are normally informed of the publication decision within eight to ten weeks.

Education Research and Perspectives

ADDRESS FOR SUBMISSION:

Clive Whitehead & Marnie O'Neill, Edtrs.
Education Research and Perspectives
The University of Western Australia
Graduate School of Education
Nedlands, WA 6907
Australia
Phone: +61 8 6488 2388
Fax: +61 8 6488 1052
E-Mail: clive.whitehead@uwa.edu.au
Web: See Guidelines
Address May Change:

PUBLICATION GUIDELINES:

Manuscript Length: 16-30
Copies Required: Three
Computer Submission: Yes Disk, Email
Format: Macintosh Office 98
Fees to Review: 0.00 US$

Manuscript Style:
    See Manuscript Guidelines

CIRCULATION DATA:

Reader: Academics
Frequency of Issue: 2 Times/Year
Copies per Issue: Less than 1,000
Sponsor/Publisher: Graduate School of
    Education
Subscribe Price: 40.00 AUS$

REVIEW INFORMATION:

Type of Review: Blind Review
No. of External Reviewers: 1
No. of In House Reviewers: 1
Acceptance Rate: 50-60%
Time to Review: 2 - 3 Months
Reviewers Comments: Yes
Invited Articles: 0-5%
Fees to Publish: 0.00 US$

MANUSCRIPT TOPICS:
Adult Career & Vocational; Art/Music; Audiology/Speech Pathology; Bilingual/E.S.L.;
Counseling & Personnel Services; Curriculum Studies; Education
Management/Administration; Educational Psychology; Educational Technology Systems;
Elementary/Early Childhood; English Literature; Foreign Language; Gifted Children; Health
& Physical Education; Higher Education; Languages & Linguistics; Library
Science/Information Resources; Reading; Religious Education; Rural Education & Small
Schools; School Law; Science Math & Environment; Secondary/Adolescent Studies; Social
Studies/Social Science; Special Education; Teacher Education; Tests, Measurement &
Evaluation; Urban Education, Cultural/Non-Traditional

MANUSCRIPT GUIDELINES/COMMENTS:

General Topics. In recent years subjects have included history and philosophy of education,
curriculum history and theory, teaching, school effectiveness, educational mentoring, female
academics, participant observation, and education as a university subject. In recent years two
post-graduate theses have been published in full as separate issues.

This journal has been published continuously by the Department of Education/Graduate School of Education since December 1950. Initially it was published as *The Educand*.

In 1961 the title was changed to *The Australian journal of Higher Education*. The present title was adopted in 1974. Throughout its history, the journal has been multi-disciplinary in outlook, with a mixture of general issues and issues devoted to special topics. The range of authors is worldwide. The journal includes articles, review essays and book reviews. Since 1991 the journal has been free of charge on the internet at:
http://www.education.uwa.edu.au

The journal is published on a bi-annual basis (in June and December) and all articles are subject to external review and report. The present joint editors and their email addresses are as follows:
A/Prof. Clive Whitehead (**Clive.Whitehead@uwa.edu.au**) and
Dr. Marnie O'Neill (**Marnie.O'Neill@uwa.edu.au**)

For information about subscriptions to the hard copy edition of the journal or contributing articles see the end pages of any issue or contact one of the joint editors by email or by addressing correspondence to:
The Editors
Education Research and Perspectives
Graduate School of Education
The University of Western Australia
35 Stirling Highway, Crawley, WA 6009.

Notes for Contributors
1. Each article should be less than 10,000 words in length.

2. Manuscripts should be submitted in both soft and hard copy.
* The soft copy to be submitted preferably in the word processing program Microsoft Word or WordPerfect in IBM or Macintosh version
* The hard copy should be an original printout in double-spaced typescript on one side only of opaque, white paper, leaving ample top and left-hand margins.

3. Tables and/or figures should be presented on separate sheets and only when essential. The position in the text should be clearly indicated.

4. The title of the article, author's name and affiliation should be set on a separate title page.

5. A mini-abstract, of not more than 100 words, should be provided at the head of the article.

6. Please also supply a three to four line autobiography (stating current academic position, institution, previous education and main research interests) for the 'Contributor's to this Issue' page.

7. Referencing: Due to the multi-disciplinary nature of the journal a variety of established forms of annotation are accepted. In each case it is imperative that authors remain *consistent* in their use of a reference style.

8. All articles submitted are subject to review and report.

Contributions should be addressed to
   The Editors, Education Research and Perspectives, Graduate School of Education
   The University of Western Australia, 35 Stirling Highway, Crawley, WA 6009 Australia

Further information on editorial matters will be supplied on application to the Editors.

Education Review

ADDRESS FOR SUBMISSION:

Gene V. Glass, Editor
Education Review
Arizona State University
College of Education
Tempe, AZ 85287-2411
USA
Phone: 480-965-2692
Fax:
E-Mail: glass@asu.edu
Web: edrev.asu.edu
Address May Change:

PUBLICATION GUIDELINES:

Manuscript Length: 11-15
Copies Required: No Paper Copies Req.
Computer Submission: Yes Email
Format: Rich Text Format
Fees to Review: 0.00 US$

Manuscript Style:
　　American Psychological Association

CIRCULATION DATA:

Reader: Academics
Frequency of Issue: 100 Times/Year
Copies per Issue: N/A
Sponsor/Publisher: College of Education,
　Arizona State University
Subscribe Price:

REVIEW INFORMATION:

Type of Review: Blind Review
No. of External Reviewers: 0
No. of In House Reviewers: 2
Acceptance Rate: 95%
Time to Review: 1 Week or Less
Reviewers Comments: Yes
Invited Articles: 50% +
Fees to Publish: 0.00 US$

MANUSCRIPT TOPICS:

Adult Career & Vocational; Art/Music; Audiology/Speech Pathology; Bilingual/E.S.L.;
Counseling & Personnel Services; Curriculum Studies; Education
Management/Administration; Educational Psychology; Elementary/Early Childhood; English
Literature; Foreign Language; Gifted Children; Health & Physical Education; Higher
Education; Languages & Linguistics; Library Science/Information Resources; Reading;
Religious Education; Rural Education & Small Schools; School Law; Science Math &
Environment; Secondary/Adolescent Studies; Special Education; Teacher Education; Tests,
Measurement & Evaluation; Urban Education, Cultural/Non-Traditional

MANUSCRIPT GUIDELINES/COMMENTS:

Education Review publishes reviews of recent books in education, covering the entire range
of education scholarship and practice. Reviews are archived and their publication announced
by means of a listserv (**EDREV@asu.edu**).

The *Education Review* is made available to the public without cost as a service of the College
of Education at Arizona State University.

Procedures

All review articles must be submitted in electronic format (either on a floppy disk or transmitted over the Internet as an attachment to an email letter to the appropriate Editor).

Long reviews:
Gene V Glass, Editor **glass@asu.edu**

Brief reviews:
Kate Corby, Brief Reviews Editor **corby@msu.edu**

Reviews in Spanish or Portuguese:
Gustavo E. Fischman, Editor for Spanish & Portugese **fischman@asu.edu**

Reviews should be submitted in a standard word-processing format (such as Microsoft Word or WordPerfect) or, preferably, in "Rich Text Format." Long review articles should be between 2,500 and 5,000 words. Reviews outside these limits may be considered at the Editor's discretion. Brief Reviews call attention to current practical books for teachers and administrators. The Brief Reviews section publishes brief evaluative summaries of books from the current and previous year.

Every review article should begin by citing the book or books to be reviewed, with full bibliographic information including authors (please include first names), copyright date, full title including any subtitle, place of publication, publisher, number of pages, ISBN Number, and price if available. For example,

Hunt, Morton. (1997). How Science Takes Stock: The Story of Meta-Analysis. N.Y: Russell Sage Foundation. Pp. xii + 210. ISBN 0-87154-389-3. $38.95

References and all other citations of published work in the review itself should follow the form specified in the *Publication Manual of the American Psychological Association* (4th Edition). See http://www.apa.org/journals/faq.html. For example,

... as argued by Hedges (1982) in his investigation into the reliability of observations in the physical sciences."

And then in the References at the end of the review, the citation of Hedges (1982) would appear as follows:

References

Hedges, L.V. (1982). How hard is hard science, how soft is soft science? The empirical cumulativeness of research. American Psychologist, 42, 443-455.

Footnotes are not permitted; auxiliary information normally included in footnotes should be included in Endnotes that appear directly before any References at the end of the review.

Submitted articles should be accompanied by a paragraph describing the review author's institutional affiliation and areas of interest.

Editorial Policy

All accepted articles are subject to copyediting by the Editor, including editing for length and format consistency, as well as editing for content. All changes will be submitted to authors for final approval before publication.

Copyright Policy

Copyright for all articles published in *ER* will be retained by the authors. Permission to use any copyrighted material in review articles, or permission to republish reviews also being published elsewhere, must be obtained by the author prior to publication in *ER*.

Criteria by Which Submitted Reviews Will Be Judged

Submitted reviews will be judged for possible publication according to the following:

Review Procedures and Criteria

Review articles are either solicited by the Editor, or offered unsolicited by reviewers. In either case, decisions on acceptance for publication are made by the Editor, who may on occasion solicit assistance from other readers in helping them make a decision. However, the articles are not typically refereed by any standard anonymous review process. In making his decision, the Editor will be guided by the following criteria:

- Does the review help readers form a clear idea of the contents of the book under consideration?
- Is the review fair and accurate in its presentation of the evidence, arguments, and methodology of the book?
- Does the review present a reasoned evaluation of the book and its conclusions?
- Is the article written in a manner that will promote understanding and further discussion? Is it respectful in tone?
- Does the article satisfy editorial standards of clarity of presentation, organization of ideas, and quality of writing?
- Does the article fit within the specific format and length requirements of this journal?

If you are interested in writing a review for *ER*, please contact the Editor at **glass@asu.edu**. *Education Review* discourages unsolicited submissions of book reviews conducted by students, advisees, colleagues, spouses, or personal friends of a book's author. Such relations place the reviewer's credibility into question and could, in certain situations, make a reviewer vulnerable to an untenable conflict of interest.

Publication of commissioned articles is presumed, but only when in the Editor's judgment the criteria listed above are satisfied. In addition, *ER* is committed to prompt turnaround times on its reviews, and commissioned articles should be completed by the agreed upon deadline. Failure to meet such deadlines removes any obligation to publish the article, although this decision remains at the Editor's discretion.

Educational Administration Quarterly

ADDRESS FOR SUBMISSION:

Diana G. Pounder, Editor
Educational Administration Quarterly
University of Utah
Dept. of Educational Leadership & Policy
1750 Campus Center Drive, Room 339
Salt Lake City, UT 84112-9254
USA
Phone: 801-581-6714
Fax: 801-585-6756
E-Mail: eaq@ed.utah.edu
Web: www.sagepub.com
Address May Change:

PUBLICATION GUIDELINES:

Manuscript Length: 25-40
Copies Required: Electronic ONLY
Computer Submission: Yes
Format: MSWord Electronic file
Fees to Review: 0.00 US$

Manuscript Style:
American Psychological Association

CIRCULATION DATA:

Reader: Academics
Frequency of Issue: 5 Times/Year
Copies per Issue: 3,001 - 4,000
Sponsor/Publisher: Sage Publications
Subscribe Price: 108.00 US$ Individual
489.00 US$ Institution
20.00 US$ Foreign Postage

REVIEW INFORMATION:

Type of Review: Blind Review
No. of External Reviewers: 3
No. of In House Reviewers: 3
Acceptance Rate: 6-10%
Time to Review: 3 Months
Reviewers Comments: Yes
Invited Articles: 6-10%
Fees to Publish: 0.00 US$

MANUSCRIPT TOPICS:
Education Management/Administration; Educational Leadership; Educational Organizations;
Higher Education; Schools; Social Studies/Social Science

MANUSCRIPT GUIDELINES/COMMENTS:

About the Journal & Editorial Policy
EAQ presents prominent empirical and conceptual articles focused on timely and critical leadership and policy issues of educational organizations. As an editorial team, we embrace traditional and emergent research paradigms, methods, and issues. We particularly promote the publication of rigorous and relevant scholarly work that enhances linkages among and utility for educational policy, practice, and research arenas, including work that examines:
a. the relationship among educational leadership structures and processes and valued organizational outcomes in educational institutions from pre-school to higher education, most notably improved teaching processes and learning outcomes;
b. improved leadership preparation and development structures and processes and assesses the relationship between leadership preparation and development and valued organizational outcomes;

c. educational environments that promote equity and social justice for students and faculty; and

d. theoretical frameworks that advance and have utility for issues such as those outlined above.

Author Submission Guidelines and Manuscript Specifications

EAQ uses an electronic submission and review process. Authors should submit by e-mail an electronic copy of the manuscript in Microsoft Word format (for PC) to **eaq@ed.utah.edu**. If electronic files cannot be e-mailed, a copy on floppy disk or CD may be mailed here:

EAQ Editor
Professor Diana G. Pounder, Ph.D.
Department of Educational Leadership & Policy
University of Utah
1705 Campus Center Drive, Room 339
Salt Lake City, UT 84112-9254

Ordinarily, manuscripts should be 25 to 40 pages in length. All tables should be included in the electronic file. Figures may be submitted in separate electronic files, preferably as TIFF or JPEG images, although we can accept with most other formats. Figures must be of sufficient resolution for high-end printing: 1200 dpi for line art, 300 dpi for grayscale, and 600 dpi for color.

Manuscripts should follow the style of the fifth edition of the *Publication Manual of the American Psychological Association* (APA). All copy should be typed, double-spaced in Times New Roman 12-point font with notes, references, tables, and figures appearing at the end of the manuscript per APA style.

Structured Abstract

Each manuscript should include a structured abstract, similar to those described by Mosteller, Navc, and Miech in the January/February 2004 *Educational Researcher* Commentary, "Why We Need a Structured Abstract in Education Research." The structured abstract for empirical manuscripts should include very brief subheaded sections such as *Purpose, Conceptual or Theoretical Framework, Research Methods/Approach (e.g. Setting, Participants, Research Design, Data Collection and Analysis), Findings,* and *Implications for Research and for Practice.* Non-empirical or conceptual manuscripts should use sub-heads appropriate to the conceptual argument or position promoted or discussed. Including section heads, abstracts should not exceed 250 words. Additionally, five key words or phrases should appear after the abstract, including an indication of the type of article (e.g. empirical paper, conceptual paper).

Author Identification

Manuscripts should include a cover sheet with the title, author's name, address, phone number, fax number, and e-mail address, along with a brief biographical statement (2-3 sentences). If the article was authored by more than one person, coauthors' names, e-mail addresses, phone numbers, and biographical statements should also be included. However, to assure appropriate blind review, the author's name or identifying information should NOT appear in headers, footers, reference list, or other portions of the manuscript text; instead,

260

Manuscript Submission. Four copies (three of which are blind copies), together with an IBM-formatted disk (or CD) that contains the electronic file of the manuscript (Microsoft Word or Acrobat PDF file format; only one electronic file for each manuscript), should be sent to: Xitao Fan, EPM Editor, Curry School of Education, University of Virginia, 287 Ruffner Hall,, 405 Emmet Street South, Charlottesville, VA 22903-2495.

For all submissions, the corresponding author must provide both his/her postal mailing address and e-mail address. Manuscripts should follow the general guidelines in the 5th edition of the *Publication Manual of the American Psychological Association*. Manuscripts should comply with the general guidelines presented in the lead of issue 4 of volume 54 of the Journal (Winter, 1994, pp. 837-847) and in supplementary "guidelines editorials" published on an occasional basis (e.g., August, 1995, pp. 525-534; April 1996, pp. 197-208; and August, 2001, pp. 517-531). Copies of these guideline editorials are available on the World Wide Web at http://www.people.virginia.edu/~xf8d. Authors are also strongly encouraged to review the recommendations of the *APA Task Force on Statistical Inference*, published in the August 1999 issue of the *American Psychologist* (http://www.apa.org/journals/amp/amp548594.html).

Various Author Guidelines editorials are available on the Web via:
http://www.people.virginia.edu/~xf8d/

Educational Assessment

ADDRESS FOR SUBMISSION:

Joan Herman, Editor
Educational Assessment
Nat'l Center for Research on Evaluation,
    Standards, and Student Testing
GSE&IS Bldg., 3rd Fl, Box 951522
300 Charles E. Young Drive North
Los Angeles, CA 90095-1522
USA
Phone: 310-794-9157
Fax: 310-825-3883
E-Mail: herman@cse.ucla.edu
Web: www.erlbaum.com
Address May Change:

PUBLICATION GUIDELINES:

Manuscript Length: 26-30+
Copies Required: Four
Computer Submission: Yes
Format: MS Word (preferred); WordPerfect
Fees to Review: 0.00 US$

Manuscript Style:
    American Psychological Association

CIRCULATION DATA:

Reader: Academics
Frequency of Issue: Quarterly
Copies per Issue: Less than 1,000
Sponsor/Publisher: Lawrence Erlbaum
    Associates
Subscribe Price: 35.00 US$ Individual
    255.00 US$ Institution

REVIEW INFORMATION:

Type of Review: Blind Review
No. of External Reviewers: 3
No. of In House Reviewers: 1
Acceptance Rate: 21-30%
Time to Review: 4 - 6 Months
Reviewers Comments: Yes
Invited Articles: 11-20%
Fees to Publish: 0.00 US$

MANUSCRIPT TOPICS:
Educational Psychology; Tests, Measurement & Evaluation

MANUSCRIPT GUIDELINES/COMMENTS:

Editorial Scope
This journal publishes original research and scholarship on the assessment of individuals, groups, and programs in educational settings. Its coverage encompasses a broad range of issues related to theory, empirical research, and practice in the appraisal of educational achievements by students and teachers, young children and adults, and novices and experts. The journal also reports on studies of conventional testing practices, discusses alternative approaches, presents scholarship on classroom practice, and debates on national assessment issues. *Educational Assessment's* stated purpose is to provide a forum for integrating conceptual and technical domains with the arenas of practice and policy, and for unifying a literature that is presently scattered over a variety of disciplines and outlets.

Audience. Educational researchers, teachers, administrators, and policy makers.

INSTRUCTIONS TO CONTRIBUTORS

Manuscript Submission

Only articles written in English will be considered. Submit four copies of your manuscript to the Editor: Joan Herman, National Center for Research on Evaluation, Standards, and Student Testing (CRESST), 300 Charles E. Young Drive North GSE&IS Building, 3rd Floor, Mailbox 951522, Los Angeles, CA 90095-1522 Phone: 310-794-9157, E-mail: **herman@cse.ucla.edu**

Prepare manuscripts according to the *Publication Manual of the American Psychological Association* (4th ed.). Type all components of the manuscript double-sided, including title page, abstract, text, quotes, acknowledgements, references, appendices, tables, figure captions, and footnotes. An abstract of 100 to 150 words should be typed on a separate page. Authors must follow the "Guidelines to Reduce Bias in Language," on pages 46-60 of the APA Manual. Four photocopies of the illustrations and the original illustrations should accompany the manuscript. All manuscripts submitted will be acknowledged promptly. Authors should keep a copy of their manuscripts to guard against loss.

Blind Review

To facilitate anonymous review, only the article title should appear on the first page of the manuscript. An attached cover page must contain the title; authorship; authors' affiliations; any statements of credit or research support; and authors; mailing addresses, phone and fax numbers, and e-mail addresses. Every effort should be made by the authors to see that the manuscript itself contains no clues to their identities.

Permissions

Authors are responsible for all statements made in their work and for obtaining permission from copyright owners to reprint or adapt a table or figure or to reprint a quotation of 500 words or more. Authors should write to original author(s) and publisher to request nonexclusive world rights in all languages to use the material in the article and in future editions. Provide copies of all permissions and credit lines obtained.

Regulations

In a cover letter, authors should state that the findings reported in the manuscript are original and have not been published previously and that the manuscript is not being simultaneously submitted elsewhere. Authors should also state that they have complied with American Psychological Association ethical standards in the treatment of their samples.

Production Notes

After a manuscript is accepted for publication, its author is asked to provide a computer disk containing the manuscript file. Files are copyedited and typeset into page proofs. Authors read proofs to correct errors and answer editors' queries.

Educational Evaluation & Policy Analysis

ADDRESS FOR SUBMISSION:

K. Wong & E. Goldring, Co-Editors
Educational Evaluation & Policy Analysis
  ELECTRONIC SUBMISSION ONLY
Vanderbilt University
Peabody # 511
230 Appleton Pl.
Nashville, TN 37203-5721
USA
Phone: 615-343-0039
Fax: 615-322-0225
E-Mail: eepa@vanderbilt.edu
Web: www.aera.net
Address May Change: 6/30/2006

PUBLICATION GUIDELINES:

Manuscript Length: 30+
Copies Required: Electronic
Computer Submission: Yes Email
Format: Word, PDF
Fees to Review: 0.00 US$

Manuscript Style:
  American Psychological Association

CIRCULATION DATA:

Reader: Academics, Administrators
Frequency of Issue: Quarterly
Copies per Issue: 5,001 - 10,000
Sponsor/Publisher: AERA - American
  Educational Research Association
Subscribe Price: 48.00 US$ Individual
  110.00 US$ Institution
  15.00 US$ Member/ $10.00 Foreign Ch.

REVIEW INFORMATION:

Type of Review: Blind Review
No. of External Reviewers: 3
No. of In House Reviewers: 0
Acceptance Rate: 11-20%
Time to Review: 4 - 6 Months
Reviewers Comments: Yes
Invited Articles: 0-5%
Fees to Publish: 0.00 US$

MANUSCRIPT TOPICS:
Education Management/Administration; Educational Psychology; Elementary/Early
Childhood; Higher Education; Secondary/Adolescent Studies; Social Studies/Social Science;
Teacher Education; Tests, Measurement & Evaluation; Urban Education, Cultural/Non-
Traditional

MANUSCRIPT GUIDELINES/COMMENTS:

Educational Evaluation and Policy Analysis (*EEPA*) publishes scholarly articles concerned
with important issues in the formulation, implementation, and evaluation of education policy.
EEPA is open to all of the diverse methodologies and theoretical orientations represented in
AERA published work. We welcome submissions focused on international and comparative
policy issues in education as well as domestic issues. Manuscripts should be written in a way
that appeals to the broad and diverse interests of the *EEPA* readership, who work in a variety
of institutional settings.

Kenneth Wong and Ellen Goldring are the co-editors of *Educational Evaluation and Policy Analysis*. *EEPA* publishes manuscripts of theoretical, methodological, or policy interest to those engaged in educational policy analysis, evaluation, and decision making. Manuscripts are accepted for consideration with the understanding that they are original material and are not under consideration for publication elsewhere.

Specifications for manuscripts can be found on the website.

Educational Forum

ADDRESS FOR SUBMISSION:

Helen McCarty, Managing Editor
Educational Forum
Kappa Delta Pi Publications
3707 Woodview Trace
Indianapolis, IN 46268-1158
USA
Phone: 317-871-4900 / 800-284-3167
Fax: 317-704-2323
E-Mail: pubs@kdp.org
Web: www.kdp.org
Address May Change:

PUBLICATION GUIDELINES:

Manuscript Length: 10
Copies Required: Four
Computer Submission: Yes
Format: No Reply
Fees to Review: 0.00 US$

Manuscript Style:
Chicago Manual of Style

CIRCULATION DATA:

Reader: Academics, Practicing Teachers
Frequency of Issue: Quarterly
Copies per Issue: 5,000
Sponsor/Publisher: Kappa Delta Pi,
International Honor Society In Education
Subscribe Price: 20.00 US$ Individual
12.00 US$ Members

REVIEW INFORMATION:

Type of Review: Blind Review
No. of External Reviewers: 3+
No. of In House Reviewers: 2
Acceptance Rate: 35%
Time to Review: 2 Months
Reviewers Comments: No
Invited Articles: 5%
Fees to Publish: 0.00 US$

MANUSCRIPT TOPICS:
Adult Career & Vocational; Art/Music; Audiology/Speech Pathology; Bilingual/E.S.L.;
Counseling & Personnel Services; Curriculum Studies; Education
Management/Administration; Educational Psychology; Educational Technology Systems;
Elementary/Early Childhood; English Literature; Foreign Language; Gifted Children; Health
& Physical Education; Higher Education; Languages & Linguistics; Library
Science/Information Resources; Reading; Religious Education; Rural Education & Small
Schools; School Law; Science Math & Environment; Secondary/Adolescent Studies; Social
Studies/Social Science; Special Education; Teacher Education; Tests, Measurement &
Evaluation; Urban Education, Cultural/Non-Traditional

MANUSCRIPT GUIDELINES/COMMENTS:

Manuscripts submitted to *The Educational Forum* should not be submitted simultaneously to
another publication, nor be under consideration by other publishers at the time of submission.
Manuscripts should be original material and not published previously.

To help facilitate the review and communication process, electronic submissions are
encouraged. They should be in IBM-compatible Microsoft Word format and sent as an e-mail

attachment or on a floppy disk. The e-mail address for submissions is **pubs@kdp.org**. Manuscripts may be sent by postal mail as long as five hard copies are enclosed; but electronic submissions are ultimately required.

All manuscripts must be formatted for blind reviewing. A separate title page with the author's name, affiliation, preferred mailing address, telephone number, fax number, and e-mail address should be provided to ensure anonymity in the review process. If more than one person has authored the manuscript, please provide contact information for all authors and indicate which person is the corresponding author.

An abstract of no more than 75 words must accompany the manuscript. Submissions should be typed double-spaced for 8½" x 11" paper. Article length should not exceed 7,000 words, including quotations and references. Pages should be numbered. *The Chicago Manual of Style*, 15th edition, should be used as a guide for formatting manuscripts and reference style. To preserve the advantages of blind reviewing, authors should avoid identifying themselves in the manuscript.

It is the author's responsibility to quote accurately and provide complete reference information, as well as secure necessary permissions. Authors of accepted papers will be requested to assign all rights to copyright to *The Forum* by means of a standard form.

Deadlines for Submissions
The Educational Forum is published the first week of January, April, July, and October. For consideration in specific issues, manuscripts should be received six months prior to the publication date.

Book Reviews
The Educational Forum also accepts unsolicited reviews on recent books. Submissions should include a brief summary of the content of the book, provide its bibliographic information (including ISBN number and total page count), and discuss its strengths and weaknesses and its contribution to the field of education.

All submissions should be addressed to:
Managing Editor
The Educational Forum
Kappa Delta Pi
3707 Woodview Trace
Indianapolis, IN 46268-1158
E-mail: **pubs@kdp.org**

Educational Gerontology

ADDRESS FOR SUBMISSION:

D. Barry Lumsden, Editor
Educational Gerontology
University of North Texas
College of Education
Box 31137
Denton, TX 76203-1337
USA
Phone: 940-565-4074
Fax: 940-369-1337
E-Mail: lumsden@unt.edu
Web: http://www.tandf.co.uk/journals
Address May Change:

PUBLICATION GUIDELINES:

Manuscript Length: 15-20
Copies Required: Three
Computer Submission: Yes
Format: WordPerfect or MSWord
Fees to Review: 0.00 US$

Manuscript Style:
American Psychological Association

CIRCULATION DATA:

Reader: Academics
Frequency of Issue: 10 Times/Year
Copies per Issue:
Sponsor/Publisher: University/Taylor & Francis
Subscribe Price: 233.00 US$ Individual
531.00 US$ Institution

REVIEW INFORMATION:

Type of Review: Blind Review
No. of External Reviewers: 3
No. of In House Reviewers: 0
Acceptance Rate: 21-30%
Time to Review: 1 - 2 Months
Reviewers Comments: Yes
Invited Articles: 0-5%
Fees to Publish: 0.00 US$

MANUSCRIPT TOPICS:

Adult Career & Vocational; Aging In General; Art/Music; Audiology/Speech Pathology; Counseling & Personnel Services; Curriculum Studies; Health & Physical Education; Higher Education; Reading; Religious Education

MANUSCRIPT GUIDELINES/COMMENTS:

Aims and Scope
This well-respected journal offers up-to-date original research in the fields of gerontology, adult education, and the social and behavioral sciences. Researchers from around the world will benefit from the exchange of ideas for both the study and practice of educational gerontology. Papers published in the journal will also serve as authoritative contributions to the growing literature in this burgeoning field. *Educational Gerontology* is the only international journal of its kind to publish eight issues per volume year.

The Institute of Scientific Information Journal Citations Report for 2002 ranks *Educational Gerontology* 22nd out of 24 journals in Gerontology (Social Science) and 69th out of 93 journals in Education & Educational Research, with an impact factor of 0.268.

268

Readership
Gerontologists, adult educators, behavioral and social scientists, and geriatricians.

INSTRUCTIONS FOR AUTHORS

Note to Authors. Please make sure your contact address information is clearly visible on the **outside** of <u>all</u> packages you are sending to Editors.

Submission of Manuscripts
Educational Gerontology: An International Journal publishes refereed materials in the fields of gerontology, adult education, and the social and behavioral sciences. According to the double-blind procedures established for critiquing papers, copies of materials received by the Editor-in-Chief are reviewed by panels appointed by the Editor-in-Chief. The peer review process consists of three or more persons knowledgeable in the areas covered by the materials. Original and two copies of each manuscript should be submitted to the editor, D. Barry Lumsden, University of North Texas, P.O. Box 311337, Denton, Texas 76203-1337.

Authors are required to submit manuscripts on disk. The disk should be prepared using MS Word or WordPerfect and should be clearly labeled with the authors' names, file name, and software program. Each manuscript must be accompanied by a statement that it has not been published elsewhere and that it has not been submitted simultaneously for publication elsewhere. Authors are responsible for obtaining permission to reproduce copyrighted material from other sources and are required to sign an agreement for the transfer of copyright to the publisher. All accepted manuscripts, artwork, and photographs become the property of the publisher.

All parts of the manuscript should be typewritten, double-spaced, with margins of at least one inch on all sides. Number manuscript pages consecutively throughout the paper. Authors should also supply a shortened version of the title suitable for the running head, not exceeding 50 character spaces. Each article should be summarized in an abstract of no more that 100 words. Avoid abbreviations, diagrams, and reference to the text.

Manuscripts, including figures, tables, and references, must conform to the specifications described in the *Publication Manual of the American Psychological Association* (5th ed., 2001). Manuscripts that do not adhere to this style will be returned for revision. Further instructions and an author template can be obtained from the journal's web page at **www.taylorandfrancis.com**.

Illustrations
Illustrations submitted (line drawings, halftones, photos, photomicrographs, etc.) should be clean originals or digital files. Digital files are recommended for highest quality reproduction and should follow these guidelines:
- 300 dpi or higher
- sized to fit on journal page
- EPS, TIFF, or PSD format only
- submitted as separate files, not embedded in text files

Tables and Figures

Tables and figures should not be embedded in the text, but should be included as separate sheets or files. A short descriptive title should appear above each table with a clear legend and any footnotes suitably identified below. All units must be included. Figures should be completely labeled, taking into account necessary size reduction. Captions should be typed, double-spaced, on a separate sheet. All original figures should be clearly marked in pencil on the reverse side with the number, author's name, and top edge indicated.

Proofs

One set of page proofs is sent to the designated corresponding author. Proofs should be checked and returned promptly.

Educational Measurement: Issues and Practice

ADDRESS FOR SUBMISSION:

Steve Ferrara, Editor
Educational Measurement: Issues and
   Practice
American Institutes for Research
1000 Thomas Jefferson St., NW
Washington, DC 20007
USA
Phone: 202-403-5431
Fax: 202-403-5001
E-Mail: sferrara@air.org
Web:
Address May Change:

PUBLICATION GUIDELINES:

Manuscript Length: 21-25
Copies Required: Five
Computer Submission: Yes
Format: ASCII, pdf, Wordperfect, MSWord
Fees to Review: 0.00 US$

Manuscript Style:
   American Psychological Association

CIRCULATION DATA:

Reader: Academics, Education Policy
   Makers, Test Developers,
   Psychometrician
Frequency of Issue: Quarterly
Copies per Issue: 2,001 - 3,000
Sponsor/Publisher: National Council of
   Measurement in Education
Subscribe Price: 40.00 US$ Individual
   65.00 US$ Institution

REVIEW INFORMATION:

Type of Review: Blind Review
No. of External Reviewers: 3+
No. of In House Reviewers: 0
Acceptance Rate: 10-20%
Time to Review: 4 - 6 Months
Reviewers Comments: Yes
Invited Articles: 0-5%
Fees to Publish: 0.00 US$

MANUSCRIPT TOPICS:
Tests, Measurement & Evaluation

MANUSCRIPT GUIDELINES/COMMENTS:

Statement of Editorial Policy
Educational Measurement: Issues and Practice publishes articles that illuminate issues in educational measurement and inform the practice of educational measurement. *EM:IP* is aimed at practitioners and users of tests and includes information about proven practices in testing, news of interest to the educational measurement community, and organizational news of NCME. Not as technical as *Journal of Educational Measurement*, *EM:IP* has as its primary purpose promoting a better understanding of and reasoned debate on timely measurement issues of practical importance to educators and the public.

EM:IP seeks manuscripts that deal with measurement issues of concern to practitioners and academics, applications of measurement techniques in educational settings, and exemplary practices. Examples of manuscripts appropriate for *EM:IP* include those dealing with specific measurement techniques for various educational objectives or controversial measurement issues; surveys of practices and changes in practices; and public critiques of testing and test use. Articles on examples of good practices in educational measurement and articles presenting contrasting views concerning the educational role of testing are welcome.

Manuscript Submission and Review Procedures
Five copies of manuscripts should be submitted. Prepare four of these for "blind" reviews by removing references to author and the author's institution. Manuscripts should be consistent with the style described in the *Publication Manual of the American Psychological Association* (4th ed., 1994). Authors should be parsimonious in the use of tables, graphs, and figures. When used, one original copy suitable for high-quality reproduction as well as four photo copies should accompany the manuscript. Avoid footnotes when possible. All manuscripts [solicited or unsolicited] that are considered for publication in the Articles section are to be sent out to at least three reviewers. Submit manuscripts to the Editor, Steve Ferrara, American Institutes for Research, 1000 Thomas Jefferson St., NW, Washington DC 20007; sferrara@air.org.

Educational Media International

ADDRESS FOR SUBMISSION:

John Hedberg, Editor-In-Chief
Educational Media International
Nanyang Technological University
Learning Sciences and Technology
National Institute of Education
1 Nanyang Walk
Singapore, 637616
Phone: +65 6790 3281
Fax: +65 6896 8038
E-Mail: jhedberg@nie.edu.sg
Web: www.tandf.co.uk/journals
Address May Change:

PUBLICATION GUIDELINES:

Manuscript Length: Apprx 5,000 Words
Copies Required: Two Prefer Electronic
   Subm
Computer Submission: Yes Email
Format: MS Word or RTF Form
Fees to Review: 0.00 US$

Manuscript Style:
   American Psychological Association

CIRCULATION DATA:

Reader: Academics, Educational Media
   Producers
Frequency of Issue: Quarterly
Copies per Issue:
Sponsor/Publisher: International Council
   for Educational Media/Routledge (Taylor
   and Francis)
Subscribe Price: 98.00 US$ Individual
   379.00 US$ Institution

REVIEW INFORMATION:

Type of Review: Blind Review
No. of External Reviewers: 2
No. of In House Reviewers: 1
Acceptance Rate: 35%
Time to Review: 2 - 3 Months
Reviewers Comments: Yes
Invited Articles: 6-10%
Fees to Publish: 0.00 US$

MANUSCRIPT TOPICS:
Adult Career & Vocational; Educational Technology Systems; Higher Education; Library Science/Information Resources

MANUSCRIPT GUIDELINES/COMMENTS:

Aims and Scope
Educational media has made a considerable impact on schools, colleges and providers of open and distance education. This journal provides an international forum for the exchange of information and views on new developments in educational and mass media. Contributions are drawn from academics and professionals whose ideas and experiences come from a number of countries and contexts.

Notes for the Guidance of Authors
The editor is always pleased to receive for consideration articles on aspects of innovation in educational media likely to be of interest to readers. It is most important that manuscripts conform strictly to the notes set out below.

1. Contributions are accepted for publication on condition that the copyright in all original materials vests in the International Council for Educational Media and that the contributor has obtained any necessary permissions and paid any fees for the use of other materials already subject to copyright. Contributors therefore undertake that their material is not a violation of any copyright and undertake to indemnify the International Council for Educational Media for any loss occasioned to the Council in consequence of any breach of this undertaking.

2. Two copies (from outside Western Europe, one non-returnable copy), should be sent to the Editor at the address shown on the title page of the journal. The manuscript should be on A4 paper, typed with 50 characters per line and lines double spaced. Please also provide manuscripts on a PC compatible 3.5" floppy disc (preferably in Word Perfect, Word or as ASCII text).

3. Manuscripts must be in English or French.

4. An abstract between 100 and 150 words should be enclosed. Authors are invited to supply abstracts in French and/or German and these will be printed with accepted papers.

5. Brief biographical notes, containing an address for correspondence, should be enclosed.

6. Footnotes should be avoided.

7. Main headings should be typed in capitals (INTRODUCTION, RESULTS, etc.). Secondary headings should be underlined.

8. Each table, diagram, illustration, etc, should be on a separate sheet, clearly labeled. Material that contains numbers should be referred to as TABLES; material containing diagrams or mostly words should be referred to as FIGURES. Each table and figure should have an explanatory legend, which should be typed at the bottom of the page. The position of each table or figure in the text should be indicated thus:

Table 1 about here

9. *All* illustrations (i.e. charts, graphs, diagrams and photographs *must* be of a high enough quality to permit immediate reproduction. Line artwork should be produced using a Vector drawing package, i.e. Adobe Illustrator, Macromedia Freehand, Corel Draw or Claris Draw with the files being supplied as eps when using Adobe Illustrator and supplied as normal when using Macromedia Freehand, Corel Draw or Claris Draw. Hard copies must also be supplied. Photographs should be glossy prints, unmarked and uncreased, with good contrast. Contributions which are otherwise acceptable may be rejected on the grounds that illustrations are of unsatisfactory quality.

10. References in the text should be made quoting the author's name, followed by the year of publication in brackets. Where reference has been made to a number of publications by an author in one year, these should be distinguished by using suffixes: 1974a, 1974b, etc. References should be listed alphabetically at the end of the paper, in the following way.

Blacklock, S (1976) *Workload*, Open University Survey Research Department, mimeograph.

Connors, B (1972) Testing innovations in course design, *British Journal of Educational Technology*, 3, 1, 48-52.

Lawless, CJ and Kirkwood A (1976a) Training the educational technologies, *British Journal of Educational Technology*, 7, 1, 54-60.

Lawless, CJ and Kirkwood, A (1976b) Individualising instructions for educational technologists. In Evans, L and Leedham, J (eds) *Aspects of Educational Technology IX*, Kogan Page, London.

Rowntree, DGF (1971) The Open University - case study in educational technology V: course production. In Packham, D *et al.* (eds) *Aspects of Educational Technology 5*, Pitman, London.

Tyler, RW (1949) *Basic Principles of Curriculum and Instruction*, University of Chicago Press, Chicago.

Notice that the titles of journals are not abbreviated, and that pagination is always given.

11. The Editor-in-Chief checks proofs of articles.

12. In all matters, the author is asked to consult the Editor *before* submitting a paper, if in any doubt.

13. Upon publication, the first named author will receive one bound copy of the journal for each contributor in addition to 25 offprints of the article to be split between him/herself and those contributors.

Educational Perspectives

ADDRESS FOR SUBMISSION:

Hunter McEwan, Editor
Educational Perspectives
University of Hawaii
College of Education
Wist Hall 113
1176 University Avenue
Honolulu, HI 96822
USA
Phone: 808-956-4242
Fax: 808-956-9100
E-Mail: epedit@hawaii.edu
Web: www.hawaii.edu/edper/
Address May Change:

PUBLICATION GUIDELINES:

Manuscript Length: 16-20
Copies Required: One
Computer Submission: Yes Email
Format: Word, RTF
Fees to Review: 0.00 US$

Manuscript Style:
   Chicago Manual of Style

CIRCULATION DATA:

Reader: Practicing Teachers, Academics
Frequency of Issue: 2 Times/Year
Copies per Issue: 1,001 - 2,000
Sponsor/Publisher: College of Education,
   University of Hawaii
Subscribe Price: 10.00 US$

REVIEW INFORMATION:

Type of Review: Editorial Review
No. of External Reviewers: No Reply
No. of In House Reviewers: No Reply
Acceptance Rate: No Reply
Time to Review: 1 - 2 Months
Reviewers Comments: No
Invited Articles: 90% +
Fees to Publish: 0.00 US$

MANUSCRIPT TOPICS:
Curriculum Studies; Education Management/Administration; Educational Technology
Systems; General Issues in Education; Health Education; Reading; School Law; Teacher
Education; Teacher Education Reform; Tests, Measurement & Evaluation

MANUSCRIPT GUIDELINES/COMMENTS:

Educational Perspectives is a theme-based publication. Information about forthcoming themes
can be obtained at the website **http://www.hawaii.edu/edper**.

Educational Perspectives, the Journal of the College of Education, University of Hawaii at
Manoa, is now in its 38th year of publication. It is a professional journal of recognized stature,
having been cited for Superior Achievement by the Educational Press Association of America
(EdPress) on six separate occasions. It is a 32-page, semiannual publication with a circulation
of 1,200. In addition to serving a local need in educational publication, *Educational
Perspectives* is in the collection of 500 colleges and universities in the United States,

276

including Stanford, Harvard, Yale, Columbia, The University of Michigan, University of California at Berkeley, and the University of California at Los Angeles.

Internationally, it is mailed to 200 educational institutions, including the College of Education (Lagos, Nigeria), Institut Nauchnoi Informatsii (Moscow, Russia) Chinese University (Hong Kiong), Institut Pedagogique National (Paris, France), University College of Dar es Salaam (Tanzania), Shanghai Normal University (Peoples Republic of China), Universita Karlova (Prague, Czech Republic), Universitas Indonesia (Jakarta), Universitetbiblioteket (Oslo, Norway), Universite de Moncton (New Brunswick, Canada), and the University of the South Pacific (Suva, Fiji).

Educational Perspectives is also received by colleges and universities in Japan, Korea, Taiwan, the Philippines, Mexico, Chile, Colombia, Australia, England, Sweden and India.

The major professional educational publication in the State of Hawaii, *Educational Perspectives* provides a forum for the discussion of educational issues in Hawaii and the Pacific, enabling dissemination of these ideas to other parts of the world.

The University of Hawaii Libraries uses *Educational Perspectives* as a one of the publications in its Gifts and Exchange Program with other colleges and universities.

Educational Perspectives is indexed nationally and internationally in the Standard Periodical Dictionary, Ulrich's International Periodicals Directory, EdPress Directory, and Xerox University microfilms (Michigan, Canada and England).

Preparing & Submitting a Manuscript
When preparing a manuscript for submission to *Educational Perspectives*, the following specifications should be followed:
- Length of manuscript 3,000 to 3,500 words.
- Manuscript should be typewritten, double-spaced.
- Manuscript should be submitted using two formats: 1) a computer program which can be converted into a MacIntosh Pagemaker 6.5 application and 2) one xeroxed copy.
- Manuscript should be documented and *Chicago Manual of Style* should be followed; footnotes and bibliography included where needed.
- Subheads are desirable.
- Suitable visual material (photographs should accompany the manuscript and should be high contrast, black and white, glossy prints, 8"x10" or contact sheets with negatives.
- Colored slides, 2"x2" may be requested for use as front cover).
- A brief biographical sketch of manuscript's author(s).
- Reworked speeches are acceptable. Reprints from other publications are not used.

All material (manuscript, photography and biography) should be submitted to:
The Editor, *Educational Perspectives,* College of Education, University of Hawaii, Wist Hall, Room 113, 1776 University Avenue, Honolulu HI 96822

Educational Policy

ADDRESS FOR SUBMISSION:

Ana M. Martinez Aleman, Editor
Educational Policy
Boston College
School of Education
Campion Hall
Chestnut Hill, MA 02467
USA
Phone: 617-552-1760
Fax: 617-552-8422
E-Mail: journal.edpolicy@bc.edu
Web:
Address May Change:

PUBLICATION GUIDELINES:

Manuscript Length: 26-30
Copies Required: Three
Computer Submission: Yes
Format: Word
Fees to Review: 0.00 US$

Manuscript Style:
American Psychological Association

CIRCULATION DATA:

Reader: Academics, Administrators
Frequency of Issue: 5 Times/Year
Copies per Issue: Less than 1,000
Sponsor/Publisher: Sage Publications
Subscribe Price: 110.00 US$ Individual
497.00 US$ Institution

REVIEW INFORMATION:

Type of Review: Blind Review
No. of External Reviewers: 2
No. of In House Reviewers: 1
Acceptance Rate: 21-30%
Time to Review: 3 Months
Reviewers Comments: Yes
Invited Articles: 0-5%
Fees to Publish: 0.00 US$

MANUSCRIPT TOPICS:
Education Management/Administration; Education Policy; Educational Technology Systems; Elementary/Early Childhood; Teacher Education; Urban Education, Cultural/Non-Traditional

MANUSCRIPT GUIDELINES/COMMENTS:

Educational Policy provides an interdisciplinary forum for improving education in primary and secondary schools, as well as in higher education and non-school settings. *Educational Policy* blends the best of educational research with the world of practice, making it a valuable resource for educators, policy makers, administrators, researcher, teachers, and graduate students. *Educational Policy* is concerned with the practical consequences of policy decisions and alternatives. It examines the relationship between educational policy and educational practice, and sheds new light on important debates and controversies within the field. You'll find that *Educational Policy* is an insightful compilation of ideas, strategies, and analyses for improving our educational system.

A regular feature is the "Reviewing Policy" section that presents a short essay by Michael W. Apple, focusing on significant new books or documents that deserve critical attention.

Articles. Essays present thought-provoking, original - and often controversial - analyses for improving educational policy.

Book Reviews. Thoughtful examinations inform you of the latest literature in the field.

Review Essays. Critical discussions compare and contrast collections of recent works.

Special Issues. Single-theme issues provide in-depth coverage of topics of current concern.

Annual Index. Alphabetical listings of authors and titles provide quick and easy reference to valuable information and ideas.

"*Educational Policy* is unique among the journals in this field. The articles address genuine issues of policy and frequently succeed in doing so in an international context. It is always a pleasure and a profit to read a journal with so clear a sense of direction." Harry Judge, *University of Oxford*

"*Educational Policy* is one of the most important and impressive journals in the field. It is essential reading for anyone concerned with the realities of education." Michael W. Apple, *University of Wisconsin, Madison*

Submission Guidelines
Manuscripts should be typewritten, double-spaced, and on one side only of white 8 ½ x 11 paper. Leave generous margins on all four sides of the page. Article title, author's name, professional title, and institutional affiliation on a separate, removable cover sheet. Only the article title should appear on subsequent pages to facilitate blind review. Authors should closely follow the *Publication Manual of the American Psychological Association* (5th edition). Tabular material should be kept to a minimum -- three to four at most. (Authors will be asked to provide camera-ready copy for charts and graphs of articles accepted for publication.) Include a 100-word abstract, as well as a listing of a few important key words, with each article. Submit three hard copies and one soft copy (on a disk or by e-mail) of the manuscript to: Editors, *Educational Policy*, School of Education, 207 Campion Hall, Boston College, Chestnut Hill, MA 02467, **journal.edpolicy@bc.edu**.

Educational Psychologist

ADDRESS FOR SUBMISSION:

Philip H. Winne & Lyn Corno, Co-Editors
Educational Psychologist
Simon Fraser University
Burnaby, BC V5A 1S6
Canada
Phone: 604-291-4858
Fax: 604-291-3203
E-Mail: winne@sfu.ca
Web:
Address May Change: 12/31/2005

PUBLICATION GUIDELINES:

Manuscript Length: 21-25
Copies Required: Five
Computer Submission: No
Format:
Fees to Review: 0.00 US$

Manuscript Style:
American Psychological Association

CIRCULATION DATA:

Reader: Academics
Frequency of Issue: Quarterly
Copies per Issue: 2,001 - 3,000
Sponsor/Publisher:
Subscribe Price: 50.00 US$
　　Free to Div. 15 APA Members

REVIEW INFORMATION:

Type of Review: Blind Review
No. of External Reviewers: 2
No. of In House Reviewers: 1
Acceptance Rate: 21-30%
Time to Review: 2 - 3 Months
Reviewers Comments: Yes
Invited Articles: 31-50%
Fees to Publish: 0.00 US$

MANUSCRIPT TOPICS:
Educational Psychology

MANUSCRIPT GUIDELINES/COMMENTS:

Editorial Scope
The scholarly essays, reviews, critiques, and theoretical and conceptual articles featured in this exceptional journal contribute to understanding issues, problems, and research concerning all aspects of educational psychology. From meta-analyses of experiments probing the effectiveness of instructional methods to historical analyses of theories and research techniques, the journal provides insightful explorations of new educational concepts and accepted educational practices. The journal, however, does not publish articles whose primary purpose is to report the methods and results of an empirical study.

Audience
Educational Psychologists, researchers, teachers, administrators, and policymakers.

Instructions to Contributors
Submission of Manuscripts. Manuscripts must be prepared in accordance with the following instructions.

280

Follow APA Style. Authors should follow the *Publication Manual of the American Psychological Association* (5th ed.) in preparing manuscripts for submission to this journal. All manuscripts must be prefaced by an abstract of 100-150 words on a separate sheet. All manuscript pages, including reference lists and tables, must be typed double-spaced. All figures must be camera ready. Authors should comply with "Guidelines to Reduce Bias in Language" as printed in the *Publication Manual*. Manuscripts that fail to conform to APA-style guidelines will be returned to the author(s).

Prepare For Blind Peer Review. All articles appearing in the *EP* are peer reviewed. Because the reviewers have agreed to participate in a blind reviewing system, authors submitting manuscripts are requested to include with each copy of the manuscript a cover sheet that shows the title of the manuscript, the names of the authors, the authors' institutional affiliations, the mailing address, the date the manuscript is submitted, and a running head. The first page of the manuscript should omit the authors' names and affiliations but should include the title of the manuscript and the date it is submitted. Footnotes containing information pertaining to the authors' identities or affiliations should be placed on separate pages. Every effort should be made by authors to see that the manuscript itself contains no clues to their identities.

Screen for Appropriateness. By submitting manuscripts to the *Educational Psychologist*, authors are confirming that the manuscripts have not been published and are not under consideration for publication elsewhere. Prior to submission, authors should determine whether their manuscripts correspond to the journal's statement of purpose--to publish essays, critiques, and articles of a theoretical/conceptual nature that contribute to our understanding of the issues, problems, and research associated with the field of educational psychology. Articles consistent with the journal's purpose include critical, integrative reviews of educational psychology research; conceptual or theoretical syntheses or analyses of educational psychology research; scientifically documented digests of educational psychology research relevant to policy issues; and documented, scholarly essays of general interest to the educational psychology community. Consistent with the journal's mission to serve as a forum for important ideas in educational psychology, articles of varying lengths and covering all aspects of educational psychology will be considered, including articles focusing on implications for educational theory, research, practice, or policy. Articles that report mainly the results of an empirical study (e.g., would be appropriate for the *Journal of Educational Psychology*) or articles that are intended mainly as practical guides (without research documentation) are inappropriate for the EP and will be returned to the authors. In addition to publishing regular articles, the journal publishes special issues that are devoted to important themes in educational psychology and keynote reviews with published peer commentary. Authors interested in the latter formats are requested to contact the editor prior to submitting a proposal for a special issue or keynote review.

Follow Copyright Laws. Authors are responsible for obtaining and providing written permission from copyright owners for reprinting previously published illustrations, tables, or lengthy quotes (500 or more words). Authors are responsible for the accuracy of the material in their manuscripts.

Submit Five Copies. Send five copies of your manuscripts (an original and four duplicates) to: Philip H. Winne and Lyn Corno, Coeditors, *Educational Psychologist*, Faculty of Education, Simon Fraser University, Burnaby, British Columbia, Canada V5A 1S6. Authors should keep a copy of the manuscript to guard against loss in the mail. After a manuscript is accepted for publication, its author is asked to provide a computer disk containing the manuscript file. Files are copyedited and typeset into page proofs. Authors read proofs to correct errors and answer editors' queries.

Educational Psychology: An Int'l Journal of Experimental Educational Psychology

ADDRESS FOR SUBMISSION:

Kevin Wheldall, Editor
Educational Psychology: An Int'l Journal of
  Experimental Educational Psychology
Macquarie University
Special Education Centre
Sydney, NSW 2109
Australia
Phone: +61 2 9850 9621
Fax: +61 2 9850 9661
E-Mail: ed.psych@speced.sed.mq.edu.au
Web: www.tandf.co.uk/journals
Address May Change:

PUBLICATION GUIDELINES:

Manuscript Length: 21-25
Copies Required: Four
Computer Submission: Yes Disk, Email
Format:
Fees to Review: 0.00 US$

Manuscript Style:
  American Psychological Association

CIRCULATION DATA:

Reader: Academics
Frequency of Issue: Bi-Monthly
Copies per Issue:
Sponsor/Publisher:
Subscribe Price: 302.00 US$
  1466.00 US$

REVIEW INFORMATION:

Type of Review: Blind Review
No. of External Reviewers: 2
No. of In House Reviewers: 0
Acceptance Rate:
Time to Review: 2 - 3 Months
Reviewers Comments: Yes
Invited Articles: No Reply
Fees to Publish: 0.00 US$

MANUSCRIPT TOPICS:
Educational Psychology

MANUSCRIPT GUIDELINES/COMMENTS:

Aims and Scope
This journal provides an international forum for the discussion and rapid dissemination of research findings in psychology relevant to education. The journal places particular emphasis on the publishing of papers reporting applied research based on experimental and behavioural studies. Reviews of relevant areas of literature also appear from time to time.

The aim of the journal is to be a primary source for articles dealing with the psychological aspects of education ranging from pre-school to tertiary provision and the education of children with special needs. The prompt publication of high-quality articles is the journal's first priority.

Instructions for Authors

Note to Authors: please make sure your contact address information is clearly visible on the outside of all packages you are sending to Editors.

Papers accepted become the copyright of the Journal, unless otherwise specifically agreed.

Manuscripts, ideally between 2000 and 8000 words, should be sent electronically to the Editors at **kevin.wheldall@mq.edu.au**. Where this is not possible, 3 copies of the article, with any illustrations, should be submitted to: Professor Kevin Wheldall, Macquarie University Special Education Centre, Macquarie University, Sydney, NSW 2109, Australia. Articles supplied as hard copy should be printed on one side of the paper, double spaced, with ample margins adhering strictly to the style guide of the American Psychological Association (APA) (fifth edition). Authors should use the Oxford Dictionary as a guide for spelling.

A cover sheet should bear the title of the contribution, name(s) of the author(s) and the address where the work was carried out. A second sheet should again give the title of the piece (without the name(s) of the author(s), to facilitate 'blind' refereeing), together with an abstract of 100 - 150 words. The full postal address, email address and fax number of the author who will check proofs and receive correspondence and offprints should also be included. All pages should be numbered. Footnotes to the text should be avoided.

Statistics. Given the experimental remit of this journal, it is expected that indications of effect size will be included by authors, where possible, so as to allow readers to form a judgement as to the importance of any experimental findings reported.

Tables and captions to illustrations. Tables must be printed out on separate sheets and not included as part of the text. The captions to illustrations should be gathered together and also printed out on a separate sheet. Tables and figures should be numbered separately. The approximate position of tables and figures should be indicated in the manuscript. Captions should include keys to symbols.

Figures. Please supply one set of artwork in a finished form, suitable for reproduction, since figures will not normally be redrawn by the publisher.

References should be indicated in the typescript by giving the author's name, with the year of publication in parentheses, as detailed in the *APA* style guide. If several papers by the same author(s) and from the same year are cited, a, b, c, etc. should be put after the year of publication. The references should be listed in full at the end of the paper in standard APA format. For example:

Adams, M. J. (1990). Beginning to read: Thinking and learning about print. Cambridge, MA: MIT Press.

Kameenui, E. J., Simmons, D. C., Baker, S., Chard, D. J., Dickson, S. V., Gunn, B., Smith, S. B., Sprick, M., & Lin, S-J. (1998). Effective strategies in teaching beginning reading. In E. J. Kameenui & D. C. Simmons (Eds.), Effective teaching strategies that accommodate diverse learners. (pp. 45-70; 194-196). New Jersey: Prentice Hall.

284

Stanovich, K. E. (1986). Matthew effects in reading: Some consequences of individual differences in the acquisition of literacy. Reading Research Quarterly, 21, 360-407.

If you have any further questions about the style for this journal, please submit your questions using the Style Queries form.

Acceptance. Upon acceptance of the paper for publication, authors will be required to resubmit their article to the editors on disk, in either PC or Apple Macintosh formats, preferably using the Microsoft Word program.

Proofs will be sent to authors if there is sufficient time to do so. They should be corrected and returned to the Joint Editors within three days. Major alterations to the text cannot be accepted.

Early Electronic Offprints. Corresponding authors can now receive their article by e-mail as a complete PDF. This allows the author to print up to 50 copies, free of charge, and disseminate them to colleagues. In many cases this facility will be available up to two weeks prior to publication. Or, alternatively, corresponding authors will receive the traditional 50 offprints. A copy of the journal will be sent by post to all corresponding authors after publication. Additional copies of the journal can be purchased at the author's preferential rate of £15.00/$25.00 per copy.

Educational Studies: A Journal in Foundations of Education

ADDRESS FOR SUBMISSION:

Rebecca Martusewicz, Editor
Educational Studies: A Journal in
   Foundations of Education
Eastern Michigan University
College of Education
313 Porter
Yspilanti, MI 48197
USA
Phone: 734-487-7210 ext 2624
Fax: 734-187-2101
E-Mail: rmartusew@emich.edu
Web: www.uakron.edu/aesa
Address May Change:

PUBLICATION GUIDELINES:

Manuscript Length: 25-30
Copies Required: Three
Computer Submission: Yes Disk, Email
Format: MSWord
Fees to Review: 0.00 US$

Manuscript Style:
   Chicago Manual of Style

CIRCULATION DATA:

Reader: Academics
Frequency of Issue: 2 Times/Year
Copies per Issue: No Reply
Sponsor/Publisher: American Educational
   Studies Association, Lawrence Erlbaum
   Associates
Subscribe Price: 35.00 US$ Individual
   150.00 US$ Institution
   65.00 US$ Indv. & $150 Inst. Foreign

REVIEW INFORMATION:

Type of Review: Juried
No. of External Reviewers: 2-4
No. of In House Reviewers: 1
Acceptance Rate: 40-50%
Time to Review: 2 - 3 Months
Reviewers Comments: Yes
Invited Articles: 11-20%
Fees to Publish: 0.00 US$

MANUSCRIPT TOPICS:
Foundations of Education; Higher Education; History, Philosophy, Policy Studies; Issues in Education; Urban Education, Cultural/Non-Traditional

MANUSCRIPT GUIDELINES/COMMENTS:

Preparing a Manuscript
Submission Guidelines for Articles: Notes and References: Provide complete, formatted references, text citations, and notes according to the *Chicago Manual of Style*, fifteenth edition. Notes that contain only bibliographic material should be incorporated into the references.

Suggested length of articles is 25 to 30 pages, double-spaced. Include an abstract with your name and address, telephone number, and e-mail address. Send four copies of the manuscript and a disk formatted in Microsoft Word 2000 to the address below.

286

Take a few moments now to make certain that your manuscript is complete and that it complies with the editorial guidelines appearing in *The Chicago Manual of Style* (15th ed.). (The manual is available from the University of Chicago Press, Direct Mail Department, 5801 South Ellis Avenue, Chicago, IL 60637; 773568-1550; www.press.uchicago.edu.) You may find it helpful to consult The Author's Manuscript section appearing on pages 49 through 62 of *The Chicago Manual of Style,* the contributor information appearing in the journal, and/or the following summary of requirements for acceptable manuscripts. If you have any questions whatsoever, please ask for clarification.

Typing. Use 8 ½ x 11-in. non-smear paper. Set all margins at 1 in. Type all components double-spaced, including title page, abstract, text, acknowledgments, references, appendixes, tables, figure captions, and notes. Indent all paragraphs and make sure the entire manuscript is neat and readable. Use superscript numbers to cite notes; do not use the automatic function for notes; type all notes on a separate page (not at the bottom of the pages on which they are cited). Type all figure captions on a separate page.

Abstract. An abstract is required, consult the Editor or the journal for the limit on length.

Notes and References. Provide complete, formatted references, text citations, and notes according to *The Chicago Manual of Style* guidelines, chapters 15 and 16. For references, use the example on p. 648 as a guide. This is the humanities style, but dates immediately follow the authors' names. For text citations, use the examples on p. 641, 16.3, and p. 643,16.10. For notes, use the example on p. 530. Notes that contain only bibliographic material should be incorporated into the references.

Figures. Submit (a) high-quality laser prints, professionally prepared black-and-white originals, or camera-ready glossy reproductions; (b) photocopies of all figures; and (c) as many computer files for these figures as you have (see Preparing a Disk). Please note that figures appearing in the journal will look only as good as what you provide. Make sure lettering and details are crisp, clear, and large enough so that they will be legible upon reduction. (Figures are reduced in size to conserve space on the printed page.)

All hard copies for which we do not have computer files will be scanned electronically, so please avoid using gray shading or dot screens in graphs. Use solid black or white or diagonal lines to distinguish columns instead.

Make sure each figure is identified. Assess whether textual information appearing on a piece of artwork might be best presented as part of the caption; alter artwork and caption accordingly.

Permissions. *You* are responsible for all statements made in your work and for obtaining permission from the copyright owner(s) to reprint or adapt a table or figure or to reprint quotes from one source totaling 500 words or more. Write to original author(s) and publisher to request nonexclusive world rights in all languages to use the material in the article and in future print and online editions. Please note that you must obtain permission for any lines of poetry or song lyrics you quote as well as for prose, and that you will be liable for any licensing fees required for such use. Provide copies of all permissions and credit lines obtained. Attached to this letter are (a) a sample permission request form you can copy/ adapt and use to secure permissions and (b) sample credit lines from *The Chicago Manual of Style*.

Concordance of Elements. Make sure your manuscript is complete and internally consistent. Each reference must be cited in text at least once; each citation must have a corresponding reference. Likewise, each figure, table, and note must be cited; if a figure, table, or note is cited in text, the corresponding element must be included with the manuscript.

Preparing a Disk

Now is the time to submit the file (as well as an ASCII version) for copyediting and typesetting. Working with an electronic manuscript allows us to capture your keystrokes-thereby maintaining the accuracy of your article and reducing the time between research and publication.

Shortening the production schedule involves combining the stages of author review of copyedited articles and subsequent review of typeset page proofs into a single review of proofs made from copyedited disk files via desktop publishing. With timely publication the concern of all involved, we assume you will (a) accept minor editorial changes that do not alter intended meanings and (b) alter page proofs only to correct errors, update publication information, and respond to editors' queries. As substantial alterations will not be made after manuscripts have been typeset, please take the time now to *make sure that your manuscript and its file are complete and identical* and that they represent your "final say."

Our first choice for format is MS word.

Macintosh and IBM users. Submit on a high-density disk containing a file in MS Word.

Other computer users. Please try to convert and transfer your file to an IBM-compatible or Mac disk; then follow directions for IBM-compatible or Mac users.

However you submit your electronic manuscript, please (a) let us know computer type (IBM-compatible, Macintosh), word processor (including version number), and file name; and (b) make sure the content of the files exactly matches that of the printed, accepted, finalized manuscript.

In addition, if your figures were prepared using a computer and you can obtain files from which the hard copies were printed, please include these on your disk (or on additional disks if they are too large) too.

If you have any questions regarding disk preparation, please contact Steve Cestaro.

Preparing a Review

Book reviews in *Educational Studies* are an important scholarly contribution to the literature of education. Reviews are one way to help evaluate the quality of scholarship, to keep other scholars informed, and to examine important issues. A review should be looked at as the opportunity to critique scholarly work. In its own right, a review can be an original and creative contribution to scholarship. Emphasis should be given to the strengths, weaknesses, and possible implications of the work being reviewed. A careful analysis of the author's scholarship and the depth and breadth of the book is desirable. The reviewer should thus draw from her/his knowledge, experience, and individual style when writing a review.

Length. The desired length is 2,000 words; please provide a word count at the end of the text.

Format. Lay out the bibliographic information and reviewer's name at the top of the first page as in the following example:

Learning Together: A History of Coeducation in American Public Schools. David Tyack and Elisabeth Hansot. New Haven, CT: Yale University Press, 1990. Pp. x, 369. $29.95; $XX.XX (Include The Cost Of A Paper Edition If There Is One).

JANE J. JONES
University of California at Santa Cruz

Deadline. Check with the editorial staff about the deadline for your submission. The editor reserves the right to edit your reviews received for publication and to reject or return for revision reviews considered wanting. You will receive one copy of the issue in which your review appears.

Taking Action
In a nutshell, now is the time for you to (a) make sure your manuscript is formatted correctly, (b) check on permissions, and (c) send the finalized manuscript - printout and disk - to the Editor.

We hope this letter has been informative, and we look forward to working with you. If you think of a way we can improve the production process, by all means let us know. We're here to help.

Sincerely,
Journal Production Department
Lawrence Erlbaum Associates, Inc.

Rebecca A. Martusewicz, Editor
Educational Studies
313 Porter
Eastern Michigan University
Yspilanti, MI 48197
(734) 487-3186
(734) 487-2101 fax
rmartusew@emich.edu

Tables/Figures From Other Sources
Authors are required to obtain permission to reproduce or adapt all or part of a table or figure from a copyrighted source. It is not necessary to obtain permission from Lawrence Erlbaum Associates, Inc. (LEA) to reproduce one table or figure from an LEA article provided you

obtain the author's permission and give full credit to LEA as copyright holder and to the author through a complete, accurate citation. When you wish to reproduce material from sources not copyrighted by LEA, contact the copyright holders to determine their requirements. If you have any doubt about the policy of the copyright holder, you should request permission. Always enclose the letter of permission when transmitting the final version of the accepted manuscript for production.

Any reproduced table or figure must be accompanied by a source note at the bottom of the reprinted table or in the figure caption giving credit to the original author and to the copyright holder. Use the following forms for tables and figures, but omit Source: in credit lines for figures. (See Chapter 15 for more information.)

Material reprinted from a journal article
Source: Reprinted, by permission of the Copyright Owner, from Author's Full Name and Co-Author's Full Name, "Title of Article," Title of Journal Volume (Year): Page Number.

Material reprinted from a book
Source: Reprinted, by permission of the Copyright Owner, from Author's Full Name and Co-Author's Full Name, Title of Book, (Place of Publication: Publisher, Year), Page Number.

Educause Quarterly

ADDRESS FOR SUBMISSION:

N. Hays, Editor
Educause Quarterly
Educause
Suite 206
4772 Walnut Street
Boulder, CO 80301
USA
Phone: 303-939-0321
Fax: 303-440-0461
E-Mail: eqeditor@educause.edu
Web: www.educause.edu/pub/eq/
Address May Change:

CIRCULATION DATA:

Reader: Academics, Managers of
   Information Technology
Frequency of Issue: Quarterly
Copies per Issue: 8,000-8,500
Sponsor/Publisher: Educause
Subscribe Price: 52.00 US$ Individual
   24.00 US$ Educause Members
   24.00 US$ Academic Library

PUBLICATION GUIDELINES:

Manuscript Length: 3,500-6,000 Words
Copies Required: One
Computer Submission: Yes (preferred)
Format: MS Word or plain text
Fees to Review: 0.00 US$

Manuscript Style:
   Chicago Manual of Style

REVIEW INFORMATION:

Type of Review: Blind Review
No. of External Reviewers: 6+
No. of In House Reviewers: 1
Acceptance Rate: 25%
Time to Review: 1 - 2 Months
Reviewers Comments: Yes
Invited Articles: 0-5%
Fees to Publish: 0.00 US$

MANUSCRIPT TOPICS:
Education Management/Administration; Educational Technology Systems; Higher Education;
Library Science/Information Resources

MANUSCRIPT GUIDELINES/COMMENTS:

Anyone in the profession (including those who are not *Educause* members) may submit
unsolicited manuscripts for publication consideration in *Educause Quarterly*. People
employed by corporations whose products and/or services are related to higher education
information technology may also contribute material for publication. All material published
must be free from endorsement or promotion of specific hardware environments and/or
proprietary software or services, whether written by corporate or campus representatives.

Who Reads *Educause Quarterly*
Educause is an international, nonprofit association for managers of information technology on
college and university campuses. The content of *EQ* relates to planning, managing and using
information resources (including technology, services, and information) in higher education,

administrative, academic, and library computing, as well as multimedia, telecommunications, and networking.

Educause members and other subscribers are involved in many different aspects of managing computing and other information resources. Their experience in the profession runs the gamut from those who have just begun, to those who have many years of experience (more than half have more than fifteen years experience).

Most of our readers are administrators or managers, with roughly three-quarters at the director level or above in their professional positions. Many have a background which includes programming, but current responsibilities, interests, and activities are often broader and more diverse. Frequently they are technical experts in one part of the field, while developing professional skills in other areas.

Publication Content
Educause publications deal with the subject of campus information technology from a use and management point of view. Areas of interest include:
- Personnel issues
- Information technology organization
- Management techniques
- Information. technology planning and policy
- End-user/departmental computing
- Executive/decision support systems
- Data administration/information management
- Application systems development
- Industry and interinstitutional partnerships
- Integrating voice, video, and data technologies
- Scholarly communication issues
- Library technology issues
- Academic computing management issues
- Use of new technologies on campus
- Hardware/software strategies and architectures
- Funding information technology
- IT in support of institutional mission
- Classroom delivery and multimedia management
- Training of staff and users
- Standards
- Information services delivery models
- Leveraging/value of information technology

Examples of appropriate material for articles, papers, or monographs include:
- Reports of research and/or data collection relevant to managing technology, preferably with analysis and assessment of the data;
- Guidelines for handling common IT challenges, problems, or professional responsibilities;

- Case studies, i.e., success or failure experiences;
- Theoretical analyses or conceptual discussions of issues facing the IT profession; and
- Explorations of some aspect of a topic related to effective management and/or use of IT in general or to a subset of the EDUCAUSE membership (e.g., small colleges, multicampus institutions,, two-year colleges, CIOs, institutional researchers, and planners)

Copyright

Once material has been accepted for publication, authors are asked to sign an author agreement form which assures Educause that the authors have the right to publish the materials, grants Educause the right to publish the work in print and electronic formats, and leaves the copyright ownership with the authors, and that the authors understand that Educause does not pay authors honoraria. The agreement also gives Educause the right to edit the material to meet the association's standards and to grant permission for educational use of the content without further author permission.

Publication

EQ is published four times a year (approximately in February, May, August, and November). Articles may be contributed at any time for publication consideration. Potential articles are reviewed by members of the Editorial Committee and those published in *EQ* are referenced in such indexing services as ERIC, Computer Literature Index, and Higher Education Abstracts. The reviewing process usually takes from six to eight weeks; author revision and the editorial/production cycle may take four to five months.

Articles in *EQ* fall into several categories. A Feature is an in-depth article that may take one of the forms listed above under publication content under examples of appropriate materials. Feature articles fall in the range of 3,000 to 6,000 words. Other types of articles (800 to 3,000 words) include Current Issues, Viewpoints, and Good Ideas. A Current Issues article is a brief overview of a timely issue facing the profession; such an article puts the designated issue into perspective and may offer insights or propose solutions. A Viewpoint article is one which expresses an author's opinion on a subject related to the field, often one about which there is some controversy. A Good Ideas article describes an application or management technique that has been successful on a campus and could be implemented by colleagues on other campuses. We also publish book reviews in the Recommended Reading department. Although as a rule we solicit these from members with a known expertise on the book topic, any reader may volunteer to write a review of a book that he or she would recommend for professional reading.

Specifications For Submitting Articles For Publication Consideration

Manuscripts should be accompanied by a letter that states that the paper is to be considered for publication in *EQ* magazine. The first page of the manuscript should include name, title, complete address, and phone number, as well as a FAX number and e-mail address, for each author. The second page should include the article title and abstract. Electronic submission is preferred, and preferred software is MS Word for Windows.

Authors must provide a biographical information including title and name institution where employed.

If the paper will include photos, they must be sent in electronic form. Publication is in black-and-white only.

The Editorial Review Process

Articles under consideration for publication as feature articles in *EQ* are sent for review to six or more of the twelve-member committee (listed on the inside front cover of each issue of the magazine). Reviewers evaluate the articles in four categories:

- Overall quality of the article
- Quality and appropriateness of the topic
- Author's knowledge and coverage of the topic (with special efforts to cover the "people" aspects of the concept or experience)
- Readability of the article.

They also provide comments concerning how the article could be improved and often make specific suggestions along those lines. (Even the best articles are usually revised before publication.)

If the article has been rated highly in terms of topic quality and author's knowledge and coverage, it is generally considered a potential for publication. The editor then shares reviewer comments and suggestions with the author and requests a revision. If the author is willing to work within the framework prescribed by the editor, the article is accepted for publication, contingent on revisions, and the revision process begins. The editor then works with the author until the article is ready for publication.

Following are some guidelines intended to convey what the editor and reviewers are looking for in articles submitted for publication. Here are a few questions used to help make a judgment as to whether an article should be pursued for publication. Each desirable attribute is followed by a description of things to avoid in writing for *EQ:*

Is the information relevant, i.e., will readers find it practical, applicable, useful? Will it serve the needs of some segment of the readership?
- Avoid relating an experience that is so peculiar and unique to your campus that it wouldn't work anywhere else.

Is the information readable, i.e., is it easy to understand, clearly and cogently presented?
- Avoid using unnecessary jargon or failing to explain the jargon you must use
- Avoid mixing chronological and how-to approaches, confusing the reader with inconsistent verb tenses throughout the article.
- Avoid the passive voice and stilted language -- keep it straightforward and simple.
- Avoid text that runs on without subdivisions or headings.

Is the subject appropriate for *EQ* readers, and has the author taken into account the expertise and interests of Educause members (e.g., are the complexity, tone, and style appropriate? has the topic been covered from a management perspective?)
- Avoid writing about a subject that is not within the purview of Educause

- Avoid relating only the technical aspects of the concepts or experience and failing to discuss the "people" and management issues.

Is the information comprehensive, i.e., does it address the major elements of a situation or idea, or reference the literature where other major elements are addressed?

- Avoid taking such a narrow view that your article doesn't take into account or acknowledge the experiences of others in the same area, or fails to draw on the published body of knowledge.

Does the information advance the reader's knowledge, i.e., does it convey a new idea or deal with an old one from a fresh or innovative perspective?

- Avoid writing on a subject that has already been covered many times before in the magazine, especially if your article adds nothing new from a practical standpoint but simply re-states conventional wisdom.

When a feature-length article is essentially the presentation of a case study, it is important that the article do more than simply tell "what we did on our campus." Case study experiences must be presented in a way that makes them generalizable to others. It is critical to be candid and reveal not only success factors but also problems encountered, especially from the point of view of offering lessons learned. It is also important to place the experience in a conceptual framework, relating it to the literature. For any kind of feature article, a list of suggested articles, books, and other publications on the same subject is especially valuable, even if you have not used these references in the article.

e-Journal of Instructional Science and Technology

ADDRESS FOR SUBMISSION:

Alan Smith, Executive Editor
e-Journal of Instructional Science and
    Technology
Phone: +61 7 46 31 2296
Fax: +61 7 46 31 2051
E-Mail: smith@usq.edu.au
Web: www.usq.edu.au/electpub/e-jist/
Address May Change:

PUBLICATION GUIDELINES:

Manuscript Length: 6-10
Copies Required: One
Computer Submission: Yes Disk, Email
Format:
Fees to Review: 0.00 US$

Manuscript Style:
    Uniform System of Citation (Harvard
    Blue Book)

CIRCULATION DATA:

Reader: Academics
Frequency of Issue: 2 Times/Year
Copies per Issue: Less than 1,000
Sponsor/Publisher: The University of
    Southern Queensland
Subscribe Price:

REVIEW INFORMATION:

Type of Review: Blind Review
No. of External Reviewers: 2
No. of In House Reviewers: 1
Acceptance Rate: 21-30%
Time to Review: 2 - 3 Months
Reviewers Comments: Yes
Invited Articles: 0-5%
Fees to Publish: 0.00 US$

MANUSCRIPT TOPICS:
Education Management/Administration; Educational Psychology; Educational Technology Systems; Higher Education; Library Science/Information Resources

MANUSCRIPT GUIDELINES/COMMENTS:

About *e-JIST*
The *e-Journal of Instructional Science and Technology* (*e-JIST*) is an international peer-reviewed electronic journal.

The *Journal* is a multi-faceted publication with content likely to be of interest to policy makers, managers, investors, professional staff, technical staff, and academics within education and training.

The editions of *e-JIST* will adopt an evolutionary style.

In the meantime, the *Journal* continues to welcome new contributions based on original work of practitioners and researchers with specific focus or implications for the design of instructional materials.

CONTRIBUTORS GUIDELINES

Papers
Presentations, in English, are solicited for consideration for publication - provided they have neither been published nor are being considered for publication, elsewhere.

Style
As much as possible, typescript should conform to the following:
- Word document
- Arial font
- 12 point
- Title of paper (Capitals, bold, centered), top of page
- Author's name (centered under title of paper)
- Sub-headings (left aligned, bold)

Based on an A4 page size use the following margins:
- Top 1"
- Bottom 1"
- Left 1.25"
- Right 1.25"
- Gutter 0"
- Header 0.5"
- Footer 0.5"

All figures and tables should be integrated in the typescript.

To assist you in the preparation of your submission a Microsoft Word template has been established. It has embedded in it, the layout and styles as specified above.

Abstract
An abstract of not more than 100 words should accompany each submission.

Submission of Articles
Submissions, which should normally be between 2000 and 6000 words, are to be forwarded by electronic mail to the Executive Editor, Alan Smith (**smith@usq.edu.au**)

Submission details
Authors' names, titles, affiliations, with complete mailing addresses, including e-mail, telephone and facsimile numbers should appear on the first page (if sent as a document attachment) or the first screen page (if sent as a direct email message) to ensure anonymity in reviewing.

Authors are completely responsible for the factual accuracy of their contributions and neither the Editorial Board of *e-JIST* nor the University of Southern Queensland accepts any responsibility for the assertions and opinions of contributors. Authors are responsible for obtaining permission to quote lengthy excerpts from previously-published articles.

Publications
All articles arc refereed by at least two experts on the subject. The Executive Editor and the Founding Editors reserve the right to suggest changes and corrections and to decide the final acceptance and publication schedule of accepted manuscripts.

English Leadership Quarterly

ADDRESS FOR SUBMISSION:

Bonita L. Wilcox, Editor
English Leadership Quarterly
PO Box 142
Cambridge Springs, PA 16403
USA
Phone: 814-398-2528
Fax: 814-398-8130
E-Mail: blwilcox@direcway.com
Web: www.NCTE.org
Address May Change: 8/1/2008

PUBLICATION GUIDELINES:

Manuscript Length: 1-20
Copies Required: One
Computer Submission: Yes Disk, Email
Format: Microsoft Word
Fees to Review: 0.00 US$

Manuscript Style:
American Psychological Association,
Camera ready, error free copy

CIRCULATION DATA:

Reader: Practicing Teachers, Academics
Frequency of Issue: Quarterly
Copies per Issue: 2,001 - 3,000
Sponsor/Publisher: National Council of
Teachers of English (NCTE) Conference
on English Leadership (CEL)
Subscribe Price: 25.00 US$

REVIEW INFORMATION:

Type of Review: Editorial Review
No. of External Reviewers: 0-1
No. of In House Reviewers: 1-2
Acceptance Rate: 11-20%
Time to Review: 2 - 3 Months
Reviewers Comments: No
Invited Articles: 0-5%
Fees to Publish: 0.00 US$

MANUSCRIPT TOPICS:

Curriculum Studies; Distance Learning; Education Management/Administration; Educational Leadership; Educational Technology Systems; Elementary/Early Childhood; English Literature; Gifted Children; Higher Education; Languages & Linguistics; Literacy Education; Reading; Secondary/Adolescent Studies; Teacher Education; Writing

MANUSCRIPT GUIDELINES/COMMENTS:

English Leadership Quarterly is a themed journal seeking manuscripts of interest to those in leadership positions in English education and literacy learning. Book reviews, software reviews, and Website reviews related to themes are encouraged.

ERS Spectrum

ADDRESS FOR SUBMISSION:

Jeanne N. Chircop, Editor
ERS Spectrum
Educational Research Service
2000 Clarendon Blvd.
Arlington, VA 22201
USA
Phone: 703-248-6226
Fax: 703-248-8410
E-Mail: jchircop@ers.org
Web: www.ers.org
Address May Change:

PUBLICATION GUIDELINES:

Manuscript Length: 11-25
Copies Required: Two
Computer Submission: Yes
Format: any
Fees to Review: 0.00 US$

Manuscript Style:
    See Manuscript Guidelines

CIRCULATION DATA:

Reader: Administrators
Frequency of Issue: Quarterly
Copies per Issue: 2,001 - 3,000
Sponsor/Publisher: Educational Research
  Service
Subscribe Price:

REVIEW INFORMATION:

Type of Review: Peer Review
No. of External Reviewers: 2
No. of In House Reviewers: 3
Acceptance Rate: 30%
Time to Review: 1-3 Months
Reviewers Comments: Yes for slight
  revision
Invited Articles: 6-10%
Fees to Publish: 0.00 US$

MANUSCRIPT TOPICS:
Education Management/Administration; Elementary/Early Childhood; Secondary/Adolescent
Studies

MANUSCRIPT GUIDELINES/COMMENTS:

Educational Research Service welcomes manuscripts for the *ERS Spectrum* from all sources. Manuscripts from practicing school administrators dealing with research and educational programs in their local school districts are especially appropriate for publication. *Spectrum* publishes original research and information for educational leadership. *Spectrum* articles cover a broad range of topics, including public school management, school policy, administrative methods, finance, personnel relations, instructional programs, and related areas.

Manuscripts submitted for publication should be based on research data, practical information, or direct experience. The editors request two copies of each submitted manuscript, typed double-spaced on 8 1/2 x 11" paper. Because of space limitations, manuscripts should be no longer than 25 pages.

300

ERS reserves the right to edit, abridge, or abstract manuscripts selected for publication. Editorial changes will be submitted to the authors for approval except when publication deadlines will not permit it. Manuscripts are accepted for publication with the understanding that they are original writings that have not been published before, and that are not currently under consideration for publication elsewhere.

The views, opinions, and data contained in the articles published in the *ERS Spectrum* are those of the respective authors, and do not necessarily represent those of the Educational Research Service or any of its sponsoring organizations.

Essays in Education

ADDRESS FOR SUBMISSION:

Timothy Lintner, Editor
Essays in Education
University of South Carolina, Aiken
471 University Parkway
Aiken, SC 29801
USA
Phone: 803-641-3564
Fax: 803-641-3698
E-Mail: tlintner@usca.edu
Web: www.usca.edu/essays/
Address May Change:

PUBLICATION GUIDELINES:

Manuscript Length: 11-15
Copies Required: Electronic
Computer Submission: Yes
Format: MS Word
Fees to Review: 0.00 US$

Manuscript Style:
     American Psychological Association

CIRCULATION DATA:

Reader: Practicing Teachers, Academics,
     Administrators
Frequency of Issue: Quarterly
Copies per Issue: No Reply
Sponsor/Publisher: No Reply
Subscribe Price: No Reply

REVIEW INFORMATION:

Type of Review: Blind Review
No. of External Reviewers: 2
No. of In House Reviewers: 1
Acceptance Rate: 30%
Time to Review: 2-4 Months
Reviewers Comments: Yes
Invited Articles: 0-5%
Fees to Publish: 0.00 US$

MANUSCRIPT TOPICS:
Adult Career & Vocational; Art/Music; Bilingual/E.S.L.; Counseling & Personnel Services;
Curriculum Studies; Education Management/Administration; Educational Psychology;
Elementary/Early Childhood; English Literature; Gifted Children; Health & Physical
Education; Higher Education; Reading; Rural Education & Small Schools; School Law;
Science Math & Environment; Secondary/Adolescent Studies; Social Studies/Social Science;
Special Education; Teacher Education; Tests, Measurement & Evaluation; Urban Education,
Cultural/Non-Traditional

MANUSCRIPT GUIDELINES/COMMENTS:

Essays in Education is a peer-reviewed electronic journal that seeks to explore the multitude
of issues that impact and influence education.

In accord with its broad focus, the journal welcomes contributions that enhance the exchange
of diverse theoretical and practical information among educators, practitioners, and
researchers around the world.

302

Beyond publishing original articles, the journal's editorial board will consider reviews of educational software, books and pedagogical materials. However, reviews must describe the practitioner's actual experiences using such materials.

Submissions to the Journal

Authors submitting works to *Essays in Education* warrant that their works are not currently under consideration by any other publication and that any portion of the work is not subject to additional copyright regulations, unless prior required consents have been obtained.

Articles are to be submitted to the editor, preferably by electronic mail.
Send to: **tlintner@usca.edu**

Editor
Essays in Education
School of Education
University of South Carolina, Aiken
471 University Parkway
Aiken, SC 29801

Cover Sheet, Title, Author Information and Key Words

Please provide a cover sheet indicating the title of the article, the author's name and institutional affiliation, and both electronic and standard addresses.

The title of the manuscript should appear on the first page of the text. Leave blank a single line and then list the author's name and institutional affiliation. Continue this format for multiple authors.

Leave a blank line, then type "KEY WORDS" and list three to six key words or phrases (separated by semicolons) that may be used to index the manuscript.

Abstracts

Each manuscript should be accompanied by an abstract. Insert the abstract between the list of key words and the beginning of the text. Abstracts should not exceed 15 lines in length.

Guidelines

Although there is no established length, scholarly articles between 15-30 pages are preferred. Though tables and graphs are welcome, these should be used sparingly within the body of the text.

Single space all copy. Insert a blank line between paragraphs, between references in the REFERENCE section, and before and after subheadings, etc.

Use the American Psychological Association (APA) format for all citations and references. Please contact the editors for any format questions that are not covered in the most recent edition of the *APA Publication Manual*.

All major headings and subheadings should be flush left.

Refereeing Process
Articles submitted for publication consideration to *Essays in Education* are peer-reviewed by three referees who are chosen from the *EIE* Editorial Board. The refereeing process is double-blind; authors and referees are anonymous to each other.

Before sending a submission to the referees, the author's name and affiliation are removed. Authors are responsible for removing any references or clues as to their identity or affiliation within the body of the paper.

Reprints of Articles
Articles included in *Essays in Education* may be reproduced for any medium for non-commercial purposes.

Evaluation and Program Planning

ADDRESS FOR SUBMISSION:

Jonathan Morell, Editor
Evaluation and Program Planning
Altarum / PO Box 14001
Ann Arbor, MI 48113-4001
For Courier Service:
3520 Green Court, Suite 300
Ann Arbor, MI 48105
USA
Phone: 735-995-1795
Fax:
E-Mail: jonny.morell@altarum.org
Web: See Guidelines
Address May Change:

PUBLICATION GUIDELINES:

Manuscript Length: 16-20
Copies Required: One
Computer Submission: Yes
Format: Word, other wp formats
Fees to Review: 0.00 US$

Manuscript Style:
    American Psychological Association

CIRCULATION DATA:

Reader: Academics
Frequency of Issue: Quarterly
Copies per Issue: Less than 1000-2000
Sponsor/Publisher:
Subscribe Price: 179.00 US$ Personal
    762.00 US$
    AEA member

REVIEW INFORMATION:

Type of Review: Blind Review
No. of External Reviewers: 2-3
No. of In House Reviewers: 1
Acceptance Rate: 50%
Time to Review: 2 - 3 Months
Reviewers Comments: Yes
Invited Articles: 21-30%
Fees to Publish: 0.00 US$

MANUSCRIPT TOPICS:
Education Management/Administration; Evaluation

MANUSCRIPT GUIDELINES/COMMENTS:

Description
Purpose and Intent of the Journal. Evaluation and Program Planning is based on the principle that the techniques and methods of evaluation and planning transcend the boundaries of specific fields and that relevant contributions to these areas come from people representing many different positions, intellectual traditions, and interests. In order to further the development of evaluation and planning, we publish articles from the private and public sectors in a wide range of areas: organizational development and behavior, training, planning, human resource development, health and mental, social services, mental retardation, corrections, substance abuse, and education. The primary goals of the journal are to assist evaluators and planners to improve the practice of their professions, to develop their skills and to improve their knowledge base.

Types of Articles Published. We publish articles, "special issues" (usually a section of an issue), and book reviews. Articles are of two types: 1) reports on specific evaluation or planning efforts, and 2) discussions of issues relevant to the conduct of evaluation and planning.

Reports on individual evaluations should include presentation of the evaluation setting, design, analysis and results. Because of our focus and philosophy, however, we also want a specific section devoted to "lessons learned". This section should contain advice to other evaluators about how you would have acted differently if you could do it all over again. The advice may involve methodology, how the evaluation was implemented or conducted, evaluation utilization tactics, or any other wisdom that you think could benefit your colleagues. More general articles should provide information relevant to the evaluator/planner's work. This might include theories in evaluation, literature reviews, critiques of instruments, or discussions of fiscal, legislative, legal or ethical affecting evaluation or planning.

Special issues are groups of articles which cover a particular topic in depth. They are organized by "special issue editors" who are willing to conceptualize the topic, find contributors, set up a quality control process, and deliver the material. Often several editors share responsibility for these tasks. Suggestions for special issues are encouraged.

Book reviews cover any area of social science or public policy which may interest evaluators and planners. As the special issues, suggestions for books and book reviewers are encouraged.

GUIDE FOR AUTHORS
Submission of Papers
All manuscripts should be submitted to the Editor-in-Chief in triplicate. Major articles should not exceed 7,000 words and must include five copies of the abstract of no more than 150 words. All manuscripts and suggestions for books to be reviewed must be mailed to: Jonathan A. Morell, Altarum, PO Box 134001, 3520 Green Court, Suite 300, Ann Arbor, MI 48113-4001, USA. The Editor can also be contacted via email at **Jonny.Morell@altarum.org**.

General
It is essential to give a fax number and e-mail address when submitting a manuscript. Articles must be written in good English. Authors should also submit an electronic copy of their paper with the final version of the manuscript. The electronic copy should match the hard copy exactly. Always keep a backup copy of the electronic file for reference and safety. Full details of electronic submission and acceptable formats can be obtained from http://authors.elsevier.comhttp://authors.elsevier. com or from Author Services at Elsevier.

Submission of an article implies that the work has not been published previously (except in the form of an abstract or as part of a published lecture or academic thesis), that it is not under consideration for publication elsewhere, and that its publication is approved by all authors and tacitly or explicitly by the responsible authorities where the work was carried out, and that, if accepted, it will not be published elsewhere in the same form, in English or in any other language, without the written consent of the Publisher. Translated material which has not previously been published in English will also be considered.

Upon acceptance of an article, authors will be asked to transfer copyright (for more information on copyright see **http://authors.elsevier.com**). This transfer will ensure the widest possible dissemination of information. A letter will be sent to the corresponding author confirming receipt of the manuscript. A form facilitating transfer of copyright will be provided. If excerpts from other copyrighted works are included, the author(s) must obtain written permission from the copyright owners and credit the source(s) in the article. Elsevier has preprinted forms for use by authors in these cases: contact ES Global Rights Department, P.O. Box 800, Oxford OX5 1DX, UK; Tel: + 44 (0) 1865 843830; fax: +44 (0) 1865 853333; e-mail: **permissions@elsevier.com** To facilitate blind review by one or more readers, all indication of authorship should appear on a detachable cover page only. Please include a brief biography of each author for major articles and brief reports, to be published in the journal. The senior author's complete mailing address for reprints, and any statements of credit or research support should appear in an introductory footnote. Please supply corresponding author's telephone and FAX numbers, and E-mail address if available.

Types of Contributions
We publish articles, "special issues" (usually a section of an issue), and book reviews. Articles are of two types: 1) reports on specific evaluation or planning efforts, and 2) discussions of issues relevant to the conduct of evaluation and planning.

Reports on individual evaluations should include presentation of the evaluation setting, design, analysis and results. Because of our focus and philosophy, however, we also want a specific section devoted to "lessons learned". This section should contain advice to other evaluators about how you would have acted differently if you could do it all over again. The advice may involve methodology, how the evaluation was implemented or conducted, evaluation utilization tactics, or any other wisdom that you think could benefit your colleagues. More general articles should provide information relevant to the evaluator/planner's work. This might include theories in evaluation, literature reviews, critiques of instruments, or discussions of fiscal, legislative, legal or ethical affecting evaluation or planning.

Special issues are groups of articles which cover a particular topic in depth. They are organized by "special issue editors" who are willing to conceptualize the topic, find contributors, set up a quality control process, and deliver the material. Often several editors share responsibility for these tasks. Suggestions for special issues are encouraged.

Book reviews cover any area of social science or public policy which may interest evaluators and planners. As the special issues, suggestions for books and book reviewers are encouraged.

Manuscript Preparation
General
Please write your text in good English (American or British usage is accepted, but not a mixture of these). Italics are not to be used for expressions of Latin origin, for example, in vivo, et al., per se. Use decimal points (not commas); use a space for thousands (10 000 and above). Print the entire manuscript on one side of paper only, using double spacing and wide (3 cm) margins. (Avoid full justification, i.e., do not use a constant right-hand margin.) Ensure

that each new paragraph is clearly indicated. Present tables and figure legends on separate pages at the end of the manuscript. If possible, consult a recent issue of the journal to become familiar with layout and conventions. Number all pages consecutively. Good quality print-outs with a font size of 12 or 10 pt are required.

Paper length. The recommended length for a paper is 5000-8000 words, plus illustrations; the preferred length for reviews and conference reports is 2500 words. Provide the following data on the title page (in the order given).

Title. Concise and informative. Titles are often used in information-retrieved systems. Avoid abbreviations and formulae where possible. The title should not exceed 50 characters (including spaces).

Author names and affiliations. Where the family name may be ambiguous (e.g.., a double name), please indicate this clearly. Present the author's affiliation addresses (where the actual work was done) below the names. Indicate all affiliations with a lower-case superscript letter immediately after the author's name and in front of the appropriate address. Provide the full postal address of each affiliation including the country name, and, if available, the e-mail address of each author. Corresponding author. Clearly indicate who is willing to handle correspondence at all stages of refereeing and publication, also post-publication. Ensure the telephone and fax numbers (with country and area code) are provided in addition to the e-mail address and the complete postal address.

Present/permanent address. If an author has moved since the work described in the article was done, or was visiting at the time, a "Present address" (or "Permanent address") may be indicated as a footnote to that author's name. The address at which the author actually did the work must be retained as the main, affiliation address. Superscript Arabic numerals are used for such footnotes.

Abstract. A concise and factual abstract is required (maximum length 200 words). The abstract should state briefly the purpose of the research, the principal results and major conclusions. An abstract is often presented separate from the article, so it must be able to stand alone. References should therefore be avoided, but if essential, they must be cited in full, without reference to the reference list. Non-standard or uncommon abbreviations should be avoided, but if essential they must be defined at their first mention in the abstract itself.

N.B. Acknowledgements. Collate acknowledgements in a separate section at the end of the article and do not, therefore, include them on the title page, as footnote to the title page or otherwise.

Arrangement of the article
Subdivision of the article. Divide your article into clearly defined and numbered sections. Subsections should be numbered 1.1 (then 1.1.1., 1.1.2.,?), 1.2., etc, (the abstract is not included in section numbering). Use this numbering also for internal cross-referencing: do not just refer to 'the text'. Any subsections may be given a brief heading. Each heading on its own separate line.

308

Text. Follow this order when typing manuscripts: Title, Authors, Affiliations, Abstract, Keywords, Main text, Acknowledgements, Appendix, References, Figure Captions, Tables (and figures) should be kept separate from the rest of the manuscript (see instructions for illustrations below). The corresponding should be identified with an asterisk and footnote. All other footnotes (except table footnotes) should be identified with superscript Arabic numerals.

Appendices. If there is more than one appendix, they should be identified as A, B, etc. Formulae and equations in appendices should be given separate numbering: (Eq.A.1), (Eq.A.2), etc.: in a subsequent appendix, (Eq.B.1) and so forth.

Acknowledgements. Please acknowledgements, including information on grants received, before the references, in a separate section, and not as a footnote on the title page.

References. See separate section, below.

Figure legends, tables, figures, schemes. Present these, in this order, at the end of the article. They are described in more details below. High-resolution graphics files must always be provided separate from the main text file (see Preparation of illustrations).

References
Responsibility for the accuracy of bibliographic citations lies entirely with the authors. Citations in the text. Please ensure that every reference cited in the text is also present in the reference list (and vice versa). Any references cited in the abstract must be given in full. Un published results and personal communications should not be in the reference list, but may be mentioned in the text. Citation of a reference as 'in press' implies that the item has been accepted for publication.

In the text refer to the author's name (without initial) and year of publication, followed - if necessary - by a short reference to appropriate pages. Examples: "Since Peterson (1988) has shown that..." "This is in agreement with results obtained later (Kramer, 1989, pp. 12-16)".

If reference is made in the text to a publication written by more than two authors the name of the first author should be used followed by "et al.". This indication, however, should never be used in the list of references. In this list names of first author and co-authors should be mentioned.

References cited together in the text should be arranged chronologically. The list of references should be arranged alphabetically on authors' names, and chronologically per author. If an author's name in the list is also mentioned with co-authors the following order should be used: publications of the single author, arranged according to publication dates -- publications of the same author with one co-author -- publications of the author with more than one co-author. Publications by the same author(s) in the same year should be listed as 1974a, 1974b, etc.

Citing and listing of web references. As a minimum, the full URL should be given. Any further information, if known (author names, dates, reference to a source publication, etc.), should also be given. Web references can be listed separately (e.g., after the reference list) under a different heading if desired, or can be included in the reference list.

Use the following system for arranging your references, please note the proper position of the punctuation:

In the text refer to the author's name (without initial) and year of publication, followed - if necessary - by a short reference to appropriate pages. Examples: "Since Peterson (1988) has shown that..." "This is in agreement with results obtained later (Kramer,1989, pp. 12-16)".

Examples: Reference to a journal publication: Van der Geer, J., Hanraads, J.A.J. ΩLupton, R.A.(2000) . The art of writing a scientific article. J Sci Commun., 163, 51-9. Reference to a book: Strunk, Jr W. ΩWhite, E.B. (1979). The elements of style (3rd ed.). New York, Macmillan.

Reference to a chapter in an edited book: Mettam, G.R. ΩAdams, L.B. (1999). How to prepare an electronic version of your article. In B.S. Jones ΩR.Z. Smith, (Eds), Introduction to the electronic age. New York: E-Publishing Inc, p.281-304.

Note shortened form for last page number. e.g., 51-9, and that for more than 6 authors the first 6 should be listed followed by 'et al'. For further details you are referred to "Uniform Requirements for Manuscripts submitted to Biomedical Journals" (J Am Med Assoc 1997;277:927-934) (see also http://www.nejm.org/general/text/requirements/1.html

Electronic format requirements for accepted articles. *General points.* We accept most wordprocessing formats, but Word, WordPerfect or LaTeX is preferred. An electronic version of the text should be submitted together with the final hardcopy of the manuscript. The electronic version must match the hardcopy exactly. Always keep a backup copy of the electronic file. Label storage media with your name, journal title, and software used. Save your files using the default extension of the program used. No changes to the accepted version are permissible without the explicit approval of the Editor. Electronic files can be stored on 3 ? inch diskette, ZIP-disk or CD (either MS-DOS or Macintosh).

Wordprocessor documents. It is important that the file saved in the native format of the wordprocessor used. The text should be in single-column format. Keep the layout of the text as simple as possible. Most formatting codes will be removed and replaced on processing the article. In particular, do not use the wordprocessor's options to justify text or to hyphenate words. However, do use bold face, italics, subscripts, superscripts, etc. Do not embed 'graphically designed' equations or tables, but prepare these using the wordprocessor's facility. When preparing tables, id you are using a table grid, use only one grid for each individual table and not a grid for each row. If no grid is used, used tabs, not spaces, to align columns. The electronic text should be prepared in a way very similar to that of conventional manuscripts (see also the Author Gateway's Quickguide: http://authors.elsevier.com). Do not import the figures into the text file but, instead, indicate their approximate locations directly in the electronic text and on the manuscript. See also the section on Preparation of electronic illustrations. To avoid unnecessary errors you are strongly advised to use the 'spellchecker' function of your wordprocessor. Although Elsevier can process most wordprocessor file formats, should your electronic file prove to be unusable, the article will be typeset from the hardcopy printout.

Preparation of illustrations

Submitting your artwork in an electronic format helps us to produce your work to the best possible standards, ensuring accuracy, clarity and a high level of detail.

- Always supply high-quality printouts of your artwork, in case conversion of the electronic artwork is problematic.
- Make sure you use uniform lettering and sizing of your original artwork.
- Save text in illustrations as "graphics" or enclose the font.
- Only use the following fonts in your illustrations: Arial, Courier, Times, Symbol.
- Number the illustrations according to their sequence in the text.
- Use a logical naming convention for your artwork files, and supply a separate listing of the files and the software used.
- Provide all illustrations as separate files and as hardcopy printouts on separate sheets.
- Provide captions to illustrations separately.
- Produce images near to the desired size of the printed version.

Files can be stored on 3 ? inch diskette, ZIP-disk or CD (either MS-DOS or Macintosh). A detailed guide on electronic artwork is available on our website:
http://authors.elsevier.com/artwork

You are urged to visit this site; some excerpts from the detailed information are given here.

Formats

Regardless of the application used, when your electronic artwork is finalised, please "save as" or convert the images to one of the following formats (Note the resolution requirements for line drawings, halftones, and line/halftone combinations are given below.): EPS: Vector drawings. Embed the font or save the text as "graphics".

TIFF: Colour or greyscale photographs (halftones): always use a minimum of 300dpi.

TIFF: Bitmapped line drawings line drawings: use a minimum of 1000dpi.

TIFF: Combinations bitmapped line/half-tone (colour or greyscale): a minimum of 500 dpi is required.

DOC, XLS, or PPT: If your electronic artwork is created in any of these Microsoft Office applications please supply "as is".

Please do not:

- Supply embedded graphics in your wordprocessor (spreadsheet, presentation) documentation;
- Supply files that are optimised for screen use (like GIF, BMP, PICT, WPG); the resolution is too low;
- Supply files that are too low in resolution;
- Submit graphics that are disproportionately large for the content.

Non-electronic illustrations
Provide all illustrations as high-quality printouts, suitable for reproduction (which may include reduction) without retouching. Number illustrations consecutively in the order in which they are referred to in the text. They should accompany the manuscript, but should not be included within the text. Clearly mark all illustrations on the back (or - in case of line drawings - on the lower front side) with the figure number and the author's name and, in cases of ambiguity, the correct orientation. Mark the appropriate position of a figure in the article.

Captions
Ensure that each illustration has a caption. Supply captions on a separate sheet, not attached to the figure. A caption should compromise a brief title (**not** on the figure itself) and a description of the illustration. Keep text in the illustrations themselves to a minimum but explain all symbols and abbreviations used.

Line drawings. Supply high-quality printouts on white paper produced with black ink. The lettering and symbols, as well as other details, should have proportionate dimensions, so as to become illegible or unclear after possible reduction; in general, the figures should be designed for a reduction factor of two to three. The degree of reduction will be determined by the Publisher. Illustrations will not be enlarged. Consider the page format of the journal when designing the illustration. Photocopies are not suitable for reproduction. Do not use any type of shading on computer-generated.

Photographs (halftones). Please supply original photographs for reproduction, printed on glossy paper, very sharp and with good contrast. Remove non-essential areas of a photograph. Do not mount photographs unless they form part of a composite figure. Where necessary, insert a scale bar in the illustration (not below it), as opposed to giving a magnification factor in the legend. Note that photocopies of photographs are not acceptable.

Colour illustrations. Submit colour illustrations as original photographs, high-quality computer prints or transparencies, close to the size expected in publication, or as 35 mm slides. Polaroid colour prints are not suitable. If, together with your accepted article, you submit usable colour figures then Elsevier will ensure, at no additional charge, that these figures will appear in colour on the web (e.g., ScienceDirect and other sites) regardless of whether or not these illustrations are reproduced in colour in the printed version. For colour reproduction in print, you will receive information regarding the costs from Elsevier after receipt of your accepted article. Further information on the preparation of electronic artwork, please see http://authors.elsevier.com/artwork. Please note: Because of technical complications which can arise by converting colour figures to 'grey scale' (for the printed version should you not opt for colour in print) please submit in addition usable black and white prints corresponding to all the colour illustrations.

Proofs
When your manuscript is received by the Publisher it is considered to be in its final form. Proofs are not to be regarded as 'drafts'. One set of page proofs in PDF format will be sent by e-mail to the corresponding author, to be checked for typesetting/editing. No changes in, or additions to, the accepted (and subsequently edited) manuscript will be allowed at this stage.

312

Proofreading is solely your responsibility. A form with queries from the copyeditor may accompany your proofs. Please answer all queries and make any corrections or additions required. Elsevier will do everything possible to get your article corrected and published as quickly and accurately as possible. In order to do this we need your help. When you receive the (PDF) proof of your article for correction, it is important to ensure that all of your corrections are sent back to us in one communication. Subsequent corrections will not be possible, so please ensure your first sending is complete. Note that this does not mean you have any less time to make your corrections, just that only one set of corrections will be accepted.

Offprints
25 offprints will be supplied free of charge. Additional offprints can be ordered at a specially reduced rate using the order form sent to the corresponding author after the manuscript has been accepted. Orders for reprints (produced after publication of an article) will incur a 50% surcharge.

Author enquiries
Authors can keep a track on the progress of their accepted article, and set up e-mail alerts informing them of changes to their manuscript's status, by using the "Track a Paper" feature of Elsevier's Author Gateway http://authors.elsevier.com. For privacy, information on each article is password-protected The author should key in the "Our Reference" code (which is in the letter of acknowledgement sent by the Publisher on receipt of the accepted article) and the name of the corresponding author. In case of problems or questions, authors may contact the Author Support Department, e-mail:authorsupport@elsevier.com.

Evaluation and Research in Education

ADDRESS FOR SUBMISSION:

Keith Morrison, Editor
Evaluation and Research in Education
Multilingual Matters Ltd.
Frankfurt Lodge
Clevedon Hall
Victorial Road, Clevedon
North Somerset, BS21 7HH
UK
Phone: +44 1275 876519
Fax: +44 1275 871673
E-Mail: info@multilingual-matters.com
Web: www.multilingual-matters.com
Address May Change:

PUBLICATION GUIDELINES:

Manuscript Length: 16-20
Copies Required: Four
Computer Submission: Yes Disk &
   Hardcopy
Format: No Reply
Fees to Review: 0.00 US$

Manuscript Style:
   , Multilingual Matters

CIRCULATION DATA:

Reader: Academics, Administrators,
   Practicing Teachers
Frequency of Issue: 3 Times/Year
Copies per Issue: Less than 1,000
Sponsor/Publisher: Multilingual Matters
   Ltd.
Subscribe Price: 75.00 US$ Individual
   220.00 US$ Library
   50.00 Pounds Indv. & 140 Pounds
   Library

REVIEW INFORMATION:

Type of Review: Editorial Review
No. of External Reviewers: 2
No. of In House Reviewers: 1
Acceptance Rate: 45%
Time to Review: 2 - 3 Months
Reviewers Comments: Yes
Invited Articles: 11-20%
Fees to Publish: 0.00 US$

MANUSCRIPT TOPICS:
Curriculum Studies; Education Management/Administration; Tests, Measurement &
Evaluation

MANUSCRIPT GUIDELINES/COMMENTS:

Evaluation & Research in Education aims to make methods of evaluation and research in
education available to teachers, administrators and research workers. Papers published in the
journal: (1) report evaluation and research findings; (2) treat conceptual and methodological
issues; and/or (3) consider the implications of the above for action. There is an extensive book
reviews section and also occasional reports on educational materials and equipment.

Guidelines for Authors of Journal Papers
Articles should not normally exceed 7000 words. Note that it is our policy not to review
papers which are currently under consideration by other journals.

They should be typed, double-spaced on A4 paper, with ample left- and right-hand margins, on one side of the paper only, and every page should be numbered consecutively. A cover page should contain only the title, thereby facilitating anonymous reviewing by two independent assessors. Authors may also wish to take precautions to avoid textual references which would identify themselves to the referees. In such cases the authors of accepted papers will have the opportunity to include any such omitted material before the paper is published.

Submissions for Work in Progress/Readers' Response/Letters to the Editor sections should be approximately 500 words in length.

Main contact author should also appear in a separate paragraph on the title page.

An abstract should be included. This should not exceed 200 words (longer abstracts are rejected by many abstracting services).

A short version of the title (maximum 45 characters) should also be supplied for the journal's running headline.

To facilitate the production of the annual subject index, a list of key words (not more than six) should be provided, under which the paper may be indexed.

Four copies of the article must be submitted.

Footnotes should be avoided. Essential notes should be numbered in the text and grouped together at the end of the article. Diagrams and Figures, if they are considered essential, should be clearly related to the section of the text to which they refer. The original diagrams and figures should be submitted with the top copy.

References should be set out in alphabetical order of the author's name in a list at the end of the article. They should be given in standard form, as in the Appendix below.

References in the text of an article should be by the author's name and year of publication, as in these examples: Jones (1987) in a paper on ... [commonest version]; Jones and Evans (1997c: 22) state that ... [where page number is required]; Evidence is given by Smith *et al.* (1984) ... [for three or more authors]. Further exploration of this aspect may be found in many sources (e.g. Brown & Green, 1982; Jackson, 1983; White, 1981a) [note alphabetical order, use of & and semi-colons].

Once the refereeing procedures are completed, authors should if possible supply a word-processor disc containing their manuscript file(s). If presented on disc, we require files to be saved:
- on an IBM-PC compatible 3.5 inch disc (5.25 inch discs also acceptable), or
- on an Apple Mac **high-density** 3.5 inch disc.
- Text should be saved in the author's normal word-processor format. The name of the word-processor program used should also be supplied. Tables and Figures should be saved in separate files.

The author of an article accepted for publication will receive page proofs for correction, if there is sufficient time to do so. This stage must not be used as an opportunity to revise the paper, because alterations are extremely costly; extensive changes will be charged to the author and will probably result in the article being delayed to a later issue. Speedy return of corrected proofs is important.

Contributions and queries should be sent to the Editors, c/o Multilingual Matters Ltd, Frankfurt Lodge, Clevedon Hall, Victoria Road, Clevedon, BS21 7HH, England.

Appendix: References
A very large majority of authors' proof-corrections are caused by errors in references. Authors are therefore requested to check the following points particularly carefully when submitting manuscripts:

- Are all the references in the reference list cited in the text?
- Do all the citations in the text appear in the reference list?
- Do the dates in the text and the reference list correspond?
- Do the spellings of authors' names in text and reference list correspond, and do all authors have the correct initials?
- Are journal references complete with volume and pages numbers?
- Are references to books complete with place of publication and the name of the publisher?

It is extremely helpful if references are presented as far as possible in accordance with our house style. A few more typical examples are shown below. Note, especially, use of upper & lower case in paper titles, use of capital letters and italic (underlining can be used as an alternative if italic is not available) in book and journal titles, punctuation (or lack of it) after dates, journal titles, and book titles. The inclusion of issue numbers of journals, or page numbers in books, is optional but if included should be as per the examples below.

Department of Education and Science (DES) (1985) *Education for All* (The Swann Report). London: HMSO.

Evans, N.J. and Ilbery, B.W. (1989) A conceptual framework for investigating farm-based accommodation and tourism in Britain. *Journal of Rural Studies* 5 (3), 257–266.

Evans, N.J. and Ilbery, B.W. (1992) Advertising and farm-based accommodation: A British case-study. *Tourism Management* 13 (4), 415–422.

Laufer, B. (1985) Vocabulary acquisition in a second language: The hypothesis of 'synforms'. PhD thesis, University of Edinburgh.

Mackey, W.F. (1980) The ecology of language shift. In P.H. Nelde (ed.) *Languages in Contact and in Conflict* (pp. 35–41). Wiesbaden: Steiner.

Marien, C. and Pizam, A. (1997) Implementing sustainable tourism development through citizen participation in the planning process. In S. Wahab and J. Pigram (eds) *Tourism, Development and Growth* (pp. 164–78). London: Routledge.

Morrison, D. (1980) Small group discussion project questionnaire. University of Hong Kong Language Centre (mimeo).

Zahn, C.J. and Hopper, R. (1985) The speech evaluation instrument: A user's manual (version 1.0a). Unpublished manuscript, Cleveland State University.

Zigler, E. and Balla, D. (eds) (1982) *Mental Retardation: The Developmental-Difference Controversy.* Hillsdale, NJ: Lawrence Erlbaum.

For more details, please e-mail us on **multi@multilingual-matters.com**.

Exceptional Children

ADDRESS FOR SUBMISSION:

Steve Graham, Editor
Exceptional Children
Vanderbilt University
Peabody College of Education
Department of Special Education
Box 328
Nashville, TN 37203-5701
USA
Phone: 301-405-6493
Fax: 301-314-9158
E-Mail: sg23@umail.umd.edu
Web:
Address May Change:

PUBLICATION GUIDELINES:

Manuscript Length: 25-35
Copies Required: Four
Computer Submission: Yes Disk, Email
Format: MSWord preferred
Fees to Review: 0.00 US$

Manuscript Style:
    American Psychological Association

CIRCULATION DATA:

Reader: Academics
Frequency of Issue: Quarterly
Copies per Issue: More than 50,000
Sponsor/Publisher: Council for Exceptional
    Children
Subscribe Price: 10.00 US$ Single Copy
    58.00 US$ Yearly

REVIEW INFORMATION:

Type of Review: Blind Review
No. of External Reviewers: 3-4
No. of In House Reviewers: 1
Acceptance Rate: 17-20%
Time to Review: 2 - 3 Months
Reviewers Comments: Yes
Invited Articles: 0%
Fees to Publish: 0.00 US$

MANUSCRIPT TOPICS:
Adult Career & Vocational; Audiology/Speech Pathology; Bilingual/E.S.L.; Elementary/Early Childhood; Gifted Children; Reading; Secondary/Adolescent Studies; Special Education; Teacher Education; Tests, Measurement & Evaluation; Urban Education, Cultural/Non-Traditional

MANUSCRIPT GUIDELINES/COMMENTS:

Purpose
Exceptional Children is the research journal of The Council for Exceptional Children. It presents research and analyses on: Education and development of exceptional infants, toddlers, children, and youth, and adults. Professional issues and policies relevant to exceptional infants, toddlers, children, youth, and adults.

The *Journal* primarily publishes five types of articles:
Research Studies report a qualitative, large-group quantitative, or single-subject design study. Effect sizes should be reported for quantitative studies.

Research Reviews involve the analysis and integration of research in one or more areas. Reviews must be comprehensive and critical. Whenever possible, effect sizes for individual studies should be reported.

Methodological Reviews systematically examine the methodological strengths and weaknesses of a specific body of literature (e.g., a methodological review of the soundness of research on teaching phonological awareness). This can include a methodological analysis of qualitative, quantitative, and single-subject design studies.

Data-Based Position Papers address an important issue (practical or theoretical) in special or gifted education. This involves analyzing and integrating the existing research literature to provide a balanced and scholarly examination of the issue.

Policy Analyses include critical analyses and research related to public policy that impact the education of exceptional infants, toddlers, children, youth, and adults.

All research that is published in *Exceptional Children* should have implications for practice, and these must be stated in the article. Manuscripts that focus on practical methods and materials for classroom use should be submitted to *Teaching Exceptional Children*, the CEC journal that is specifically for teachers of children with disabilities and children who are gifted.

Exceptional Children does not publish descriptions of instructional procedures or classroom materials, accounts of personal experiences, letters to the editor, book or test reviews, and single case studies. Nondatabased reports on innovative techniques, programs, or models as well as studies involving a pretest-posttest only design with no comparison condition are also not published in *Exceptional Children*. Investigations involving questionnaires and survey are generally not published unless the sample is representative of the population being studied.

Writing for *Exceptional Children*
While *Exceptional Children* is the research journal, its articles are read by a much broader audience than just researchers. Therefore, articles written for *Exceptional Children* need to be written for this broader audience. Articles should not be viewed as shortened versions of dissertation or technical reports, but rather as a way to inform other researchers, school administrators, state department personnel, service providers, teachers, parents, and others about your research and its implications for practice. Articles must be clear and concise.

To best meet the needs of the broader audience, consider the following questions as you prepare your manuscript:

Introduction
- Why is your research needed?
- What are 2 to 3 key points the reader needs to understand before reading about what you did?
- Is the tone positive?
- Have you successfully communicated in less than 5 pages, and ideally in 2 to 3 pages?

Methodology
- Have you provided enough general information in a way that a lay reader can understand what you have done?
- Have you provided a source of further information about methodology for the researcher who wants to replicate your research?

Results
- Have you organized your results in a way that promotes the understanding of your findings?
- Have you provided the necessary details for the researcher without making it difficult for others to read?

Discussion
- What are the 2 to 3 key points that need to be made about your findings?
- What limitations are there on your research and its findings?
- What are the practical implications of your findings?
- What are the next steps to be taken?

Manuscript Requirements
Before submitting a manuscript to *Exceptional Children*, please review the Author Checklist below. This will help ensure that your manuscript is not screened out or returned before review.

- Manuscript is consistent with the purpose of the journal.
- Manuscript conforms to APA format (see *APA Publication Manual*, 5th edition, 2001) particularly:
  1. Manuscript is double spaced, with 1" margins (12 font type preferred).
  2. All pages are numbered in sequence, starting with the title page.
  3. Effect size information is provided for quantitative studies.

- All references in text are listed and in complete agreement with text citations.
- Abstract is not more than 120 words long.
- The first page of the manuscript contains the running head, title of the article, authors' names, affiliations, date of submission, address of submitting author (including street name for overnight delivery), phone number, fax number, and e-mail address. The second page duplicates the first page except that only the running head and title are included.
- An exact electronic copy of the manuscript on a 3½" disk is included and saved as either a Microsoft Word (preferred) or RTF file. The label on the disk includes an abbreviated title, the authors' names, file names, date submitted for review, and word processing program.
- All word processing codes are removed from the electronic version of the manuscript for apostrophes, quotation marks, hyphens, and so forth.

- Cover letter states that manuscript is original and not previously published, all authors have given consent to submit the manuscript to Exceptional Children, and the manuscript is not under consideration elsewhere.
- The cover letter indicates if the data from this manuscript is part of a larger study or if any part of the data has been included in another manuscript. The cover letter must provide a full explanation if either of these situations exist.

Review Process

Selection of manuscripts for publication is based on a blind peer review process. However, all manuscripts are screened first. Those manuscripts that do not meet the manuscript requirements, or that are not consistent with the purpose of the journal, are not forwarded for peer review. The author either is notified that the manuscript is not acceptable for Exceptional Children, or is requested to make changes in the manuscript so that it meets requirements. Copies of the manuscript are not returned to the author in either case.

Manuscripts that are not screened out and that are consistent with the purpose of the journal are sent out for peer review. Reviewers will not know the identity of the author.

Based on the blind reviews, the Associate editors and/or co-editors will communicate the results of that review to the author. The decision that is communicated to the author will be one of the following:

- Acceptable, with routine editing
- Acceptable, with revisions indicated by the action editor
- Revise and resubmit
- Unacceptable

When a decision is made that a manuscript is unacceptable for *Exceptional Children*, it may be recommended that it be sent to a journal of one of the CEC Divisions. This recommendation does not mean that the manuscript would be automatically accepted by a Division journal; the manuscript would have to go through the review process again.

Exceptional Parent

ADDRESS FOR SUBMISSION:

Laura Apel, Managing Editor
Exceptional Parent
65 East Route 4
River Edge, NJ 07661
USA
Phone: 201-489-4111 ext. 212
Fax: 201-489-0074
E-Mail: laura@eparent.com
Web: www.eparent.com
Address May Change:

PUBLICATION GUIDELINES:

Manuscript Length: 6-10
Copies Required: One
Computer Submission: Yes Email
Format:
Fees to Review: 0.00 US$

Manuscript Style:
   See Manuscript Guidelines

CIRCULATION DATA:

Reader: Practicing Teachers, Parents;
   Healthcare Providers
Frequency of Issue: Monthly
Copies per Issue: Over 65,000
Sponsor/Publisher: Psy-Ed Corp
Subscribe Price: 39.95 US$

REVIEW INFORMATION:

Type of Review: Editorial Review
No. of External Reviewers: 0
No. of In House Reviewers: 2
Acceptance Rate: 6-10%
Time to Review: Over 6 Months
Reviewers Comments: No
Invited Articles: No Reply
Fees to Publish: 0.00 US$

MANUSCRIPT TOPICS:
Audiology/Speech Pathology; Behavioral, Developmental Disabilities; Educational
Psychology; Elementary/Early Childhood; Gifted Children; Special Education

MANUSCRIPT GUIDELINES/COMMENTS:

Exceptional Parent publishes articles on a broad scale of social, psychological, legal, political,
technological, financial, and educational concerns faced by families of children with
disabilities.

Our primary audience is parents. We strive to maintain respect and consideration for both the
professional and the parent who want to work together in understanding the child's disability.
Therefore, our tone is "How to work together." As journalists we examine ALL sides of
controversial issues.

Our tone is generally upbeat, but we also recognize that our audience is no stranger to
difficulties and realities.

Exceptional Parent advises; it does not preach. We try as much as possible to avoid saying "You must..." or "You should..." Rather, we suggest, "A good way of doing this is...," or "You can."

Exceptional Parent's Style

We try to use language geared toward the consumer/reader who has a high-school diploma (i.e., McCall's, Woman's Day, Newsweek) as opposed to professional, medical or business journals (i.e., JAMA, Business Week, New England Journal of Medicine.) Professional Journal style-with reference to studies and imbedded footnotes--is unacceptable. Therefore, professional jargon and specialized terminology is discouraged. If there is a term parents will be coming across on a regular basis ("intervention," "aspirate" "URL," "OBRA Trust"), it needs to be "translated" into everyday or ordinary terms.

Sensitivity

Because our readers are professionals as well as parents, we write about "the child" rather than "your specific child."

We try to be as sensitive to our readers as possible. We speak of "children with disabilities" or "children with special needs" rather than "disabled children" or "handicapped children."

We avoid discussion of what could have been done to prevent a disability. Our readers are interested in what they can do now.

If you write about a child with a specific disability, it should be worded in such a way that it reaches out to all families that have children with disabilities. Think to yourself, "What information can my story contain that will be of use to other parents of any child with a disability?" Also, please give a brief description of any disabilities that are mentioned.

The approach our publication takes is

1. Parents are the best experts on their children.
2. *Exceptional Parent* offers practical information and advice that readers can use to make life easier and happier when caring for a child or young adult with special needs.
3. *Exceptional Parent* is also a valuable resource for educational and health care professionals.

Technical Hints

Disorders, diseases and disabilities are used in lower case, unless they are "named after" someone. Therefore, we capitalized Down syndrome (always lower-case syndrome) because Dr. Down is the person who identified it. We use multiple sclerosis in the lower case because it defines a condition.

Please be sure to spell-check your article before sending it to us!! Fact checking is also very important! Be sure to check all names, dates, and addresses. For example, Kodak is really referred to as Eastman Kodak. Please be as thorough as possible, the more accurate the information, the more professional the article will be.

Article lengths vary. Approximately 1200-1800 words would be appropriate. Please indicate if there is any artwork (art is: printed pictures, paper-copy illustrations, slides, and transparencies) that should accompany the article if selected for publication. It is not necessary to send artwork with the submitted manuscript, but a brief description or photocopies of the artwork are welcome.

Please remember, to include author "bio" information that will be included in total word count. This information consists of the name and pertinent background of the author. This should be no longer than three or four sentences.

Copy should be typed and double-spaced, preferably in 12 pt. type and provided on Mac disc in a Word compatible program. Copy should be sent to:

Exceptional Parent, c/o Manuscript Submission, 65 East Route 4, River Edge, NJ 07661

Copy can also be e-mailed to **epedit@aol.com**. The review process can vary from six months to a year.

Photos
Pictures and illustrations should be clearly labeled with the name(s) of the person/people, the activity, or the subject-matter shown. This is so the pictures and/or illustrations can be easily captioned and fit into the story. Put names in order of appearance in pictures. For example, Brenda (right) and John (left). People should be identified by name, relationship to a child if shown, home address (city/state), age of child, and the activity they are involved in (school, vacation, play, etc.).

Please do not write directly on the back of photographs. Include on the label, the name and address of the person who is sending the pictures and the title of the article for which they are intended. Slides and transparencies should be numbered and described on a separate sheet of paper. Please note, **we cannot guarantee that art will be returned**.

A picture should be accompanied by written permission to publish. An address and phone number should also be supplied. We need the permission of everyone in a photo(s)! *Enclosed please find a permission form for you to copy.

Include with your article a list of all sources you contacted, their telephone numbers, and copies of any materials you used (i.e., an article from another magazine, a photocopy of a technical or medical definition).

We also need the addresses of all those mentioned in the article so that we may send them a copy of the magazine.

Other materials
Our emphasis is on family over clinical experience. Personal anecdotes, quotes, or sidebars are encouraged because they bring "life" to the articles. Our readers need to identify with the story and the child/young adults disability on some level. Whether it has to do with siblings, advocacy etc., it should help as many parents as possible!

Exceptionality - A Special Education Journal

ADDRESS FOR SUBMISSION:

Edward J. Sabornie, Editor
Exceptionality - A Special Education
   Journal
North Carolina State University
College of Education
Poe Hall
Campus Box 7801
Raleigh, NC 27695-7801
USA
Phone: 919-515-1777
Fax: 919-515-6978
E-Mail: edward_sabornie@ncsu.edu
Web: See Guidelines
Address May Change:

PUBLICATION GUIDELINES:

Manuscript Length: 26-30
Copies Required: Five
Computer Submission: No
Format: NA
Fees to Review: 0.00 US$

Manuscript Style:
   American Psychological Association

CIRCULATION DATA:

Reader: Academics
Frequency of Issue: Quarterly
Copies per Issue: Less than 1,000
Sponsor/Publisher: Lawrence Erlbaum, Inc.
Subscribe Price: 45.00 US$ Individuals

REVIEW INFORMATION:

Type of Review: Editorial Review
No. of External Reviewers: 0-3
No. of In House Reviewers: 1
Acceptance Rate: 11-30%
Time to Review: 1 - 2 Months
Reviewers Comments: Yes
Invited Articles: 21-30%
Fees to Publish: 0.00 US$

MANUSCRIPT TOPICS:
Adult Career & Vocational; Educational Psychology; Gifted Children; Reading; Science Math & Environment; Secondary/Adolescent Studies; Special Education; Teacher Education; Tests, Measurement & Evaluation

MANUSCRIPT GUIDELINES/COMMENTS:

Website: **https://www.erlbaum.com/shop/tek9.asp?pg=products&specific=9036-2835**

Editorial Scope. The purpose of *Exceptionality* is to provide a forum for presentation of current research and professional scholarship in special education. Areas of scholarship published in the journal include quantitative, qualitative, and single-subject research designs examining students and persons with exceptionalities, as well as reviews of the literature, discussion pieces, invited works, position papers, theoretical papers, policy analyses, and research syntheses. Appropriate data-based papers include basic, experimental, applied, naturalistic, ethnographic, and historical investigations. Papers that describe assessment, diagnosis, placement, teacher education, and service delivery practices will also be included. Manuscripts accepted for publication will represent a cross section of all areas of special education and exceptionality and will attempt to further the knowledge base and improve services to individuals with disabilities and gifted and talented behavior.

Audience. Education researchers, education professionals interested in students at risk, developmental and school psychologists, neuropsychologists, medical personnel involved with students and persons with exceptionalities, social workers, teachers, and higher education students in education.

Instructions to Contributors

Manuscript Submission. Only manuscripts written in English will be considered. Submit five manuscript copies to the Editor, Dr. Edward J. Sabornie, North Carolina State University, College of Education and Psychology, Poe Hall, Campus Box 7801, Raleigh, NC 27695-7801. Prepare manuscripts according to the *Publication Manual of the American Psychological Association* (5th ed.). Type all components of the manuscript double-spaced, including the title page, abstract, text, quotes, acknowledgments, references, appendixes, tables, figure captions, and footnotes. An abstract of fewer than 200 words should be typed on a separate page. Authors should comply with the "Guidelines to Reduce Bias in Language," which appears on pages 46 to 53 of the *APA Manual.* Five photocopies of the illustrations and the original illustrations should accompany the manuscript. All manuscripts submitted will be acknowledged promptly. Authors should keep a copy of their manuscript to guard against loss.

Peer Review Policy. The editorial board evaluates manuscripts with regard to scientific rigor and importance of the implications for practice or policy. To accelerate the review process, reviewers only provide comments to authors whose manuscripts are found acceptable for publication. In this way, we are able to provide author feedback in approximately 6 weeks from the time of receipt of the manuscript. Authors who prefer that their identities and affiliations be masked are responsible for requesting blind review. Every effort should be made by the authors to see that the manuscript itself contains no clues to their identities.

Permissions. Authors are responsible for all statements made in their work and for obtaining permission from copyright owners to reprint or adapt a table or figure or to reprint a quotation of 500 words or more. Authors should write to the original author(s) and publisher to request nonexclusive world rights in all languages for use of the material in the article and in future editions. Provide copies of all permissions and credit lines obtained.

Regulations. In a cover letter, authors should state that the findings and ideas reported in the manuscript are original and have not been published previously and that the manuscript is not being simultaneously submitted elsewhere. Authors should also state that they have complied with American Psychological Association ethical standards in the treatment of their samples.

Production Notes. After a manuscript is accepted for publication, the author is asked to provide a computer disk containing the manuscript file. Files are copyedited and typeset into page proofs. Authors read proofs to correct errors and answer editors' queries. Authors may order reprints of their articles only when they return page proofs.

FORUM: for promoting 3-19 comprehensive education

ADDRESS FOR SUBMISSION:

Clyde Chitty, Editor
FORUM: for promoting 3-19
  comprehensive education
19 Beaconsfield Road, Bickley
Bromley, Kent, BR1 2BL
UK
Phone: +44 (0) 20 7919-7300
Fax: +44 (0) 20 7919-7313
E-Mail: journals@triangle.co.uk
Web: www.triangle.co.uk
Address May Change:

PUBLICATION GUIDELINES:

Manuscript Length: 6-10
Copies Required: Two
Computer Submission: Yes , Disk
Format: No Reply
Fees to Review: 0.00 US$

Manuscript Style:
  See Manuscript Guidelines

CIRCULATION DATA:

Reader: Practicing Teachers,
  Administrators, Parents, Governors
Frequency of Issue: 3 Times/Year
Copies per Issue: No Reply
Sponsor/Publisher: Triangle Journals Ltd.
Subscribe Price: 28.00 US$ Individual
  60.00 US$ Institution
  18.00 Pounds Indv. & 42 Pounds Inst.

REVIEW INFORMATION:

Type of Review: Blind Review
No. of External Reviewers: 1
No. of In House Reviewers: 1
Acceptance Rate: 75%
Time to Review: 1 - 2 Months
Reviewers Comments: Yes
Invited Articles: No Reply
Fees to Publish: 0.00 US$

MANUSCRIPT TOPICS:
Education Management/Administration; Government Educational Policy

MANUSCRIPT GUIDELINES/COMMENTS:

About the Journal
FORUM has for over forty years been the pre-eminent focal point in the United Kingdom for topical and informed analysis - very often highly forthright and critical - of all aspects of government policy as it influences the education of children from primary through to higher education. *FORUM* - a journal-cum-magazine - vigorously campaigns for the universal provision of state-provided education, and seeks to identify and expose all attempts to overturn the gains of the past thirty years. Every teacher, headteacher, administrator, parent, or governor should read this exciting publication.

Contributions are not drawn only from the familiar sources in universities and colleges, but also in large numbers from teachers, writing of their own experiences in the classroom.

That *FORUM* is an excellent means of keeping up-to-date with events within the education scene in Britain is born out by the fact that although, naturally, the vast majority of its readers arc teachers within the UK, about 20% of all subscribers live outside the country.

FORUM: for promoting 3-19 comprehensive education is published three times a year in Spring, Summer and Autumn, those three issues constituting one volume.

How to Contribute
Editorial correspondence, including typescript articles (1500–2000 words), contributions to discussion (800 words maximum), and books for review, should be addressed to: Professor Clyde Chitty [**c.chitty@gold.ac.uk**], 19 Beaconsfield Road, Bickley, Bromley, Kent BR1 2BL, United Kingdom. Telephone: 0181-464 4962. Please send two copies and enclose a stamped addressed envelope.

328

Futurist

ADDRESS FOR SUBMISSION:

Cynthia G. Wagner, Managing Editor
Futurist
7910 Woodmont Avenue, Suite 450
Bethesda, MD 20814
USA
Phone: 301-656-8274
Fax: 301-951-0394
E-Mail: cwagner@wfs.org
Web: www.wfs.org
Address May Change:

PUBLICATION GUIDELINES:

Manuscript Length: 16-20
Copies Required: One
Computer Submission: Yes Disk, Email
Format: MS Word / US English
Fees to Review: 0.00 US$

Manuscript Style:
    Chicago Manual of Style

CIRCULATION DATA:

Reader: Academics, Business Persons
Frequency of Issue: Bi-Monthly
Copies per Issue: 10,001 - 25,000
Sponsor/Publisher: World Future Society
Subscribe Price: 20.00 US$ Student
    55.00 US$ Institution
    45.00 US$ Member / $55 Non-member

REVIEW INFORMATION:

Type of Review: Editorial Review
No. of External Reviewers: 0
No. of In House Reviewers: 3
Acceptance Rate: 21-30%
Time to Review: 4 - 6 Months
Reviewers Comments: No
Invited Articles: 6-10%
Fees to Publish: 0.00 US$

MANUSCRIPT TOPICS:
Adult Career & Vocational; Educational Technology Systems; Futures Studies; General Trends; Innovations; Health & Physical Education; Higher Education; Science Math & Environment; Social Studies/Social Science

MANUSCRIPT GUIDELINES/COMMENTS:

The Futurist is constantly looking for articles to publish, both by established authorities and new authors. Articles must pass the following tests:

1. **Subject Matter**
The article should have something new and significant to say about the future, not merely repeat what has already been said before. For example, an article noting that increasing air pollution may damage human health is something everyone has already heard. Writers for *The Futurist* should remember that the publication focuses on the future, especially the period five to 50 years ahead.

The Futurist does not publish fiction or poetry. An exception is occasionally made for scenarios presenting fictionalized people in future situations. These scenarios are kept brief.

The Futurist covers a wide range of subject areas--virtually everything that will affect our future or will be affected by the changes the future will bring. Past articles have focused on topics ranging from technology, planning, resources, and economics, to religion; the arts, values, and health. Articles we avoid include: (A) overly technical articles that would be of little interest to the general reader; (B) opinion pieces on current government issues; (C) articles by authors with only a casual knowledge of the subject being discussed.

2. Author's Knowledge of the Subject

Authors should provide some biographical material, which should indicate their qualifications to write about a particular subject.

3. Quality of Writing

Make points clearly and in a way that holds the reader's interest. A reader should not have to struggle to guess an author's meaning or wade through lots of unnecessary words in the process. Use concrete examples and anecdotes to illustrate the points made; nothing is duller than a page of generalities unrelieved by specific examples. Keep sentences short, mostly under 25 words. Avoid the jargon of a particular trade or profession; when technical terms are necessary, be sure to explain them.

The Futurist's copyeditors use the University of Chicago Press's *A Manual of Style* and *Merriam Webster's Unabridged Dictionary* as guidelines on spelling and style.

Authors can get a feel for *The Futurist's* style by reviewing recent issues, available in many large libraries, bookstores, and newsstands. Sample copies may be purchased from the Society for $7.95 each, prepaid.

Writer's Guidelines for the Futurist

Submissions. The editors prefer to read completed manuscripts but will consider queries that include a strong thesis, detailed outline, and summary of the author's expertise on the proposed topic.

Manuscripts submitted must be typed, **double-spaced**, and accompanied by a self-addressed, stamped envelope to be considered or returned. A brief "about the author" note is recommended. E-mailed submissions are acceptable. **Do not** submit manuscripts by fax. Simultaneous queries or submissions are acceptable; please make note of this in your cover letter.

Length of Articles. Articles in *The Futurist* generally run 1,000 to 4,000 words, but both longer and shorter articles are acceptable.

Opinion pieces about the future may be submitted to "Future View," *The Futurist's* guest editorial column; these normally should be no longer than 800 words.

Photographs and Drawings. *The Futurist* is very interested in photographs, drawings, or other materials that might be used to illustrate articles. Color slides or glossy prints (either color or black and white) are acceptable, as are digital images. *The Futurist is* not responsible for damage to materials during the mailing process. All such materials must be accompanied by a self-addressed, stamped envelope or mailing tube with sufficient postage to be returned.

Response Time. The editors will make every attempt to respond to all queries and manuscript submissions as soon as possible, but please allow at least three weeks for queries and three months for manuscripts.

In certain cases, the editors of *The Futurist* may show manuscripts to the editors of other World Future Society publications, including *Futures Research Quarterly, Future Times,* and the *Forums* on the Society's Web site. This may further delay response, but will increase the author's opportunities for publication.

Withdrawal of Manuscript from Planned Publication. Authors may withdraw a manuscript from the publication process provided written notice is given at least seven weeks before the date of publication. At the same time, the editors reserve the right to withdraw from publication any previously accepted material.

Compensation. Authors of articles are provided 10 free copies of the issue in which their work appears and the right to purchase additional copies at the lowest multiple rate ($3 each).

The Futurist does NOT offer financial compensation for articles.

Send all submissions to:
  Managing Editor
  The Futurist
  World Future Society,
  7910 Woodmont Avenue, Suite 450
  Bethesda, MD 20814, U.S.A
  E-mail: **cwagner@wfs.org**.

Gender and Education

ADDRESS FOR SUBMISSION:

Christine Skelton, Editor
Gender and Education
University of Newcastle upon Tyne
Department of Education
St. Thomas Street
Newcastle upon Tyne, NE1 7RU
UK
Phone: +44 1912 226535
Fax: +44 1912 228170
E-Mail: gender.education@ncl.ac.uk
Web: http://www.tandf.co.uk/journals
Address May Change:

PUBLICATION GUIDELINES:

Manuscript Length: 21-25 3,000-7,000
  Words
Copies Required: Four
Computer Submission: Yes Email
Format: No Reply
Fees to Review: 0.00 US$

Manuscript Style:
  See Manuscript Guidelines

CIRCULATION DATA:

Reader: Academics
Frequency of Issue: Quarterly
Copies per Issue:
Sponsor/Publisher: Carfax Publishing
  (Taylor & Francis Group)
Subscribe Price: 204.00 US$ Individual
  1125.00 US$ Institution

REVIEW INFORMATION:

Type of Review: Blind Review
No. of External Reviewers: 2
No. of In House Reviewers: 1
Acceptance Rate: 11-20%
Time to Review: 2 - 3 Months
Reviewers Comments: Yes
Invited Articles: 0-5%
Fees to Publish: 0.00 US$

MANUSCRIPT TOPICS:
Educational Psychology; Gender/Education; Gender/Education

MANUSCRIPT GUIDELINES/COMMENTS:

This journal publishes articles and shorter, more polemic 'viewpoints' from throughout the world which contribute to feminist knowledge, theory, consciousness, action and debate. All articles and viewpoints are submitted to at least two referees before acceptance for publication.

Notes for Contributors
The Editors welcome a variety of contributions that focus on gender as a category of analysis in education and that further feminist knowledge, theory, consciousness, action and debate. Education will be interpreted in a broad sense to cover both formal and informal aspects, including nursery, primary and secondary education; youth cultures inside and outside schools; adult, community, further and higher education; vocational education and training; media education; parental education. Contributors are asked to avoid unnecessary or mystifying jargon and to use non-sexist and non-racist language.

332

Manuscripts should be sent to Christine Skelton, Department of Education, University of Newcastle upon Tyne, St Thomas' Street, Newcastle upon Tyne, NE1 7RU, UK. Manuscripts may be of two main types: articles, ideally between 3000 and 7000 words, and viewpoints, usually up to 3000 words, that are more polemical in tone and possibly based on the life experiences, ideas and views of the writer. Please state clearly whether your contribution is intended for the Viewpoint slot. All manuscripts submitted are subjected to independent refereeing.

Manuscripts should not presently be under consideration for publication elsewhere and can only be considered if four complete copies of each manuscript are submitted, though in cases of hardship, two will suffice. They should be typed on one side of the paper, double spaced, with ample margins and bear the title of the contribution plus an abstract of 100-150 words. In order to protect anonymity, name(s) of the author(s) and institutional address, if any, should appear on a separate title page. The full postal address of the author who will check proofs and receive correspondence and offprints should also be included. All pages should be numbered. Footnotes to the text should be avoided wherever this is reasonably possible. The approximate total number of words should be specified on the title page.

Tables and captions to illustrations. Tables should be typed out on separate sheets and not included as part of the text. The captions to illustrations should be gathered together and also typed out on a separate sheet. Tables should be numbered with Roman numerals, and figures with Arabic numerals. The approximate position of tables and figures should be indicated in the manuscript. Captions should include keys to symbols.

Figures. Please supply one set of artwork in a finished form, suitable for reproduction. If this is not possible, figures will be redrawn by the publishers.

References should be indicated in the typescript by giving the author's name with the year of publication in parentheses. If several papers by the same author and from the same year are cited, a, b, c, etc., should be placed after the year of publication. References should be listed in full at the end of the paper in the following standard form:

For books: ARNOT, M. (2000) *Reproducing Gender* (London, Routledge Falmer).
For articles: BENJAMIN, S. (2000) Challenging masculinities: disability and achievement in testing times, *Gender and Education*, 13(1), pp.39-55.

For chapters   MAHONY, P. (1998) Girls will be girls and boys will be first, in D. Epstein,
within books: J. Elwood, V. Hey & J. Maw (Eds) *Failing Boys?* (Buckingham, Open University Press).

Titles of journals should not be abbreviated.

Proofs will be sent to authors if there is sufficient time to do so. They should be corrected and returned to the Editor within three days. Major alterations to the text cannot be accepted.

Offprints. Fifty offprints of each paper are supplied free. Additional copies may be purchased and should be ordered when the proofs are returned. Offprints, together with a complete copy of the relevant journal issue, are sent by accelerated surface post about three weeks after publication.

Government Union Review

ADDRESS FOR SUBMISSION:

David Y. Denholm, Editor
Government Union Review
Public Service Research Foundation
320 D Maple Avenue East
Vienna, VA 22180
USA
Phone: 703-242-3575
Fax: 703-242-3579
E-Mail: info@psrf.org
Web: www.psrf.org
Address May Change:

PUBLICATION GUIDELINES:

Manuscript Length: 21-30
Copies Required: Two
Computer Submission: Yes
Format: MSWord
Fees to Review: 0.00 US$

Manuscript Style:
    Chicago Manual of Style

CIRCULATION DATA:

Reader: Academics
Frequency of Issue: Quarterly
Copies per Issue: 2,001 - 3,000
Sponsor/Publisher: Public Service Research
    Foundation
Subscribe Price: 0.00 US$

REVIEW INFORMATION:

Type of Review: Editorial Review
No. of External Reviewers: 0
No. of In House Reviewers: 2
Acceptance Rate: 70%
Time to Review: 1 - 2 Months
Reviewers Comments: No
Invited Articles: 31-50%
Fees to Publish: 0.00 US$

MANUSCRIPT TOPICS:
Education Management/Administration; Public Sector Labor Relations

MANUSCRIPT GUIDELINES/COMMENTS:

Harvard Civil Rights-Liberties Law Review

ADDRESS FOR SUBMISSION:

Heather Butterfield, Ajay Krishnan, Eds.
Harvard Civil Rights-Liberties Law Review
Harvard University
Harvard Law School
Hastings Hall
Cambridge, MA 02138
USA
Phone: 617-495-4500
Fax: 617-495-2148
E-Mail: hlscrc@law.harvard.edu
Web: See Guidelines
Address May Change:

PUBLICATION GUIDELINES:

Manuscript Length: More than 20
Copies Required: One
Computer Submission: No
Format: N/A
Fees to Review: 0.00 US$

Manuscript Style:
    Uniform System of Citation (Harvard
    Blue Book)

CIRCULATION DATA:

Reader: Academics
Frequency of Issue: 2 Times/Year
Copies per Issue: 1,001 - 2,000
Sponsor/Publisher: Harvard University
Subscribe Price: 28.00 US$
    34.00 US$ Foreign Surface
    46.00 US$ Foreign Airmail

REVIEW INFORMATION:

Type of Review: Editorial Review
No. of External Reviewers: 3+
No. of In House Reviewers: 0
Acceptance Rate: 6-10%
Time to Review: 1 - 2 Months
Reviewers Comments: Yes
Invited Articles: 6-10%
Fees to Publish: 0.00 US$

MANUSCRIPT TOPICS:
Civil Rights, Civil Liberties Law; School Law; Social Studies/Social Science; Urban Education, Cultural/Non-Traditional

MANUSCRIPT GUIDELINES/COMMENTS:

Journal's Website: **http://www.law.harvard.edu/students/orgs/crcl/**

The *Harvard Civil Rights-Civil Liberties Law Review (CR-CL)*, one of Harvard Law School's cutting-edge journals, is a dynamic journal that seeks to capture and analyze the current issues impacting individual civil rights and civil liberties. Founded in 1966 as an instrument to advance personal freedoms and human dignities, *CR-CL* has become the nation's leading progressive law journal. *CR-CL* seeks to act as a catalyst for dialogue and progressive thought, publishing innovative legal scholarship from various perspectives and in diverse fields of study.

In recent years *CR-CL* has published articles by professors, practitioners, and students on varied topics including zoning the homeless, political lawyering, and the right to revolution.

These and other subjects continue to be some of the most exciting and rapidly developing areas of the law, and we believe that the dialogue provided by *CR-CL* and other progressive journals will help to shape the future.

CR-CL welcomes the submission of manuscripts, as well as ideas for comments and articles. Manuscripts will be returned only if a self-addressed, stamped envelope is enclosed with the manuscript. *CR-CL* does not currently accept submissions by e-mail. Please address submissions to

Harvard Civil Rights-Civil Liberties Law Review
Harvard Law School
Cambridge, MA 02138

It is preferred that manuscripts be double-spaced and that footnotes follow the text rather than appear at the bottom of textual pages. In matters of citation and style, *CRCL* follows *A Uniform System of Citation*, Harvard Law Review Association, Gannett House, Cambridge, Massachusetts 02138, and the *United States Government Printing Office Style Manual*.

Harvard Educational Review

ADDRESS FOR SUBMISSION:

Manuscript Editor
Harvard Educational Review
Harvard University
Harvard Graduate School of Education
8 Story Street, 1st Floor
Cambridge, MA 02138
USA
Phone: 617-495-3432
Fax: 617-496-3584
E-Mail: hepg@harvard.edu
Web: gseweb.harvard.edu/~hepg/her.html
Address May Change:

PUBLICATION GUIDELINES:

Manuscript Length: 15,000 words
Copies Required: Three + disk or cd-rom
Computer Submission: No
Format: See Guidelines
Fees to Review: 0.00 US$

Manuscript Style:
   Chicago Manual of Style, American
   Psychological Association

CIRCULATION DATA:

Reader: Academics
Frequency of Issue: Quarterly
Copies per Issue: 10,001 - 25,000
Sponsor/Publisher: Harvard University
Subscribe Price: 59.00 US$ Individual
   139.00 US$ Institution

REVIEW INFORMATION:

Type of Review: Blind Review
No. of External Reviewers: 0
No. of In House Reviewers: 3+
Acceptance Rate: 1-5%
Time to Review: Over 6 Months
Reviewers Comments: No
Invited Articles: 31-50%
Fees to Publish: 0.00 US$

MANUSCRIPT TOPICS:
Adult Career & Vocational; Art/Music; Bilingual/E.S.L.; Education
Management/Administration; Higher Education; Languages & Linguistics; Teacher
Education; Tests, Measurement & Evaluation; Urban Education, Cultural/Non-Traditional

MANUSCRIPT GUIDELINES/COMMENTS:

The *Harvard Educational Review* accepts contributions from teachers, practitioners, policymakers, scholars, and researchers in education arid related fields, as well as from informed observers. In addition to discussions and reviews of research and theory, *HER* welcomes articles that reflect on teaching and practice in educational settings in the United States and abroad. Authors can elect to indicate whether they are submitting their manuscript as an article, a Voices Inside Schools article, an essay review, or a book review. *HER* has a two stage review process. Manuscripts that pass the initial stage are then considered by the full Editorial Board and receive detailed written feedback. It is the policy of the *Review* to consider for publication only articles that are not simultaneously being considered elsewhere. Please follow our guidelines in preparing your manuscript for submission.
   (**http://gseweb.harvard.edu/hepg/guidelines.html**).

1. Authors must submit *three copies* of the manuscript, including a one-page abstract. Manuscripts will be returned only if a stamped, self-addressed envelope is included at the time of submission. In addition, please include a clearly labeled 3.5-inch disk or cd-rom containing an electronic version of the manuscript in Microsoft Word format. If you do not have access to MS Word, please contact us to make other arrangements.
2. Manuscripts are considered *anonymously*. The author's name must appear only on the title page; any references that identify the author in the text must be deleted.
3. HER accepts manuscripts of *up to 15,000 words* and reserves the right to return any manuscript that exceeds that length.
4. All text must be *double-spaced*, and type size must be at least *12 point with 1" margins on both sides*.
5. Quoted material is extracted in the text when it is more than 45 words, unless the editors determine otherwise.
6. Authors should refer to *The Chicago Manual of Style* for general questions of style, grammar, punctuation, and form. Chicago should also be referred to for footnotes of theoretical, descriptive, or essay-like material.
7. For technical and research manuscripts, authors should use the *Publication Manual of the American Psychological Association* for reference and citations format.
8. *The Uniform System of Citation*, published by the *Harvard Law Review*, should be used for articles that rely heavily on legal documentation. Because this form is not easily adaptable to other sources, it is usually combined with *The Chicago Manual of Style* as necessary.
9. Authors should select the style most suitable for their manuscripts and adhere consistently to that style. The Editors reserve the right to request that authors use an alternative style if the one chosen seems inappropriate. Styles may not be combined, with the exception of legal citations.
10. *References must be in APA format*. We request that authors provide complete references, including page citations in book reviews. Authors should be certain that citations and footnotes in the text agree with those in the references.
11. As a generalist journal, *HER* discourages the use of technical jargon. We encourage authors to minimize the use of underlining, parentheses, italics, and quotation marks for emphasis in the text. Footnotes should be as few and as concise as possible. Tables and figures should be kept to a minimum.

Voices Inside Schools

The purpose of this section is to provide a forum devoted to the voices of teachers, students, and others committed to education within the school community broadly defined who interact with students and who have important knowledge and expertise about life inside schools gained through practice, reflection, and/or research. We value the writing of adults and students who have intimate and first-hand experience with teaching and learning.

Submissions for the Voices Inside Schools section are written by teachers and other professionals in the field of education about their own practice, and by students about their own educational experiences. In the past, *HER* has published articles by practitioners on a wide variety of issues: a Black educator's experiences teaching writing as a process to minority students, a literacy educator teaching women in a correctional facility, a university professor describing the content and pedagogy of her course on AIDS, and a school principal reflecting on school restructuring. Authors may choose to present their perspective through a range of formats, from data-driven to more reflective essays.

Please visit our Voices Inside Schools page for more information.

Book Reviews

HER also accepts reviews of recent publications (within the last 2 publication years) about education. Book reviews, in which the author reviews a book related to education, should be 8-12 double-spaced pages. *HER* also publishes essay reviews, in which one or more books in a particular field are analyzed and the implications for future research and practice are discussed. These essays should range from 15-20 pages. More detailed guidelines for book and essay reviews are available from the *HER* office. Please call 617-495-3432, or write to the address above.

Higher Education

ADDRESS FOR SUBMISSION:

Higher Education
Springer
Higher Education Editorial Office
PO Box 17
Dordrecht, 3300 AA
The Netherlands
Phone: (+31) 78 6576 208
Fax: (+31) 78 6576 377
E-Mail: tamara.welschot@springer-sbm.com
Web: www.kluweronline.com
Address May Change:

PUBLICATION GUIDELINES:

Manuscript Length: 6000 words
Copies Required: Electronic only
Computer Submission: Yes See Guidelines
Format: N/A
Fees to Review: 0.00 US$

Manuscript Style:
    See Manuscript Guidelines

CIRCULATION DATA:

Reader: Academics
Frequency of Issue: 8 Times/Year
Copies per Issue: 1,001 - 2,000
Sponsor/Publisher: Springer
Subscribe Price: 328.00 US$ Individual
    717.00 US$ Institution

REVIEW INFORMATION:

Type of Review: Editorial Review
No. of External Reviewers: 2
No. of In House Reviewers: 1
Acceptance Rate: 20%
Time to Review: 4 - 6 Months
Reviewers Comments: Yes
Invited Articles: Special Issues
Fees to Publish: 0.00 US$

MANUSCRIPT TOPICS:
Higher Education

MANUSCRIPT GUIDELINES/COMMENTS:

For questions related to any aspect of this journal, please contact:

Tamara Welschot, Senior Publishing Editor: Springer
Phone: (+31) 78 6576 208
Fax: (+31) 78 6576 377
P.O. Box 17
3300 AA Dordrecht
The Netherlands
Email: **Tamara.Welschot@springer-sbm.com**

Higher Education is recognised as the leading international journal of Higher Education studies, publishing eight separate numbers each year. Since its establishment in 1972, *Higher Education* has followed educational developments throughout the world in universities, polytechnics, colleges, and vocational and education institutions. It has actively endeavoured to report on developments in both public and private Higher Education sectors. Contributions have come from leading scholars from different countries while articles have tackled the problems of teachers as well as students, and of planners as well as administrators.

While each Higher Education system has its own distinctive features, common problems and issues are shared internationally by researchers, teachers and institutional leaders. *Higher Education* offers opportunities for exchange of research results, experience and insights, and provides a forum for ongoing discussion between experts. *Higher Education* publishes authoritative overview articles, comparative studies and analyses of particular problems or issues. All contributions are peer reviewed.

Springer now offers authors, editors and reviewers of *Higher Education* the option of using our fully web-enabled online manuscript submission and review system. To keep the review time as short as possible (no postal delays!), we encourage authors to submit manuscripts online to the journal's editorial office. Our online manuscript submission and review system offers authors the option to track the progress of the review process of manuscripts in real time. Manuscripts should be submitted to:**http://high.edmgr.com**.

The online manuscript submission and review system for *Higher Education* offers easy and straightforward log-in and submission procedures. This system supports a wide range of submission file formats: for manuscripts -Word, WordPerfect, RTF, TXT and LaTex; for figures - TIFF, GIF, JPEG, EPS, PPT, and Postscript.

NOTE: By using the online manuscript submission and review system, it is NOT necessary to submit the manuscript also in printout + disk. In case you encounter any difficulties while submitting your manuscript on line, please get in touch with the responsible Editorial Assistant by clicking on "CONTACT US" from the tool bar.

Manuscript Presentation
The journal's language is English. British English or American English spelling and terminology may be used, but either one should be followed consistently throughout the article. Manuscripts should be printed or typewritten on A4 or US Letter bond paper, one side only, leaving adequate margins on all sides to allow reviewers' remarks. Please double-space all material, including notes and references. Quotations of more than 40 words should be set off clearly, either by indenting the left-hand margin or by using a smaller typeface. Use double quotation marks for direct quotations and single quotation marks for quotations within quotations and for words or phrases used in a special sense.

Number the pages consecutively with the first page containing:
- running head (shortened title)
- title
- author(s)
- affiliation(s)
- full address for correspondence, including telephone and fax number and
- e-mail address

342

Abstract
All articles should include an abstract of 100-150 words and should normally be no longer than 6000 words including references and tables. The abstract should not contain any undefined abbreviations or unspecified references. As the abstract and key words will be used to select appropriate reviewers, it is essential to make them as informative as possible.

Key Words
Please provide 5 to 10 key words or short phrases in alphabetical order.

Figures and Tables
Submission of electronic figures. In addition to hard-copy printouts of figures, authors are requested to supply the electronic versions of figures in either Encapsulated PostScript (EPS) or TIFF format. Many other formats, e.g., Proprietary Formats, PiCT (Macintosh) and WMF (Windows), cannot be used and the hard copy will be scanned instead.

Figures should be saved in separate files without their captions, which should be included with the text of the article. Files should be named according to DOS conventions, e.g., 'figure1.eps'. For vector graphics, EPS is the preferred format. Lines should not be thinner than 0.25pts and in-fill patterns and screen should have a density of at least 10%. Font-related problems can be avoided by using standard fonts such as Times Roman and Helvetica. For bitmapped graphics, TIFF is the preferred format but EPS is also acceptable. The following resolutions are optimal: black-and-white line figures - 600 - 1200 dpi; line figures with some grey or coloured lines - 600 dpi; photographs - 300 dpi; screen dumps - leave as is. Higher resolutions will not improve output quality but will only increase file size, which may cause problems with printing; lower resolutions may compromise output quality. Please try to provide artwork that approximately fits within the typeset area of the journal. Especially screened originals, i.e. originals with grey areas, may suffer badly from reduction by more than 10-15%.

Avoiding Problems with EPS Graphics
Please always check whether the figures print correctly to a PostScript printer in a reasonable amount of time. If they do not, simplify your figures or use a different graphics program.

If EPS export does not produce acceptable output, try to create an EPS file with the printer driver (see below). This option is unavailable with the Microsoft driver for Windows NT, so if you run Windows NT, get the Adobe driver from the Adobe site (www.adobe.com).

If EPS export is not an option, e.g., because you rely on OLE and cannot create separate files for your graphics, it may help us if you simply provide a PostScript dump of the entire document.

How to set up for eps and postscript dumps under windows
Create a printer entry specifically for this purpose: install the printer 'Apple Laserwriter Plus' and specify 'FILE': as printer port. Each time you send something to the 'printer' you will be asked for a filename. This file will be the EPS file or PostScript dump that we can use.

The EPS export option can be found under the PostScript tab. EPS export should be used only for single-page documents. For printing a document of several pages, select 'Optimise for portability' instead. The option 'Download header with each job' should be checked.

Submission of hard-copy figures
If no electronic versions of figures are available, submit only high-quality artwork that can be reproduced as is, i.e., without any part having to be redrawn or re-typeset. The letter size of any text in the figures must be large enough to allow for reduction. Photographs should be in black-and-white on glossy paper. If a figure contains colour, make absolutely clear whether it should be printed in black-and-white or in colour. Figures that are to be printed in black-and-white should not be submitted in colour. Authors will be charged for reproducing figures in colour.

Each figure and table should be numbered and mentioned in the text. The approximate position of figures and tables should be indicated in the margin of the manuscript. On the reverse side of each figure, the name of the (first) author and the figure number should be written in pencil; the top of the figure should be clearly indicated. Figures and tables should be placed at the end of the manuscript following the Reference section. Each figure and table should be accompanied by an explanatory legend. The figure legends should be grouped and placed on a separate page. Figures are not returned to the author unless specifically requested.

In tables, footnotes are preferable to long explanatory material in either the heading or body of the table. Such explanatory footnotes, identified by superscript letters, should be placed immediately below the table.

Section Headings
First-, second-, third-, and forth-order headings should be clearly distinguishable but not numbered.

Appendices
Supplementary material should be collected in an Appendix and placed before the Notes and Reference sections.

Notes
Please use endnotes rather than footnotes. Notes should be indicated by consecutive superscript numbers in the text and listed at the end of the article before the References. A source reference note should be indicated by means of an asterisk after the title. This note should be placed at the bottom of the first page.

Cross-Referencing
In the text, a reference identified by means of an author's name should be followed by the date of the reference in parentheses and page number(s) where appropriate. When there are more than two authors, only the first author's name should be mentioned, followed by 'et al.'. In the event that an author cited has had two or more works published during the same year, the reference, both in the text and in the reference list, should be identified by a lower case letter like 'a' and 'b' after the date to distinguish the works.

344

Examples:
Winograd (1986, p. 204)
(Winograd 1986a, b)
(Winograd 1986; Flores et al. 1988)
(Bullen and Bennett 1990)

Acknowledgements
Acknowledgements of people, grants, funds, etc. should be placed in a separate section before the References.

References
References to books, journal articles, articles in collections and conference or workshop proceedings, and technical reports should be listed at the end of the article in alphabetical order (see examples below). Articles in preparation or articles submitted for publication, unpublished observations, personal communications, etc. should not be included in the reference list but should only be mentioned in the article text (e.g., T.Moore, personal communication).

References to books should include the author's name; year of publication; title; page numbers where appropriate; publisher; place of publication, in the order given in the example below.

Das, M.S. (1972). *Brain Drain Controversy and International Students.* Lucknow: Lucknow Publishing House.

References to articles in an edited collection should include the author's name; year of publication; article title; editor's name; title of collection; first and last page numbers; publisher; place of publication., in the order given in the example below.

Foster, P. (1987). 'The contribution of education to development', in Psacharopoulos, G. (ed.), *Economics of Education: Research and Studies.* Oxford: Pergamon Press, pp. 93-100.

References to articles in conference proceedings should include the author's name; year of publication; article title; editor's name (if any); title of proceedings; first and last page numbers; place and date of conference; publisher and/or organization from which the proceedings can be obtained; place of publication, in the order given in the example below.

Carroll, D.C. (1987). 'Student financial assistance and consequences'. *Presented at the 147th annual meeting of the American Statistical Association*, San Francisco.

References to articles in periodicals should include the author's name; year of publication; article title; full title of periodical; volume number (issue number where appropriate); first and last page numbers, in the order given in the example below.

James, L.R., Joyce, W.F. and Slocum, J.R. (1988). 'Organisations do not cognize', *Academy of Management Review* 13(1), 129--132.

References to technical reports or doctoral dissertations should include the author's name; year of publication; title of report or dissertation; institution; location of institution, in the order given in the example below.

Andrieu, S.C. (1991). *The Influence of Background, Graduate Experience, Aspirations, Expected Earnings, and Financial Commitment on Within-Year Persistence of Students Enrolled in Graduate Programs.* Doctoral dissertation, University of New Orleans.

Proofs
Proofs will be sent to the corresponding author. One corrected proof, together with the original, edited manuscript, should be returned to the Publisher within three days of receipt by mail (airmail overseas).

Offprints
Fifty offprints of each article will be provided free of charge. Additional offprints can be ordered by means of an offprint order form supplied with the proofs.

Page Charges and Colour Figures
No page charges are levied on authors or their institutions. Colour figures are published at the author's expense only.

Copyright
Authors will be asked, upon acceptance of an article, to transfer copyright of the article to the Publisher. This will ensure the widest possible dissemination of information under copyright laws.

Permissions
It is the responsibility of the author to obtain written permission for a quotation from unpublished material, or for all quotations in excess of 250 words in one extract or 500 words in total from any work still in copyright, and for the reprinting of figures, tables or poems from unpublished or copyrighted material.

Springer Open Choice
In addition to the normal publication process (whereby an article is submitted to the journal and access to that article is granted to customers who have purchased a subscription), Springer now provides an alternative publishing option: Springer Open Choice. A Springer Open Choice article receives all the benefits of a regular subscription-based article, but in addition is made available publicly through Springer's online platform SpringerLink. To publish via Springer Open Choice, upon acceptance please visit www.springeronline.com/openchoice to complete the relevant order form and provide the required payment information. Payment must be received in full before publication or articles will publish as regular subscription-model articles. We regret that Springer Open Choice cannot be ordered for published articles.

Higher Education in Europe

ADDRESS FOR SUBMISSION:

Daniel Lincoln, Senior Editor
Higher Education in Europe
UNESCO-CEPES
39 Stirbei Voda Street
R-70732 Bucharest,
Romania
Phone: +40 21 313 0839
Fax: +40 21 312 3567
E-Mail: d.lincoln@cepes.ro
Web: www.tandf.co.uk/journals
Address May Change:

PUBLICATION GUIDELINES:

Manuscript Length: 21-25 5,000 Words
Copies Required: One
Computer Submission: Yes Disk, Email
Format: No Reply
Fees to Review: 0.00 US$

Manuscript Style:
  American Psychological Association,
  Harvard Method

CIRCULATION DATA:

Reader: Academics, Administrators, Grad
  Students, Policy Makers
Frequency of Issue: Quarterly
Copies per Issue:
Sponsor/Publisher: UNESCO Carfax
  (Taylor & Francis Group)
Subscribe Price: 96.00 US$ Individual
  450.00 US$ Institution

REVIEW INFORMATION:

Type of Review: Peer Review
No. of External Reviewers: Varies
No. of In House Reviewers: Varies
Acceptance Rate: 75%
Time to Review: 1 - 2 Months
Reviewers Comments: Yes
Invited Articles: 50% +
Fees to Publish: 0.00 US$

MANUSCRIPT TOPICS:
Education Management/Administration; Higher Education

MANUSCRIPT GUIDELINES/COMMENTS:

Journal's Website: **www.cepes.ro**

Topics Include. All aspects of Governance, Organizational Management, and International Cooperation in Higher Education

Aims and Scope
Higher Education in Europe is a quarterly review published on behalf of UNESCO European Centre for Higher Education (CEPES). It is a scholarly publication dealing with major problems and trends in contemporary higher education. It presents information, interpretations, and criticism in regard to current developments in the field. While focusing primarily on Europe and North America within the context of the other activities of the Centre, it regularly features contributions from other regions of the world as well.

Instructions for Prospective Authors. Persons wishing to publish in the review should send their proposals to the Editor and request a copy of the guidelines for the preparation of articles. Unsolicited articles and book review manuscripts will not be returned. All correspondence should be addressed to the Editor, UNESCO-CEPES, 39 Stirbei-Voda Street, R-70732 Bucharest, Romania; or by E-mail to **d.lincoln@cepes.ro** preferably as a Word-for-Windows, Word Perfect 5.1, or rich text format attachment. Finally, texts can be sent by computer diskette, preferably in Word-for-Windows or in Word Perfect 5.1.

Articles should be typed, double-space, with normal margins and should not exceed 5000 words. Notes, references, and bibliography should be presented separately, according to the so-called Harvard or APA Method. A list of "References" appearing at the end of the text should give full names of authors, full original titles (with English, French, or Russian translation, if appropriate), publisher, place of publication, date of publication, and page numbers. Charts, diagrams, tables, and graphs can be presented in a compatible Word for Windows format or produced by hand in black ink. They should be presented on separate pages, their respective positions indicated in the text. References in the text should only indicate the author's surname, date of publication, and page number, if necessary.

UNESCO-CEPES would be grateful to receive manuscripts not only in English but accompanied by French and Russian translations if possible.

The text of an article should be preceded by an abstract of approximately 100 words. The author's name, address, and a brief biography should be given on a separate sheet of paper.

Higher Education Quarterly

ADDRESS FOR SUBMISSION:

Heather Eggins, Editor
Higher Education Quarterly
c/o Society for Research into Higher
  Education
76 Portland Place
London, W1B 1NT
UK
Phone: +44 2 072 725584
Fax: +44 2 072 630016
E-Mail: heather.eggings@strath.ac.uk
Web: www.blackwellpublishers.co.uk
Address May Change:

PUBLICATION GUIDELINES:

Manuscript Length: 5000-8000 words
Copies Required: Three
Computer Submission: Yes Disk
Format: MSWord
Fees to Review: 0.00 US$

Manuscript Style:
  See Manuscript Guidelines

CIRCULATION DATA:

Reader: Academics, Administrators,
  National Policy Makers
Frequency of Issue: Quarterly
Copies per Issue: Less than 1,000
Sponsor/Publisher: Society for Research
  into Higher Education/ Blackwell
  Publishers, Inc.
Subscribe Price: 480.00 US$

REVIEW INFORMATION:

Type of Review: Editorial Review
No. of External Reviewers: 2
No. of In House Reviewers: 1
Acceptance Rate: 21-30%
Time to Review: 4 - 6 Months
Reviewers Comments: Yes
Invited Articles: 11-20%
Fees to Publish: 0.00 US$

MANUSCRIPT TOPICS:
Education Management/Administration; Education Policy; Higher Education

MANUSCRIPT GUIDELINES/COMMENTS:

Higher Education Quarterly publishes articles concerned with policy, strategic management and ideas in higher education. A substantial part of its contents is concerned with reporting research findings in ways that bring out their relevance to senior managers and policy makers at institutional and national levels, and to academics who are not necessarily specialists in the academic study of higher education. The *Higher Education Quarterly* also publishes papers that are not based on empirical research but give thoughtful academic analyses of significant policy, management or academic issues.

Papers from countries other than the UK, especially those from other European countries, that highlight issues of international concern are particularly welcomed.

How to Submit Your Article
Papers accepted become the copyright of Blackwell Publishers.

Manuscripts should be sent to the General Editor, Professor Heather Eggins c/o Society for Research into Higher Education, 76 Portland Place, London W1B 1NT, UK.

Books for review and reviews should be sent to Dr. Paul Trowler, Department of Educational Research, Lancaster University, Lancaster LA1 4YL, UK.

Authors should submit articles on 3.5 floppy disc (where possible) and also present *three* copies of their manuscript, typed on single-sided A4 paper, double spaced, with ample margins, bearing the title of the article, name(s) of the author(s) and the address where the work was carried out. Each article should be accompanied by an abstract of 100-150 words on a separate sheet, together with a biographical note of about 30 words. A note should appear at the end of the last page indicating the total number of words in the article (including those in the Abstract and References).

Tables and Captions to Illustrations. Tables must be typed out on separate sheets and not included as part of the text. The captions to illustrations should be numbered by Roman numerals, and figures by Arabic numerals. The approximate position of tables and figures should be indicated in the manuscript. Captions should include keys to symbols.

Figures. .Figures involving line drawings will be redrawn by the publisher unless the author specifically requests that the original be used.

References. References should be indicated in the typescript by giving the author's name, with the year of publication in parenthesis. If several papers by the same author and from the same year are cited, a, b, c, etc should be put after the year of publication. The references should be listed in full at the end of the article in the following standard form

Clark, Burton, R. (Ed.)(1985), *The School and the University: An International Perspective* Berkeley, University of California Press.

Shinn, Christine Helen (1986), *Paying the Piper: The Development of the University Grants Committee 1919-1946* London, Falmer Press.

Neave, Guy (1986), On Shifting Sands, Changing Priorities and Perspectives in European Higher Education from 1984 to 1986, *European Journal of Education*, pp.7-24.

Titles of journals should not be abbreviated.

Proofs will be sent to authors if there is sufficient time to do so. They should be corrected and returned to the Editorial Office within three days. Major alterations of the text cannot be accepted.

Free copies. Authors will receive six copies of the issue in which their article appears.

Industry and Higher Education

ADDRESS FOR SUBMISSION:

John Edmondson, Editor
Industry and Higher Education
IP Publishing, LTD.
Coleridge House
4-5 Coleridge Gardens
London, NW6 3QH
UK
Phone: 44 207-372-2600
Fax: 44 207-372-2253
E-Mail: jedmondip@aol.com
Web: www.ippublishing.com
Address May Change:

PUBLICATION GUIDELINES:

Manuscript Length: 16-20
Copies Required: Three
Computer Submission: Yes Disk, Email
Format: Any commonly used software
Fees to Review: 0.00 US$

Manuscript Style:
    See Manuscript Guidelines

CIRCULATION DATA:

Reader: Academics
Frequency of Issue: Bi-Monthly
Copies per Issue:
Sponsor/Publisher:
Subscribe Price: 462.00 US$

REVIEW INFORMATION:

Type of Review: Blind Review
No. of External Reviewers: 2
No. of In House Reviewers: 1
Acceptance Rate: 40%
Time to Review: 1 - 2 Months
Reviewers Comments: Yes
Invited Articles: 6-10%
Fees to Publish: 0.00 US$

MANUSCRIPT TOPICS:
Adult Career & Vocational; Continuing Education; Curriculum Studies; Education Management/Administration; Technology Transfer

MANUSCRIPT GUIDELINES/COMMENTS:

Notes for authors
Please send all submissions to John Edmondson, *Industry and Higher Education*, In Print Publishing Ltd, Coleridge House, 4-5 Coleridge Gardens, London NW6 3QH, UK. Phone: +44 20 7372 2600 Fax: +44 7372 2253. E-mail: **jedmondip@aol.com**. For more details about *Industry and Higher Education*, see **www.ippublishing.com**.

Industry and Higher Education is an international bimonthly journal. It is concerned with policy and practice in relation to all types of collaboration between business and higher education.

Type and length of contributions
The major part of the journal is taken up by papers between 4,000 and 8,000 words long. These should be analytical and evaluative in approach and not simply descriptive. Other contributions include opinion or 'viewpoint' pieces (1,500-3,000 words); case studies of specific ventures or programmes (1,500-3,000 words); brief factual summaries of reports, agency programmes, educational institutions, etc (1,000-2,000 words); and letters to the editors.

Presentation
Submissions should be double-spaced, printed on one side of the paper in one column. Two hard copies should be accompanied by an electronic version on disk (please state the software used). The *title page* should contain full names of the authors, their professional status or affiliation and the address to which they wish correspondence to be sent. There should be an *abstract* of about 100 words at the beginning of the paper. The text should be organized under appropriate *cross-headings* and where possible these should not be more than 800 words apart.

Between 3 and 6 keywords should appear below the abstract, highlighting the main topics of the paper.

References should follow the Harvard system. That is, they should be shown within the text as the author's surname (or authors' surnames) followed by a comma and the year of publication, all in round brackets: for example, (Smith, 1998). At the end of the article a bibliographical list should be supplied, organized alphabetically by author (surnames followed by initials - all authors should be named). Bibliographic information should be given in the order indicated by the following examples:

• *Articles*: Collins, Steven W. (2001), 'Academic research and regional innovation: insights from Seattle, Washington', Industry and Higher Education, Vol 15, No 3, pp 217–221.

• *Books*: Roberts, E.B., ed (1991), Entrepreneurs in High Technology, Oxford University Press, Oxford.

Notes should be numbered consecutively in the text and typed in plain text at the end of the paper (not as footnotes on text pages)

Figures and tables should be presented separately on separate sheets at the end of the text. Each figure or table must be referred to in the text - the first reference will be used to locate the figure or table in the final printed version.

Copyright
Unless otherwise indicated, articles are received on the understanding that they are original contributions, and have not been published or submitted for publication elsewhere. The editors reserve the right to edit or otherwise alter contributions, but authors will see proofs before publication. Wherever possible, authors are asked to assign copyright to IP Publishing Ltd. Relevant authors' rights are protected.

Infant Mental Health Journal

ADDRESS FOR SUBMISSION:

Joy Osofsky, Editor
Infant Mental Health Journal
Louisiana State University
Health Science Center
Division of Psychiatry
1542 Tulane Avenue
New Orleans, LA 70112
USA
Phone: 504-568-6004
Fax: 504-568-6246
E-Mail: imhj@lsuhsc.edu
Web:
Address May Change:

PUBLICATION GUIDELINES:

Manuscript Length: 20-25
Copies Required: Three
Computer Submission: No
Format: N/A
Fees to Review: 0.00 US$

Manuscript Style:
American Psychological Association

CIRCULATION DATA:

Reader: Academics, Counselors, Social
Workers
Frequency of Issue: 6 Times/Year
Copies per Issue: Less than 1,000
Sponsor/Publisher:
Subscribe Price: 95.00 US$
107.00 US$ Outside North America

REVIEW INFORMATION:

Type of Review: Blind Review
No. of External Reviewers: 2
No. of In House Reviewers: 0
Acceptance Rate: 50%
Time to Review: 4 - 6 Months
Reviewers Comments: Yes
Invited Articles: No Reply
Fees to Publish: 0.00 US$

MANUSCRIPT TOPICS:
Educational Psychology; Elementary/Early Childhood

MANUSCRIPT GUIDELINES/COMMENTS:

Reader. Counselors, Early Childhood Education Specialists, Nurses, Physicians, Psychologists, and Public Health Workers

The *IMHJ* publishes research articles, literature reviews, program descriptions/evaluations, clinical studies, and book reviews that focus on infant social-emotional development, care giver-infant interactions, contextual and cultural influences on infant and family development, and all conditions that place infants and/or their families at-risk for less than optimal development. The *IMHJ* is dedicated to an interdisciplinary approach to the optimal development of infants and their families, and, therefore, welcomes submissions from all disciplinary perspectives.

Manuscripts (An original and three copies) should be submitted to the Editor typed, with double spacing throughout and ample margins. Blind reviewing will be used. Each copy of the paper should include a cover sheet with the following information: Title of manuscript, name of author(s), and author(s) affiliation. The title should appear on the abstract and on the first page of text. Information about the identity of the author(s) contained in footnotes should appear on the title page only. The title page is not included when the manuscript is sent out for review. A cover letter to the Editor should accompany the paper: it should request a review and indicate that the manuscript has not been published previously or submitted elsewhere.

An abstract of approximately 150 words must be included. Tables and figures must be sufficiently clear so that they can be photographed directly. (Black and white glossy prints are acceptable.) Letter quality or near letter-quality print must be used for computer-prepared manuscripts.

Style must conform to that described by the *American Psychological Association Publication Manual*, Fourth Edition, 1994 revision (American Psychological Association, 1200 Seventeenth Street, N.W., Washington, D.C. 20036). Authors are responsible for final preparation of manuscripts to conform to the APA style.

Manuscripts are reviewed by the Editor, Associate Editor(s), members of the Editorial Board, and invited reviewers with special knowledge of the topic addressed in the manuscript. The Editor retains the right to reject articles that do not conform to conventional clinical or scientific ethical standards. Normally, the review process is completed in 3 months. Nearly all manuscripts accepted for publication require some degree of revision. There is no charge for publication of papers in the *Infant Mental Health Journal*. The publisher may levy additional charges for changes in proof other than correction of printers errors. Proof will be sent to the corresponding author and must be read carefully because final responsibility for accuracy rests with the author(s). Author(s) must return corrected proof to the publisher in a timely manner. If the publisher does not receive corrected proof from the author(s), publication will still proceed as scheduled.

Additional questions with regard to style and submission of manuscripts should be directed to the Editor.

Intelligence

ADDRESS FOR SUBMISSION:

Douglas K. Detterman, Editor
Intelligence
Case Western Reserve University
Department of Psychology
10900 Euclid Avenue
Cleveland, OH 44106-7123
USA
Phone: 216-368-2680
Fax: 216-368-4891
E-Mail: dkd2@po.cwru.edu
Web:
Address May Change:

PUBLICATION GUIDELINES:

Manuscript Length: 21-25
Copies Required: Four
Computer Submission: Yes
Format: N/A
Fees to Review: 0.00 US$

Manuscript Style:
American Psychological Association

CIRCULATION DATA:

Reader: , Researchers
Frequency of Issue: 6 Times/Year
Copies per Issue: 1,001 - 2,000
Sponsor/Publisher: International Society for
Intelligence Research/ Elsevier Science
Publishing Co.
Subscribe Price: 113.00 US$ Individual
269.00 US$ Library
75.00 US$ ISIR Membership Included

REVIEW INFORMATION:

Type of Review: Editorial Review
No. of External Reviewers: 3
No. of In House Reviewers: 0
Acceptance Rate: 50%
Time to Review: 2 - 3 Months
Reviewers Comments: Yes
Invited Articles: 0-5%
Fees to Publish: 0.00 US$

MANUSCRIPT TOPICS:
Experiments; Human Intelligence; Tests, Measurement & Evaluation

MANUSCRIPT GUIDELINES/COMMENTS:

Guide for Authors
The journal *Intelligence* publishes papers reporting work that makes a substantial contribution to an understanding of the nature and function of intelligence. Varied approaches to the problem will be welcome. Theoretical and review articles will be considered if appropriate, but preference will be given to original research. In general, studies concerned with application will not be considered appropriate unless the work also makes a contribution to basic knowledge.

For submission, send *four copies* of all manuscripts to the Editor, Douglas K. Detterman, Department of Psychology, Case Western Reserve University, 10900 Euclid Ave., Cleveland, OH 44106-7123. A blind review will be conducted upon the request of the author. Intelligence will also, on a trial basis, accept electronic submissions. The paper, in MS Word or PDF format, should be submitted to **Intelligence_Journal@HotMail.com**

Manuscripts should conform to the conventions specified in the fifth edition (2001) of the *Publication Manual of the American Psychological Association* (750 First St. NE, Washington, DC 20002-4242) with the exceptions listed below.

1. **Preparation of Manuscript**. Please double space *all* material. Manuscripts should be typewritten on 8 1/2 x 11 in. bond paper, *one side only*, ragged right margin, leaving 1-in. margins on all sides. Number pages consecutively with the title page as page 1, and include a brief abstract from 100 to 150 words as page 2. All tables and other end-of-paper matter, except art, should be numbered also.

2. **Illustrations**. Submit only clear reproductions of artwork. Authors should retain original artwork until a manuscript has been accepted in its final version. All figures must be in a camera-ready form. All artwork should be placed in the manuscript. Authors must provide high-quality figures, preferably laser printed, typeset, or professionally inked. Photographs must be black and white glossies. The largest figure that can be accommodated is 5 x 7 in., so please keep this in mind when constructing artwork. Colour Reproduction: submit colour illustrations as original photographs, high-quality computer prints or transparencies, close to the size expected in publication, or as 35 mm slides. Polaroid colour prints are not suitable. *If, together with your accepted article, you submit usable colour figures then Elsevier will ensure, at no additional charge, that these figures will appear in colour on the web (e.g., ScienceDirect and other sites) regardless of whether or not these illustrations are reproduced in colour in the printed version.* For colour reproduction in print, you will receive information regarding the costs from Elsevier after receipt of your accepted article. For further information on the preparation of electronic artwork, please see http://authors.elsevier.com/artwork.

Please note. Because of technical complications which can arise by converting colour figures to "grey scale" (for the printed version should you not opt for colour in print) please submit in addition usable black and white prints corresponding to all the colour illustrations.

3. **Numbering of Figures and Tables**. Each figure and table must be mentioned in the text and must be numbered consecutively using Arabic numerals in the order of its appearance in the text. On the reverse side of every figure *write the name of the author and the figure number*. A brief title should be typed directly above each table. Please indicate in the manuscript approximately where you wish each table or figure to be placed.

4. **Footnotes**. Footnotes should be used sparingly and indicated by consecutive numbers in the text. Material to be footnoted should be typed separately and submitted with the manuscript following the figure legends. Acknowledgments, grant numbers, an author correspondence address, E-mail, and any change of address should be given in a separate, asterisked footnote, which will appear at the end of text.

5. **References**. Contributors should refer to the *APA Publication Manual* for the correct listing of references in the text and reference list. The only exception is that unpublished references should not be treated as reference notes, but listed in the same format as published references. All references must be closely checked in text and lists to determine that dates and spellings are consistent. Please note that the names of *all* authors should be given in the list of

356

references, and "et al." used only in the text. Examples for journals, unpublished papers, and books (in that order) are given below:

Atkinson, R. C., & Shiffrin, R. M. (1971). The control of short-term memory. *Scientific American, 225*, 82-90.

Lightburn, L. T. (1955). *The relation of critical fusion frequency to age.* Unpublished doctoral dissertation, University of New Jersey.

Riesen, A. H. (1966). Sensory deprivation. In E. Stellar & J. M. Sprague (Eds.), *Progress in physiological psychology* (pp 105-112). New York: Academic

6. **Spelling, Terminology, and Abbreviations**. American spelling, rather than British, is preferred. The Third Edition of *Webster's Unabridged Dictionary* is the standard reference work when in doubt. Please try to avoid jargon and, whenever possible, abbreviations that are not commonly accepted.

7. **Role of corresponding author**. The corresponding authors of a manuscript for *Intelligence* has the duty to ensure that all the named authors have seen and approved the original and any revised version of the paper and are in agreement with its content before it is submitted to the Editorial Office. Each author should have participated sufficiently in the work to take public responsibility for the content. The corresponding author should also ensure that all those who have contributed to the research are acknowledged appropriately either as co-author or in the Acknowledgements. In addition, the corresponding author has the prime responsibility for ensuring the paper is correctly prepared according to the Guide for Authors. Submitted manuscripts not complying with the Guide for Authors may be returned to the authors for possible revision and resubmission.

Upon acceptance of an article, authors will be asked to transfer copyright (for more information on copyright see http://authors.elsevier.com). This transfer will ensure the widest possible dissemination of information. A letter will be sent to the corresponding author confirming receipt of the manuscript. A form facilitating transfer of copyright will be provided. If excerpts from other copyrighted works are included, the author(s) must obtain written permission from the copyright owners and credit the source(s) in the article. Elsevier has preprinted forms for use by the authors in these cases: contact ELSEVIER, Global Rights Department, P.O. Box 800, Oxford, OX5 IDX, UK; phone: (444) 1865 843830, e-mail: permissions@elsevier.com

8. **Affiliation, Running Head**. Please include under your name on the title page the institutions with which you are connected, your complete mailing address, E-mail, and credits to any other institution where the work may have been done. A shortened version of your title, suitable for alternate page headings, should be typed underneath your affiliation and identified as *Running Head*.

9. **Acceptance**. Upon acceptance we request an IBM compatible disk, spell checked and stripped of all embedded graphics. Graphics should be saved in a separate eps, tiff, or ps file. The accuracy of the disk and page proofs is the author's responsibility.

10. **Offprints**. The lead author will be provided 25 free copies of his or her article.

11.**Supplementary data**. Elsevier now accepts electronic supplementary material to support and enhance your scientific research. Supplementary files offer the author additional possibilities to publish supporting applications, movies, animation sequences, high-resolution images, background datasets, sound clips and more. Supplementary files supplied will be published online alongside the electronic version of your article in Elsevier web products, including ScienceDirect:http://www.sciencedirect.com. In order to ensure that your submitted material in directly usable, please ensure that data is provided in one of our recommended file formats. Authors should submit the material in electronic format together with the article and supply a concise and descriptive caption for each file. For more detailed instructions please visit our Author Gateway at http://authors.elsevier.com.

12. **Enquiries**. Authors can keep track on the progress of their accepted article, and set up e-mail alerts, informing them of changes to their manuscript's status, by using the "track a Paper" feature of Elsevier's Author Gateway http://authors.elsevier.com. For privacy, information on each article is password protected. The author should key in the "Our References" code (which is in the letter of acknowledgement sent by the publisher on receipt of the accepted article) and the name of the corresponding author. In case of problems or questions, authors may contact the Author Service Department.

E-mail: authorsupport@elsevier.com.

Intercultural Education

ADDRESS FOR SUBMISSION:

Barry van Driel, Editor-In-Chief
Intercultural Education
236 San Carlos Ave. # 1
Sausalito, CA
USA
Phone: 415-332-3273
Fax:
E-Mail: barry@iaie.org
Web: www.tandf.co.uk/journals
Address May Change:

PUBLICATION GUIDELINES:

Manuscript Length: 3000-6000 words
Copies Required: One Word document
Computer Submission: Yes
Format: MSWord
Fees to Review: 0.00 US$

Manuscript Style:
See Manuscript Guidelines

CIRCULATION DATA:

Reader: Counselors, Teacher Trainers,
Practicing Teachers, Academics
Frequency of Issue: 5 Times/Year
Copies per Issue:
Sponsor/Publisher: IAIE, Int'l Association
for Intercultural Education; Carfax
Publishing (Taylor & Francis Group)
Subscribe Price: 218.00 US$ Individual
661.00 US$ Institution

REVIEW INFORMATION:

Type of Review: Editorial Review
No. of External Reviewers: 25
No. of In House Reviewers: 2
Acceptance Rate: 35%
Time to Review: 1 - 2 Months
Reviewers Comments: Yes
Invited Articles: 21-30%
Fees to Publish: 0.00 US$

MANUSCRIPT TOPICS:
Bilingual/E.S.L.; Conflict Management; Curriculum Studies; Education
Management/Administration; Higher Education; Human Rights Education; Intercultural
Education; Multicultural Education; Teacher Education

MANUSCRIPT GUIDELINES/COMMENTS:

Journal's Website: www.iaie.org

Aims and Scope
Intercultural Education is a global forum for the analysis of issues dealing with education in
plural societies. It provides educational professionals with the knowledge and information that
can assist them in contributing to the critical analysis and the implementation of intercultural
education. Topics covered include: terminological issues, education and multicultural society
today, intercultural communication, human rights and anti-racist education, pluralism and
diversity in a democratic frame work, pluralism in post-communist and in post-colonial
countries, migration and indigenous minority issues, refugee issues, language policy issues,
curriculum and classroom organization, and school development.

Manuscripts
(Hard copy and a version on disk, preferably in Word format) should be sent to: Barry van Driel, 236 San Carlos Ave. #1, Sausalito, CA, USA or by email to: **barry@iaie.org**.

All articles will be refereed by members of the editorial board, which may lead to suggestions for the improvement of the article. The author's final draft will be edited and corrected by the journal's final editor.

Main articles should be between 3,000 and 6,000 words, including a short biographical note of the author(s), and with one's address for correspondence including fax and e-mail at the end of the article.

Books for review, originally written in English, should be addressed to Sven Sierens, Center for Intercultural Education, Sint Pietersnieuwstraat, B-9000 Ghent, Belgium; Email: fa855025@skynet.be

Electronic Submission
Authors should send the final, revised version of their articles in electronic disk form. We prefer to receive disks in Microsoft Word in a PC format.

Tables and captions to illustrations
Tables and captions to illustrations must be typed out on separate sheets and not included as part of the text.

Figures
Please, supply one set of artwork in a finished form, suitable for reproduction.

References
These should be indicated in the typescript by giving the author's name, with the year of publication in parentheses. If several papers by the same author and from the same year are cited, a, b, c, etc. should be put after the year of publication. The references should be listed in full, including pages, at the end of the paper in the following standard form:

For books: FRYER, P. (1984) **Staying Power.** London: Pluto Press.

For articles: HAARMANN, H. (1995) Multilingualism and ideology: the historical experiment of Soviet language politics. **European Journal of Intercultural Studies,** 5, 3, pp. 16-17.

For chapters within books: JONES, C. (1992) Cities diversity and education. In: COULBY, D. & JONES, C. (Eds) **The World Yearbook of Education 1992.** London: Kogan Page.

Titles of journals and names of publishers, etc. should **not** be abbreviated. Acronyms for the names of organizations, examinations, etc. should be preceded by the title in full.

End notes should be kept to a minimum. They should be numbered consecutively throughout the article, and should immediately precede the 'References' section.

360

Offprints. Fifty offprints of each paper are supplied free. Additional copies may be purchased and should be ordered when the proofs are returned. Offprints, together with a complete copy of the relevant journal issue, are sent by accelerated surface post about three weeks after publication.

Copyright. It is a condition of publication that authors vest copyright in their articles, including abstracts, in Taylor & Francis Ltd. This enables us to ensure full copyright protection and to disseminate the article, and the journal, to the widest possible readership in print and electronic formats as appropriate.

Authors may, of course, use the article elsewhere **after** publication without prior permission from Carfax, provided that acknowledgement is given to the Journal as the original source of publication, and that Carfax is notified so that our records show that its use is properly authorized.

International Electronic Journal for Leadership in Learning

ADDRESS FOR SUBMISSION:

J. Kent Donlevy, Editor
International Electronic Journal for
   Leadership in Learning
University of Calgary
Graduate Division of Edu. Research
Faculty of Education
Calgary, AB
Canada
Phone:
Fax: 403-282-3005
E-Mail: iejll@ucalgary.ca
Web: www.ucalgary.ca/~iejll
Address May Change:

PUBLICATION GUIDELINES:

Manuscript Length: 16-20
Copies Required: No Paper Copy Required
Computer Submission: Yes Email Required
Format: Word
Fees to Review: 0.00 US$

Manuscript Style:
   American Psychological Association

CIRCULATION DATA:

Reader: Practicing Teachers, Academics,
   Administrators
Frequency of Issue: 24 Times/Year
Copies per Issue: 5,001 - 10,000
Sponsor/Publisher: Univ. of Calgary Press,
   Assn. for Supervision & Curr. Devel,
   Center for Leadership in Learning
Subscribe Price: 0.00 US$ Online

REVIEW INFORMATION:

Type of Review: Blind Review
No. of External Reviewers: 3
No. of In House Reviewers: 1
Acceptance Rate: 21-30%
Time to Review: 2 - 3 Months
Reviewers Comments: Yes
Invited Articles: 0-5%
Fees to Publish: 0.00 US$

MANUSCRIPT TOPICS:
Education Management/Administration; Higher Education; Urban Education, Cultural/Non-Traditional

MANUSCRIPT GUIDELINES/COMMENTS:

The International Electronic Journal for Leadership in Learning (IEJLL) promotes the study and discussion of substantive leadership issues that are of current concern in educational communities. Preference is given to articles, reviews, and commentary that focus upon issues with a significant impact upon life in schools. Prospective authors should submit work that will be of interest to a broad readership, including teachers, administrators, members of governance bodies, parents, community members, department of education personnel, and academics. In addition, the *IEJLL* seeks to promote responses from readers in the form of postings to its associated electronic mail discussion group, The Change Agency Listserver, as well as commentary posted to the *IEJLL* Talkback Forum.

General Guidelines

The *IEJLL* is a refereed electronic journal intended for a broad audience of persons interested in leadership in learning. Our audience includes members of government education departments, school boards, school councils, faculties of education, parent organizations, and school staffs.

Submissions can take various forms:
- articles on current quantitative or qualitative research
- reports on innovative programs
- position papers
- reflective commentaries on published submissions

The *"International Electronic Journal for Leadership in Learning" (IEJLL)* welcomes submissions that address the following themes:
- Integrating technology into teaching and learning.
- Exploring the potential of the principalship.
- Professional development and its effects on teacher practice and student achievement.
- The role administrators play in being supporters/advocates of growth.
- School funding and ownership models.
- Morality in education.
- The growing incidence of special needs students and how best to meet this challenge.
- The next generation of accountability.
- School-based decision making, school councils and new conceptualizations of professional power.
- Teacher burnout - a real or exaggerated phenomenon?
- The relative influence of certified versus noncertified teachers and support staff.
- Looming shortages in the pool of potential principals, superintendents, and teacher-leaders.
- How should the work of educators change?
- Role of teachers' associations in providing educational leadership.
- Language policy and how schools accommodate students from language minority backgrounds

Submissions that address additional topics relevant to educational leadership are also welcome.

Submissions to the *IEJLL* should not exceed 5000 words excluding references. Authors are strongly encouraged to utilize the multimedia potential of web-based publication. Articles may initiate electronic conversations among readers and authors. These conversations will be facilitated by e-mail links to the author and to The Change Agency Listserver. Submissions must adhere to the guidelines of the *Publication Manual of the American Psychological Association* (Fourth Edition) and *IEJLL* Ethical Guidelines for Authors and/or Respondents.

References to other electronic journals and sites should contain web site addresses (URLs).

Abstract
Include an abstract of no more than 100 words identifying the essence of the submission. Abstracts will be published independently from the article for readers to "browse" before choosing an article to view/read.

Authorship Information
A brief autobiography of the author should accompany the submission in a separate file to facilitate a blind review process. Include such information as academic background, current position, professional affiliation, mailing address, area of current interest or research and other interests. E-mail addresses are expected as are WWW addresses for authors' home pages, if applicable.

Sending Your Work
The *IEJLL* is committed to making effective use of electronic delivery for timely communication. Therefore, the IEJLL is unable to accept paper submissions.

Acceptable Electronic Format for Submissions
Rich Text Format (RTF) files with embedded graphics and charts are preferred. ASCII, Text files, or DOS Text files are acceptable. In the latter case, diagrams and charts should be submitted using ASCII characters. Graphics submitted in GIF or JPEG format are preferred. Authors who are interested in including sound and/or video are encouraged to discuss such submissions with the Editorial Committee. The Editorial Committee is very interested in investigating the expanding opportunities of the electronic medium.

Submissions can be sent to *IEJLL* one of two ways:
* Through e-mail to **IEJLL@ucalgary.ca**
* By sending computer files on a 3.5" floppy disk to:
  The International Electronic Journal for Leadership in Learning, c/o Graduate Division of Educational Research, The Faculty of Education, University of Calgary, 2500 University Drive NW, Calgary, Alberta, T2N 1N4

Publishing Policy: Copyright
1. Once a paper has been accepted for publication in the *IEJLL*, the author transfers copyright to the *IEJLL*. Ten months following publication in the *IEJLL*, authors will be granted the right to republish their works, in whole or in part, provided that formal permission to republish is sought from the *IEJLL*, and provided that appropriate citation of the original publication is made, including a reference to the Internet address for the archived *IEJLL* version of the work.

2. Readers are responsible for referencing the *IEJLL* when using information derived from it.

3. The *IEJLL* grants reproduction rights for noncommercial educational purposes with the provision that full acknowledgment of the source is noted on each copy.

4. The *IEJLL* retains the right to archive published submissions in an electronic format for an indefinite period.

364

Ethical Responsibilities and Requirements of Authors
When the Editorial Committee receives submissions, they will assume the following:

1. Authors have presented complete and accurate accounts of the research performed.

2. Authors have provided complete and accurate citations and, where appropriate, related their work to that of others.

3. Authors have ensured the safety of research participants.

4. Authors have used inclusive language.

5. All authors of a paper have contributed significantly to the work done.

6. When articles contain material (tables, figures, charts, etc.) that is protected by copyright, authors have secured written permission form the holder of the copyright.

7. The authors have disclosed any information which may affect publication of the submission. This includes the disclosure of any related articles published previously or under consideration for publication in this or other journals.

8. If submissions are accepted by the *IEJLL*, authors will not republish the article in other journals for a period of ten months. After this time period, submissions may be republished if appropriate reference is made to the original publication.

9. The authors have archived the original research data used in the production of research articles; these data may be requested by the Editorial Committee or other researchers.

International Journal of Artificial Intelligence in Education

ADDRESS FOR SUBMISSION:

Paul Brna, Editor
International Journal of Artificial
   Intelligence in Education
Phone: 0 191 243 7609
Fax:
E-Mail: paul.brna@unn.ac.uk
Web: www.ijaied.org
Address May Change: 7/1/2008

PUBLICATION GUIDELINES:

Manuscript Length: 30+
Copies Required: Four
Computer Submission: Yes Disk, Email
Format: Word, LaTeX
Fees to Review: 0.00 US$

Manuscript Style:
   American Psychological Association

CIRCULATION DATA:

Reader: Academics, Industrial Researchers
Frequency of Issue: Quarterly
Copies per Issue: Less than 1,000
Sponsor/Publisher: International Artificial
   Intelligence in Education Society
Subscribe Price: 155.00 US$
   50.00 US$ IAIED Society Members

REVIEW INFORMATION:

Type of Review: Blind Review
No. of External Reviewers: 3
No. of In House Reviewers: 0
Acceptance Rate: 21-30%
Time to Review: 2 - 3 Months
Reviewers Comments: Yes
Invited Articles: 0-5%
Fees to Publish: 0.00 US$

MANUSCRIPT TOPICS:
Educational Technology Systems; Learning and ICTs

MANUSCRIPT GUIDELINES/COMMENTS:

Scope
IJAIED publishes papers concerned with the application of AI to education. It aims to help the development of principles for the design of computer-based learning systems. Its premise is that such principles involve the modelling and representation of relevant aspects of knowledge, before implementation or during execution, and hence require the application of AI techniques and concepts.

IJAIED has a very broad notion of the scope of AI and of a 'computer-based learning system', as indicated by the following list of topics considered to be within the scope of *IJAIED*:

- adaptive and intelligent multimedia and hypermedia systems
- agent-based learning environments
- AIED and teacher education
- architectures for AIED systems
- assessment and testing of learning outcomes
- authoring systems and shells for AIED systems

- bayesian and statistical methods
- case-based systems
- cognitive development
- cognitive models of problem-solving
- cognitive tools for learning
- computer-assisted language learning
- computer-supported collaborative learning
- dialogue (argumentation, explanation, negotiation, etc.)
- discovery environments and microworlds
- distributed learning environments
- educational robotics
- embedded training systems
- empirical studies to inform the design of learning environments
- environments to support the learning of programming
- evaluation of AIED systems
- formal models of components of AIED systems
- help and advice systems
- human factors and interface design
- instructional design principles
- instructional planning
- intelligent agents on the internet
- intelligent courseware for computer-based training
- intelligent tutoring systems
- knowledge and skill acquisition
- knowledge representation for instruction
- modelling metacognitive skills
- modelling pedagogical interactions
- motivation
- natural language interfaces for instructional systems
- networked learning and teaching systems
- neural models applied to AIED systems
- performance support systems
- practical, real-world applications of AIED systems
- qualitative reasoning in simulations
- situated learning and cognitive apprenticeship
- social and cultural aspects of learning
- student modelling and cognitive diagnosis
- support for knowledge building communities
- support for networked communication
- theories of learning and conceptual change
- tools for administration and curriculum integration
- tools for the guided exploration of information resources
- virtual learning environments
- virtual reality based learning systems

- visual, graphical and other innovative interfaces
- web-based AIED systems

Guidelines

The following guidelines are intended for the benefit of potential *IJAIED* authors and reviewers, although we must always bear in mind that AIED is still a young and evolving field and it is not the aim to lay down 'rules of good practice' which inhibit original research.

A major factor is that AIED is an inter-disciplinary field and thus the *IJAIED* readership includes people with widely differing background knowledge and interests. There is therefore an obligation on all *IJAIED* authors to make their papers accessible to the broad spectrum of *IJAIED* readers. Specialist terms should be explained, theories in particular fields should be briefly summarised, etc. Where it is difficult to do this in the space available, references should be provided.

Although AIED itself is inter-disciplinary, when the main focus of a paper is towards one particular established discipline, then that paper must follow the precepts of that discipline. For example, if a paper presents a behavioural study of students using some system to support claims about improved learning, then it must conform to the standards developed in behavioural science, e.g. there should be a comparison with a control group, the variance in the data must be dealt with somehow, and so on. Other examples are discussed below.

On the other hand, it is not reasonable to expect that authors will meet all the standards of all disciplines outside their main focus. Of course a paper should not violate or ignore such standards but it need not go into irrelevant detail to meet them. For example, the behavioural study mentioned above need not include a theoretical analysis of the algorithms underlying the system which is the basis for the study.

There are many different kinds of paper which may be written for *IJAIED*, each with their own requirements. But first we should try to identify what all *IJAIED* papers have in common. In general terms, *IJAIED* papers are concerned with the application of AI techniques and concepts to educational issues. Indeed many *IJAIED* papers could be titled 'The application of X to Y' where X and Y are clearly within the fields of AI and Education respectively.

However, this is much too simplistic: AI is much more than a collection of techniques and concepts. It is a rather complex methodology (or set of methodologies) concerned with issues many of which (such as the nature of knowledge and learning) are intrinsically related to education. Sometimes an *IJAIED* paper may not be able to point to specific AI techniques but rather is imbued with the spirit of an AI approach to the problem. Naturally, such a paper should make it clear what insights and benefits come from adopting an AI point of view.

In addition, as AIED evolves it develops techniques, concepts and methodologies of its own, which while originally derived from AI may no longer be considered part of AI itself. For example, AIED now routinely uses concepts such as model tracing, mal-rule, etc. and refers to classic AIED systems such as SOPHIE and GUIDON which may well not be discussed at all in standard AI texts. In such cases it is not necessary for *IJAIED* papers to establish the bona-

368

fide AI pedigree of such terms. It is entirely to be expected and welcomed that AIED research will spawn its own concepts and paradigms which can be assumed common knowledge for AIED researchers.

The phrase 'to educational issues' above is also too simplistic. Education is also a complex subject. Generally, AIED has interpreted 'education' rather narrowly as concerned with learning, teaching, training and the like, rather than with the broader cultural matters which educationalists have in mind. As AIED evolves and its achievements become more significant maybe it will address itself to educational theory and philosophy (and of course such papers would be welcome in *IJAIED*). In addition, the educational process involves more than the direct concern with learning - there are, for example, various administrative activities, such as timetabling, which when tackled as an AI application would also lie within *IJAIED's* scope.

Generally, it is necessary for *IJAIED* papers to identify the (educational) problem they are addressing, to describe the kinds of learning and teaching which a system is intended to provide and if appropriate to give some evidence of benefits. Again, as the field evolves these links may be left implicit or indirect. For example, we can assume that an analysis of student modelling or a description of some new student modelling technique is intended to lead to improvements when applied to a tutoring system or learning environment without this needing to be made explicit. Similarly, as techniques develop and become standard so AI-based authoring tools or shells will be specified which are only indirectly concerned with learning and teaching.

As the journal title 'AI in Education' indicates, the impetus and flow of ideas in AIED has been from AI to education. On the whole, educationalists have been reactive, criticising AI approaches, rather than proactive, using their own perspectives to propose system designs. This will change as the field is successful. Naturally, *IJAIED* would welcome and encourage educationalists to explain the implications of their own understanding of knowledge, learning and teaching for AIED and AI generally. (It is noticeable that other social scientists such as sociologists, psychologists, anthropologists, etc. have been less reticent in advising the AI field.)

After these general comments, we can now consider the different kinds of *IJAIED* paper separately (although of course not all papers will fit neatly into one category).
* A system description. The system described would be an AI-based learning environment, authoring tool or other system with an educational purpose. Some aspect of the system would be novel (or standard components would be combined in some novel way) and the benefits of that novelty would be demonstrated, typically through some study of the system in use. While it should be discussed how the system's design derives from theoretical principles, a design itself is not a research result: it must be demonstrated through an implementation. Merely using conventional AI tools (such as AI programming languages) to support normal educational practice is not AIED research. Teaching AI is not usually AIED research either.
* A component description. Here the technical details of a new method for implementing some component of an AI-based learning environment would be discussed, including some formal specification or pseudocode. If the focus is on the technical properties then these would be presented following good computer science and HCI practice. The

benefits of the method would be shown by some theoretical or experimental study, the latter not necessarily involving the evaluation of a complete system, since the components which are not a focus of the study may not be fully implemented. If the component is not a standard one then some discussion of its relevance should be given.

- A theoretical study. As AIED research progresses it may become possible to give formal, mathematical analyses of the properties of systems. Such an analysis may just provide a cleansing of the messiness of an actual implementation, but to be of more interest to *IJAIED*, some new insight should result - for example, some precise clarification of the effect of design choices, a detailed comparison of the power of two systems or techniques, a derivation of some predicted outcome from the use of a system, etc.

- An experimental study. There are many kinds of experimental study, ranging from preliminary studies of learners intended to inform the design of a learning environment through to large-scale summative evaluations of completed systems. There are also empirical studies of teachers intended to lead to principles to support the development of systems. In all cases, the relevance to AIED must be made clear and the study itself must follow the standard practices of behavioural science.

- A review. An acceptable review would be comprehensive and balanced. To be comprehensive, the review must be of a topic which can be adequately covered in a journal-length paper: a reader must be confident that no significant work in the field discussed has been omitted. To be balanced, the review must discuss work in proportion to its importance and derive conclusions justified by the field as a whole. A review is not just a catalogue of relevant work: it is an analysis based on some informative conceptual framework. *IJAIED* prefers reviews which are timely, that is, are concerned with some emerging issue, not ones which give a historical perspective on some long-standing topic.

- A methodological study. Such a paper develops a new conceptualization of the AIED field, or some aspect of it. It would explore the implications of some educational, sociological, AI or other paradigm for AIED. It may explore the impact or influence of some of the more philosophical aspects of AI within educational theory and practice. It may be more speculative than other kinds of paper but it would at least identify clearly the implications for AIED if the arguments presented are considered sound.

- A viewpoint. Because AIED is a somewhat controversial field, *IJAIED* welcomes 'viewpoint' papers in which the normal standards of objectivity and expectations of results are relaxed in order that an author can present a challenge to the prevailing orthodoxy. Viewpoints may be polemical and less balanced than a review but the arguments must be clearly presented and based upon a deep understanding of the relevant issues. Ideally, they should serve to provoke discussion among the readership. Often a viewpoint will be published together with one or more short responses to it in order to initiate such a debate. A paper submitted as a viewpoint should be clearly identified as such because the reviewing criteria are different from 'normal' papers.

Finally, it may help intending authors to know the questions which reviewers are asked to answer. These are:

- Is the subject of the paper suitable for *IJAIED*?
- Is the content of the paper likely to be of interest to and appropriate for *IJAIED* readers?
- Is the paper technically sound and accurate in its AI and Education content?

370

- Is this a new and original contribution? Does the author make clear what this contribution is?
- Are the major claims and conclusions substantiated? Have the ideas or systems been tested or evaluated sensibly?
- Is the paper clear, explicit, and well-organised? Is the length appropriate for the content? Are there any gaps or redundancies?
- Are the title and abstract informative?
- Does the paper adequately refer to related work? Are the references complete and necessary?

Formatting instructions: Information for Authors
Potential authors should examine recent issues of the *Journal* to assess the type of material covered and the presentation style and should also consult the document on the scope and standards of *IJAIED*.

IJAIED articles are to be published on the WWW as well as on paper. Therefore, we expect that all papers will eventually be submitted in a WWW-compatible form and take advantage of the facilities offered by the WWW. At the moment, however, authors may submit the first versions of papers in the traditional paper form, if it is preferred. We do, however, encourage authors to begin adapting papers for WWW publication - reviewers will take account of the rather experimental nature of WWW publication. As papers will also be published in a paper form authors must ensure that the printed form is suitable for such publication.

Submission of a paper represents certification by the author that the article is not being considered nor has been published elsewhere.

Below are general details for the paper, followed by details for hardcopy submission and for electronic submission, and then details for the final version of the paper, if it is accepted.

GENERAL DETAILS
Layout. Authors are advised to consult the section below giving details for the layout of the final version of the paper (if accepted) - it is not essential to follow those instructions for the first submission but it may avoid later work if they are.

General. Papers should conform to the APA style as specified in the *Publication Manual of the American Psychological Association* available from APA, 1200 17th Street, N.W., Washington, DC 20036 USA.

Length. In general, articles should not exceed 10000 words (with figures considered equivalent to the number of words possible in the space occupied).

Sections. Articles should be subdivided into unnumbered sections and sub-sections using short, meaningful subheads.

Abstract. An informative, comprehensive abstract of 75 to 200 words must be included. This abstract should succinctly summarize the major points of the paper and the author's conclusions.

Citations. Examples of references cited within the text of articles are as follows: (Williams, Allen, & Jones, 1978) or (Moore, 1990; Smith, 1991) or Terrell (1977).

Quotations. Quoted material of more than two lines should be set in a narrower width than the remainder of the text. At the close of the quotation, give the complete source including page numbers. Where necessary, it is the author's responsibility to obtain written permission from the copyright holders to quote or reproduce material from another publication.

Tables and Figures. Tables and figures should be included in the text at appropriate places. Captions should be provided at the top of each table, and figure captions should be below the figure. (See section on the final submission.)

Equations. Equations should be prepared carefully, use separate lines and centre each equation. If a reference is needed in the text, refer to it as Equation 1, etc., and number each equation, placing this number on the right hand side of the equation, e.g.

$$z=f(x,y) \qquad (1)$$

Program Listings. Program listings should be avoided unless they are essential and add significantly to the article. If included, they must be formatted exactly as they are to appear - usually, using a fixed width font, e.g.

```
while x=0 do
  begin
  readln(y);
  ...
  end
```

Acknowledgments. Financial support for work reported or a grant under which a study was made should be noted in the Acknowledgments. Appreciation to individuals for assistance with the manuscript or with the material reported may also be included. Any acknowledgements should appear just before the references and be formatted in the same manner as a section.

References. Authors are responsible for checking the accuracy of all references and that all references cited in the text also appear in the References section. All references should be in alphabetical order by author (unnumbered), as shown below. Use the following style when referencing a book, an article in a periodical or in conference proceedings:

Bull, S., Brna, P., & Pain, H. (1995). Extending the scope of the student model. User Modeling and User-Adapted Interaction, 5, 45-65.

O'Shea, T., & Self, J. A. (1983). Learning and Teaching with Computers: Artificial Intelligence in Education. Englewood Cliffs, NJ: Prentice-Hall.

372

Vassileva, J., Greer, J., McCalla, G., Deters, R., Zapata, D., Mudgal, C., & Grant, S. (1999). A Multi-Agent Design of a Peer-Help Environment. In S. Lajoie & M. Vivet (Eds.) Artificial Intelligence in Education (pp. 38-45). Amsterdam: IOS Press.

SUBMISSION OF THE FIRST VERSION OF THE PAPER
The first version of the paper may be submitted on paper or electronically.

Paper submission
Four copies of the manuscript should be submitted. Manuscripts should be typed on 8.5 x 11 inch or A4 paper with a minimum 1.25 inch left margin. A title sheet should precede the first page of the article and give the title of the article, name of author(s), institutional mailing address (including department, institution, city, state, code, and country), or other affiliation. Include the telephone and fax numbers and e-mail address of the contact author.

Send four copies of the article to:
Prof. Paul Brna, The Editor, *IJAIED*, School of Informatics, Northumbria University, Newcastle upon Tyne NE1 8ST, UK

Electronic submission
This should by email as an attached file (using the standard facilities provided by mail programs such as Eudora, Pegasus, Mozilla, etc.). We would prefer the document to be submitted as a Microsoft Word file, but if this is not possible then we will also accept RTF and LaTeX.

SUBMISSION OF THE FINAL VERSION OF THE PAPER
The final version of the paper should be sent by email to **IJAIED@paulbrna.sdeom.co.uk**. If this is not possible then the paper should be sent by post recorded on a CD-ROM in either PC or Mac format.

In either case, please include text files (e.g. LaTeX source files), word processed form and PDF version along with all figures sent as separate files in a proper graphical format - TIFF, GIF, JPG, EPS, etc. This is in addition to the figures appearing in the paper as normal.

It may be necessary to send a printed version by post. The printed form should be posted to the address given above.

We would prefer the paper to be submitted as a Microsoft Word document. An *IJAIED* style file can be downloaded here. If Word format is not possible then we will also accept RTF and Latex. Ideally, all authors should also submit an HTML version of their paper. This would be particularly useful if you are not submitting in our preferred format (Microsoft Word).

Layout of the Paper
It is essential that authors follow these guidelines for the final version of the paper since we do not have the resources to do extensive reformatting. The paper will be printed pretty much as it is submitted. If a paper submitted as a final version does not have a satisfactory layout it will not be accepted as the final version.

Page Set-up. Use pages of A4 size, with the text falling within a space of 16cm by 22cm.

Fonts and Sizes. The recommended type font is Times New Roman. As a second choice, use Times. Only for tables and figures (illustrations) you may use Helvetica, Univers or other sans-serif fonts. Keep italics and/or bold for special text parts.

Recommended type font sizes:
- For the title: 16 pts.
- For authors names and addresses, headings and subheadings: 12 pts.
- For the main text (including headings and captions): 11 pts.
- For footnotes, references, figures and tables: 10 pts.

Title. Type the title approx. 2 cm below the first line of the page. Left justify the title on the page. Leave approx 1 cm between the title and the name(s) of the author(s) typed left-justified and bold 12pt. Continuing straight after, type the address(es) for correspondence left-justified in italics. Please include email addresses and URLs when possible in the address on separate lines and italicised.

Abstract. The abstract should be in 11pt, not indented and begin with the emboldened word "Abstract." There should be two blank lines before and after.

General Layout. Use single line spacing. The main text (including the abstract) should be fully justified. Start a new paragraph by indenting it 0.75 cm from the left margin (and not by inserting a blank line), except under a heading and subheading. Only use italics if you want to emphasise specific parts of the main text.

Headings. Headings, subheadings and subsubheadings should be left-justified. Do not include references to the literature, illustrations or tables in headings and subheadings. A HEADING should be in bold and capitals, with two blank lines before and one blank line after it. A Subheading should be in bold and lowercase, with one blank line before and after it. A Subsubheading should be in bold and italics, with one blank line before and after it.

Illustrations and Tables. All illustrations must be numbered consecutively (i.e., not section-wise), using Arabic numbers. All illustrations should be centred, except for very small figures (no wider than 7 cm), which may be placed side by side. Centre figure captions beneath the figure, e.g.

Fig. 4. A caption.

Do not assemble figures at the back of your article, but place them as close as possible to where they are mentioned in the main text. To avoid technical problems that arise mainly with figures, all figures must also be sent as separate files in a proper graphical format - GIF, JPG, EPS, etc. All tables must be numbered consecutively (in Arabic numbers). Table headings should be placed above the table, e.g.

Table 4
A caption

374

References. References should be listed in alphabetical order at the end of your paper (under the heading 'REFERENCES') but before any appendix. They should be in 10 point.

Reprints
Upon publication, each author will receive a complimentary copy of the journal issue in which the article appears.

International Journal of Continuing Engineering Education & Life Long Learning

ADDRESS FOR SUBMISSION:

M.A. Dorgham, Editor
International Journal of Continuing
   Engineering Education & Life Long
   Learning
IEL Editorial Office
The Pastures, Yardley Road
Olney
Buckinghamshire, MK46 5EL
UK
Phone: +44 1234 240 519
Fax: +44 1234 240 515
E-Mail: m.dorgham@inderscience.com
Web: www.inderscience.com
Address May Change:

PUBLICATION GUIDELINES:

Manuscript Length: 16-20
Copies Required: Three
Computer Submission: Yes
Format: MS Word
Fees to Review: 0.00 US$

Manuscript Style:
   See Manuscript Guidelines

CIRCULATION DATA:

Reader: Academics, Business Persons
Frequency of Issue: 16 Times/Year
Copies per Issue: 10,001 - 25,000
Sponsor/Publisher: Inderscience, Ltd.
   Initiated by UNISCO
Subscribe Price:
   See Website

REVIEW INFORMATION:

Type of Review: Editorial Review
No. of External Reviewers: 3
No. of In House Reviewers: 0
Acceptance Rate: 18%
Time to Review: 2 - 3 Months
Reviewers Comments: Yes
Invited Articles: 10%
Fees to Publish: 0.00 US$

MANUSCRIPT TOPICS:
Science Math & Environment; Urban Education, Cultural/Non-Traditional

MANUSCRIPT GUIDELINES/COMMENTS:

Reader Type. Academics, Business Persons, Policy Makers, Managers and Professional in Industry and related Business.

The *International Journal of Technology Management* (IJTM) aims to provide a refereed and authoritative source of information in the field of managing with technology, and the management of engineering, science and technology. The journal seeks to establish channels of communication between Government departments, technology executives in industry, commerce and related business, and academic experts in the field.

Objectives
The objectives of the journal are to develop, promote and coordinate the science and practice of Technology Management. It also aims to help professionals working in the field, engineering and business educators and policy-makers to contribute, to disseminate information and to learn from each other's work. The international dimension is emphasized in order to overcome cultural and national barriers and to meet the needs of accelerating technological change and changes in the global economy.

Readership
The journal provides a vehicle to help professionals, academics, researchers and policy makers, working in the field of technology management, engineering and business education, to disseminate information and to learn from each other's work.

Contents
The journal publishes original papers, review papers, technical reports, case studies, conference reports, management reports, book reviews, notes, commentaries, and news. Special Issues devoted to important topics in Technology Management will occasionally be published.

Commentaries on papers and reports published in the Journal are encouraged. Authors will have the opportunity to respond to the commentary on their work before the entire treatment is published.

Contribution may be by submission or invitation, and suggestions for special issues and publications are welcome.

Subject coverage
- Competitiveness and cooperation
- Knowledge assets
- Globalization
- Productivity, efficiency and quality
- Sourcing
- Strategic planning
- Strategic technology management and policies
- R&D and design management: its interaction with corporate strategy, technology and planning; its interface with production and marketing; managing a worldwide R&D system
- Role of multinational corporation
- Role of innovation and new technology
- Information technology
- Business/government relations
- Management of production systems
- Factory and office automation
- R&D/manufacturing/marketing and after-market interface
- International technology management policy and strategy
- Technology transfer and licensing

- Legal aspects and financial considerations in international technology management
- Investment patterns and opportunities
- Technology monitoring, audit and evaluation
- Technology relations and trends, especially in the Far East, South Pacific and Third World markets.

Submission of papers

Papers, case studies, technical and conference reports, etc. are invited for submission, together with a brief abstract (100-150 words) and 1-10 keywords that reflect the content. Authors may wish to send in advance abstracts of proposed papers along with cover letters/e-mails (see requirements below). Please refer to notes for intending authors for more detailed guidance.

Please submit your manuscript with a cover letter/e-mail containing the following imperative statements:
1. Title and the central theme of the article.
2. Journal for which publication is intended.
3. Which subject/theme of the Journal the material fits.
4. Why the material is important in its field and why the material should be published in this Journal.
5. Nomination of up to four recognized experts who would be considered appropriate to review the submission. Please state
   - the names, title, addresses, phone, fax, and email addresses of these reviewers
   - the expertise of each reviewer relating to your paper
   - your relationship with each of them.

6. The fact that the manuscript contains original unpublished work and is not being submitted for publication elsewhere.

Note that
- Any non-English speaking author should have his/her paper proofread by a professional technical writer for grammatical and spelling corrections as well as the readability of the paper, before submitting it to the Editor.

A complete submission must include the following components in three separate MS-Word/Word for Windows files, plus hard copy with high quality black and white artwork for all figures, as indicated:
- the cover letter complying to the format of the sample letter
- the title page, including authors' full mailing, e-mail addresses and biographical details, attached to each of the hard copies
- three hard copies of the manuscript (title, abstract, keywords, article, references) without authors' names unless they are in the References section
- an electronic copy of the manuscript containing all details
- a hard copy of the Assignment of Copyright statement, duly signed.

These files should be submitted to: The Editor-in-Chief, *IEL* EDITORIAL OFFICE, address above; Email : **editorial@inderscience.com**

Papers may also be sent directly to the relevant Editor, with copies to the Editorial Office, above Each paper submitted to Inderscience Enterprises Limited is subject to the following review procedure:

- It is reviewed by the editor for general suitability for this publication.
- If it is judged suitable, two reviewers are selected and a double-blind review process takes place
- Based on the recommendations of the reviewers, the editor then decides whether the particular article should be acceptable as it is, revised or rejected.

NOTES FOR INTENDING AUTHORS

Formal conditions of acceptance

- Papers will only be published in English.
- Each typescript must be accompanied by a statement that it has not been submitted for publication elsewhere in English.
- Previous presentation at a conference, or publication in another language, should be disclosed.
- All papers are refereed, and the Editor-in-Chief reserves the right to refuse any typescript, whether on invitation or otherwise, and to make suggestions and/or modifications before publication.
- Typescripts which have been accepted become the property of the publisher. It is a condition of acceptance that copyright shall be vested in the publisher.
- The publisher shall furnish authors of accepted papers with proofs for the correction of printing errors. The proofs shall be returned within 14 calendar days of submittal. The publishers shall not be held responsible for errors which are the result of authors' oversights.

Typescript preparation

- The original typescript should be submitted electronically in A4 size format, with double-spaced typing and a wide margin on the left, following the submission requirements described on the Journal's website.
- A final paper which would exceed 6000 words or occupy more than 15 pages of the Journal may be returned for abridgement.
- A complete typescript should include, in the following order: *title, author(s), address(es), abstract, keywords, biographical notes, introduction, text, acknowledgements, references and notes, tables, figure captions, figures.*

Electronic copy

- The preferred word processing program is Microsoft's Word or Word for Windows.
- Figures in the final accepted manuscript may be included in the electronic text file and also provided as separate files, but must also be accompanied by high-resolution hard copy printout.

International context

- It should not be assumed that the reader is familiar with specific national institutions or corporations.
- Countries and groupings of countries should be referred to by their full title (for example, 'China', 'Europe' and 'America' are all ambiguous).
- Special attention should be paid to identifying units of currency by nationality.
- Acronyms should be translated in full into English. (See also 'Translated works' below.)

Title, abstract, keywords, addresses, biographical notes
Please assist us by following these guidelines:
- Title : as short as possible
- Abstract: approximately 100 words, maximum 150
- Keywords : approximately 10 words or phrases
- Address : position, department, name of institution, full postal address
- Biographical notes : approximately 100 words per author, maximum 150.

References and notes
Inderscience journal uses a numbering system in which references and notes are placed in the same sequence.
- In the text, a reference is indicated by a number in square brackets, e.g. [3]. This system avoids footnotes. Full references and short notes should then be placed in number order at the end of the text.
- References should be made only to works that are published, accepted for publication (not merely 'submitted'), or available through libraries or institutions. Any other source should be qualified by a note regarding availability.
- Full reference should include *all authors' names and initials, year of publication, title of paper, title of publication* (underlined), *volume and issue number* (of a journal), *publisher and form* (book, conference proceedings), *page numbers.*
- Notes should make a specific point, and be short and succinct.

Figures
- All illustrations, whether diagrams or photographs, are referred to as Figures and are numbered sequentially. Please place them at the end of the paper, rather than interspersed in text.
- Originals of line diagrams will be photographically reduced and used directly. All artwork for figures must be black and white and prepared to the highest possible standards. Bear in mind that lettering may be reduced in size by a factor of 2 or 3, and that fine lines may disappear.

Translated works
- Difficulty often arises in translating acronyms, so it is best to spell out an acronym in English (for example, IIRP - French personal income tax).
- Similarly, labels and suffixes need careful attention where the letters refer to words which have been translated.
- The names of mathematical functions may change in translation - check against an English or American mathematical reference text.

Units of measurement
- Inderscience journal follows the *Système* International for units of measurement.
- Imperial units will be converted, except where conversion would affect the meaning of a statement, or imply a greater or lesser degree of accuracy.

Appendix 1 : Sample Cover Letter/E-mail [the example used is the IJEB, a sister journal for IJTM]

January 1, 2003
Dear Editor of the *[please type in journal title or acronym]*:

Enclosed is a paper, entitled "**Mobile Agents for Network Management.**" Please accept it as a candidate for publication in the *[journal title]*. Below are our responses to your submission requirements.

1. Title and the central theme of the article.
Paper title: "**Mobile Agents for Network Management.**" This study reviews the concepts of mobile agents and distributed network management system. It proposes a mobile agent-based implementation framework and creates a prototype system to demonstrate the superior performance of a mobile agent-based network over the conventional client-server architecture in a large network environment.

2. Which subject/theme of the Journal the material fits
New enabling technologies (if no matching subject/theme, enter 'Subject highly related to *[subject of journal]* but not listed by *[please type in journal title or acronym]*)

3. Why the material is important in its field and why the material should be published in [please type in journal title or acronym]?
The necessity of having an effective computer network is rapidly growing alongside the implementation of information technology. Finding an appropriate network management system has become increasingly important today's distributed environment. However, the conventional centralized architecture, which routinely requests the status information of local units by the central server, is not sufficient to manage the growing requests. Recently, a new framework that uses mobile agent technology to assist the distributed management has emerged. The mobile agent reduces network traffic, distributes management tasks, and improves operational performance. Given today's bandwidth demand over the Internet, it is important for the *[journal title/acronym]* readers to understand this technology and its benefits. This study gives a real-life example of how to use mobile agents for distributed network management. It is the first in the literature that reports the analysis of network performance based on an operational prototype of mobile agent-based distributed network. We strongly believe the contribution of this study warrants its publication in the *[journal title/acronym]*.

4. Names, addresses, and email addresses of four expert referees.

Prof. Dr. William Gates	Assoc Prof. Dr. John Adams
Chair Professor of Information Technology	Director of Network Research Center

321 Johnson Hall
Premier University Lancaster, NY 00012
-6666, USA
phone: +1-888-888-8888
fax: +1-888-888-8886
e-mail: wgates@lancaster.edu
Expertise: published a related paper
("TCP/IP and OSI: Four Strategies
for Interconnection") in CACM, 38(3),
pp. 188-198. Relationship: I met Dr. Gate
only once at a conference in 1999. I didn't
know him personally.

College of Business Australian University
123, Harbor Drive Sydney,
Australia 56789
phone: +61-8-8888-8888
fax: +61-8-8888-8886
e-mail: jadams@au.edu.au
Expertise: published a related paper
("Creating Mobile Agents") in IEEE
TOSE, 18(8), pp. 88-98.
Relationship: None. I have never
met Dr. Adams.

Assoc Prof. Dr. Chia-Ho Chen
Chair of MIS Department
College of Management
Open University.
888, Putong Road
Keelung, Taiwan 100
phone: +886-2-8888-8888
fax: +886-2-8888-8886
e-mail: chchen@ou.edu.tw
Expertise: published a related paper
("Network Management for E-Commerce")
in IJ Electronic Business, 1(4), pp. 18-28.
Relationship: Former professor, dissertation
chairman.

Mr. Frank Young
Partner, ABC Consulting
888, Seashore Highway
Won Kok, Kowloon
Hong Kong
phone: +852-8888-8888
fax: +852-8888-8886
e-mail: fyoung@abcc.com
Expertise: Mr. Young provides
consulting services extensively to his
clients regarding network management
practices. Relationship: I have worked
with Mr. Young in several consulting
projects in the past three years.

Finally, this paper is our original unpublished work and it has not been submitted to any other journal for reviews.

Sincerely,
Johnny Smith

Appendix 2 : Assignment of Copyright
Inderscience Enterprises Ltd, trading as Inderscience Publishers, of World Trade Center Building, 29 Route de Pre-Bois, (Case Postale 896) CR1215 Geneve 15, Switzerland ("Inderscience")

Please read the notes overleaf and fill in, sign and send this form with the paper manuscript of your Article. This assignment comes into effect if your Article is accepted for publication.

So that we can ensure both the widest dissemination and protection of material published in Inderscience's journals, we ask authors to assign world-wide copyright in both print and other media in their papers, including abstracts, to Inderscience. This enables us to ensure copyright protection against infringement, and to disseminate your article, and our journals, as widely as possible.

382

1. In consideration of the undertaking set out in paragraph 2, and upon acceptance by Inderscience for publication in the Journal, the Author as beneficial owner hereby assigns to Inderscience the copyright in the Article entitled:

_____

by _____
to be published in _____('the Journal')
for the full legal term of copyright. This assignment includes the right to publish (subject to paragraphs 3 and 4) the material in the article in electronic form; the Article may be published in printed, online, CD-ROM, microfiche or in other form.

2. Inderscience hereby undertakes to prepare and publish the Article named in paragraph 1 in the *Journal*.

3. The Editor of the Journal and Inderscience are empowered to make such editorial changes as may be necessary to make the Article suitable for publication. Every effort will be made to consult the Author if substantive changes are required.

4. The Author hereby asserts his/her moral rights under the UK Copyright Designs and Patents Act 1988 to be identified as the Author of the Article.

5. The Author warrants that the Article is the Author's original work, has not been published before, and is not currently under consideration for publication elsewhere; and that the Article contains no libellous or unlawful statements and that it in no way infringes the rights of others, and that the Author, as the owner of the copyright, is entitled to make this assignment.

6. If the Article was prepared jointly by more than one author, the Author warrants that he/she has been authorised by all co-authors to sign this agreement on their behalf.

Signed by the Author _____
Date _____

Assignment of Copyright: Explanatory Notes
Inderscience's policy is to acquire copyright for all contributions, for the following reasons:
a. ownership of copyright by a central organisation helps to ensure maximum international protection against infringement;
b. requests for permission to reproduce articles in books, course packs or for library loan can be handled efficiently and with sensitivity to changing library and reader needs. This relieves authors of a time-consuming and costly administrative burden.
c. the demand for research literature to be delivered in electronic form, whether on-line or on CD-ROM, can be met efficiently, with proper safeguards for authors, editors and journal owners.

There are opportunities to reach institutions (e.g., companies, schools and public libraries) and individual readers that are unlikely to subscribe to the printed journal. Inderscience works with other organisations to publish, where appropriate, in on-line or off-line databases and services, or to deliver copies of individual articles. It has also registered the Journal with the

Copyright Licensing Agency, which offers centralised licensing arrangements for photocopying. Income received from all of these sources is used to further the interests of the Journal.

Once accepted for publication, your Article will be published in conventional printed form in the Journal, and will be stored electronically to enable Inderscience to publish the journal on-line, in order to meet increasing library and faculty demand, and to deliver it as an individual article copy or as part of a larger collection of articles to meet the specific requirements of a particular market. Assignment of copyright signifies agreement to Inderscience making such arrangements.

It may be that the Author is not able to make the assignment solely by him- or herself:
a. If it is appropriate, the Author's employer may sign this agreement. The employer may reserve the right to use the Article for internal or promotional purposes (by indicating on this agreement) and reserve all rights other than copyright.
b. If the Author is a UK Government employee, the Government will grant a non-exclusive licence to publish the Article in the Journal in any medium or form provided that Crown Copyright and user rights (including patent rights) are reserved.
c. If the Author is the employee of a government (except the UK Government) and the work was done in that capacity, the assignment applies only to the extent allowed by applicable law.

Under the UK's Copyright Design and Patents Act 1988, the Author has the moral right to be identified as the author wherever the Article is published, and to object to its derogatory treatment or distortion. Inderscience encourages assertion of this right, as it represents best publishing practice and is an important safeguard for all authors. Clause 4 asserts the Author's moral rights, as required by the Act.

The *Journal* will permit the Author to use the Article elsewhere after publication, provided acknowledgement is given to the Journal as the original source of publication.

Thank you for reading these notes. This assignment will enable Inderscience to ensure that the Article will reach the optimum readership.

International Journal of Educational Advancement

ADDRESS FOR SUBMISSION:

Brenda Rouse, Publishing Editor
International Journal of Educational
    Advancement
Henry Stewart Publications
Museum House
25 Museum Street
London, WC1A 1JT
UK
Phone: +44 (0) 207-323-2916
Fax: +44 (0) 207-323-2918
E-Mail: brenda@hspublications.co.uk
Web: www.henrystewart.co.uk
Address May Change:

PUBLICATION GUIDELINES:

Manuscript Length: 3500-6000 words
Copies Required: One
Computer Submission: Yes
Format: MS Word
Fees to Review: 0.00 US$

Manuscript Style:
    , Vancouver Referencing Style

CIRCULATION DATA:

Reader: Academics, Business Persons
Frequency of Issue: Quarterly
Copies per Issue: Less than 1,000
Sponsor/Publisher: Henry Stewart
    Publications - Owner
Subscribe Price: 250.00 US$

REVIEW INFORMATION:

Type of Review: Blind Review
No. of External Reviewers: 2
No. of In House Reviewers: 1
Acceptance Rate: 21-30%
Time to Review: 2 - 3 Months
Reviewers Comments: Yes
Invited Articles: 11-20%
Fees to Publish: 0.00 US$

MANUSCRIPT TOPICS:
Alumni Relations; Communication; Direct Marketing; Education
Management/Administration; Marketing Theory & Applications; Non-Profit Organizations;
Public Administration; Public Relations; Strategic Management Policy

MANUSCRIPT GUIDELINES/COMMENTS:

Spelling. American spelling (e.g., -ize and -yze endings, behavior, center, defense, traveled,
aging, practice and license (noun and verb), etc.), but n.b. use dialogue and catalogue.

Avoid Latin plurals for words with a more common English alternative (e.g., use syllabuses,
forums, formulas rather than syllabi, fora, formulae).

Punctuation. Double quotation marks except for quotes within quotes, which have single
quotation marks.

Periods and commas precede closing quotation marks, but colons and semicolons do not.

Serial commas should be used in lists with "and" or "or" (e.g., "Tom, Dick, and Harry").

Ellipses should be three points only—do not enclose them in square brackets.

Contractions and abbreviations should both be followed by periods (e.g., Mr., Mrs., vol., eds.).

Hyphens should be used in compound adjectives and adverbs (e.g., fund-raising efforts, fast-rising profits) but not with adverbs ending in -ly (e.g., poorly written work) and not in combination with prefixes such as non, pre, post, multi, unless followed by an upper-case letter (e.g., postsecondary education, post-Soviet Russia).

Extracts. Shorter quotations (under about 60 words) will be kept within the text; longer ones should be indented and should not have quotation marks.

Italics. Use italics for titles of books and journals and for foreign or Latin words or phrases (except for well-known terms that are generally used in English like "per capita" or "gratis"). Use italics (sparingly) rather than bold or upper-case for emphasis.

Abbreviations. Spell out all except very well-known abbreviations (e.g., USA or NATO) on the first use. Do not use periods for abbreviations and acronyms that are all in upper-case. Use "for example," "that is," and "and so on" or "and so forth" in the text rather than "e.g.," "i.e.," and "etc."

Capitals. Do not use capitals for titles unless you are speaking of a particular person (e.g., "the job of a president ..." but "President Clinton").

Use capitals for North, South, East, and West only when part of the name of a geographical area (e.g., "West Virginia" but "in the west of the country").

Numbers. Numbers should be written out in full up to 100; but percentages and precise measurements, money etc., should be in figures (e.g., forty-five students, $45, 120 pounds, 92 percent).
- Numbers of four or more digits should have commas (e.g., 3,000 and 67,000).
- Centuries should be written in full (e.g., nineteenth century).
- Write "the 1960s" rather than "the 1960's" or "the sixties".

Dates. Use the form June 11, 1999.

Inclusive Language, etc. Avoid noninclusive language but do not use "s/he" or use masculine and feminine pronouns alternately. It is often better to pluralize (e.g., instead of "the scholar should check his sources" use "scholars should check their sources"), but use "he or she, his or hers" when it's unavoidable. Do not use "man" for people or the human race in general and try to avoid terms like "manpower" (use e.g., "staff" or "personnel" or "human resources"). Be sensitive in using terms referring to members of ethnic minority groups and people with disabilities.

International Journal of Leadership in Education

ADDRESS FOR SUBMISSION:

Duncan Waite, Editor
International Journal of Leadership in
    Education
Texas State University
EAPS
601 University Drive
San Marcos, TX 78666-4685
USA
Phone: 512-245-8918 or 512-245-2575
Fax: 512-245-8872
E-Mail: ijle@txstate.edu
Web: www.tandf.co.uk/journals
Address May Change:

PUBLICATION GUIDELINES:

Manuscript Length: 26-30
Copies Required: Four
Computer Submission: Yes
Format: MSWord/English
Fees to Review: 0.00 US$

Manuscript Style:
    See Manuscript Guidelines

CIRCULATION DATA:

Reader: Academics, Administrators
Frequency of Issue: Quarterly
Copies per Issue:
Sponsor/Publisher: Taylor & Francis Ltd
Subscribe Price: 136.00 US$ Individual
    369.00 US$ Institution

REVIEW INFORMATION:

Type of Review: Blind Review
No. of External Reviewers: 3+
No. of In House Reviewers: 2
Acceptance Rate: 30%
Time to Review: 3-4 Months
Reviewers Comments: Yes
Invited Articles: 10%
Fees to Publish: 0.00 US$

MANUSCRIPT TOPICS:
Adult Career & Vocational; Curriculum Studies; Education Management/Administration; Educational Leadership; Elementary/Early Childhood; Higher Education; Rural Education & Small Schools; Secondary/Adolescent Studies; Teacher Education; Urban Education, Cultural/Non-Traditional

MANUSCRIPT GUIDELINES/COMMENTS:

The Journal Presents
* Cutting-edge writing on instructional supervision, curriculum and teaching development, and educational administration
* An alternative voice: reports of alternative theoretical perspectives, alternative methodologies, and alternative experiences of leadership
* A broad definition of leadership, including teachers-as-leaders, shared governance, site-based decision making, and community-school collaborations

- An international medium for the publication of theoretical and practical discussions of educational leadership. across a range of approaches, as these relate to ethical. political, epistemological and philosophical issues
- A forum for rescarchers and 'practitioner-researchers' to consider conceptual, methodological, and practical issues in a range of professional and service settings and sectors.

Submission of Papers

Before preparing your submission, please visit our website for a complete style guide; contact details are given below.

Four copies of papers for consideration should be sent to the Editor at the editorial office, address below, arranged in a form suitable for blind peer review, with all author identifiers removed from the text proper, and included only on a cover sheet.

Papers are accepted for consideration on condition that you will accept and warrant the following conditions. In order to ensure both the widest dissemination and protection of material published in our journal, we ask authors to assign the rights of copyright in the articles they contribute. This enables Taylor & Francis Ltd to ensure protection against infringement.

1. In consideration of the publication of your Article, you assign us with full title guarantee all rights of copyright and related rights in your Article. So that there is no doubt, this assignment includes the right to publish the Article in all forms, including electronic and digital forms, for the full legal term of the copyright and any extension or renewals. You shall retain the right to use the substance of the above work in future works, including lectures, press releases and reviews provided that you acknowledge its prior publication in the journal.

2. We shall prepare and publish your Article in the *Journal*. We reserve the right to make such editorial changes as may be necessary to make the Article suitable for publication; and we reserve the right not to proceed with publication for whatever reason. In such an instance, copyright in the Article will revert to you.

3. You hereby assert your moral rights to be identified as the author of the Article according to the UK Copyright Designs & Patents Act 1988.

4. You warrant that you have secured the necessary written permission from the appropriate copyright owner or authorities for the reproduction in the Article and the journal of any text, illustration. or other material. You warrant that, apart from any such third party copyright material included in the Article, the Article is your original work, and cannot be construed as plagiarizing any other published work, and has not been and will not be published elsewhere.

5. In addition you warrant that the Article contains no statement that is abusive, defamatory, libelous, obscene, fraudulent, nor in any way infringes the rights of others, nor is in any other way unlawful or in violation of applicable laws.

388

6. You warrant that any patient. client or participant mentioned in the text has given informed consent to the inclusion of material pertaining to themselves, and that they acknowledge that they cannot be identified via the text.

7. If the Article was prepared jointly with other authors, you warrant that you have been authorized by all co authors to sign this Agreement on their behalf, and to agree on their behalf the order of names in the publication of the Article.

Fifty complimentary offprints of your article will be sent to the principal or sole author of articles; book reviewers will be sent three complimentary offprints. Larger quantities may be ordered at a special discount price. An order form will accompany the proof, which must be completed and returned, irrespective of whether you require additional copies. All authors (including co-authors and book reviewers) will receive a complimentary copy of the issue in which their article appears.

Editorial Office
Duncan Waite, PhD, Editor. The International Journal *of Leadership in* Education, EAPS. Texas State University. 601 University Drive. San Marcos. TX 78666, USA. Tel: +I S12 245 8918; email: **IJLE@txstate.edu**

Please refer to the following website for the journal style guide
http://www.educationarena.com/

For more information on our journals and books publishing, visit our Taylor & Francis website http://www.tandf.co.uk

If you are unable to access the website please write to:
Journals Editorial, Taylor & Francis Ltd. I I New Fetter Lane. London EC4P 4EE, UK

International Journal of Sustainability in Higher Education

ADDRESS FOR SUBMISSION:

Walter Leal Filho, Editor
International Journal of Sustainability in
  Higher Education
Technical University Hamburg-Harburg
Technology Transfer (TUHH/TuTech)
Schellerrdamm 4,
Germany
Phone: +49 40 766 18059
Fax: +49 40 766 18078
E-Mail: leal@tu-harburg.de
Web: www.emeraldinsight.com/ijshe.htm
Address May Change:

PUBLICATION GUIDELINES:

Manuscript Length: 6-10
Copies Required: Three
Computer Submission: Yes Disk, Email
Format: MSWord/English
Fees to Review: 0.00 US$

Manuscript Style:
  Chicago Manual of Style

CIRCULATION DATA:

Reader: Academics
Frequency of Issue: Quarterly
Copies per Issue: 1,001 - 2,000
Sponsor/Publisher: Emerald Group
  Publishing Limited
Subscribe Price: 589.00 Pounds
  1459.00 AUS$
  1019.00 US$

REVIEW INFORMATION:

Type of Review: Editorial Review
No. of External Reviewers: 2
No. of In House Reviewers: 0
Acceptance Rate: 11-20%
Time to Review: 1 - 2 Months
Reviewers Comments: Yes
Invited Articles: 6-10%
Fees to Publish: 0.00 US$

MANUSCRIPT TOPICS:
Higher Education

MANUSCRIPT GUIDELINES/COMMENTS:

The *International Journal of Sustainability in Higher Education* is a fully-refereed academic journal. Published in conjunction with the Association of University Leaders for a Sustainable Future (ULSF), the journal aims at addressing environmental management systems (EMS), sustainable development and Agenda 21 issues at higher education institutions, worldwide. It intends to act as an outlet for papers dealing with curriculum greening and methodological approaches to sustainability. In addition, the journal will report on initiatives aimed at environmental improvements in universities, and the increased competitiveness of self-regulatory mechanisms such as environmental auditing and maintaining EMS. IJSHE disseminates case studies, projects and programmes whilst still considering the market opportunities available.

Guidelines for Submissions

IJSHE publishes original papers in the field of sustainability, including environmental management systems, curriculum greening and operational aspects of environmental improvements at higher education institutions. The Journal shall publish state-of-the-art papers, that reflect new concepts, ideas and changes brought about by those engaged in pursuing sustainability and working in related disciplines.

In addition to papers and articles, book reviews, news items and features will be published. For submissions other those related to papers and articles, please contact the relevant editors to discuss the format of your submission. Letters to the editor will be published on approval by the editorial board.

Submission of manuscripts (papers and articles)

One (1) original and two (2) copies of each manuscript, which has not been published elsewhere before, should be submitted to the editor. *IJSHE* considers all manuscripts on the strict condition that they have been submitted only to it, that they have not been published already, nor are they under consideration for publication, nor in press elsewhere. All accepted manuscripts, photographs, and artwork become the property of the publisher. Exceptions to this may be negotiated on exceptional cases.

Transfer of copyright

Authors are responsible for obtaining permission to reproduce copyrighted material from other sources and are required to sign an agreement for the transfer of copyright to the publisher (JAR form). This form is available from the Editor.

MCB seeks to retain copyright of the articles it publishes, without the author giving up their rights to use their own material (to republish or reproduce their article on paper or electronically, subject to acknowledgement of first publication details). Please see MCB's Authors' Charter for full details.

Preparation of Manuscripts

Manuscripts should be concise, yet sufficiently detailed to permit critical review. Page 1 of the paper should contain the paper/article title, the names and institutional affiliations of all authors, and the name and complete mailing address, telephone, fax and e-mail of the person to whom all correspondence and proofs should be sent. Accepted manuscripts in their final, revised versions should also be submitted as electronic word processing files on disk.

Page 2 should contain an abstract, which should not exceed 250 words. Articles for publication may only be submitted in English. Manuscripts should also adhere to the following structure:

Keywords

Identify important subjects covered by the paper which are not listed in the Title. Authors must provide from three to ten alphabetised keywords or two-word key phrases. They should be placed following the Abstract.

Headings

All headings for sections and subsections should be typed in lowercase letters and placed on separate lines. Do not underline any headings.

References

References to other publications should be complete and in Harvard style. They should contain full bibliographical details and journal titles should not be abbreviated. For multiple citations in the same year use a, b, c immediately following the year of publication. References should be shown within the text by giving the author's last name followed by a comma and year of publication all in round brackets, e.g. (Fox, 1994). At the end of the article should be a reference list in alphabetical order as follows

(a) for books

surname, initials and year of publication, title, publisher, place of publication, e.g.Casson, M. (1979), Alternatives to the Multinational Enterprise, Macmillan, London.

(b) for chapter in edited book

surname, initials and year, "title", editor's surname, initials, title, publisher, place, pages, e.g.Bessley, M. and Wilson, P. (1984), "Public policy and small firms in Britain", in Levicki, C. (Ed.), Small Business Theory and Policy, Croom Helm, London, pp.111-26. Please note that the chapter title must be underlined.

(c) for articles

surname, initials, year "title", journal, volume, number, pages, e.g.Fox, S. (1994) "Empowerment as a catalyst for change: an example from the food industry", Supply Chain Management, Vol 2 No 3, pp. 29-33.

If there is more than one author list surnames followed by initials. All authors should be shown.

Electronic sources should include the URL of the electronic site at which they may be found, as follows:

Neuman, B.C.(1995), "Security, payment, and privacy for network commerce", IEEE Journal on Selected Areas in Communications, Vol. 13 No.8, October, pp.1523-31. Available (IEEE SEPTEMBER) http://www.research.att.com/jsac/

Notes/Endnotes should be used only if absolutely necessary. They should, however, always be used for citing Web sites. They should be identified in the text by consecutive numbers enclosed in square brackets and listed at the end of the article. Please then provide full Web site addresses in the end list.

Tables

Each table should be typed on a separate page, and numbered consecutively with Roman numerals. The headings should be sufficiently clear so that the meaning of the data will be understandable without reference to the text. Explanatory footnotes to tables are encouraged and they should be indicated by lowercase, italic, superscript letters, beginning with ` in each table. Do not use vertical lines to separate columns.

392

Illustrations (Figures)
The number of illustrations (line drawings, wherever possible) should be limited to the minimum needed to clarify the text. Double documentation in figures and tables is not acceptable. Graphs must have a professionally prepared quality. Clear printouts from laser printers (or equivalent devices) on quality paper are acceptable. No part of the drawing should be typewritten. Individual figures should be prepared at approximately 15 x 18 cm size; they will be reduced to the printing width of 12.5 cm, and all elements in the drawing should be clearly legible at this reduction. The letters and symbols should be approx. 2 mm high after reduction. It is preferable to include the legend of symbols in the graph. All terms, abbreviations, and symbols must correspond with those in the text.

Each illustration should be identified by the authors' names and figure number, preferably written in a clear corner area. One original set of all figures (photographs, line drawings) must be submitted as sharp, glossy, high quality prints (Xerox-type prints are not accepted) along with three xerographic copies of the originals. Photographs should exhibit a high contrast. Arrows, letters, and numbers should be inserted preferably with template rub-on letters. Micrographs should have an internal magnification marker: the magnification should also be stated in the legend. High resolution graphics which are too large to submit on a 3 1/2 disk may be sent by email attached file direct to the Editor/Managing Editor.

Bionotes
A short bionote should be provided on a separate sheet and be located at the beginning of a paper.

Reprints
Each author will receive on request, up to 10 copies of the journal in which they paper is published, to a maximum of 20 copies per article. Reprints of an individual article may be ordered from Emerald Press. Please visit the Reprints and Permission page.

International Journal of Testing

ADDRESS FOR SUBMISSION:

John Hattie, Editor
International Journal of Testing
University of Auckland
Faculty of Education
PO Box 92019
Auckland,
New Zealand
Phone: 64 9 373 7599 x 82496
Fax: 64 9 308 2355
E-Mail: ijt@auckland.ac.nz
Web: www.leaonline.com/loi/ijt
Address May Change:

PUBLICATION GUIDELINES:

Manuscript Length: 30+
Copies Required: Five
Computer Submission: Yes Preferred,
  Email
Format: MSWord, WordPerfect
Fees to Review: 0.00 US$

Manuscript Style:
  American Psychological Association

CIRCULATION DATA:

Reader: Academics
Frequency of Issue: Quarterly
Copies per Issue: No Reply
Sponsor/Publisher: American Psychological
  Assn, Div 15 Educ Psych, Intl Testing
  Commission, Lawrence Erlbaum Assoc.
Subscribe Price: 55.00 US$ Indv US/Can
  225.00 US$ Inst US/Can, $255 All
  Other
  85.00 US$ Indv All Other Countries

REVIEW INFORMATION:

Type of Review: Blind Review
No. of External Reviewers: 2
No. of In House Reviewers: 0
Acceptance Rate: 0-5%
Time to Review: 2 - 3 Months
Reviewers Comments: Yes
Invited Articles: 0-5%
Fees to Publish: 0.00 US$

MANUSCRIPT TOPICS:
Counseling & Personnel Services; Educational Psychology; Tests, Measurement & Evaluation

MANUSCRIPT GUIDELINES/COMMENTS:

Statement of Purpose
The International Journal of Testing (IJT) is dedicated to the advancement of theory, research, and practice in the area of testing and assessment in psychology, education, counseling, organizational behavior, human resource management, and related disciplines. *IJT* publishes original articles addressing theoretical issues, methodological approaches, and empirical research as well as integrative interdisciplinary reviews of testing-related topics and reports of current testing practices. All papers will be peer-reviewed and should be of interest to an international audience. Examples of topics appropriate for *IJT* include: (a) new perspectives in test development and validation; (b) issues concerning the qualification and training of test users and test developers; (c) recent trends in testing and measurement arising in a particular field or discipline; (d) comparisons of national/regional differences in test practices; (e) methods and procedures in adapting tests for use in new languages or cultural groups; (f)

international assessment projects or other international studies in which testing constitutes an essential element; (g) testing culturally and/or linguistically heterogeneous populations; and (h) internationalization of testing (e.g., personnel selection for global organizations, Internet applications, and international copyrights of tests and test adaptations). In addition to regular articles, short communications of topics relevant to an international audience will be considered for publication in *IJT*. Substantive comments on articles previously published in *IJT* will also be considered and the authors of the original articles will have an opportunity to reply. Announcements of activities (e.g., conferences, symposia, and training workshops) in the area of testing and measurement are welcomed. Reviews of books and software relevant to testing and measurement as well as reviews of widely used tests will appear regularly in the journal. Reviews should be descriptive and evaluative; comparative reviews are encouraged.

Audience
Scholars, professionals, and graduate students interested in test development and test use. Practitioners conducting assessments in human behavior in psychology, education, counseling, organizational behavior, personnel selection, human resource management, and related disciplines.

Manuscript Preparation
Manuscripts must be prepared according to the *Publication Manual of the American Psychological Association* (5"' ed.). On the first page, indicate the full title of the article, a running head (less than 50 characters), the word count of the manuscript, submission date, and the author(s) name(s), affiliations(s), and complete mailing address(es).

All articles appearing in the *IJT* are peer reviewed, and the reviewers have agreed to participate in a blind reviewing system. The second page of the manuscript, therefore, should omit the authors' names and affiliations but should include the title of the manuscript, running head, and submission date. Footnotes containing information pertaining to the authors' identities or affiliations should be placed on separate pages. Every effort should be made by authors to see that the manuscript itself contains no clues to their identities.

All manuscripts must be prefaced by an abstract of 100-150 words on a separate sheet, as well as a maximum of six key words. All manuscript pages, including references lists and tables, must be typed double-spaced. Pages must be numbered consecutively. Define acronyms and abbreviations used in the manuscript when first mentioned. Print each figure and table on a separate page. All figures must be camera-ready. Authors should comply with "Guidelines to Reduce Bias in Language" as printed in the *Publication Manual*. Manuscripts that fail to conform to APA-style guidelines will be returned to the author(s). MSWord or WordPerfect files are preferred.

Manuscript Submission
Electronic submission is preferred. For more information about electronic submission, please see **www.education.auckland.ac.nz/staff/j.hattie**. To submit paper copies, please send five copies of your manuscripts (an original and four duplicates) to: John Hattie, Editor, *International Journal of Testing*, Faculty of Education, University of Auckland, Private Bag 92019, Auckland, New Zealand.

Permissions

All manuscripts submitted must contain material that has not been published and is not being considered elsewhere. Authors are responsible for all statements made in their work, for obtaining permission from copyright owners for reprinting or adapting a table or figure, and also for reprinting a quotation of more than 500 words. Copies of all permissions must be provided prior to publication. Figures must be provided in camera-ready form.

Production Notes

After a manuscript has been accepted for publication, authors are requested to send to the Editor: (a) two paper copies of the final version; (b) an electronic file of the final version on diskette; (c) a statement of verification that the paper and electronic copies are replications of the same final version; (d) the signed publication and copyright transfer agreement form; and (e) figures in camera-ready form. Copy-edited page proofs will be sent to the authors for review and correction before publication.

International Journal on E-Learning

ADDRESS FOR SUBMISSION:

Gary Marks, Editor
International Journal on E-Learning
 ONLINE SUBMISSIONS ONLY
AACE
PO Box 3728
Norfolk, VA 23514-3728
USA
Phone: 757-623-7588
Fax: 703-997-8760
E-Mail: pubs@aace.org
Web: www.aace.org
Address May Change:

PUBLICATION GUIDELINES:

Manuscript Length: Max/30 pages
Copies Required: No Paper Copy Required
Computer Submission: Yes Online Subm.
 Only
Format: MSWord, html, rtf
Fees to Review: 0.00 US$

Manuscript Style:
 American Psychological Association

CIRCULATION DATA:

Reader: , See Guidelines
Frequency of Issue: Quarterly
Copies per Issue: 1,000-1,800
Sponsor/Publisher: AACE-Assn. For the
 Advancement of Computers in Education
Subscribe Price: 85.00 US$ Individual
 120.00 US$ Institution

REVIEW INFORMATION:

Type of Review: Blind Review
No. of External Reviewers: 2-4
No. of In House Reviewers: 2
Acceptance Rate: 11-20%
Time to Review: 2-4 Months
Reviewers Comments: Yes
Invited Articles: 15-25%
Fees to Publish: 0.00 US$

MANUSCRIPT TOPICS:
Distance Education; Educational Technology Systems; Higher Education; Knowledge
Management; On-line Learning; Science Math & Environment

MANUSCRIPT GUIDELINES/COMMENTS:

Reader. Researchers, Developers and Practitioners in Corporate, Government, Healthcare and
Higher Education.

Advances in technology and the growth of e-learning to provide educators and trainers with
unique opportunities to enhance learning and teaching in corporate, government, healthcare,
and higher education. *IJEL* serves as a forum to facilitate the international exchange of
information on the current research, development, and practice of e-learning in these sectors.

Please read through the guidelines below before submitting your paper.

Journal Content

Contributions for all journals may include research papers, case studies, tutorials, courseware experiences, evaluations, review papers, and viewpoints.

General Guidelines

Material must be original, scientifically accurate, and in good form editorially. The manuscript should be informative, summarizing the basic facts and conclusions, and maintaining a coherence and unity of thought.

Tutorial or how-to-do-it articles should preferably include a section on evaluation. Controversial topics should be treated in a factually sound and reasonably unbiased manner.

The format of headings, tables, figures, citations, references, and other details should follow the (APA) style as described in the Publication Manual of the *American Psychological Association*, 5th edition, available from APA, 750 1st St., NE, Washington, DC 20002 USA.

Preview

Manuscripts sent to the Editor for review are accepted on a voluntary basis from authors. Before submitting an article, please review the following suggestions. Manuscripts received in correct form serve to expedite the processing and prompt reviewing for early publication.

Spelling, punctuation, sentence structure, and the mechanical elements of arrangements, spacing, length, and consistency of usage in form and descriptions should be studied before submission. Due to the academic focus of AACE publications, the use of personal pronoun (I, we, etc.) and present tense is strongly discouraged.

Pre-publication

No manuscript will be considered which has already been published or is being considered by another journal.

Copyright

These journals are copyrighted by the Association for the Advancement of Computing in Education. Material published and so copyrighted may not be published elsewhere without the written permission of AACE.

Author Note(s)

Financial support for work reported or a grant under which a study was made should be noted just prior to the Acknowledgments. Acknowledgments or appreciation to individuals for assistance with the manuscript or with the material reported should be included as a note to appear at the end of the article prior to the References.

Handling of Manuscripts

All manuscripts are acknowledged upon receipt. Review is carried out as promptly as possible. The manuscript will be reviewed by at least two members of the Editorial Review Board, which takes approximately five months. When a decision for publication or rejection is made, the senior author or author designated to receive correspondence is notified. At the time of notification, the author may be asked to make certain revisions in the manuscript, or the Editor may submit suggested revisions to the author for approval.

Presentation

Accepted Submission File Formats. All submissions must be sent in electronic form using the Article Submission Form. **No hard copy submission papers will be accepted.** Do NOT submit compressed files. Do not use any word processing options/tools, such as--strike through, hidden text, comments, merges, and so forth.

Submit your manuscript in either of the following formats:
- **DOC**- Microsoft Word (preferred)
- RTF - Rich Text Format

Manuscripts should be double-spaced and a font size of 12 is preferred.

Length. In general, articles should not exceed 30 double-spaced pages. Long articles or articles containing complex material should be broken up by short, meaningful subheads.

Title sheet. Do NOT include a title sheet. Manuscripts are blind reviewed so there should be no indication of the author(s) name on the pages.

Abstract. An informative, comprehensive abstract of 75 to 200 words must accompany the manuscript. This abstract should succinctly summarize the major points of the paper, and the author's summary and/or conclusions.

Tables, Figures & Graphics

All tables and figure graphics must be embedded within the file and of such quality that when printed be in camera-ready form (publication quality). Within the submitted file, number and type captions centered at the top of each table. Figures are labeled at the bottom of the figure, left justified, and numbered in sequence.

Any graphics that go in the article must be submitted as separate files. The highest quality master (e.g. TIF) is preferred. Additionally, the graphics must also be embedded in the correct locations within the document so the copyeditors know the proper placement. Please note that any graphics created in Microsoft Word must also be submitted as separate files.

Graphics, tables, figures, photos, and so forth, must be sized to fit a 6" x 9" publication with margins of: top, 1" inside 1" outside, .75" and bottom, 1" an overall measurement of 4.5 X 6.75 is the absolute limit in size. A table or figure sized on a full size 8.5 by 11 piece of paper does not always reduce and remain legible. Please adhere to the size stipulation or your manuscript will be returned for graphics/figures or tables to be re-done.

Quotations

Copy all quoted material exactly as it appears in the original, indicating any omissions by three spaced periods. At the close of the quotation, give the complete source including page numbers. A block quote must be a minimum of 40 words or four lines, single spaced.

Terminology and Abbreviations
Define any words or phrases that cannot be found in Webster's Unabridged Dictionary. Define or explain new or highly technical terminology. Write out the first use of a term that you expect to use subsequently in abbreviated form. Abbreviations (i.e., e.g., etc.) are only acceptable in parenthesis, otherwise they must be spelled out, that is, for example, and so forth, respectively. Please avoid other foreign phrases and words such as via.

Program Listings
Program listings will appear with the published article if space permits. Listings should be publication quality. The brand of computer required should be included. Lengthy program listings (more than four 6 x 9 pages) can not be published, but may be made available from the author; a note to that effect should be included in the article.

Citations
Citations should strictly follow *American Psychological Association* (APA) style guide. Examples of references cited within the texts of articles are as follows: (Williams, Allen, & Jones, 1978) or (Moore, 1990; Smith, 1991) or Terrell (1977). In citations, "et al." can only be used after all authors have been cited or referenced with the exception of six or more authors. As per APA all citations must match the reference list and vice versa. Over use of references is discouraged.

References
Authors are responsible for checking the accuracy of all references and that all references cited in the text also appear in the Reference section. All references should be in alphabetical order by author (unnumbered) *American Psychological Association* (APA), 5th edition, style. Citation examples (1) book and (2) periodical:

Knowles, M. (1975). *Self-directed learning: A guide for learners and teachers*. New York: Association Press.

Raybould, B. (1995). Performance support engineering: An emerging development methodology for enabling organizational learning. *Performance Improvement Quarterly*, 8(1), 7-22.

Citing Electronic Media
The following forms for citing on-line sources are taken from the APA Publication Guidelines, Appendix 3-A, Section I (pp. 218-222). Please see the APA manual for additional information on formatting electronic media. A block quote must be a minimum of 40 words or four lines, single spaced (not 20 and double spaced as is presently noted). In citations, et al., can only be used after all authors have been cited or referenced. As per APA all citations must match the reference list and vice versa.

Elements of references to on-line information
Author, I. (date). Title of article. Name of Periodical [On-line], xx. Available: Specify path

Author, I., & Author, I. (date). Title of chapter. In Title of full work [On-line]. Available: Specify path

Author, I., Author, I., & Author, I. (date). Title of full work [On-line]. Available: Specify path

The date element should indicate the year of publication or, if the source undergoes regular revision, the most recent update; if a date cannot be determined, provide an exact date of your search. (p. 219)

An availability statement replaces the location and name of a publisher typically provided for text references. Provide information sufficient to retrieve the material. For example, for material that is widely available on networks, specify the method used to find the material, such as the protocol (Telnet, FTP, Internet, etc.), the directory, and the file name. (p. 219)

Other Electronic Media
Author, I. (Version number) [CD-ROM]. (date). Location of producer/distributor: Name of producer/distributor.

Author, I. (date). Title of article [CD-ROM]. Title of Journal, xx, xxx-xxx. Abstract from: Source and retrieval number

Author, I. (date). Name of Software (Version number) [Computer software]. Location of Location of producer/distributor: Name of producer/distributor.

After the title of the work, insert in brackets as part of the title element (i.e., before the period) the type of medium for the material (current examples include CD-ROM, Electronic data tape, cartridge tape, and computer program). (p. 220)

Include the location and name of the producer and distributor if citing an entire bibliographic database. (p. 220)

Post-publication
Upon publication, the contact author will receive complimentary copies of the journal issue in which the article appears for distribution to all of the co-authors.

Please carefully read and adhere to these guidelines. Manuscripts not submitted according to the guidelines will be rejected and returned to the author.

International Migration Review

ADDRESS FOR SUBMISSION:

Mark J. Miller, Editor
International Migration Review
Center for Migration Studies
209 Flagg Place
Staten Island, NY 10304-1122
USA
Phone: 718-351-8800
Fax: 718-667-4598
E-Mail: imr@cmsny.org
Web: www.cmsny.org
Address May Change:

PUBLICATION GUIDELINES:

Manuscript Length: 26-30
Copies Required: Four
Computer Submission: Yes
Format: MS Word/ Excel - IBM
    Compatible
Fees to Review: 0.00 US$

Manuscript Style:
    See Manuscript Guidelines

CIRCULATION DATA:

Reader: Academics
Frequency of Issue: Quarterly
Copies per Issue: 2,001 - 3,000
Sponsor/Publisher:
Subscribe Price: 39.00 US$ Individual
    80.00 US$ Institution
    54.00 US$ & $95 Foreign

REVIEW INFORMATION:

Type of Review: Blind Review
No. of External Reviewers: 3
No. of In House Reviewers: 2
Acceptance Rate: 11-20%
Time to Review: 2 - 3 Months
Reviewers Comments: Yes
Invited Articles: 0-5%
Fees to Publish: 0.00 US$

MANUSCRIPT TOPICS:
Immigration and Refugee Studies; Social Studies/Social Science

MANUSCRIPT GUIDELINES/COMMENTS:

Editorial Procedure
In order to provide impartiality in the selection of manuscripts for publication, all papers deemed appropriate for *IMR* are sent out anonymously to readers. To protect anonymity, the author's name and affiliation should appear only on a separate cover page. *IMR* has the right to first publication of all submitted manuscripts. Manuscripts submitted to *IMR* cannot be submitted simultaneously to another publication. Submission of a manuscript to *IMR* is taken to indicate the author's commitment to publish in this *Review*. No paper known to be under jurisdiction by any other journal will be reviewed by *IMR*. Authors are not paid for accepted manuscripts. If manuscripts are accepted and published, all rights, including subsidiary rights, are owned by the Center for Migration Studies. The author retains the right to use his/her article without charge in any book of which he/she is the author or editor after it has appeared in the *Review*.

402

Preparation of Copy

1. Type all copy - including indented matter, footnotes, and references – double-spaced on white paper.

2. Footnotes must be typed as endnotes, preceding references. Footnotes should include grant numbers or credits, if applicable, but should not include author's affiliation.

3. Include an abstract of not more than 100 words summarizing the findings of the paper.

4. Four copies of the manuscript are required and should be addressed to: Editor, International Migration Review, Center for Migration studies, 209 Flagg Place, Staten Island, NY 10304-1199. Manuscripts are not returned to authors. Only upon acceptance of the manuscript will a computer disk be requested.

5. Please prepare tables using Microsoft Excel or Microsoft Word. Save each table in a separate file. Table headings must be typed in large/small caps, with principal words capitalized (example enclosed). Insert location notes at the appropriate places in the text, *e.g.,* "Table 1 about here." Tables should not contain more than 20 two-digit columns, or the equivalent. Please use commas in numbers more than three digits. Do not use any demarcation lines within tables, *i.e.,* to separate sections, panels, etc. The data source should be listed first at the bottom of the table, followed by notes, if applicable.

6. Figures created in graphics programs, such as Adobe Illustrator or Aldus Free Hand, must be provided in high-resolution (300 dpi) EPS (Encapsulated PostScript File), TIFF (Tag Image File Format) or PDF (Portable Document Format) files. In the alternative, a high-resolution (300 dpi) camera-ready laser proof is acceptable.

7. We prefer MS Word and MS Excel. If you have any questions regarding submission of articles, please call Mrs. Patricia Delgado, IMR Secretary, at (718) 351-8800. All disks should be IBM-compatible. Please indicate programs used on disk label.

Format of References in Text

All references to monographs, articles, and statistical sources are to be identified at an appropriate point in the text by last name of author, year of publication, and pagination where appropriate all within parentheses. Footnotes are to be used only for substantive observations. Specify subsequent citations of the same source in the same way as the first one; do not use ibid, op cit., or loc cit.

1. When author's name is in the text: Duncan (1969). When author's name is not in the text: Gouldner, 1963)

2. Pagination follows year of publication: (Lipset, 1964:61-64).

3. For more than three authors, use et al. For institutional authorship, supply minimum identification from the beginning of the complete citation: (U.S. Bureau of the Census, 1963:117).

4. With more than one reference to an author in the same year, distinguish them by use of letters (a, b) attached to year of publication: (Levy, 1965a:311).

5. Enclose a series of references within a single pair of parentheses, separated by semicolons: (Johnson, 1942; Perry, 1947; Linguist, 1984).

Forms of References in Appendix:
List all items alphabetically by author and, within author(s), by year of publication beginning with the most recent year, in an appendix titled "REFERENCES. For multiple author or editor listings (more than two), give the first author only *and* add ct al. Use italics for titles of books and journals. For examples, see text of articles published in the *Review*.

Abstract and/or Key words (page 2)

If the submission is an essay, it must be accompanied by an abstract: a short summary (approx. 150 words) typed double-spaced on a separate sheet. Both essays and notes should be attended by a list of five key words defining the content of the text. These will help in its evaluation. In the case of acceptance the abstract will be translated by the Editorial Office into the four other languages for inclusion at the beginning of the essay.

Biographical note (page 3)

If the submission is an essay or study, a brief biographical note of some 5-8 typewritten lines should also be included. It should give: full name, major professional qualifications, relevant past positions and present position (with dates), main field(s) of research. It must also include the authors full address and, if available, e-mail address.

Main text

- The title of the essay or note should appear once more at the beginning of the main text. The authors name should not appear.
- The main text should be prepared for blind review. There should be no references identifying the author in any way at all.
- The relative importance of headings and subheadings in essays should be clear.

Use of the term **Introduction** should be avoided. Four types of heading can be used:

- Main Heading (H1) **bold**, with two lines of extra spacing above and one below.
- Second-order Heading (H2) italicized, with extra spacing above and below.
- Third-order Heading (H3) italicized, with extra spacing above and no spacing below.
- Fourth-order Heading (H4) italicized, ending with a full stop and with text following on the same line.

In addition,

- The location of figures and tables should be indicated in the text.
- New paragraphs should be indicated by clear indentation.
- Quoted passages longer than 3 lines should be indented throughout.
- The use of endnotes should be avoided; footnotes are not acceptable. However, if essential, endnotes should be designated by superscript numbers consecutively throughout the manuscript and placed in **Notes** after the main text. The endnote function of the word-processing system must be employed for this purpose.
- Italicization. Single foreign words and phrases are italicized, although authors are requested to substitute the native term for the foreign one whenever possible. A definition of the foreign term should be supplied the first time it is used.
- No other formatting should be employed.

Following the main text

- **Notes** (if any) should be listed in numerical order and placed after the main text.
- **Appendix** (if any) should follow the **Notes**.

407

References

The **References** should be arranged alphabetically. They should be typed double-spaced and given in the text as: author and year of publication, for example: (Wilson 1966; Olsen 1966a, b; Stodolsky and Lesser 1993: 580). For the list of References follow the style shown below:

Essays and studies in journals
Roberts, Peter. 1999. The Future of the University. *International Review of Education* 45(1): 65-85.
Forrester, Keith, Nick Frost, and Keven Ward. 2000. Researching Work and Learning: A Birds Eye View. *International Review of Education* 46(6): 483-489.

Books
Bernardo, Allan B. I. 1998. *Literacy and the Mind. The Contexts and Cognitive Consequences of Literacy Practice.* Hamburg: UNESCO Institute for Education.

Hill, Dave, and Mike Cole (eds.). 2001. *Schooling and Equality. Fact, Concept and Policy.* London: Kogan Page.

Essays in books
Jewett, Alfred E. 1987. Participant Purposes for Engaging in Physical Activity. In: *Myths, Models, and Methods in Sport Pedagogy*, ed. by George T. Barrette, 87-100. Champaign, IL: Human Kinetics

Dunn, Judy, and Jane Brown. 1991. Becoming American or English? Talking about the Social World in England and the United States. In: *Cultural Approaches to Parenting*, ed. by Marc H. Bornstein, 155-172. Hillsdale, NJ: Lawrence Erlbaum Associates.

Citations in languages other than English, French and German should include a translation of the title in parentheses, thus
Esipov, Boris P. (ed.). 1967. *Osnovy didaktiki* [Bases of Didactics]. Moscow: Prosveshchenie.

Websites should be cited as follows
http://www.unesco.org/education/uie/publications/uiestud8.shtml, accessed August 4, 2004.

Note that first names of authors must be included along with date and place of publication and publisher for books as well as the pagination of the essay and the full name of the editor for anthologies.

Titles, including those of journals, should not be abbreviated; subtitles should be included.

All other cases should be treated in accordance with these examples.

If there is both a list of **Notes** and a list of **References**, all bibliographical details should be included in the **References** and not repeated in the **Notes**.

Book reviews

The same rules of style and presentation apply to book reviews. Each review should be headed by the details of the book, as follows:

NASH, GARY B. 1997. *History on Trial*. New York: Alfred A. Knopf. 318 pp. ISBN 0-679-44687-7.

In length, book reviews should not exceed 800 words.

Where two or more books are reviewed together the review can be commensurately longer.

Book reviews can be in English, French or German. The books reviewed are normally in one of those languages, but books in other languages can also be considered for review on a case-by-case basis.

Offprints

Authors of essays, studies and notes will receive 50 complimentary offprints of their publication in addition to a copy of the issue of the journal in which their contribution is published. Authors of book reviews will receive a complimentary copy of the issue in which their review appears.

International Review of Research in Open and Distance Learning

ADDRESS FOR SUBMISSION:

Terry Anderson, Editor
International Review of Research in Open
    and Distance Learning
Athabasca University - Canada's Open U.
Centre for Distance Education
1 University Drive
Athabasca, AB T9S 3A3
Canada
Phone: 780-421-2536
Fax: 780-497-3416
E-Mail: paulah@athabascau.ca
Web: www.irrodl.org
Address May Change:

PUBLICATION GUIDELINES:

Manuscript Length: 21-35
Copies Required: One
Computer Submission: Yes Email
Format: MSWord, Rich Text Format
Fees to Review: 0.00 US$

Manuscript Style:
    American Psychological Association

CIRCULATION DATA:

Reader: Practicing Teachers, Academics,
    Researchers
Frequency of Issue: 2 -6 Times/Year
Copies per Issue: 5000+
Sponsor/Publisher: Athabasca University -
    Canada's Open University
Subscribe Price: 0.00 US$

REVIEW INFORMATION:

Type of Review: Blind Review
No. of External Reviewers: 3
No. of In House Reviewers: 1-2
Acceptance Rate: 11-20%
Time to Review: 1-7 Months
Reviewers Comments: Yes
Invited Articles: 21-30%
Fees to Publish: 0.00 US$

MANUSCRIPT TOPICS:
Higher Education; Online Learning & Teaching; Open & Distance Education

MANUSCRIPT GUIDELINES/COMMENTS:

International Review of Research on Open and Distance Learning (IRRODL) is an open source, refereed e-journal to advance theory, research and practice in open and distance learning worldwide. The aim of IRRODL is to disseminate scholarly information to scholars and practitioners of open and distance learning worldwide.

IRRODL welcomes submissions relating to open and distance learning from around the world for three sections of the journal:

    The Main section consists of refereed, scholarly articles, featuring advances in theory, research and/or best practice in open and distance learning
    The Research section, consists of refereed, scholarly articles of research or practice that support existing theory, research, and/or practice in open and distance learning

The Notes section features book reviews, technical reviews (Technical Notes) and shorter articles or abstracts which are not refereed, featured as:

- Field Notes. news and happenings from the "field"
- Conference Notes. announcements and reports of open and distance learning conferences and other professional development activities

Documentation

Manuscripts will conform to APA standard. Consult the *Publication Manual of the American Psychological Association* (5th ed., 2001).Follow the author-date method of citation in text. In addition, provide page numbers for all direct quotes.

Prepare an unnumbered reference list in alphabetical order by author. When there is more than one article by the same author(s), list the latest paper first. References should include the names of all contributing authors. The following are examples of the basic reference list format:

Periodical: Surname, A. A. (year). Article title. Title of Periodical, Volume (issue), inclusive page numbers.

Book: Surname, A. A. (year). Title of book. Publisher location: Publisher name.

Online sources: As for printed sources, as far as information is available. Include WWW information in a retrieval statement at the end of the reference (Retrieved Month date, year: URL). [link to http://www.apa.org/journals/webref.html/]

For all other cases, please refer to the *APA Manual*.

Authors are responsible for accuracy of all references and to ensure that any references cited in the text also appear in the reference section. Notes, if necessary, must appear at the end of the article (before reference list) as endnotes. Please use the endnote feature provided by your word processor.

Style

Submissions must be in English. Either British or American spelling is acceptable, but usage must be consistent throughout. Please spell check all submissions.

Please refer to the *APA Manual* for advice on ways to reduce bias in language.

To abbreviate the name of an organization or agency to the initial letters, use capitals and no periods (e.g., YWCA). For first occurrence, provide the full name with abbreviation in parentheses; use abbreviation as required after that.

Italics may be used to identify special terms or to indicate special emphasis. Please use this feature sparingly.

411

Copyright
IRRODL welcomes manuscripts that have not been published in other journals. Manuscripts accepted for publication become the copyright of Athabasca University.

By submitting their articles, authors grant *IRRODL* the right to publish, distribute, archive, and retrieve their material. Authors retain the right to use their own material for purely educational and research purposes. In all subsequent publications, whether in whole or part, *IRRODL* must be acknowledged as the original publisher. Authors are required to complete and submit *IRRODL*'s Release and Copyright Assignment form prior to publication.

Permission and Acknowledgment
Authors are responsible for obtaining permission to quote copyrighted material. At the end of your article, please acknowledge sources of funding/support, other participants and copyright holders who have given permission to use their material.

Length
Manuscripts intended for the Main section should be in the 5000-7000 word range (excluding references). Manuscripts for Notes may range from 50 words for items such as conference announcements, to 2000 words for reports and book reviews.

Review Process
The review process takes 1 - 3 months, depending on the quality of submission (foreign submissions may take longer, as they are edited for English usage prior to sending them to review; domestic (e.g., US, UK, Australian and Canadian submissions typically take less time to peer review, as they are not edited for English usage prior to review). After that time, contact the Managing Editor regarding the status of your submission.

Articles will be subject to blind review by three reviewers, who will look for:

- significance of the problem
- applicability and interest to the field (relevance beyond case presented?)
- originality and contribution to open and distance learning (implications
- for other work?)
- appropriateness of method
- literature review
- complete, clear and well organized presentation
- accurate and useful interpretation
- sound argument and analysis

After completion of the review process, *IRRODL* Editors will send their decision by e-mail. A detailed written summary of the reviewers' comments will be provided in cases where article have been accepted for publication, or where changes are requested by the editor before publication.

Once a manuscript is accepted and authors have made the recommended changes on their submissions, *IRRODL* Editors will conduct a thorough review and copy edit before publishing any article. We reserve the right to make editorial changes ed to correct errors or to conform to *IRRODL* standards.

Tables/Figures/URLs
Tables and figures must be of publication quality, clearly labeled and numbered in sequence. They should be placed in the correct location within the body of your article.

Book Reviews
Book reviews must include (in this order): title, author, place of publication, publisher, date of publication, ISBN and number of pages. Book reviews must not contain footnotes; incorporate all references into the text of your review.

Submitting Manuscripts
All submissions must be paginated and have a cover page. Please indicate total word count and whether the submission is intended for the peer reviewed Main or Research Notes Sections. For submissions to Notes, please indicate topic area – book review, field, or conference.

Send submissions as an email attachment to **irrodl@athabascau.ca**. Submissions will be acknowledged via email on receipt.

Manuscripts should be a Word file, prepared in Normal style. Manuscripts may also be submitted in Rich Text Format (RTF). Avoid text formatting.

Manuscripts must be accompanied by:
- an abstract (no more than 150 words)
- 6 to 8 key terms (e.g., self-directed learning, instructional design,
- learner support)
- a short (50 word) biography for each author, complete with e-mail address
- a separate title page which must include:
- complete title of the paper -- 10-12 words
- name(s) of author(s) and institutional affiliation(s)
- running head for publication (maximum 50 characters) and
- an author note with departmental affiliation, acknowledgments and
- contact information (telephone, fax and e-mail)

Include the title of the manuscript at the top of the first page of text.

References to locations, persons, organizations or any other information that might serve to identify the authors must be excluded from manuscripts submitted for review.

Contributing authors will be expected to participate in an online IRRODL Web Conference for 45 days after publication.

Internet and Higher Education (The)

ADDRESS FOR SUBMISSION:

Laurie P. Dringus, Editor
Internet and Higher Education (The)
Nova Southeatern University
Grad. Sch. of Computer & Info. Sciences
Carl DeSantis Building 4th floor
3100 College Avenue
Ft. Lauderdale, FL 33314
USA
Phone: 954-262-2073
Fax: 954-262-3915
E-Mail: laurie@nova.edu
Web: www.scis.nova.edu/ihe
Address May Change:

PUBLICATION GUIDELINES:

Manuscript Length: 21-25
Copies Required: Four
Computer Submission: Yes Disk, Email
Format: Word; in English
Fees to Review: 0.00 US$

Manuscript Style:
    American Psychological Association

CIRCULATION DATA:

Reader: Practicing Teachers, Academics,
    Administrators
Frequency of Issue: Quarterly
Copies per Issue: 1,001 - 2,000
Sponsor/Publisher: Elsevier Science
    Publishing Co.
Subscribe Price: 75.00 US$ Individual
    224.00 US$ Institution

REVIEW INFORMATION:

Type of Review: Blind Review
No. of External Reviewers: 2
No. of In House Reviewers: 1
Acceptance Rate: 21-30%
Time to Review: 1-3 Months
Reviewers Comments: Yes
Invited Articles: 6-10%
Fees to Publish: 0.00 US$

MANUSCRIPT TOPICS:
Education Management/Administration; Educational Technology Systems; Higher Education; Internet and Education; Online Learning & Teaching

MANUSCRIPT GUIDELINES/COMMENTS:

The Internet and Higher Education is a quarterly journal designed to reach those faculty, staff, and administrators charged with the responsibility of enhancing instructional practices and productivity via the use of Information Technology (IT) and the Internet. It will seek and publish scholarly papers grounded in theory, dealing with: (1) Any coursework in digital form via the Internet; the use of the Internet to create learning organizations; experiments with hypertext systems; the use of Internet-based activities designed to foster increased faculty and administrative output. (2) Social and theoretical commentary which critically examines issues related to the deployment of IT via the Internet to enhance instruction and institutional productivity, such as racial and gender issues related to technology; the impact of hypertext systems on traditional communication systems and cognitive structures; and socioeconomic aspects of Internet access in the Information Era.

414

Submissions

Manuscripts being submitted for publication should be mailed to Dr. Laurie P. Dringus, Editor, *The Internet and Higher Education*, Graduate School of Computer and Information Sciences, Nova Southeastern University, Carl DeSantis Building 4th floor, 3100 College Avenue, Ft. Lauderdale, Florida, USA, 33314-7796. E-mail: **laurie@nova.edu**. It is preferred that authors submit via email with the manuscript as a Word file. Authors submitting in hardcopy should submit four copies of the manuscript and include an e-mail return address if possible. All submissions will be promptly acknowledged. Hardcopy or electronic submissions must follow the manuscript requirements below. Currently, *The Internet and Higher Education* is a print journal, therefore, *accepted* manuscripts must match precisely in hardcopy and in electronic form.

Manuscript Requirements

Manuscripts should be in English, and should be double spaced throughout, with at least one inch margins. The main text of the paper should be presented in 12pt type (Times Roman preferred). Manuscripts should be between 10 and 30 pages in length and should contain, after the title page, an abstract of 100-150 words, and keywords indicated under the abstract.. The name(s), affiliation(s), address(es), and phone and fax number(s) of the author(s) should appear on a separate cover page. To ensure anonymity in the review process, names of the author(s) should not appear elsewhere in the manuscript. *The Internet and Higher Education* uses an in-text author/date documentation style based on the latest edition of the *Publication Manual of the American Psychological Association*. Thus all material for which the author desires to provide documentation should be followed by the cited author's name, date of publication, and page number; i.e. (Alter, 1990, pp. 4-6), or (Geertz, 1992).

References

All references cited should be listed alphabetically in a separate section at the end of the manuscript. The format of citations should follow the *APA Manual*, pp. 181-222.

Tables

Tables, graphs, and figures should accompany the manuscript on separate sheets in the back of the paper and should not be incorporated into the text. Authors should indicate on the paper's margin where the graphic material should go in the text. If authors are submitting electronic versions, tables should be included in the same file as the manuscript. These should appear at the end of the file. Graphics in .gif and other special formats should be submitted as separate files from the manuscript file. *The Internet and Higher Education* does not publish footnotes and none should be used.

Review Process

Manuscripts are peer reviewed by members of the Editorial Board and a group of outside readers. The editor relies heavily on their recommendations but makes the final decision on acceptance of manuscripts. The review process usually takes one to three months. Manuscripts will not be returned and authors should retain the originals of their papers.

Publication
Upon acceptance authors will be expected to assign copyright to Elsevier Science and to supply a digital copy of their manuscript on a 3 1/2in. disk formatted for use with an IBM compatible PC. Files should be in WordPerfect or Word format with version indicated --- no Macs please. Any art or graphics should be in separate files. Art should be supplied as camera-ready copy. For further details of the electronic formats which we accept (and other details established by Elsevier Science), please see http://www.elsevier.nl/locate/disksub. *Content of disk must match hardcopy manuscript precisely.* When the article has been accepted for publication and is in production, contact Elsevier Science at authorsupport@elsevier.ie for author information; manuscript status may also be tracked using **Oasis**, Elsevier's web-based database: www.elsevier.nl/oasis.

Journal for Specialists in Group Work

ADDRESS FOR SUBMISSION:

Donald E. Ward, Editor
Journal for Specialists in Group Work
Pittsburg State University
Department of Psychology and Counseling
Pittsburg, KS 66762
USA
Phone: 620-235-4530
Fax: 620-235-6102
E-Mail: dward@pittstate.edu
Web: http://asgw.org/jsgw/jsgw.htm
Address May Change:

PUBLICATION GUIDELINES:

Manuscript Length: 16-30
Copies Required: One After Acceptance
Computer Submission: Preferred
Format: PC-compatible Microsoft Word
Fees to Review: 0.00 US$

Manuscript Style:
American Psychological Association

CIRCULATION DATA:

Reader: Academics, Group Practitioners
Frequency of Issue: Quarterly
Copies per Issue: 1500-2500
Sponsor/Publisher: Association for
Specialists in Group Work/Taylor &
Francis
Subscribe Price: 68.00 US$ Individual
224.00 US$ Institution incl. on-line

REVIEW INFORMATION:

Type of Review: Blind Review
No. of External Reviewers: 3
No. of In House Reviewers: 1
Acceptance Rate: 45-55%
Time to Review: 2 - 3 Months
Reviewers Comments: Yes
Invited Articles: 0-5%
Fees to Publish: 0.00 US$

MANUSCRIPT TOPICS:
Adult Career & Vocational; Art/Music; Counseling & Personnel Services; Group Work;
Urban Education, Cultural/Non-Traditional

MANUSCRIPT GUIDELINES/COMMENTS:

Topics Include: Career & Vocational; Children & Adults; Counseling, Therapy Guidance,
Psychoeducational, Preventative, Support, , Work/Task, and Process Groups; International
Group Work; Group Research

The Journal for Specialists in Group Work invites articles of interest to the readers and
membership. To contribute to the journal, follow these guidelines. Manuscripts should be well
organized and concise so the development of ideas is logical. Avoid dull, stereotyped writing
and aim at the clear and interesting communication of ideas. All manuscripts should include
information describing applicability of the topic to group work practitioners.

Authors are expected to submit the manuscript for review as a PC-compatible, Microsoft
Word file. In addition, a hard copy is required upon acceptance.

The title of the article should appear on a separate page accompanying the manuscript. Include on this page the names of the authors followed by a paragraph that repeats the names of the authors and gives their titles and institutional affiliations and a paragraph that provides author contact information for the contact author.

Article titles and headings within the article should be concise.

Manuscripts should be submitted as PC-Compatible, Microsoft Word files in 12-point Times New Roman font.

Include a 100-word abstract of the manuscript that conveys the main message to the reader. Four or five keywords should be included at the bottom of the Abstract page to facilitate electronic access to the article.

Double-space all material, including references and extensive quotations. Allow 1" margins.

Adhere to guidelines to reduce bias in language against persons on the basis of gender, sexual orientation, racial or ethnic group, disability or age by referring to the fourth edition of the APA publication manual. Also, use terms such as client, student, or participant rather than subject.

Do not use footnotes.

References should follow the *Publication Manual of The American Psychological Association* (fifth edition). Check all references for completeness; adequate information should be given to allow the reader to retrieve the referenced material from the most available source. All references cited in text must be listed in the reference section and vice versa. Direct quotations must have page numbers cited.

Lengthy quotations (generally 300-500 cumulative words or more from one source) require written permission from the copyright holder for reproduction. Adaptation of tables and figures also requires reproduction approval from the copyrighted source. It is the author's responsibility to secure such permission, and a copy of the publisher's written permission must be provided to the journal editor immediately upon acceptance of the article for publication by AAC.

Tables should be kept to a minimum. Include only essential data and combine tables wherever possible. Each table should be on a separate page following the reference section of the article. Final placement of the tables is at the discretion of the production editor; in all cases, tables will be placed after the first reference to the table in the text. Supply figures (graphs, illustrations, Line drawings) as camera-ready art (prepared by a commercial artist on glossy or repro paper), with sans serif text no smaller than 8 points.

Never submit material that is under consideration by another publication.

418

For other questions of format or style, refer to the 2001 (fifth) edition of the *Publication Manual of the American Psychological Association*. Copies may be ordered from APA, 750 First St. N.E., Washington, DC 20002-4242.

Journal articles are edited within a uniform style for correctness and consistency of grammar, spelling, and punctuation. In some cases, manuscripts are reworded for conciseness or clarity of expression. Authors bear the responsibility for the accuracy of references, tables, and figures.

Journal of Accounting Education

ADDRESS FOR SUBMISSION:

James E. Rebele, Editor
Journal of Accounting Education
Robert Morris University
School of Business
6001 University Boulevard
Moon Township, PA 15108
Phone: 412-269-4894
Fax: 412-262-8672
E-Mail: rebele@rmu.edu
Web: www.elsevier.com/locate/jaccedu
Address May Change:

PUBLICATION GUIDELINES:

Manuscript Length: 11-15
Copies Required: Four
Computer Submission: No
Format:
Fees to Review: 0.00 US$

Manuscript Style:
Chicago Manual of Style

CIRCULATION DATA:

Reader: Academics
Frequency of Issue: Quarterly
Copies per Issue: 2,001 - 3,000
Sponsor/Publisher: Elsevier
Subscribe Price: 96.00 US$ Individual
386.00 US$ Institution

REVIEW INFORMATION:

Type of Review: Blind Review
No. of External Reviewers: 2
No. of In House Reviewers: 0
Acceptance Rate: 11-20%
Time to Review: 2 - 3 Months
Reviewers Comments: Yes
Invited Articles: 6-10%
Fees to Publish: 0.00 US$

MANUSCRIPT TOPICS:

Curriculum Studies; Educational Technology Systems; Higher Education; Tests, Measurement & Evaluation

MANUSCRIPT GUIDELINES/COMMENTS:

Description

The *Journal of Accounting Education* (*JAEd*) is a refereed journal dedicated to promoting excellence in teaching and stimulating research in accounting education internationally. The journal provides a forum for exchanging ideas, opinions, and research results among accounting educators around the world. The journal is divided into four sections. Papers in the "Main Articles" section present in-depth analyses of the topics discussed. The "International Prospectives" section is designed to provide an awareness of the internationally educational environment including changes and developments in countries and regions around the world. The "Teaching and Educational Notes" section is designed to further the goal of providing a forum. This section contains short papers with information of interest to readers of *JAEd*. The "Case Section" provides a vehicle for dissemination of material for use in the classroom. The case material should aid in providing a positive learning experience for both student and professor and should be available for general use. Topics covered in *JAEd* include: faculty

420

evaluations, microcomputers, innovative teaching methods, results of classroom experiments, and changes in the education process, among others. Also, articles written by non-accounting faculty are published if they deal with education in general or include some aspect of accounting education.

Journal of Adult Development

ADDRESS FOR SUBMISSION:

Thomas Peters, Managing Editor
Journal of Adult Development
Clark University
Heinz Werner Institute for
  Developmental Analysis
950 Main Street
Worcester, MA 01610
USA
Phone:
Fax:
E-Mail: tpeters@clark.edu
Web: www.wkap.nl/series.htm/pasap
Address May Change:

PUBLICATION GUIDELINES:

Manuscript Length: 1-25
Copies Required: Four
Computer Submission: No
Format: N/A
Fees to Review: 0.00 US$

Manuscript Style:
  American Psychological Association

CIRCULATION DATA:

Reader: Academics
Frequency of Issue: Quarterly
Copies per Issue: 1,001 - 2,000
Sponsor/Publisher: Plenum Publishing
  (Kluwer Academic)
Subscribe Price: 362.00 US$ Institution

REVIEW INFORMATION:

Type of Review: Blind Review
No. of External Reviewers: 3
No. of In House Reviewers: 1
Acceptance Rate: 30%
Time to Review: 6-9 Months
Reviewers Comments: Yes
Invited Articles: 0-50%
Fees to Publish: 0.00 US$

MANUSCRIPT TOPICS:
Adult Career & Vocational; All topics as related to Career Development; Counseling &
Personnel Services; Education Management/Administration; Educational Psychology; Higher
Education; Social Studies/Social Science; Tests, Measurement & Evaluation; Urban
Education, Cultural/Non-Traditional

MANUSCRIPT GUIDELINES/COMMENTS:

Journal of Adult Development is a transdisciplinary forum for the publication of peer reviewed
original papers on biological, psychological (cognitive, affective, valuative, behavioral),
and/or sociocultural development in young, middle, or late adulthood. The journal publishes
theoretical and empirical articles, book reviews, and letters. Toward an integrated perspective,
the journal encourages both basic and applied contributions to knowledge as well as
quantitative and/or qualitative approaches to inquiry.

Instructions to Authors

1. Manuscripts, in quadruplicate and in English, should be submitted to:
   Thomas Peters, Managing Editor, *Journal of Adult Development,* Clark University, Heinz Werner Institute for Developmental Analysis, 950 Main Street, Worchester, MA 01610.

Authors should include a cover letter that states the paper's relevance to the scope of the journal and should submit the manuscript in a form appropriate to the blind review process. In addition to hard copy (manuscripts), authors are encouraged to submit disks using MSWord 2000, if possible.

2. Submission is a representation that the manuscript has not been published previously and is not currently under consideration for publication elsewhere. A statement transferring copyright from the authors (or their employers, if they hold the copyright) to Plenum Publishing Corporation/Kluwer Academic Publishers will be required before the manuscript can be accepted for publication. The Editor will supply the necessary forms for this transfer. Such a written transfer of copyright, which previously was assumed to be implicit in the act of submitting a manuscript, is necessary under the U.S. Copyright Law in order for the publisher to carry through the dissemination of research results and reviews as widely and effectively as possible.

3. Type double-spaced on one side of 8 1/2 X 11 inch white paper using generous margins on all sides, and submit the original and three copies (including, where possible, copies of all illustrations and tables).

4. A title page is to be provided and should include the title of the article, author's name (no degrees), author's affiliation, and suggested running head. The affiliation should comprise the department, institution (usually university or company), city, and state (or nation) and should be typed as a footnote to the author's name. The suggested running head should be less than 80 characters (including spaces) and should comprise the article title or an abbreviated version thereof. For office purposes, the title page should include the complete mailing address and telephone number of the one author designated to review proofs.

5. An abstract is to be provided, preferably no longer than 150 words.

6. A list of 4-5 key words is to be provided directly below the abstract. Key words should express the precise content of the manuscript, as they are used for indexing purposes.

7. Illustrations (photographs, drawings, diagrams, and charts) are to be numbered in one consecutive series of Arabic numerals. The captions for illustrations should be typed on a separate sheet of paper. Photographs should be large, glossy prints, showing high contrast. Drawings should be prepared with India ink. Either the original drawings or good-quality photographic prints are acceptable. Artwork for each figure should be provided on a separate sheet of paper. Identify figures on the back with author's name and number of the illustration.

8. Tables should be numbered (with Roman numerals) and referred to by number in the text. Each table should be typed on a separate sheet of paper. Center the title above the table, and type explanatory footnotes (indicated by superscript lowercase letters) below the table.

9. List references alphabetically at the end of the paper and refer to them in the text by name and year in parentheses. References should include (in this order): last names and initials of all authors, year published, title of article, name of publication, volume number, and inclusive pages. The style and punctuation of the references should conform to strict *APA style*-illustrated by the following examples:

Journal Article

Pilisuk, M., Montgomery, M. B., Parks. S. H., & Acredolo, C. (1993). Locus of control, life stress, and social networks: Gender differences in the health status of the elderly. *Sex Roles, 28,* 147-166.

Book

Hart, D.A. (1992*). Becoming men The development of aspirations, values, and adaptational styles,* New York: Plenum Press.

Contribution to a Book

Haviland, J. M., & Walker-Andrews, A. S. (1992). Emotion socialization: A view from development and ethology. In V. e. Van Hasselt & M. Hersen (Eds.), *Handbook of social development: A lifespan perspective* (pp. 29-49). New York: Kluwer Academic/Plenum Press.

10. Footnotes should be avoided. When their use is absolutely necessary, footnotes should be numbered consecutively using Arabic numerals and should be typed at the bottom of the page to which they refer. Place a line above the footnote, so that it is set off from the text. Use the appropriate superscript numeral for citation in the text.

11. In general, the journal follows the recommendations of the 2001 *Publication Manual of the American Psychological Association* (Fifth Edition), and it is suggested that contributors refer to this publication.

12. After a manuscript has been accepted for publication and after all revisions have been incorporated, manuscripts may be submitted to the Editor's Office on personal-computer disks. Label the disk with identifying information --kind of computer used, kind of software and version number, disk format and file name of article, as well as abbreviated journal name, authors' last names, and (if room) paper title. Package the disk in a disk mailer or protective cardboard. The disk must be the one from which the accompanying manuscript (finalized version) was printed out. The Editor's Office cannot accept a disk without its accompanying, matching hard-copy manuscript. Disks will be used on a case-by-case basis -- where efficient and feasible.

13. The journal makes no page charges. Reprints are available to authors, and order forms with the current price schedule are sent with proofs.

Journal of Agricultural Education

ADDRESS FOR SUBMISSION:

Greg Miller, Editor
Journal of Agricultural Education
Iowa State University
201 Curtiss Hall
Ames, IA 50011
USA
Phone: 515-294-2583
Fax: 515-294-0530
E-Mail: gsmiller@iastate.edu
Web: http://pubs.aged.tamu.edu/jae/
Address May Change: 12/31/2006

CIRCULATION DATA:

Reader: Academics, Administrators
Frequency of Issue: Quarterly
Copies per Issue: Less than 1,000
Sponsor/Publisher: American Association
 for Agricultural Education
Subscribe Price: 0.00 US$ AAAE Member
 120.00 US$ Individual
 150.00 US$ Foreign

PUBLICATION GUIDELINES:

Manuscript Length: 16-20
Copies Required: Four
Computer Submission: No
Format:
Fees to Review: 0.00 US$

Manuscript Style:
 American Psychological Association

REVIEW INFORMATION:

Type of Review: Blind Review
No. of External Reviewers: 2
No. of In House Reviewers: 1
Acceptance Rate: 21-30%
Time to Review: 4 - 6 Months
Reviewers Comments: Yes
Invited Articles: 0-5%
Fees to Publish: 0.00 US$

MANUSCRIPT TOPICS:

Adult Career & Vocational; Curriculum Studies; Education Management/Administration; Educational Technology Systems; Environment-Agricultural Education; Higher Education; Rural Education & Small Schools; Science Math & Environment; Teacher Education; Tests, Measurement & Evaluation; Urban Education, Cultural/Non-Traditional

MANUSCRIPT GUIDELINES/COMMENTS:

Editorial Policy

The *Journal of Agricultural Education* is a publication of the American Association for Agricultural Education (AAAE). And is published four times a year. The *Journal* publishes blind, peer-reviewed manuscripts addressing current trends and issues, descriptions or analyses of innovations, research, philosophical concerns, and learner/program evaluation in agricultural education, including extension and international agricultural education. The submission of empirically-based manuscripts that report original quantitative or qualitative research, manuscripts based on historical or philosophical research, and reviews/synthesis of empirical or theoretical literature are encouraged. The *Journal* will not consider any manuscript that has been published by or is under consideration by another journal. All or part of this issue and previous issues may be reproduced only for educational purposes.

Subscriptions
All AAAE members receive the *Journal*. Nonmember subscriptions are $120 per year, (includes library rate postage) and foreign/overseas subscriptions are $150 per year (includes airmail postage to foreign/overseas addresses). Back issues are $10 per copy when copies are available. Subscriptions and back issue requests should be addressed to the Business Manager (for address see website). Articles from the *Journal* are indexed in the *Current Index to Journals of Education* (CITE) and are accessible through ERIC.

Manuscript Submission
Submit manuscripts to the Editor at any time. Authors should submit:
A. A Cover letter

B. A separate title page that includes the manuscript title and the name, mailing address, phone number, facsimile number, and e-mail address for all authors.

C. Four copies of the manuscript prepared for blind review (no references to authors' names or institutional affiliation):
1. The first page of the manuscript should include the following:
    a. Manuscript title
    b. An abstract (no more than 200 words)
    c. The introduction/theoretical base section of the manuscript should start
    d. Immediately after the abstract (on page 1).

2. Manuscripts, including tables/figures, must be no more than twenty (20) typed, double-spaced pages, including tables, figures and references. Times Roman 12 point font with one inch margins should be used. Tables and figures should be placed within the body of the manuscript as soon as feasible after their first mention in the text. Page numbers should be centered at the bottom of each page.

3. Authors should ensure that tables, figures and references are prepared according to the guidelines in the *Publication Manual of the American Psychological Association* (5th Edition, 2001). The font size for all text in tables and figures must be at least 12 point. Patterns rather than colors should be used for the bars in bar charts and for the "pie slices" in pie charts. Authors should ensure that table notes are formatted according to the APA Manual. Consult the APA manual for all other questions concerning manuscript style and the reporting of data analyses. Authors should report effect sizes in the manuscript and tables when reporting statistical significance.

D. The cover letter, title page and four copies of the manuscript should be mailed to the Editor at Iowa State University, 201 Curtiss Hall, Ames, Iowa 50011. The lead author will receive a letter confirming that the manuscript has been received. In most cases, the lead author will be notified of the results of the review process within 3-4 months.

Journal of American College Health

ADDRESS FOR SUBMISSION:

Martha Wedeman, Managing Editor
Journal of American College Health
Heldref Publications
1319 Eighteenth Street N.W.
Washington, DC 20036-1802
USA
Phone: 202-296-6267 ext 214
Fax: 202-296-5149
E-Mail: jach@heldref.org
Web: www.heldref.org/
Address May Change:

PUBLICATION GUIDELINES:

Manuscript Length: See Below
Copies Required: Two
Computer Submission: Yes
Format: MS Word and 2 Hard Copies
Fees to Review: 0.00 US$

Manuscript Style:
, JAMA, Index Medicus

CIRCULATION DATA:

Reader: Academics
Frequency of Issue: Bi-Monthly
Copies per Issue: 3,000-3,500
Sponsor/Publisher: American College
    Health Assn./ Heldref Publications, Inc.
Subscribe Price: 80.00 US$ Individual
    156.00 US$ Institution
    16.00 US$ Add for Outside USA

REVIEW INFORMATION:

Type of Review: Blind Review
No. of External Reviewers: 3
No. of In House Reviewers: 0
Acceptance Rate: 20-30%
Time to Review: 4 - 6 Months
Reviewers Comments: Yes
Invited Articles: 0-5%
Fees to Publish: 0.00 US$

MANUSCRIPT TOPICS:
Adult Career & Vocational; Clinical Medicine; Counseling & Personnel Services; Educational Psychology; Health & Physical Education; Higher Education

MANUSCRIPT GUIDELINES/COMMENTS:

Scope of the Journal
Binge drinking, campus violence, eating disorders, sexual harassment: today's college students face challenges their parents never imagined. The *Journal of American College Health,* the only scholarly publication devoted entirely to college students' health, focuses on these issues, as well as use of tobacco and other drugs, sexual habits, psychological problems, and student gambling. Published in cooperation with the American College Health Association, *The Journal of American College Health is* must reading for physicians, nurses, health educators, and administrators who are involved with students every day. Parents and secondary school educators will also find the *journal* a useful resource in preparing students for future campus life. The *journal* includes major research articles, clinical and program notes, practical accounts of developing prevention strategies, and lively viewpoint articles on controversial issues. Recent articles on alcohol abuse, designated drivers, and a theme issue on men's health have attracted widespread media attention.

Guidelines for Authors

The Journal of American College Health provides a medium for the exchange of information relating to health in institutions of higher education. The *journal* publishes articles encompassing many areas of this broad field, including clinical and preventive medicine, dentistry, environmental and community health and safety, health promotion and education, management and administration, mental health, nursing, pharmacy, sports medicine, and consumer-related issues in these areas.

The *Journal of American College Health is* intended for college health professionals: physicians, physician assistants, psychologists, nurses, health educators, counselors, and professionals interested in adolescent and young adult health issues; college and university administrators and student affairs personnel; and students as peer educators, preprofessionals, and consumers.

The *journal* publishes (a) scientific or research articles presenting significant new data, insights, or analyses; (b) state-of-the-art reviews in areas of interest; (c) clinical and program notes that share experiences or interesting cases or report on innovative procedures; (d) brief reports, viewpoints, editorials, book reviews, and letters to the editor.

Types of Articles

Major Articles

Theoretical, scientific, and research manuscripts and reviews are eligible for consideration as major articles. The editors encourage submission of manuscripts reflecting new contributions to knowledge or interpretations rather than studies that simply confirm previous observations. The preferred length is 15 to 20 double-spaced pages, including tables, figures, and references.

Clinical and Program Notes

The *journal* is fully refereed and applies the highest standards to all submissions. It encourages spontaneous and informal communications in the form of clinical and program notes that report on clinical experiences, new or especially interesting ideas and services, or requests for collaboration in clinical studies. Program notes run 4 to 7 double-spaced pages, including a brief abstract, but do not usually include tables or figures; references must conform to the style used in major articles.

Viewpoint

Viewpoint is a forum for the expression of opinions and points of view. Manuscripts can vary in length from 4 to 10 pages, but our preference is for concise presentations. Abstracts, tables, and figures are unnecessary. References, when needed to support the discussion, should follow the same format as that used in major articles.

Letters to the Editor in response to published articles are also welcome. They should be brief (500 –1,000 words) and they may be edited.

428

Submission
Submit manuscripts electronically to the managing editor (jach@heldref.org) as double-spaced Word files with minimal formatting in Times. Do not use word-processing styles, forced section or page breaks, or automatic footnotes or references.

Provide a letter indicating that the manuscript has not been submitted simultaneously to any other publication.

Follow the *American Medical Association Manual of Style,* 9th edition, Baltimore: Williams & Wilkins; 1998, in matters of medical and scientific usage. We do not use American Psychological Association (APA) style.

Titles should be short, specific, and clear. An abstract of no more than 150 words and 3 to 5 key words should precede the text of the article. Divide text in major articles into sections headed Method, Results, and Comment.

Use a separate page for authors' names, academic degrees, affiliations, position, telephone, fax, electronic mail numbers, and postal addresses; indicate the name of the corresponding author.

Submit tables and figures as separate files. Use them sparingly as nonredundant enhancements of the text. Send figures in their original source file and mail hard copies of tables and figures to the managing editor. Provide written permission from publishers and authors to reprint or adapt previously published tables or figures.

Indicate approval of the appropriate institutional review board (IRB) for all studies involving human participants and describe how participants provided informed consent.

Proofread carefully, double checking all statistics, numbers, symbols, references, and tables. Authors are responsible for the accuracy of all material submitted.

Editorial Process
All submissions are blind reviewed by at least one consulting or ad hoc reviewer, the statistical editor when appropriate, and an executive editor. This procedure often takes about 4 months. The managing editor will notify authors of the decision—accept, return for revisions (major or minor), or rejection. Review comments will be sent to the author. When the reviews have been completed, the managing editor will notify the corresponding author of the editors' decision as to whether the manuscript is to be accepted, rejected, or sent back for revisions (minor or substantial). The editors will not normally consider rejected manuscripts.

Heldref reserves the right to edit accepted manuscripts for clarity, coherence, style, and felicitous usage. Authors receive an edited draft to proofread, respond to queries, and correct errors that may have been introduced in the editing process. Extensive changes and rewriting are not permitted at this stage.

Accepted manuscripts are usually published within 1 year of acceptance. Each author receives 2 complimentary copies of the issue in which the article appears. Additional copies *of* the journal or reprints are available to authors at a reduced price (minimum order 50).

References

Authors should cite references consecutively in the text, using a superscript at the *end of* the article in the numerical order in which the source is first cited. List references by number at the end of the text with titles of journals listed in the abbreviated forms shown in *Index Medicus,* as in the following examples.

Journals
1. Engwal D, Hunter R, Steinberg M. Gambling and other risk behaviors on university campuses. *J Am Coll Health*. 2004(6):245–255.

Books
2. Bernstein TM. The Careful Writer: A Modern Guide to English Usage. New York: Atheneum; 1965.

Other
References to unpublished material should be noted parenthetically in the text (e.g., James Jackson, PhD, unpublished data, personal communication, September 12, 2004).

Quoted material must include the page on which it appeared in the referenced source (e.g., 7((p27).

Submit all manuscripts to the Managing Editor, *The Journal of American College Health*, 1319 Eighteenth Street, NW, Washington, DC 20036-1802; Phone: 202-296-6267; Fax: 202-296-5149.

Website: www.heldref.org/html/body_jach.html

Journal of Applied Developmental Psychology

ADDRESS FOR SUBMISSION:

Ann McGillicuddy-Delisi, Editor
Journal of Applied Developmental
Psychology
c/o Editorial Office Manager
Lafayette College
Easton, PA 18042-1781
USA
Phone: 610-330-5859
Fax: 610-330-5349
E-Mail: japd@lafayette.edu
Web: http://www.sciencedirect.com
Address May Change:

PUBLICATION GUIDELINES:

Manuscript Length: 30+
Copies Required: Three
Computer Submission: Yes Disk, Email
Format: Word
Fees to Review: 0.00 US$

Manuscript Style:
American Psychological Association

CIRCULATION DATA:

Reader: Academics, Counselors
Frequency of Issue: Bi-Monthly
Copies per Issue: No Reply
Sponsor/Publisher:
Subscribe Price: 384.00 US$

REVIEW INFORMATION:

Type of Review: Blind Review
No. of External Reviewers: 2
No. of In House Reviewers: 0
Acceptance Rate: No Reply
Time to Review: 2 - 3 Months
Reviewers Comments: Yes
Invited Articles: 0-5%
Fees to Publish: 0.00 US$

MANUSCRIPT TOPICS:
Developmental Psychology; Educational Psychology; Elementary/Early Childhood

MANUSCRIPT GUIDELINES/COMMENTS:

This mission statement for the journal that is based on both historical context of the field when the journal was first founded in 1980 and on an analysis of future directions for applied developmental psychology. The journal itself has grown from the first volume of 4 issues per year totaling 300 pages per volume, to 750 pages per volume over 6 annual issues that now reflect a variety of different formats (e.g., special topic issues) to address increasingly diverse topics. This growth reflects the changes that have occurred in the field of developmental psychology. Students are now trained explicitly in applied developmental psychology in some graduate programs, and many developmental researchers who were trained in basic research currently train the next generation of scholars for careers in applied fields, and engage in research with an applied emphasis themselves. *The Journal of Applied Developmental Psychology* has adapted to these and other changes in the field and, we hope, has taken a leadership role in the evolution of this area of science.

Purpose

The purpose of The *Journal of Applied Developmental Psychology* is to disseminate knowledge of developmental phenomena that contribute to practices and policies that can be meaningfully applied to issues of behavioral science. As was the case at its inception, a broad definition of development is used and we continue to emphasize the synergistic relationship between research and application. Manuscripts that focus on a variety of developmental processes such as genetic, neuropsychological, perceptual, cognitive, communicative, social, contextual, and cultural variables at any point across the lifespan are welcomed. The journal remains committed to promoting the application of findings presented in published papers to real life social problems of infants, children, adolescents, and adults. The journal is committed to reporting basic and applied science that has broad impact.

Manuscripts Solicited

The journal primarily seeks papers that present theoretically based empirical studies that can have a meaningful impact. However, position papers, critical reviews, and theoretical analyses that can be translated into action are also considered. We seek submissions from a range of contributors who work in a variety of settings around the world. Papers should present well-designed research representing a variety of professional specializations (clinical, cognitive, social, biological, etc.) and applied dimensions (treatment and preventive interventions, social policy, program evaluation, training initiatives, etc.). In addition, the book review editor periodically selects relevant books to be reviewed in the journal.

Purposes and Procedures for Reviews

The identity of authors and of reviewers of the highest caliber will be held confidential in an effort to prevent discrimination based on professional status, gender, age, racial origin, culture, sexual preference, religious belief, language, disability, economic status, or political views. Reviews will be constructive with the goals of fostering the development of new questions and methodologies as well as providing critical feedback to authors.

In order to be responsive to a particular event or a salient social issue, a topic will be occasionally selected for a special article or as the focus of an entire issue. In some cases, special action editors will be appointed in order to ensure that the most relevant and innovative research ideas and methodologies are presented.

Audience

Developmental scientists, including psychologists, social workers, educators, social policy analysts, counselors and clinicians, medical practitioners, practitioner-researchers, academics, research and program evaluators, medical practitioners who work in pediatric and geriatric settings, those who evaluate disabilities, collaborate with schools, design interventions, interpret research findings and translate them into relevant policy, and who work in various capacities in policy and child advocacy organizations will find their needs and interests addressed by *The Journal of Applied Developmental Psychology*.

Summary

The Journal of Applied Developmental Psychology seeks to publish research of the highest quality in a manner that makes the findings and implications of basic research understandable and applicable without sacrificing the complexity of the relationships among involved constructs and variables. The journal will be a vehicle for promoting optimal human development by introducing provocative articles that enable readers to use the knowledge generated by the research to improve policy and practice.

Guide for Authors

The Journal of Applied Developmental Psychology is intended as a forum for communication between researchers and practitioners working in life-span human development fields. Articles describing application of empirical research from social and behavioral disciplines bearing on human development are appropriate. Conceptual and methodological reviews and position papers which facilitate application of research results to such settings as educational, clinical, and the like, are also welcome. Recommendations for intervention or for policy are appropriate when data based.

Review of manuscripts. Authors should remove any identifying information from the manuscript. All necessary information pertaining to identification, title, institutional affiliation, etc. should be on a cover page and only the title of the manuscript should appear on the first page of the manuscript. Authors should guarantee that the manuscript is an original submission and only to this journal.

Authors must follow the guidelines described in the fifth edition (1994) of the *Publication Manual of the American Psychological Association* (1200 Seventeenth St. NW, Washington, DC 20036). Instructions for typing, preparation of tables, figures, and references are all described in the manual. Manuscripts should conform to the conventions specified in the manual with the following advisements:

1. **Preparation of manuscript**. Please double space all material. Manuscripts should be typewritten on 8 ½ x 11 inches bond paper, leaving 1-in. margins on all sides. Number pages consecutively with the title page as page 1, and include a brief abstract from 100 to 150 words as page 2.

2. **Illustrations**. All illustrations and figures are to be submitted in a form suitable for reproduction without retouching or redrawing. The area of the typed page will be 4 ½ x 7 inches, and no illustration can exceed these margins. If photos are to be used, glossies should be submitted, no larger than 8 x 10. Original inked drawings reproduce best, and are preferable, but if these are not available, same-size matte photostats are acceptable. Do not enlarge or reduce art. This will be done by the printer.

3. **Numbering of figures and tables**. All tables and figures must be numbered consecutively using Arabic numbers. Ditto for tables. All tables and figures must be cited in text, and an indication for placement must be given. Every figure should be identified on the back or in a margin with a figure number, the name of the author, and the word "TOP." All figures must have captions, which should be typed on a separate sheet of paper. Each table should be typed on a separate sheet of paper, and should have a brief descriptive title. Tables should be clearly ruled horizontally to indicate levels of column headings. Vertical ruling is discouraged.

4. **Footnotes**. Footnotes should be used sparingly and indicated by consecutive superscript numbers in the text. Material to be footnoted should be typed separately and submitted with the manuscript following the figure legends.

5. **References**. Use the *APA Publication Manual* for the correct listing of references.

6. **Spelling, Terminology, Abbreviations**. Standard United States spelling and punctuation should be used throughout. Follow Merriam Webster's Collegiate Dictionary (10th ed.) for spelling and hyphenation of words. Please avoid jargon wherever possible. Avoid abbreviations that are not commonly accepted.

7. **Permissions**. Contributors are responsible for obtaining permission from copyright owners if they use an illustration, table, or lengthy quote from material that has been published elsewhere. Contributors should write to both the publisher and author of material they are seeking permission to reproduce.

8. **Affiliation**. Please include under your name on the title page the institution with which you are connected, your complete mailing address, and credits to any other institution where the work may have been done. Underneath your affiliation, please also include a shortened version of your title that can be used as a running head.

9. **Acceptance**. Upon acceptance, we request an IBM compatible disk, spell checked and stripped of all embedded graphics. Graphics are to be saved in a separate file, an eps, tiff, or ps file. The accuracy of the disk and page proofs is the authors' responsibility.

10. **Offprints**. The only opportunity contributors have to order offprints is when page proofs are returned.

11. **Three copies of ms. should be sent to**: Tanya Allison-Kewley, Office Manager, *Journal of Applied Developmental Psychology* Office, Psychology Department, Oechsle Hall, Lafayette College, Easton, PA 18042-1781 Phone: +1 610-330-5859 Fax: +1 610-330-5349 E-mail: **jadp@lafayette.edu**

Journal of Applied Psychology

ADDRESS FOR SUBMISSION:

Sheldon Zedeck, Editor
Journal of Applied Psychology
University of California
Department of Psychology
Berkeley, CA 94720-1650
USA
Phone: 510-642-5292
Fax: 510-642-7130
E-Mail: zedeck@socrates.berkeley.edu
Web: www.apa.org/journals/apl.htm
Address May Change:

PUBLICATION GUIDELINES:

Manuscript Length: 26-30
Copies Required: Four
Computer Submission: No
Format: N/A
Fees to Review: 0.00 US$

Manuscript Style:
American Psychological Association

CIRCULATION DATA:

Reader: Academics
Frequency of Issue: Bi-Monthly
Copies per Issue: 3,001 - 4,000
Sponsor/Publisher: American Psychological
Association
Subscribe Price: 158.00 US$ Individual
394.00 US$ Institution
77.00 US$ APA Member

REVIEW INFORMATION:

Type of Review: Blind Review
No. of External Reviewers: 2
No. of In House Reviewers: 0
Acceptance Rate: 11-20%
Time to Review: 2 - 3 Months
Reviewers Comments: Yes
Invited Articles: 0-5%
Fees to Publish: 0.00 US$

MANUSCRIPT TOPICS:
Tests, Measurement & Evaluation

MANUSCRIPT GUIDELINES/COMMENTS:

The *Journal of Applied Psychology* is devoted primarily to original investigations that contribute new knowledge and understanding to fields of applied psychology other than clinical and applied experimental or human factors. The journal considers quantitative investigations of interest to psychologists doing research or working in such settings as universities, industry, government, urban affairs, police and correctional systems, health and educational institutions, transportation and defense systems, labor unions, and consumer affairs. A theoretical or review article may be accepted if it represents a special contribution to an applied field. Topics appropriate for the *Journal of Applied Psychology* include personnel selection, performance measurement, training, work motivation, job attitudes, eyewitness accuracy, leadership, drug and alcohol abuse, career development, the conflict between job and family demands, work behavior, work stress, organizational design and interventions, technology, polygraph use, the utility of organizational interventions, consumer buying behavior, and cross-cultural differences in work behavior and attitudes. The specific topics addressed, however, change as a function of societal and organizational change; studies of human behavior in novel situations are also encouraged.

Mail manuscripts to:
Dr. Sheldon Zedeck
Editor, *Journal of Applied Psychology*
Department of Psychology
University of California
Berkeley, CA 94720-1650

Authors must submit five (5) copies of the manuscript. The copies should be clear, readable, and on paper of good quality. A dot matrix or unusual typeface is acceptable only if it is clear and legible. In addition to addresses and phone numbers, authors should supply electronic mail addresses and fax numbers, if available, for potential use by the editorial office and later by the production office. Authors should keep a copy of the manuscript to guard against loss.

The journal will accept submissions in masked (blind) review format only. Each copy of a manuscript should include a separate title page with author names and affiliations, and these should not appear anywhere else on the manuscript. Furthermore, author identification notes should be typed on the title page (see *Manual*). Authors should make every reasonable effort to see that the manuscript itself contains no clues to their identities. Manuscripts not in masked format will not be reviewed.

Articles submitted for publication in the *Journal of Applied Psychology* are evaluated according to the following criteria: (a) significance of contribution, (b) technical adequacy, (c) appropriateness for the journal, and (d) clarity of presentation. In addition, articles must be clearly written in concise and unambiguous language and must be logically organized. The goal of APA primary journals is to publish useful information that is accurate and clear.

Authors should prepare manuscripts according to the *Publication Manual of the American Psychological Association* (5th ed.). Articles not prepared according to the guidelines of the *Manual* will not be reviewed. All manuscripts must include an abstract containing a maximum of 960 characters and spaces (which is approximately 120 words) typed on a separate sheet of paper. Typing instructions (all copy must be double-spaced) and instructions on preparing tables, figures, references, metrics, and abstracts appear in the *Manual*. Also, all manuscripts are copyedited for bias-free language (see chap. 2 of the *Publication Manual*). Original color figures can be printed in color provided the author agrees to pay half of the associated production costs.

The journal will publish both regular articles, or Feature Articles, and Research Reports. Authors can refer to recent issues of the journal for approximate length of Feature Articles. (Total manuscript pages divided by 4 provides an estimate of total printed pages.) Longer articles will be considered for publication, but the contribution they make must justify the number of journal pages needed to present the research. Research Reports feature shorter manuscripts that make a distinct but relatively narrow contribution, such as important replications or studies that discuss specific applications of psychology. Authors may request Research Report status at the time of submission, or the editor may suggest that a regular-

436

length submission be pared down to Research Report length. Research Reports are limited to no more than 17 pages of text proper; these limits do not include the title page, abstract, references, tables, or figures. Different printers, fonts, spacing, margins, and so forth can substantially alter the amount of text that can be fit on a page. In determining the length limits of Research Reports, authors should count 25–26 lines of text (60 characters per line) as the equivalent of one page.

Authors are required to obtain and provide to APA all necessary permissions to reproduce any copyrighted work, including, for example, test instruments and other test materials or portions thereof.

APA policy prohibits an author from submitting the same manuscript for concurrent consideration by two or more publications. In addition, it is a violation of APA Ethical Principles to publish "as original data, data that have been previously published" (Standard 6.24). As this journal is a primary journal that publishes original material only, APA policy prohibits as well publication of any manuscript that has already been published in whole or substantial part elsewhere. Authors have an obligation to consult journal editors concerning prior publication of any data upon which their article depends.

In addition, APA Ethical Principles specify that "after research results are published, psychologists do not withhold the data on which their conclusions are based from other competent professionals who seek to verify the substantive claims through reanalysis and who intend to use such data only for that purpose, provided that the confidentiality of the participants can be protected and unless legal rights concerning proprietary data preclude their release" (Standard 6.25). APA expects authors submitting to this journal to adhere to these standards. Specifically, authors of manuscripts submitted to APA journals are expected to have their data available throughout the editorial review process and for at least 5 years after the date of publication.

Authors will be required to state in writing that they have complied with APA ethical standards in the treatment of their sample, human or animal, or to describe the details of treatment. A copy of the APA Ethical Principles may be obtained by writing the APA Ethics Office, 750 First Street, NE, Washington, DC 20002-4242 (or see "Ethical Principles," December 1992, *American Psychologist,* Vol. 47, pp. 1597-1611).

APA requires authors to reveal any possible conflict of interest in the conduct and reporting of research (e.g., financial interests in a test procedure, funding by pharmaceutical companies for drug research).

Journal of Applied Research in the Community College

ADDRESS FOR SUBMISSION:

Mary Kinnick, Editor
Journal of Applied Research in the
    Community College
Portland State University
Graduate School of Education
PO Box 751
Portland, OR 97207
USA
Phone: 503-287-6959
Fax: 503-725-3200
E-Mail: kinnickm@pdx.edu
Web: www.ncccrp.org
Address May Change: 8/31/2006

PUBLICATION GUIDELINES:

Manuscript Length: 16-20
Copies Required: One
Computer Submission: Yes Preferred
Format: Word
Fees to Review: 0.00 US$

Manuscript Style:
    American Psychological Association

CIRCULATION DATA:

Reader: Academics, Administrators,
    Institutional Researchers
Frequency of Issue: 2 Times/Year
Copies per Issue: Less than 1,000
Sponsor/Publisher: National Community
    College Council for Research and
    Planning (NCCCRP)
Subscribe Price: 35.00 US$
    50% Less NCCCRP Member

REVIEW INFORMATION:

Type of Review: Blind Review
No. of External Reviewers: 2
No. of In House Reviewers: 2
Acceptance Rate: 37%
Time to Review: 2 - 3 Months
Reviewers Comments: Yes
Invited Articles: 6-10%
Fees to Publish: 0.00 US$

MANUSCRIPT TOPICS:
Education Management/Administration; Higher Education; Tests, Measurement & Evaluation

MANUSCRIPT GUIDELINES/COMMENTS:

Introduction
The Graduate School of Education, Postsecondary, Adult and Continuing Education program, is honored to house the *Journal of Applied Research in the Community College*. The *Journal* is edited under the direction of Dr. Mary Kinnick, Professor, PACE program and assisted by Heather Burns, managing editor and doctoral student at Portland State University. Dr. Christine Cress, Assistant Professor, PACE program, serves on the editorial advisory board. The Associate Editors are Susan Bach, Portland Community College; Melissa Banks, Clackamas Community College; Juliette Stoering, Portland State University; and Dan Walleri, Mt. Hood Community College.

438

The *Journal of Applied Research in the Community College* is a refereed journal sponsored by the National Council of Research and Planning (NCRP), an affiliated council of the American Association of Community Colleges. The purpose of the biannual journal is to serve the needs and interests of institutional researchers and planners in the community college as well as those of administrators, faculty, policy makers and others with an interest in the community college.

Call for Manuscripts
Journal of Applied Research in the Community College
Research, Assessment, Planning

The Purpose
The *Journal of Applied Research in the Community College* is a refereed journal sponsored by the National Council of Research and Planning, an affiliated council of the American Association of Community Colleges. The purpose of the biannual journal is to serve the needs and interests of institutional researchers and planners in the community college as well as those of administrators, faculty, policy makers and others with an interest in the community college. The journal communicates innovative practices in applied research, planning and assessment that support educational and administrative decision making at the institutional, state and national levels. The journal publishes manuscripts that describe the objectives, methods and findings of studies conducted to assess student outcomes, evaluate programs and services, identify community educational needs, project the impact of proposed legislation or otherwise provide information needed by those shaping and setting educational and administrative policy for community colleges. Besides providing insights into emerging policy issues, articles accepted for publication describe research, planning and assessment models, tools and techniques that can be adapted by those working in other settings.

The Process
Manuscripts should be 10 to 20 pages in length (double-spaces) and should be sent to the Executive Editor on computer diskette. Each manuscript should be accompanied by an abstract of 150 words or less, along with a brief biographical sketch of the author(s). Manuscripts submitted to the *Journal* must not be under consideration by other publishers.

All manuscripts should conform to the guidelines as outlined in the *APA Style Manual*, fifth edition. All manuscripts will be submitted for blind review to selected members of an editorial advisory board, which consists of community college policy makers and researchers.

Where to Send
Send manuscripts to the Executive Editor:
Mary Kinnick
Professor, Postsecondary, Adult and Continuing Education
Graduate School of Education
Portland State University
PO Box 751 Portland, OR 97207
kinnickm@pdx.edu
(503) 725-4627

Journal of Applied School Psychology

ADDRESS FOR SUBMISSION:

Charles A. Maher, Editor
Journal of Applied School Psychology
Rutgers University
Grad.Sch./Applied & Profess. Psycology
152 Frelinghusyen Road
Piscataway, NJ 08854
USA
Phone: 732-445-2000x103
Fax: 732-445-4888
E-Mail: camaher@rci.rutgers.edu
Web: www.haworthpressinc.com
Address May Change:

PUBLICATION GUIDELINES:

Manuscript Length: 21-25
Copies Required: Three
Computer Submission: Yes
Format: Wordperfect, MSWord
Fees to Review: 0.00 US$

Manuscript Style:
American Psychological Association

CIRCULATION DATA:

Reader: Academics, Administrators, School
& Other Practicing Psychologists
Frequency of Issue: 2 Times/Year
Copies per Issue: 5,001 - 10,000
Sponsor/Publisher: Haworth Press, Inc.
Subscribe Price: 60.00 US$ Individual
81.00 US$ Institution
87.00 US$ Library

REVIEW INFORMATION:

Type of Review: Blind Review
No. of External Reviewers: 3
No. of In House Reviewers: 2
Acceptance Rate: 21-30%
Time to Review: 2 - 3 Months
Reviewers Comments: Yes
Invited Articles: 11-20%
Fees to Publish: 0.00 US$

MANUSCRIPT TOPICS:
Assessment; Bilingual/E.S.L.; Counseling & Personnel Services; Educational Psychology; Educational Technology Systems; Gifted Children; School Psychology; Special Education; Staff Development; Tests, Measurement & Evaluation

MANUSCRIPT GUIDELINES/COMMENTS:

About the Journal
A biannual journal with an applied focus, the *Journal of Applied School Psychology* includes up-to-the-minute, practical information that assists practicing school psychologists and related professionals in performing the wide range of service delivery tasks for which they are responsible and for which they must coordinate their efforts, in areas of assessment, instruction, counseling, staff development, and organizational development.

Informative and instructive articles are aimed at school psychologists, social workers, other special service providers, school supervisors, directors, and administrators. All of these groups will find topics of interest, such as
• reviews of applied educational research and relevant literature

440

- descriptions of successful programs
- policy perspectives on current and future issues and trends
- guidelines for designing, implementing, and evaluating special service programs

This invaluable professional resource helps readers
- assess individual pupils and groups to determine their special educational needs
- design individualized and group programs
- assist regular and special classroom teachers in fostering academic achievement and functional living of special students
- enhance the social and emotional development of pupils through preventive and remedial approaches
- help school administrators to develop smoothly functioning organizational systems
- foster the physical well-being of special students
- involve parents and families in special programs
- educate and train school staff to more effectively educate special needs students

About the Editor
Charles A. Maher, PsyD. is Professor of Psychology at the Graduate School of Applied and Professional Psychology at Rutgers University where he served eight years as Chairperson of the Department of Applied Psychology. He is actively involved, both nationally and internationally, as a consultant to schools, private corporations, government agencies, and professional sports organizations. His consultation programs and services encompass a broad area including educational planning, professional self management, enhancement of the psychoeducational performance of individuals and groups, and sport psychology. He is a recipient of the 1991 Capital Award of the National Leadership Council for principled leadership, business professionalism, and success achievement. He is a fellow of the American Psychological Association, American Psychological Society, and the American Association of Applied Preventive Psychology.

1. **Original articles only**. Submission of a manuscript to this Journal represents a certification on the part of the author(s) that it is an original work and that neither this manuscript nor a version of it has been published elsewhere nor is being considered for publication elsewhere.

2. **Manuscript length**. Your manuscript may be approximately 20 typed pages double-spaced (including references and abstract). Lengthier manuscripts may be considered, but only at the discretion of the Editor. Sometimes, lengthier manuscripts may be considered if they can be divided up into sections for publication in successive Journal issues.

3. **Manuscript style**. References, citations, and general style of manuscripts for this Journal should follow the Chicago style (as outlined in the latest edition of the *Manual of Style* of the University of Chicago Press). References should be double-spaced and placed in alphabetical order.

If an author wishes to submit a paper that has been already prepared in another style, he or she may do so. However, if the paper is accepted (with or without reviewer's alterations), the author is fully responsible for retyping the manuscript in the correct style as indicated above.

Neither the Editor nor the Publisher is responsible for re-preparing manuscript copy to adhere to the Journal's style.

4. Manuscript preparation.
Margins: leave at least a one-inch margin on all four sides.
Paper: use clean white, 8-1/2" x 11" bond paper.
Number of copies: 3 (the original plus two photocopies).
Cover page: Important-staple a cover page to the manuscript indicating only the article title (this is used for anonymous refereeing).
Second "title page": enclose a regular title page but do not staple it to the manuscript. Include the title again, plus:

- Full authorship
- An ABSTRACT of about 100 words. (Below the abstract provide 3-10 key words for index purposes).
- An introductory footnote with authors' academic degrees, professional titles, affiliations, mailing addresses, and any desired acknowledgment of research support or other credit.

5. Return envelopes. When you submit your three manuscript copies, also include:

- A 9" x 12" envelope, self-addressed and stamped (with sufficient postage to ensure return of your manuscript);
- A regular envelope, stamped and self-addressed. This is for the Editor to send you an "acknowledgement of receipt" letter.

6. Spelling, grammar, and punctuation. You are responsible for preparing manuscript copy which is clearly written in acceptable scholarly English, and which contains no errors of spelling grammar, or punctuation. Neither the Editor nor the Publisher is responsible for correcting errors of spelling and grammar: the manuscript, after acceptance by the Editor, must be immediately ready for typesetting as it is finally submitted by the author(s). Check your paper for the following common errors:

- Dangling modifiers
- Misplaced modifiers
- Unclear antecedents
- Incorrect or inconsistent abbreviations Also, check the accuracy of all arithmetic calculations, statistics, numerical data, text citations, and references.

7. Inconsistencies must be avoided. Be sure you are consistent in your use of abbreviations terminology, and in citing references, from one part of your paper to another.

8. Preparation of tables, figures, and illustrations. All tables, figures, illustrations, etc. must be "camera-ready." That is, they must be cleanly typed or artistically prepared so that they can be used either exactly as they are or else used after a photographic reduction in size. Figures, tables, and illustrations must be prepared on separate sheets of paper. Always use black ink and professional drawing instruments. On the back of these items, write your article title and the journal title lightly in pencil, so they do not get misplaced. In text, skip extra lines and indicate where these figures and tables are to be placed (please do not write on face of art).

Photographs are considered part of the acceptable manuscript and remain with Publisher for use in additional printings.

9. **Alterations Required By Referees And Reviewers.** Many times a paper is accepted by the Editor contingent upon changes that are mandated by anonymous specialist referees and members of the Editorial Board. If the Editor returns your manuscript for revisions, you are responsible for retyping any sections of the paper to incorporate these revisions (if applicable, revisions should also be put on disk).

10. **Typesetting.** You will not be receiving galley proofs of your article. Editorial revisions, if any, must therefore be made while your article is still in manuscript. The final version of the manuscript will be the version you see published. Typesetter's errors will be corrected by the production staff of The Haworth Press. Authors are expected to submit manuscripts, disks, and art that are free from error.

11. **Electronic media.** Haworth's in-house type-setting unit will now be able to utilize your final manuscript material as prepared on most personal computers and word processors. This will minimize typographical errors and decrease overall production timelag.

A. Please continue to send your first draft and final draft copies of your manuscript to the journal Editor in print format for his/her final review and approval;

B. Only after the journal editor has approved your final manuscript, you may submit the final approved version both on:
- Printed format ("hard copy")
- Floppy diskette

C. Please make sure that the disk version and the hard copy (printed cony) are exactly the same.

D. Wrap your floppy diskettes in a strong diskette wrapper or holder, and write on the outside of the package:
- The brand name of your computer or word processor
- The word-processing program that you used to create your article, book chapter, or book
- File name

The benefits of this procedure are many with speed and accuracy being the most obvious. We look forward to working with you on this, knowing we will be able to serve you more efficiently in the future.

12. **Reprints.** The senior author will receive one copy of the journal issue and 10 complimentary reprints of his or her article. The junior author will receive one copy of the issue. These are sent several weeks after the journal issue is published and in circulation. An order form for the purchase of additional reprints will also be sent to all authors at this time. (Approximately 4-6 weeks is necessary for the preparation of reprints.) Please do not query the Journal's Editor about reprints. ALl such questions should be sent directly to The Haworth Press, Inc., Production Department, 21 East Broad Street, West Hazleton, PA 18201. To order

additional reprints (minimum: 50 copies), please contact The Haworth Document Delivery Center, 10 Alice Street, Binghamton, New York 13904-1580 (607) 722-5857.

13. **Copyright.** Copyright ownership of your manuscript must be transferred officially to The Haworth Press, Inc. before we can begin the peer-review process. The Editor's letter acknowledging receipt of the manuscript will be accompanied by a form fully explaining this. All authors must sign the form and return the original to the Editor as soon as possible. Failure to return the copyright form in a timely fashion will result in delay in review and subsequent publication.

Journal of Broadcasting & Electronic Media

ADDRESS FOR SUBMISSION:

Donald G. Godfrey, Editor
Journal of Broadcasting & Electronic Media
Arizona State University
Walter Cronkite School of Journalism
and Mass Communications
P O Box 851304
Tempe, AZ 85287-1305
USA
Phone: 480-965-8661
Fax: 480-965-7041
E-Mail: don.godfrey@asu.edu
Web: www.beaweb.org
Address May Change:

PUBLICATION GUIDELINES:

Manuscript Length: 15-30
Copies Required: Four
Computer Submission: No
Format: MS Word
Fees to Review: 0.00 US$

Manuscript Style:
American Psychological Association

CIRCULATION DATA:

Reader: Academics, Administrators,
Professionals
Frequency of Issue: Quarterly
Copies per Issue: 2,001 - 3,000
Sponsor/Publisher: Broadcast Education
Association
Subscribe Price: 40.00 US$
50.00 US$ Foreign
25.00 US$ Student

REVIEW INFORMATION:

Type of Review: Blind Review
No. of External Reviewers: 3
No. of In House Reviewers: 0
Acceptance Rate: 11-20%
Time to Review: 2 - 3 Months
Reviewers Comments: Yes
Invited Articles: 0-5%
Fees to Publish: 0.00 US$

MANUSCRIPT TOPICS:
Broadcasting and electronic media; Criticism; History; Law; Research; Social Studies/Social Science

MANUSCRIPT GUIDELINES/COMMENTS:

The *Journal of Broadcasting & Electronic Media* is an international quarterly devoted to advancing, research, knowledge, and understanding of communication and the electronic media. The *Journal* invites submissions of original research that examine a broad range of issues concerning the electronic media, including their historical, technological, economic, policy, cultural, and social dimensions. Scholarship that extends a historiography, tests theory, or that fosters innovative perspectives on topics of importance to the field, is particularly encouraged. The *Journal* is open to a diversity of theoretic paradigms and methodologies.

Submitted work is evaluated according to the quality of its conceptualization; the importance of the topic to scholars, policy makers, and practitioners; the lasting contribution it will make to electronic media studies; and the research execution. Key considerations of research execution include the research design, soundness of the research procedure, and the clarity of presentation. The Editor reserves the right not to send manuscripts out for review that fall outside the scope of the *Journal* or make an insignificant contribution to the field.

1. It is assumed that only the original work of the author will be submitted for *Journal* consideration. Any manuscript submitted must not be under consideration by another publication. Papers presented first at conferences or symposia should be carefully revised prior to submission for publication in the *Journal*.

2. Four copies of the manuscript should be submitted. The author should retain the original. Manuscripts will not be returned.

3. The published journal follows APA style, but manuscripts may be submitted in APA, MLA or *The Chicago Manual of Style*. Upon acceptance manuscripts must be prepared by the author in strict accordance with the current edition of the *Publication Manual of the American Psychological Association*. Nonsexist language should be used.

4. Because manuscripts are reviewed blindly, author identification should be on the title page only. The title page should include the following: the complete title; author name(s); corresponding postal addresses, electronic mail addresses, and telephone numbers; and any necessary credits. Any further references that might identify the author(s) should be removed from the manuscript.

5. The second page of the manuscript should consist of an abstract of 75 to 100 words. The text of the manuscript (including its title) should begin on the next page, with the remaining pages numbered consecutively with running heads.

6. Notes and references should be double-spaced on pages following the text of the manuscript, and follow the formats of the current edition of the *Publication Manual of the American Psychological Association*. Notes should be kept to a minimum. Complete citations for references should be supplied.

7. Clear, economical, and orderly expression is expected of submissions to the *Journal*. Most *Journal* submissions should be circa 25 pages, including references and tables. Brevity is encouraged.

8. The number of tables should be kept to a minimum. No table should be included if the equivalent information can be communicated in a few sentences in the text. If the author wishes to offer large or esoteric tables for interested readers, their availability from the author should be indicated in a text note. Graphic material, other than tables, should be submitted in camera ready form if the manuscript is accepted for publication.

9. Authors normally will have an editorial decision within 3–4 months. Because manuscripts are sent to expert referees for evaluation, the consideration time may vary.

446

10. The Editor reserves the right to make minor changes in any accepted manuscript that do not alter the substantial meaning or results of the article or the expressed views of the author. Authors will be given the opportunity to approve all such changes and can withdraw their manuscript from consideration at any time.

11. The Broadcast Education Association holds copyright to all issues of the *Journal of Broadcasting & Electronic Media.* The Executive Director of the Association must grant permission for reproduction in any form of any of the contents of the *Journal.* The address is: Executive Director, Broadcast Education Association, 1771 N Street, NW, Washington, D. C., 20036.

12. Research manuscripts and correspondence should be addressed to: Donald G. Godfrey, Editor, *Journal of Broadcasting & Electronic Media,* Walter Cronkite School of Journalism & Mass Communications, Arizona State University, Box 871305, Tempe, AZ 85287-1305.

Inquiries and correspondence about book/video/electronic-media reviews or critical essays should be addressed to: Michael D. Murray, Review and Criticism Editor, *Journal of Broadcasting & Electronic Media,* School of Journalism, 4505 Maryland Parkway, Las Vegas, NV 89154-5007.

Journal of Business and Training Education

ADDRESS FOR SUBMISSION:

Betty A. Kleen, Editor
Journal of Business and Training Education
Nicholls State University
Information Systems Department
PO Box 2042
Thibodaux, LA 70310
USA
Phone: 985-448-4191
Fax: 985-448-4922
E-Mail: betty.kleen@nicholls.edu
Web:
Address May Change:

PUBLICATION GUIDELINES:

Manuscript Length: 6-15 double-spaced
Copies Required: Computer submission
Computer Submission: Yes
Format: Microsoft Word
Fees to Review: 0.00 US$

Manuscript Style:
American Psychological Association

CIRCULATION DATA:

Reader: Academics, Practicing Teachers,
Trainers/Business & Industry
Frequency of Issue: 1-2 Times/Year
Copies per Issue: Less than 1,000
Sponsor/Publisher: Louisiana Association
of Business Educators
Subscribe Price: 10.00 US$

REVIEW INFORMATION:

Type of Review: Blind Review
No. of External Reviewers: 3
No. of In House Reviewers: 0
Acceptance Rate: 21-30%
Time to Review: 2 - 3 Months
Reviewers Comments: Yes
Invited Articles: 0-5%
Fees to Publish: 0.00 US$

MANUSCRIPT TOPICS:
Adult Career & Vocational; Business Education/Office Training

MANUSCRIPT GUIDELINES/COMMENTS:

Call for Papers
The Louisiana Association of Business Educators invites business educators and trainers to contribute articles for publication in the *Journal of Business and Training Education*, a national refereed publication. Manuscripts should deal with topics of interest to educators (at both the secondary and post-secondary levels) and to trainers in business and industry. Submission of manuscripts dealing with practical topics are encouraged, as are research based or theoretical papers. Book reviews are accepted. Occasionally, invited authors' papers will be published. The Journal is listed in *Cabell's Directory of Publishing Opportunities.*

Manuscripts will be selected through a blind review process. Manuscripts should not have been published or be under current consideration for publication by another journal. The manuscripts should range from 6 to 15 double-spaced typed pages of 12 point type-size, including tables and references. Manuscripts must be prepared using the style format in the

Publication Manual of the American Psychological Association, Fifth Edition, 2001. Remove all personal and institutional identification from the body and title of the paper. The Title Page is to include the title of the manuscript, a 50-100 word abstract and the running header. The following information needs to be included in the email message accompanying the manuscript: Title of manuscript; and for each author, full name, position title, place of employment, city, state, zip code, telephone numbers and e-mail address.

Journal of Business Communication

ADDRESS FOR SUBMISSION:

Steve Ralston, Editor
Journal of Business Communication
University of Michigan - Flint
Department of Communication
4116 WSW Building
Flint, MI 48507
USA
Phone: 810-766-6679
Fax: 810-766-6834
E-Mail: See Guidelines
Web:
Address May Change:

PUBLICATION GUIDELINES:

Manuscript Length: Average 30
Copies Required: No Reply
Computer Submission: Yes
Format: After Ms. Acceptance
Fees to Review: 0.00 US$

Manuscript Style:
American Psychological Association

CIRCULATION DATA:

Reader: Academics
Frequency of Issue: Quarterly
Copies per Issue: 2,001 - 3,000
Sponsor/Publisher: Association for
Business Communication
Subscribe Price: 60.00 US$

REVIEW INFORMATION:

Type of Review:
No. of External Reviewers: 3
No. of In House Reviewers: 2
Acceptance Rate: 11-20%
Time to Review: 2 - 3 Months
Reviewers Comments: Yes
Invited Articles: 0-5%
Fees to Publish: 0.00 US$

MANUSCRIPT TOPICS:
Adult Career & Vocational; Education Management/Administration; Higher Education; Social Studies/Social Science; Tests, Measurement & Evaluation

MANUSCRIPT GUIDELINES/COMMENTS:

The *Journal of Business Communication (JBC)* publishes manuscripts that contribute to knowledge and theory of business communication as a distinct, multifaceted field approached through the administrative disciplines, the liberal arts, and the social sciences. Accordingly, *JBC* seeks manuscripts that address all areas of business communication including but not limited to business composition/technical writing, information systems, international business communication, management communication, and organizational and corporate communication. In addition, *JBC* welcomes submissions concerning the role of written, verbal, nonverbal and electronic communication in the creation, maintenance, and performance of profit and not for profit business. *JBC* accepts all rigorous research methods, including but not limited to qualitative, quantitative, and critical. *JBC* conducts blind reviews. Papers reviewed for publication in *JBC* are examined by the Editor, an Associate Editor and two subject-matter experts.

Types of Manuscripts Published
- Traditional scholarly studies of 15-35 pages, excluding references, notes, and appendices.
- Commentaries of 10-14 pages, excluding references, notes, and appendices.
- Book reviews. To inquire about reviewing a book, contact the Book Review Editor.

Submitting Manuscripts
Electronic submission of manuscripts is **strongly encouraged.** Electronic submission will greatly expedite the review of your manuscript. Save manuscripts as a Word, WordPerfect, or rich text file. Attach the file to an e-mail and send to the Editor. Title your e-mail: <YourName.*JBC*>. Include your name and contact information in the email message. In addition, two documents should be attached: A cover page and the complete manuscript (consult instructions that follow).

Traditional submission. Submit 2 copies of the cover page and 4 complete copies of the manuscript to the Editor.

Manuscript Preparation
Submissions must be original materials not under consideration or published elsewhere. Write the manuscript in English, following the format specified in the *Publication Manual Of The American Psychological Association* (5th edition). Authors may use either U.S. or British spelling, but use U.S. punctuation.

Remove all personal and institutional identification from the body of the manuscript.

On the cover page, include:
- Manuscript title.
- Name, institutional affiliation, mailing address, e-mail address, and telephone and fax numbers for each author.
- Information about the manuscript's history, such as public presentations, publication of any part of the manuscript, and if the manuscript is drawn from a thesis or dissertation.

On the second page, include the manuscript's title and an abstract (150 words or fewer).

Start the body of the paper on the third page

Check the paper and references for accuracy. Write clearly and concisely using inclusive language. *Refer to your own research in the 3rd person, e.g., Smith (2000) shows that . . .*

If your article is accepted, you will be asked to provide
- Some additional text formatting
- An electronic copy of the article (if not originally submitted electronically).
- A camera-ready copy of any images (or to pay actual production costs).
- Author notes.
- A brief biography of all authors.
- 5-6 keywords for the manuscript.

- If you used human subjects, include either a copy of the approval form of your institution's committee on the ethical treatment of human subjects or a statement showing that you have complied with principles 6.06-6.20 of the American Psychological Association's "Ethical Principles of Psychologists And Code of Conduct" (APA, 1992).

Steven M. Ralston, Editor
Journal of Business Communication
University of Michigan-Flint
Department of Communication
4116 WSW Building
Flint, MI 48507
Phone: 810-766-6679; Facsimile: 810-766-6834
E-mail 1: **JBC@list.flint.umich.edu**; E-Mail 2: **JBCED@yahoo.com**

Melinda Knight, Book Review Editor
Journal of Business Communication
University of Rochester,
Simon School, Box 270100
Rochester, NY 14627-0100
Phone: 716-273-4817. Facsimile: 716-273-3268
E-mail: **knight@simon.rochester.edu**

Notes

Notes

Notes

Notes

Notes

Notes

Notes

Notes

Cabell's Directories
of Publishing Opportunities in Business

NINTH EDITION 2004-2005

Accounting
Economics & Finance
Management
Marketing

To order Hardcopy or On-line versions - visit
www.cabells.com